LIABILITY FOR TRANSBOUNDARY POLLUTION AT THE INTERSECTION OF PUBLIC AND PRIVATE INTERNATIONAL LAW

This book focuses on how public and private international law address civil liability for transboundary pollution. In public international law, civil liability treaties promote the implementation of minimum procedural standards in domestic tort law. This approach implicitly relies on private international law to facilitate civil litigation against transboundary polluters. Yet this connection remains poorly understood. Filling the gap, this book engages in a meaningful dialogue between the two areas and explores how domestic private international law can reflect the policies developed in international environmental law. It begins with an investigation of civil liability in international environmental law. It then identifies preferable rules of civil jurisdiction, foreign judgments and choice of law for environmental damage, using Canadian private international law as a case study and making extensive references to European law. Liability for transboundary pollution is a contentious issue of the law, both in scholarship and practice: international lawyers both private and public as well as environmental lawyers will welcome this important work.

Volume 12 in the series Hart Monographs in Transnational and International Law

Hart Monographs in Transnational and International Law

Series Editor: Craig Scott, Professor of Law, Osgoode Hall Law School of York University, Toronto

The objective of this series is to publish high-quality scholarship in public international law and private international law, as well as work that adopts "transnational law" as its thematic, theoretical or doctrinal focus. The series strives to be a leading venue for work of the following sort:

*critical reappraisals of foundational concepts and core doctrinal principles of both public and private international law, and their operation in practice, including insights drawn from general legal theory;

*analysis and development of conceptions of 'transnational law', including in relation to the role of unofficial law and informal processes in transnational regulation and in relation to theories and studies of 'governance' in transnational spheres; and

*empirical studies of the emergence, evolution and transformation of international and/or transnational legal orders, including accounts and explanations of how law is constructed within different communities of interpretation and practice.

In relation to the first of these categories, the series especially welcomes monographs that explore the interactions between the ever-integrating fields of public and private international law. Of special interest are explorations of the extent to which these interactions are structured by higher-order principles and policies, on the one hand, and by politics and the exercise of various forms of power, on the other hand.

The series is open to work not only by law scholars but also by scholars from cognate disciplines.

Recent titles in this series

Volume 7: The Concept of Unity in Public International Law
Mario Prost

Volume 8: Interlocking Constitutions: Towards an Interordinal Theory of National, European and UN Law
Luis I Gordillo

Volume 9: Transnational Terrorism and State Accountability: A New Theory of Prevention
Vincent-Joël Proulx

Volume 10: Transconstitutionalism
Marcelo Neves translated by Kevin Mundy

Volume 11: The Institutional Problem in Modern International Law
Richard Collins

Volume 12: Liability for Transboundary Pollution at the Intersection of Public and Private International Law
Guillaume Laganière

Liability for Transboundary Pollution at the Intersection of Public and Private International Law

Guillaume Laganière

•HART•
OXFORD • LONDON • NEW YORK • NEW DELHI • SYDNEY

HART PUBLISHING
Bloomsbury Publishing Plc
Kemp House, Chawley Park, Cumnor Hill, Oxford, OX2 9PH, UK
1385 Broadway, New York, NY 10018, USA
29 Earlsfort Terrace, Dublin 2, Ireland

HART PUBLISHING, the Hart/Stag logo, BLOOMSBURY and the Diana logo are trademarks of Bloomsbury Publishing Plc

First published in Great Britain 2022

A catalogue record for this book is available from the British Library.

Library of Congress Cataloging-in-Publication data

Names: Laganière, Guillaume, author.

Title: Liability for transboundary pollution at the intersection of public and private international law / Guillaume Laganière.

Description: Oxford, UK ; New York, NY : Hart Publishing, an imprint of Bloomsbury Publishing, 2022. | Includes bibliographical references and index.

Identifiers: LCCN 2021052594 (print) | LCCN 2021052595 (ebook) | ISBN 9781509951154 (hardback) | ISBN 9781509951192 (paperback) | ISBN 9781509951161 (Epub) | ISBN 9781509951178 (pdf)

Subjects: LCSH: Liability for environmental damages. | Transboundary pollution—Law and legislation. | Conflict of laws—Pollution. | Environmental law, International.

Classification: LCC K955 .L34 2022 (print) | LCC K955 (ebook) | DDC 344.04/6—dc23/eng/20211105

LC record available at https://lccn.loc.gov/2021052594

LC ebook record available at https://lccn.loc.gov/2021052595

ISBN: HB: 978-1-50995-115-4
ePDF: 978-1-50995-117-8
ePub: 978-1-50995-116-1

Typeset by Compuscript Ltd, Shannon

To find out more about our authors and books visit www.hartpublishing.co.uk. Here you will find extracts, author information, details of forthcoming events and the option to sign up for our newsletters.

Preface

THIS BOOK IS based on my doctoral dissertation written at McGill University (2015–2020). The catalyst for my dissertation – and this book – came during my master studies at the University of Cambridge in 2012–2013. Private international law was my primary research interest at the time, but I was keen to study environmental issues, which I had not done so far in law school; I therefore signed up for a class on international environmental law. Throughout the year, we discussed the international regulation of air and water pollution, biodiversity, climate change, waste management, nuclear energy, and other fascinating subjects. It struck me that private actors were involved in almost all areas. It also struck me that enforcement mechanisms – including liability – were often described as lacklustre or insufficiently developed in international environmental law. Most textbooks identified domestic liability regimes as one of the solutions, but only depending on the rules of private international law in force in any given state. We did not discuss those rules much further. This is by no means a criticism of the excellent teaching I received: as I later learned first-hand, a teacher simply cannot cover everything in class. But the connection between the two areas of the law sparked my interest. I was a private international lawyer with a keen interest in environmental issues and a willingness to delve deeper into international environmental law. If I ever embarked on a doctoral project (or even a book), it would be to help fill this gap – not for the sake of filling the gap, but to find new ways of approaching the liability conundrum in international environmental law and to explain exactly how private international law deals with transboundary environmental problems. This project, I hoped, would also connect with ongoing work on the role of private international law in global governance.

The project stayed in the back of my mind as I graduated and moved on to law practice. I eventually returned to academia and began my doctorate. As I worked on my dissertation, climate change lawsuits against governments and corporations proliferated around the world, keeping my subject relevant but also making it more complex from a private international law perspective. Six years later, as this book is being published, I can say that I answered some of the questions I asked myself when I began the project. I hope that this book convinces others – public and private international lawyers alike – to study the connections between international environmental law and private international law.

Guillaume Laganière
Montreal
July 2021

Acknowledgements

I wish to thank the following people, who supported me throughout the years and made this book possible.

My doctoral supervisor at McGill University, Professor Geneviève Saumier; members of my supervisory committee, Professors Jaye Ellis and Catherine Walsh; and members of my examination and defence committee, Professors Jutta Brunnée, Richard Janda, Sébastien Jodoin and Sara Seck.

My colleagues at Université du Québec à Montréal's Faculty of Law, and former colleagues at Woods LLP.

My friends and family – my mother Céline, my father Benoît, Diane, Benjamin, Myriam, Étienne and especially Stéphanie.

This research was supported in part by the Social Sciences and Humanities Research Council of Canada

Conseil de recherches en sciences humaines du Canada

Social Sciences and Humanities Research Council of Canada

Canada

Table of Contents

PART 2
TRANSBOUNDARY POLLUTION IN CANADIAN PRIVATE INTERNATIONAL LAW

List of Abbreviations

GENERAL

ABA	American Bar Association
CBA	Canadian Bar Association
CEC	Commission for Environmental Cooperation
EC	European Commission
ECJ	European Court of Justice
EPA	Environmental Protection Agency
EU	European Union
HCCH	Hague Conference on Private International Law
ICJ	International Court of Justice
IIL	Institute of International Law
IJC	International Joint Commission
ILA	International Law Association
ILC	International Law Commission
ITLOS	International Tribunal for the Law of the Sea
IUCN	International Union for Conservation of Nature
OECD	Organisation for Economic Co-operation and Development
ULCC	Uniform Law Conference of Canada
UNCC	United Nations Compensation Commission
UNECE	United Nations Economic Commission for Europe
UNEP	United Nations Environment Programme
UNGA	United Nations General Assembly
UNSC	United Nations Security Council

CANADIAN LEGISLATION AND CASE LAW REPORTS*

Neutral Citations

ABCA	Alberta Court of Appeal
ABQB	Alberta Court of Queen's Bench
BCCA	British Columbia Court of Appeal
BCSC	British Columbia Supreme Court
FC	Federal Court
FCA	Federal Court of Appeal
MBCA	Manitoba Court of Appeal
ONCA	Ontario Court of Appeal
ONSC	Ontario Superior Court of Justice
QCCA	Quebec Court of Appeal
QCCS	Quebec Superior Court
SCC	Supreme Court of Canada
SKCA	Saskatchewan Court of Appeal

Paper Reports

BCLR	British Columbia Law Reports
CELR	Canadian Environmental Law Reports
CNLR	Canadian Native Law Reporter
CPC	Carswell's Practice Cases
DLR	Dominion Law Reports
NWTR	Northwest Territories Reports
OR	Ontario Reports
RDJ	Revue de droit judiciaire
RJQ	Recueils de jurisprudence du Québec

* McGill Law Journal, *Canadian Guide to Uniform Legal Citation*, 9th edn (Toronto, Thomson Reuters, 2018).

SCR	Supreme Court of Canada Reports
WLR	Western Law Reporter
WWR	Western Weekly Reports

Legislation

CCP	Code of Civil Procedure (Quebec)
CCQ	Civil Code of Quebec
CCSM	Continuing Consolidation of the Statutes of Manitoba
CQLR	Compilation of Québec Laws and Regulations
RRO	Revised Regulations of Ontario
RSBC	Revised Statutes of British Columbia
RSC	Revised Statutes of Canada
RSNB	Revised Statutes of New Brunswick
RSNWT (Nu)	Revised Statutes of the Northwest Territories (as duplicated for Nunavut)
RSO	Revised Statutes of Ontario
RSPEI	Revised Statutes of Prince Edward Island
RSY	Revised Statutes of the Yukon
SBC	Statutes of British Columbia
SC	Statutes of Canada
SM	Statutes of Manitoba
SNL	Statutes of Newfoundland and Labrador
SNS	Statutes of Nova Scotia
SNWT	Statutes of the Northwest Territories
SO	Statutes of Ontario
SPEI	Statutes of Prince Edward Island
SQ	Statutes of Quebec
SS	Statutes of Saskatchewan
SY	Statutes of the Yukon

Courts

Dist Ct	District Court (Ontario)
Div Ct	Divisional Court (Ontario)
Gen Div	Court of Justice, General Division (Ontario)
H Ct J	High Court of Justice (Ontario)
SC	Supreme Court (provincial)
SC (AD)	Supreme Court (Appellate Division) (provincial)
Sup Ct	Superior Court (provincial)

International Materials, Legislation, Jurisprudence and Government Documents

INTERNATIONAL MATERIALS

Treaties and Other Agreements

Jurisprudence

Arguments

United Nations

Resolutions of the General Assembly

Resolutions of the Security Council

Declarations

Guidelines, Principles and Other Instruments

Meetings

Reports

Compliance Committee of the UNECE

International Law Commission

Draft Articles

Reports

Hague Conference on Private International Law

Council of Europe

World Bank

Organisation for Economic Co-operation and Development

International Law Association

Institute of International Law

Commission for Environmental Cooperation

International Union for Conservation of Nature

American Bar Association and Canadian Bar Association Working Group

Other Organisations

LEGISLATION

Canada

Constitution

Statutes

Regulations

Uniform Legislation

United Kingdom

Statutes

United States

Federal Statutes

State Statutes

European Union

JURISPRUDENCE

Canada

Judgments

Arguments

United Kingdom

United States

Australia

Germany

Netherlands

European Union

GOVERNMENT DOCUMENTS

Canada

Legislative Debates

Law Reform Publications

Other Documents

United Kingdom

United States

European Union

Introduction

I. CONTEXT

THIS BOOK CONCERNS clouds of smoke stretching over borders and toxic waste flowing down international rivers and lakes; facilities located here but emitting greenhouse gas that affect the lives of millions there; nuclear fallout causing environmental destruction in multiple territories; and even the legitimate day-to-day operations of a plant located at the border. Most states have detailed legal regimes regulating incidents that occur within their borders. Domestic laws impose preventive measures, regulatory oversight and criminal penalties on polluters, and provide civil remedies to local populations who seek to take legal action against them.[1] But the interdependence of natural ecosystems reveals the obvious transboundary implications of pollution.[2] And when pollution spans political borders, environmental law suddenly becomes unstable.[3] If the harmful activity happened in state *x* but the victim suffered harm in state *y*, who should be held liable, by whom and under what set of rules? As one commentator puts it, 'The problem is not only that pollution and resource degradation cross national borders, but also that decision-making in one country can affect the environment in another country'.[4]

In some cases, the absence of an all-encompassing international authority creates regulatory gaps[5] which result in the significant under-regulation of transboundary pollution, particularly in the global commons. In other cases, it creates regulatory overlap which results in conflicting assertions of extraterritorial authority.[6] These gaps and overlaps lead to regulatory competition.[7]

[1] See generally M-E Arbour, 'Liability Law and Nuisance in the Civil Law Tradition' in L Paddock, DL Markell and NS Bryner (eds), *Elgar Encyclopedia of Environmental Law*, vol 4: Compliance and Enforcement of Environmental Law (Cheltenham, Edward Elgar, 2017); L Collins and H McLeod Kilmurray, 'Common Law Tools to Protect the Environment' in Paddock, Markell and Bryner (ibid).

[2] *References re Greenhouse Gas Pollution Pricing Act* 2021 SCC 11 [12].

[3] See generally S Jayakumar et al (eds), *Transboundary Pollution: Evolving Issues of Law and Policy* (Cheltenham, Edward Elgar, 2015).

[4] M Anderson, 'Transnational Corporations and Environmental Damage: Is Tort Law the Answer?' (2002) 41 *Washburn Law Journal* 399, 399.

[5] R Wai, 'Transnational Liftoff and Juridical Touchdown: The Regulatory Function of Private International Law in a Global Age' (2002) 40 *Columbia Journal of Transnational Law* 209, 250–58.

[6] S-L Hsu and AL Parrish, 'Litigating Canada-U.S. Transboundary Harm: International Environmental Lawmaking and the Threat of Extraterritorial Reciprocity' (2007) 48 *Virgnia Journal of International Law* 1.

[7] TW Merrill, 'Golden Rules for Transboundary Pollution' (1997) 46 *Duke Law Journal* 931, 968–70.

They can also lead in some cases to the much maligned (but historically debated[8]) race to the bottom in which environmental standards decrease to the benefit of disaggregated private actors moving somewhat autonomously across jurisdictions.[9]

Gaps and overlaps mean that the persons threatened with or affected by transboundary pollution face many procedural uncertainties when they seek the liability of a polluter through litigation. They must determine where to sue for injunctive relief or compensation. They must assess the applicable law under the choice of law rules of the forum, as well as the territorial scope of local environmental statutes. They must deal with the enforcement of a judgment abroad if the defendant fails to comply and has no assets in the jurisdiction.

The near-mythical *Trail Smelter* arbitration between Canada and the United States over the toxic fumes of a Canadian facility at the border illustrates the difficulties associated with the process.[10] The case is widely considered a cornerstone of public international law, yet it arose out of a private dispute between the operator of the smelter in Canada and the individuals affected by pollution in the United States. Neither Canadian nor American courts, however, would have had jurisdiction under the rules of private international law in force at the time.[11] Governments eventually took up the issue and initiated an interstate dispute-resolution process, which quickly overshadowed an essentially private nuisance dispute and left the jurisdictional problem unaddressed.

Arbitrators issued their final award in 1941 but litigation resumed many years later over the very same smelter, amid a citizen suit under the Comprehensive Environmental Response, Compensation, and Liability Act (CERCLA)[12] and unilateral action by American authorities. The *Pakootas* lawsuit targeted the operator of the facility, Teck Cominco, for the contamination of the United States side of the Columbia River, and sought to enforce remediation orders issued in the United States. The defendant, Teck Cominco, argued that the lawsuit was inappropriate insofar as it involved an American agency targeting, under American law, a company operating in Canada. Courts denied Teck Cominco's 'extraterritoriality' argument and allowed the lawsuit to proceed in the United States in 2006.[13] The judicial saga continued for years. In September 2018, the

[8] H Zhao and R Percival, 'Comparative Environmental Federalism: Subsidiarity and Central Regulation in the United States and China' (2017) 6 *Transnational Environmental Law* 531, 540–41.

[9] U Grušić, 'International Environmental Litigation in EU Courts: A Regulatory Perspective' (2016) 35 *Yearbook of European Law* 180, 187–88.

[10] *Trail Smelter (United States v Canada)* (1941) 3 RIAA 1905.

[11] WF Baber and RV Bartlett, *Global Democracy and Sustainable Jurisprudence: Deliberative Environmental Law* (Cambridge, MIT Press, 2009) 88. This is widely reported in the literature, typically by relying on the account of John Erskine Read, who advised the Canadian Ministry of External Affairs during the dispute and was later appointed to the International Court of Justice: JE Read, 'The *Trail Smelter* Dispute' (1963) 1 *Canadian Yearbook of International Law* 213, 222.

[12] Comprehensive Environmental Response, Compensation, and Liability Act of 1980, Pub L No 96-510, 94 Stat 2767 (1980) (codified as amended at 42 USC § 9601–9628) (CERCLA).

[13] *Pakootas v Teck Cominco Metals Ltd* 452 F (3d) 1066 (9th Cir 2006), *certiorari* denied 552 US 1095 (2008).

United States Court of Appeals for the Ninth Circuit held Teck Cominco liable for more than eight million USD in clean-up costs incurred by plaintiffs, and the Supreme Court refused to hear the case.[14] The heated debate that took place in courthouses and among scholars and commentators as a result of the *Pakootas* lawsuit (and Teck's activities generally)[15] shows that while the stakes in the *Trail Smelter* saga may have evolved, the legal treatment of the underlying issue remains frustratingly elusive.

Gaps and overlaps are also amplified by the vast discrepancy in the environmental laws applied around the globe. Discrepancies may appear minor among developed and friendly neighbours such as Canada and the United States, or within the European Union. After all, regulatory architecture and enforcement priorities may vary, but what is outright prohibited in one is rarely allowed in the other. Canadian regulations on vehicle emissions, for instance, go as far as to incorporate American standards by reference.[16] Yet policymakers can disagree on reasonable environmental priorities, and their policy choices seldom benefit from scientific certainty. Regulatory disparities inevitably follow, even among friendly and like-minded countries such as Canada and the United States.

Gaps and overlaps affect the prospect of liability, an important tool of compliance with environmental law. Victims fundamentally seek to hold polluters liable for breaching their statutory duties or deviating from basic standards of diligence, to obtain redress for the damage that ensues and to prevent it from continuing. They can avail themselves of a variety of causes of action, loosely referred to as 'environmental torts'.[17] But this process becomes particularly difficult when the polluting act and its consequences do not occur in a single jurisdiction. Environmental laws may clash, overlap or suffer from a lack of enforcement such that polluters escape liability towards victims.[18]

Addressing this problem ideally requires an international legal regime that prevents as many gaps and overlaps as possible from arising in the first place. Such international legal regime could also deal robustly and effectively with the gaps and overlaps that remain inevitable. This would ensure that polluters causing transboundary damage are never in a better position than polluters causing damage only in the state in which they operate. The issue of liability, however, has proven to be excessively difficult and controversial in international law. States committed in Stockholm (1972)[19] and

[14] *Pakootas v Teck Cominco Metals Ltd* 905 F (3d) 565 (9th Cir 2018), *certiorari* denied 139 S Ct 2693 (2019).

[15] See n 351 (ch 4) below.

[16] On-Road Vehicle and Engine Emission Regulations, SOR/2003-2.

[17] *Smith v Inco Ltd* 2012 ONSC 5094 [95], affd 2013 ONCA 724, leave to appeal to SCC refused [2014] 2 SCR vii (defining 'environmental tort' as 'the collective use of several traditional causes of action for the purpose of advancing environmental claims').

[18] Wai, 'Transnational Liftoff and Juridical Touchdown' (2002) 251.

[19] Declaration of the United Nations Conference on the Human Environment (16 June 1972) UN Doc A/CONF 48/14/Rev 1 ('Stockholm Declaration') principle 22.

Rio (1992 and 2012)[20] to developing international liability law and compensation for victims of transboundary pollution. Their governments later recognised in Malmö the importance of compliance, liability and enforcement in ensuring environmental protection.[21]

States, however, have repeatedly failed to meet their commitments. Today, there is still no general international liability regime for transboundary pollution. Scholars explored early on how state responsibility applied to transboundary pollution and other hazardous human activities such as space exploration.[22] But states have jealously maintained their sovereignty over natural resources and consistently avoided articulating a clear doctrine of state responsibility for environmental damage.[23] Today, the difficulties in applying the rules of state responsibility to an environmental dispute remain legion.[24] Forty-nine years have now passed since Stockholm. Determining whether these decades of hesitation come from conceptual confusion or a lack of political interest has become a rhetorical question that simply fails to advance the environmental agenda.

Since Stockholm, states have chosen to focus on preventive measures rather than compensation, or have deliberately avoided state responsibility by imposing civil liability on private persons (typically the operator of a facility) through civil liability treaties. The International Law Commission (ILC) took the same stance in its 2006 Principles on the Allocation of Loss. This set of principles – analysed in this book – calls for states to ensure the availability of 'prompt and adequate compensation' for victims of transboundary pollution and to adjust their rules of private international law accordingly.[25] They come from a prominent organisation mandated by the United Nations (UN) to promote

[20] Rio Declaration on Environment and Development (13 June 1992) UN Doc A/CONF.151/26/Rev.1(Vol 1) ('Rio Declaration') principle 13. At the Rio+20 Summit of the United Nations Conference on Sustainable Development in 2012, states reaffirmed the principles expressed in the Rio Declaration and their commitment to fully implement them: The future we want, UNGA Res 66/288 (27 July 2012) UN Doc A/RES/66/288.

[21] Malmö Ministerial Declaration (Malmö, 31 May 2000) UN Doc UNEP/GC/DEC/SS.VI/1 (2000), para 3.

[22] KB Hoffman, 'State Responsibility in International Law and Transboundary Pollution Injuries' (1976) 25 *International and Comparative Law Quarterly* 709; LFE Goldie, 'International Principles of Responsibility for Pollution' (1970) 9 *Columbia Journal of Transnational Law* 283.

[23] J Brunnée, 'Of Sense and Sensibility: Reflections on International Liability Regimes as Tools for Environmental Protection' (2004) 53 *International and Comparative Law Quarterly* 351, 352–54; SE Gaines, 'International Principles for Transnational Environmental Liability: Can Developments in Municipal Law Help Break the Impasse?' (1989) 30 *Harvard International Law Journal* 311, 313; N Sachs, 'Beyond the Liability Wall: Strengthening Tort Remedies in International Environmental Law' (2008) 55 *UCLA Law Review* 837, 838.

[24] J Peel, 'Unpacking the Elements of a State Responsibility Claim for Transboundary Pollution' in Jayakumar et al, *Transboundary Pollution* (2015) 75–76.

[25] Principles on the allocation of loss in the case of transboundary harm arising out of hazardous activities, annexed to GA Res 61/36 (4 December 2006) UN Doc A/RES/61/36 ('ILC Principles on the Allocation of Loss').

the codification and progressive development of international law,[26] and whose reports are presented to the UN General Assembly (UNGA).

Relying on civil liability makes sense. While prevention is always preferable, ex post facto remedies nonetheless help internalise the costs of pollution, provide incentives for compliance and act as a back-up to regulatory efforts.[27] Furthermore, the dynamics of transboundary pollution reflect a conflict between industrial firms – from small operators to large multinationals – and private victims, fuelled only indirectly by the states' political settings. On this view, claiming compensation from a government for pollution caused by the industry undermines the polluter-pays principle.[28] Advancing civil liability thus seems sensible and realistic given the dearth of sufficiently precise and enforceable rules binding states. But even this modest alternative approach to state responsibility has proven difficult to accept. States have rejected most civil liability treaties other than for marine oil pollution and nuclear incidents. Victims of environmental damage still struggle to obtain redress while corporations freely externalise the environmental consequences of their activities in other jurisdictions. Liability for transboundary pollution remains an 'empty abstraction' in international law.[29]

Attempts at creating international liability regimes for transboundary pollution ought to be taken seriously, but optimism has waned after the failure of too many regimes. As time passed, negotiators gradually put their faith in domestic liability regimes to address the gaps and overlaps in the regulation of transboundary pollution. Priorities shifted from substantive regulation at an international level to the articulation of minimum procedural standards destined to be implemented in domestic law. The shift is pragmatic, not dogmatic. It does not question the legitimacy or adequacy of international environmental law, but settles for the implementation of its underlying policies into domestic law to achieve a form of accountability that is otherwise out of reach, at least for now. Environmental liability thus slowly but surely became a laboratory of paramount importance for the study of the interactions between domestic and international law.

Regulatory coordination under the umbrella of international law can effectively achieve what we expect from an international liability regime – allocating

[26] Statute of the International Law Commission, GA Res 174 (II) (21 November 1947) UN Doc A/519 ('Statute of the ILC'), Art 1(1).

[27] Sachs, 'Beyond the Liability Wall' (2008) 845–46; Brunnée, 'Sense and Sensibility' (2004) 365–66.

[28] A Boyle and C Redgewell, *Birnie, Boyle and Redgewell's International Law and the Environment*, 4th edn (Oxford, Oxford University Press, 2021) 232; AE Boyle, 'Globalising Environmental Liability: The Interplay of National and International Law' (2005) 17 *Journal of Environmental Law* 3, 8. cf J Brunnée, 'International Legal Accountability Through the Lens of the Law of State Responsibility' (2005) 36 *Netherlands Yearbook of International Law* 3, 36 (cautioning against relieving the states from the legal consequences of their own actions by focusing exclusively on non-state actors).

[29] 'Developments in the Law: International Environmental Law' (1991) 104 *Harvard Law Review* 1484, 1500. At the very least, its development 'remains largely an aspiration': Boyle and Redgewell, *International Law and the Environment* (2021) 355.

the burdens and benefits of activities that are potentially harmful yet condoned by the states for political or economic reasons.[30] It rests on the idea that 'the international legal system must be able to influence the domestic policies of states and harness national institutions in pursuit of global objectives'.[31] But an important piece of the puzzle is missing. Most proposals implicitly rely on private international law to facilitate 'good' forum shopping: for instance, how to maintain a claim under the jurisdiction of a domestic court or to apply a law that is favourable to compensation. In fact, the doctrines designed to operationalise what the ILC referred to as a duty to ensure prompt and adequate compensation primarily involve the reform of private international law. Yet little meaningful dialogue between public and private international law occurs over these issues. Only one scholar has gone as far as to explicitly link a state's duty to ensure prompt and adequate compensation of environmental damage with the procedural standards found in private international law.[32] The connection remains frustratingly undertheorised.

A useful and often overlooked way to approach gaps and overlaps in transboundary environmental protection is to ensure that private international law reflects the policies entrenched in international environmental law, particularly that of prompt and adequate compensation. Private international law 'provides rules for governing people, relationships, or situations that in some way or another cannot be confined within the remit of any one particular [s]tate or territory'.[33] We refer to these rules as 'conflict rules'. Private international law, as it is generally conceived today in the United Kingdom and in Canada,[34] has three branches: jurisdiction; choice of law; and the recognition and enforcement of foreign judgments. 'Jurisdiction' refers to the possibility for a domestic court to hear a transboundary dispute on the basis of a sufficient connection with the forum. 'Choice of law' refers to the law applied by the court to that dispute (local or foreign). 'Enforcement of foreign judgments' refers to the ability of a domestic court to recognise a foreign civil judgment as if it were its own, such that it can be enforced against the assets of the defendant in the forum.

Suggesting that private international law offers appropriate tools to deal with the consequences of transboundary pollution is hardly a novel proposition. But this proposition depends on an acute understanding of its regulatory

[30] J Ebbesson, 'Piercing the State Veil in Pursuit of Environmental Justice' in J Ebbesson and P Okowa (eds), *Environmental Law and Justice in Context* (Cambridge, Cambridge University Press, 2009) 275–77.

[31] A-M Slaughter and W Burke-White, 'The Future of International Law Is Domestic (or, The European Way of Law)' (2006) 47 *Harvard International Law Journal* 327, 328.

[32] R Lefeber, *Transboundary Environmental Interference and the Origin of State Liability* (The Hague, Kluwer Law International, 1996) 260–69.

[33] H Muir Watt, 'Private International Law's Shadow Contribution to the Question of Informal Transnational Authority' (2018) 25 *Indiana Journal of Global Legal Studies* 37, 38.

[34] A Briggs, *The Conflict of Laws*, 4th edn (Oxford, Oxford University Press, 2019) 4–6; SGA Pitel and NS Rafferty, *Conflict of Laws*, 2nd edn (Toronto, Irwin Law, 2016) 1.

function, the implementation of environmental policy through conflict rules, and the ways in which this process relates to the articulation of liability standards for transboundary pollution. We lack this understanding. This book provides the missing piece of the puzzle – one that sheds new light on existing proposals to hold polluters liable for transboundary pollution – and by treating the ILC Principles on the Allocation of Loss as the contemporary benchmark that they can be.

II. A STUDY OF PRIVATE INTERNATIONAL LAW AND GLOBAL GOVERNANCE

The proposals in this book find their inspiration in the ongoing work on private international law and global governance.[35] Current research seeks to improve the response of private international law to global challenges such as the regulation of transnational corporations or the protection of natural ecosystems, positing that the field can help deal with those challenges alongside public law and public international law. Horatia Muir Watt's work, for instance, seeks to redefine the role of private international law on the premise that it can no longer ignore the private causes of injustice affecting the world.[36] Her project involves the deconstruction of the walls surrounding private international law and the revision of its centuries-old methods. She posits that 'Private autonomy should be concerned with responsibility as much as it means freedom of parochialism; [that] voice should be given to affected communities; [that] multiple legalities should be re-anchored; [and that] process-based methodology should give way to clear preferences'.[37] As explained in chapter two, the regulatory failings of private international law in today's globalised world should not be overstated. The discipline already plays a role in the substantive regulation of transnational actors and phenomena. How it can do so in environmental law, however, remains unclear.

This book expands the reflection on private international law and global governance and identifies its implications for the regulation of transboundary pollution. It investigates civil jurisdiction and choice of law to create an

[35] M Lehmann, 'Regulation, Global Governance and Private International Law: Squaring the Triangle' (2020) 16 *Journal of Private International Law* 1; H Muir Watt and DP Fernández Arroyo (eds), *Private International Law and Global Governance* (Oxford, Oxford University Press, 2014). Global governance can be broadly defined as 'the mechanisms, public or private, formal or informal, which induce some form of discipline on the part of both institutional and private actors in the pursuit of their own political and economic goals'. H Muir Watt, 'Further Terrains for Subversive Comparisons: The Field of Global Governance and the Public/Private Divide' in PG Monateri (ed), *Methods of Comparative Law* (Cheltenham, Edward Elgar, 2012) 272, fn 10.

[36] H Muir Watt, 'Private International Law Beyond the Schism' (2011) 2 *Transnational Legal Theory* 347, 347. See also Muir Watt and Fernández Arroyo, *Global Governance* (ibid).

[37] Muir Watt, 'Beyond the Schism' (2011) 428.

alignment with the objectives pursued by international liability regimes dealing with transboundary pollution. This approach rests on the idea that private international law has a substantive 'regulatory function'.[38] This theory, extensively developed by Robert Wai and Horatia Muir Watt[39] and explained in chapter two, frames private international law as a means to preserve and increase global welfare through the allocation of regulatory authority, in order to respond to important international concerns such as 'distributive justice, democratic political governance, or effective transnational regulation'.[40]

Wai's account of private international law describes regulation as occurring through 'touchdown points': *domestic* areas such as tort law where third parties seek compensation for the externalities of *transnational* conduct.[41] Thus 'Decisions of courts and legislators can enable regulation of transnational business networks by instituting different kinds of legal liability and facilitating other forms of direct action by non-state actors'.[42] His work ultimately allows us to conceptualise private international law as part of a representative process relied upon by marginalised individuals and groups to regulate private conduct and complement domestic public regulation.[43] From this perspective, 'expanding rather than limiting such [private] claims is a defensible policy goal to increase possibilities for contestation of transnational private actors by other private actors'.[44] As explained in chapter two, this proposition offers a sound theoretical basis for solving the liability conundrum in international environmental law.

III. SCOPE OF THE BOOK

This book addresses the problem of transboundary pollution generally, in the sense of an act which occurs in one place and has consequences in another. It does, however, focus on the *civil* liability of private parties (or public authorities acting in a private capacity). It also focuses on Canadian law as a case study.

[38] Wai (n 5).

[39] H Muir Watt, 'Choice of Law in Integrated and Interconnected Markets: A Matter of Political Economy' (2003) 9 *Columbia Journal of European Law* 383, 399–408.

[40] Wai (n 5) 266.

[41] ibid.

[42] ibid 268.

[43] R Wai, 'Transnational Private Law and Private Ordering in a Contested Global Society' (2005) 46 *Harvard International Law Journal* 471, 479–81.

[44] R Wai, 'Private v Private: Transnational Private Law and Contestation in Global Economic Governance' in Muir Watt and Fernández Arroyo (n 35) 49. See also R Wai, 'Conflicts and Comity in Transnational Governance: Private International Law as Mechanism and Metaphor for Transnational Social Regulation Through Plural Legal Regimes' in C Joerges and E-U Petersmann (eds), *Constitutionalism, Multilevel Trade Governance and International Economic Law* (Oxford, Hart, 2011).

Transboundary pollution as an act which occurs in one place and has consequences in another. Transboundary pollution is 'a physical externality or spillover that crosses state lines'.[45] It 'occurs when a potentially harmful environmental agent is released in one political jurisdiction (the source state) and physically migrates through a natural medium such as air, water, or soil to another political jurisdiction (the affected state)'.[46] For the purposes of this book, transboundary pollution only entails that the harmful act or activity occurs in one place and that the damage occurs either partly in that place and partly, or completely, in another.[47] The first scenario is the most common because transboundary pollution typically involves continuous damage beginning in one place and eventually crossing a border (or several, depending on how diffuse the problem is). The *Bier* case, a notorious dispute brought by Dutch plaintiffs over the discharge of waste salts in the Rhine by a company operating in France, offers a good example.[48] The second scenario recalls the classic example of a gun fired across a border by a person in state *x*, causing an injury to a person in state *y*. Here, the act and the injury are completely disassociated. Both scenarios, however, involve a foreign element – a legally relevant point of contact with a foreign state which triggers the rules of private international law focused on in this book.

Two forms of 'transboundary pollution' fall outside the scope of this book. The first is damage to the global commons, which raises special considerations – chiefly the legal interest to sue without having personally suffered damage – and does not involve, strictly speaking, a conflict of domestic laws or jurisdictions.[49] Excluding the global commons does not leave us only with trivial or anectodal forms of transboundary pollution: issues as significant as climate change can be approached not only as a global regulatory challenge, but also as distinct occurrences of transboundary damage calling for private remedies in certain circumstances.[50]

[45] Merrill, 'Golden Rules' (1997) 968.

[46] ibid. This book uses 'state of origin' to refer to a source state.

[47] This book refers to environmental 'damage', 'harm' or 'injury' as encompassing any form of damage recoverable under the law designated by choice of law rules – for instance, damage to human health or property, economic losses such as deprivation of profits, the cost of preventive and restoration measures, or even damage to the environment itself. These concepts, of course, are complex and abundantly discussed in public international law and domestic tort law. See generally M Bowman and AE Boyle (eds), *Environmental Damage in International and Comparative Law: Problems of Definition and Valuation* (Oxford, Oxford University Press, 2002).

[48] Case 21/76 *Handelskwekeriz GJ Bier BV v Mines de potasse d'Alsace* [1976] ECR I-1735.

[49] M Fallon, B Fauvarque-Cosson and S Francq, 'Le régime du risque transfrontière de la responsabilité environnementale: en marche vers un droit spécial des conflits de lois?' in G Viney and B Dubuisson (eds), *Les responsabilités environnementales dans l'espace européen: point de vue franco-belge* (Brussels, Bruylant, 2006) 602.

[50] Sachs (n 23) 901. See generally HM Osofsky, 'Is Climate Change "International"? Litigation's Diagonal Regulatory Role' (2009) 49 *Virginia Journal of International Law* 585.

The second form of 'transboundary pollution' excluded from the scope of this book is local pollution caused by a private actor with some degree of connection to a foreign entity – typically transnational corporations that caused environmental damage abroad through the actions of their subsidiaries, agents or other related entities.[51] Business-related human rights violations, including environmental damage, raise complex issues of private international law due to the transnational nature of the entities involved (not to mention other issues such as parent liability in corporate law).[52] The damage itself, however, remains local. Cases of transboundary pollution, by contrast, more often hinge on the territorial connections with the polluting activity or the damage suffered by the victim than the domicile of the corporate wrongdoer. They involve what is described in this book as 'complex torts' or '*pure* transboundary damage'.

Civil liability of the polluter in private (international) law. This book builds on the idea that holding polluters liable for their actions in private law[53] (and specifically tort law[54]) is a sensible approach to provide victims with remedies and further the objectives of international liability regimes, assuming we understand how jurisdiction and choice of law reflect those objectives. This private approach to transboundary pollution typically unfolds in litigation before domestic courts between private parties. While individual interests do not always align with the protection of the environment per se, it is believed that actions by private individuals have legitimate regulatory implications and can supplement (or even replace) state intervention. Prominent figures such as the former Secretary General of the Hague Conference on Private International Law (HCCH) Hans van Loon note that 'transnational tort law has gained increased prominence in environmental matters [and] its role may well further expand in light of the concerns about climate change'.[55] But the value of private law as a response to transboundary pollution is by no means self-evident.

[51] eg *Okpabi v Royal Dutch Shell plc* [2021] UKSC 3; *Vedanta Resources plc v Lungowe* [2019] UKSC 20.

[52] See generally C Kessedjian and H Cantú Rivera (eds), *Private International Law Aspects of Corporate Social Responsibility* (Cham, Springer, 2020); G van Calster, 'Environmental Law and Private International Law' in E Lees and JE Viñuales (eds), *The Oxford Handbook of Comparative Environmental Law* (Oxford, Oxford University Press, 2019).

[53] D Howarth, 'Environmental Law and Private Law' in Lees and Viñuales, *Comparative Environmental Law* (ibid) 1093–95.

[54] Ziff notes that property law is equally important and often flies under the radar when discussing environmental protection: B Ziff, 'Environmental Protection and the Abject Failures of the Common Law' (2020) 71 *University of New Brunswick Law Journal* 3, 5–6.

[55] H van Loon, 'The Global Horizon of Private International Law' (2016) 380 *Recueil des cours de l'Académie de droit international* 9, 98. See also H van Loon, 'The Present and Prospective Contribution of Global Private International Law Unification to Global Legal Ordering' in F Ferrari and DP Fernández Arroyo (eds), *Private International Law: Contemporary Challenges and Continuing Relevance* (Cheltenham, Edward Elgar, 2019) 231–34; H van Loon, 'Principles and Building Blocks for a Global Legal Framework for Transnational Civil Litigation in Environmental Matters' (2018) 23 *Uniform Law Review* 298.

As explained in chapter two, considerable scholarly debate has occurred over this proposition.

Regardless of the stance taken in this regard, however, all-or-nothing proposals ought to be avoided. There is no need to pit (1) regulation against civil liability, (2) public law against private law, or (3) domestic law against international law. First, clearing up the conceptual problems associated with liability for transboundary pollution and emphasising the potential role of civil liability and litigation does not imply the rejection of preventive and regulatory approaches. We may disagree on the extent to which regulation and civil liability respectively contribute to deterrence or environmental protection, but civil liability plays *some* role in this process. At a minimum, it 'can guide the implementation and interpretation of regulation, fill gaps in regulatory regimes, and provide alternative avenues and new innovations to protect environmental values and incentivise sustainable development of natural resources'.[56] Litigation can prevent damage, mobilise public interest, highlight legislative deficiencies and provide a forum where citizens can be heard should their political representatives not be listening.[57] Simply put, civil liability acts as a safety valve in case of regulatory or political failure. This book deals with the significant public policy implications of this safety valve in a transboundary context, where gaps and overlaps increase the risk of state failure.

Second, and in a similar vein, focusing on private law does not imply that public law serves no purpose in regulating transboundary pollution or providing remedies, nor that it is necessarily ineffective in doing so. In any event, environmental law is difficult to pin down as either public or private. Landowners, for instance, used private law as a source of legal remedies long before states enacted the first comprehensive environmental statutes.[58] Undeniably, 'Liability for loss or damage is an elementary feature of a legal system' and 'an important part of most systems of environmental law'.[59] The point is not 'to pit one discipline against another, or to wage a battle of academic expertise'.[60] Private law remedies can – and should – coexist with other mechanisms rooted in public law (public participation in administrative decision-making processes, for instance) or international law (citizen submissions under trade agreements, for instance).

[56] D Grinlinton, 'The Continuing Relevance of Common Law Property Rights and Remedies in Addressing Environmental Challenges' (2017) 62 *McGill Law Journal* 633, 636. See generally DA Kysar, 'The Public Life of Private Law: Tort Law as a Risk Regulation Mechanism' (2018) 9 *European Journal of Risk Regulation* 48.

[57] Wai, 'Transnational Private Law and Private Ordering' (2005) 481–82.

[58] M Wilde, *Civil Liability for Environmental Damage: Comparative Analysis of Law and Policy in Europe and the US*, 2nd edn (Alphen on the Rhine, Kluwer Law International, 2013) 3–4.

[59] Boyle and Redgewell (n 28) 225; Boyle, 'Globalising Environmental Liability' (2005) 3.

[60] Muir Watt (n 36) 355. See also J Connell, 'Trans-National Environmental Disputes: Are Civil Remedies More Effective for Victims of Environmental Harm?' (2007) 10 *Asia Pacific Journal of Environmental Law* 39, 47.

Finally, positing a lack of consensus over existing international environmental liability instruments does not imply that we should stop working towards an international solution. As Sand puts it:

> [M]ost transnational environmental fact situations require a multilevel regulatory approach, because their 'public' international law features tend to be inextricably mixed with equally relevant aspects of international and comparative private law, commercial law, administrative law, human rights, and even criminal law.[61]

This book does not purport to identify the flaws of public international law, beyond the failure of most environmental liability instruments to achieve consensus. Assigning responsibility to the state may still be a valid response to transboundary pollution, even though the private sector, not the state, is often directly responsible for environmental damage. It may also be useful to incorporate liability rules into a wide-ranging treaty. This book does not settle these issues. It focuses instead on the private law aspects of environmental liability, particularly those that are unique to transboundary pollution: jurisdiction and choice of law. They are important for two reasons. First, private international law is inextricably bound to the regulation of transboundary pollution itself: by allocating regulatory authority, it either weakens or strengthens domestic regulatory oversight on polluters.[62] Second, many cross-border environmental lawsuits hinge on victims' ability to find a court with jurisdiction and a favourable cause of action under domestic law. Again, these are matters of private international law, crucial to the viability of a private action and scrutinised by litigants before they even commence proceedings.[63]

Of course, overcoming jurisdictional and choice of law challenges is not an end in itself. Applying substantive tort law to complex environmental problems – whether local or transboundary – raises enormous difficulties and may not always be the best option, or even a viable one. It also raises important questions on the legitimacy of judicial intervention, particularly in relation to politically sensitive issues such as climate change.[64] While this book focuses on private international law and transboundary pollution, other challenges must be kept in mind – challenges for which private international law offers no answers, and which a purely private angle may struggle to overcome.

Canada as a case study. This book starts by engaging with international environmental law, private international law and their mutual relationship. It then focuses on Canadian private international law as a case study. Canada is a federation in which each province and territory is considered a distinct

[61] PH Sand, 'The Evolution of Transnational Environmental Law: Four Cases in Historical Perspective' (2012) 1 *Transnational Environmental Law* 183, 186–87.

[62] Ebbesson, 'Piercing the State Veil' (2009) 282.

[63] CO García-Castrillón, 'International Litigation Trends in Environmental Liability: A European Union-United States Comparative Perspective' (2011) 7 *Journal of Private International Law* 551, 565.

[64] eg L Burgers, 'Should Judges Make Climate Change Law?' (2020) 9 *Transnational Environmental Law* 55.

state for the purposes of private international law.[65] This means that 'transboundary' pollution can occur even within its borders, much like in the United States.[66] While environmental regulation falls under shared federal and provincial jurisdiction,[67] private international law is essentially provincial.[68] Quebec comprehensively codified its rules of private international law in the Civil Code of Quebec (CCQ).[69] Other provinces resort to the common law, at times supplemented by particular statutes.

There are good reasons to focus on Canada. The country shares with the United States the longest international border on the planet and the world's largest surface freshwater system on which millions of Canadians and Americans rely.[70] Contaminants move in both directions. Today, for instance, 'Over fifty percent of air pollution in the Province of Ontario – more than ninety percent in some municipalities – originates in the United States'.[71] Canada and the United States sides deal with transboundary issues through a wide variety of legal and political means.[72] While the two governments – as well as Mexico – generally cooperate in a peaceful setting, incidents do happen and can lead to litigation. This history of Canada-United States environmental litigation goes in fact much beyond the *Trail Smelter* arbitration: there is also an extensive history of civil litigation between the two countries. The *Pakootas* case is a notorious and recent example,[73] but others exist. For instance, a First Nation sued in the United States two corporations that operated aluminum plants in the state of New York, alleging that the plants emitted airborne pollutants which settled on the Canadian side of the border where they lived.[74] An Ontario resident brought a private prosecution against a Detroit electricity provider that operated two coal-fired power plants in Eastern Michigan which contaminated the St-Clair River with mercury.[75] Another group of Ontario

[65] *Club Resorts Ltd v Van Breda* 2012 SCC 17 [21].

[66] eg *International Paper Co v Ouellette* 479 US 481 (1987).

[67] *R v Hydro-Québec* [1997] 3 SCR 213, 286.

[68] HP Glenn, 'Justice Louis LeBel and the Private International Law of a Diverse Federation' (2015) 70 *Supreme Court Law Review (2d)* 47. The words 'Canadian private international law' should therefore be understood as the rules of private of international law in force in the relevant province or territory. The same goes for the words 'Canadian law'. The word 'province' is also used as a shorthand for Canadian provinces *and* territories (Yukon, Northwest Territories and Nunavut).

[69] Civil Code of Quebec CQLR c CCQ-1991 (CCQ), Arts 3076ff. Relevant statutory provisions of Canadian private international law are available online and reprinted in J Basedow et al (eds), *Encyclopedia of Private International Law*, vol 4 (Cheltenham, Edward Elgar, 2017) 3046.

[70] ND Hall, 'Transboundary Pollution: Harmonizing International and Domestic Law' (2007) 40 *University of Michigan Journal of Law Reform* 681, 682–683.

[71] ML Banda, 'Regime Congruence: Rethinking the Scope of State Responsibility for Transboundary Environmental Harm' (2019) 103 *Minnesota Law Review* 1879, 1880.

[72] See generally CA Cooper, 'The Management of International Environmental Disputes in the Context of Canada-United States Relations: A Survey and Evaluation of Techniques and Mechanisms' (1986) 24 *Canadian Yearbook of International Law* 247.

[73] *Pakootas* 2006 (n 13).

[74] *Canadian St Regis Band of Mohawk Indians v Reynolds Metals* [1981] 3 CNLR 33 (ND NY).

[75] *Edwards v DTE Energy Co* [2008] OJ No 4433 (Lexis Advance Quicklaw) (Ont Sup Ct).

residents settled a lawsuit against the company's ancestor for transboundary air pollution.[76] Yet another group of Ontario residents sued three American steel manufacturers that operated seven plants across the Detroit River from Canada, claiming that the noxious air pollutants emitted from their facilities represented a nuisance for Canadians.[77] Canadian public authorities have also had their share of court time in the United States.[78]

The Canada-United States border thus offers a unique setting to study the jurisdictional aspects of transboundary environmental litigation. While this book's focus remains on Canadian law (and not American law), it also relies on a variety of sources and instruments from European countries, including the Rome II Regulation and its much-discussed choice of law rule for environmental damage, openly driven by environmental policy.[79]

IV. OBJECTIVES OF THE BOOK

This book explores how states implement international environmental policy through domestic rules on jurisdiction and choice of law, and how this process relates to the articulation of international liability standards for transboundary pollution. International environmental lawyers are aware of private international law's potential relevance in solving the liability conundrum, but they rarely delve deep into the intricacies of the field.[80] Private international lawyers, on their part, are certainly aware of the many challenges raised by transboundary pollution,[81] but they rarely pay attention to their international backdrop, including the *states'* duty to ensure that victims obtain prompt and adequate compensation. Contemporary private international law almost invariably fails to ponder the efforts at crafting an international liability regime that would attract consensus. Yet the two bodies of law interact in obvious ways.[82] International environmental law frequently and explicitly points to private international law as part of the solution, most recently in the ILC Principles on the Allocation

[76] 'Edison Pays 300 Claims for Fallout' *Windsor Star* (7 September 1973) A3.

[77] *Michie v Great Lakes Steel Division, National Steel Corp* 495 F (2d) 213 (6th Cir 1974), *certiorari* denied 419 US 997 (1974).

[78] eg *Her Majesty the Queen in Right of the Province of Ontario v United States Environmental Protection Agency* 912 F (2d) 1525 (DC Cir 1990) (lawsuit against the Environmental Protection Agency for failure to take action in relation to acid rain affecting Canada); *United States of America v Hooker Chemicals & Plastics Corporation* 101 FRD 444 (WD NY 1984) (intervention by the province of Ontario in proceedings brought by American authorities against a chemical company over a landfill located next to a drinking-water treatment plant and polluting Lake Ontario).

[79] Regulation (EC) 864/2007 of the European Parliament and of the Council of 11 July 2007 on the law applicable to non-contractual obligations (Rome II) [2007] OJ L199/40 ('Rome II Regulation'), Art 7.

[80] Boyle and Redgewell (n 28) 330–35; Boyle (n 28) 9–16.

[81] eg C von Bar, 'Environmental Damage in Private International Law' (1997) 268 *Recueil des cours de l'Académie de droit international* 291.

[82] See generally R Wolfrum, C Langenfeld and P Minnerop, *Environmental Liability in International Law: Towards a Coherent Conception* (Berlin, Erich Schmidt, 2005).

of Loss.[83] We must take these signals seriously, in light of the shifting emphasis towards civil liability and the contrasting failure of most liability treaties to achieve consensus.

To do so, it is necessary to go back in time. Active discussions took place in the 1970s over transboundary pollution in the midst of the 1977 OECD Recommendation on equal access and non-discrimination in relation to 'transfrontier pollution'[84] and the adoption of the 1974 Convention on the Protection of the Environment (Nordic Convention) by Scandinavian countries.[85] Both instruments require that foreign victims of pollution have the same access to courts and remedies as local victims of pollution in the state of origin (the state of origin being one of the contracting states). Early proposals relied heavily on private international law. They occurred precisely while environmental protection was finding a place of its own on the international agenda, and transboundary issues such as acid rain, ozone depletion and nuclear incidents were being discussed. Yet many of these proposals were never fully studied nor implemented. Private international law (and indeed private law generally) faded in the background as international treaty-making hit full speed. Follow-up projects under the auspices of the Hague Conference on Private International Law and the International Law Association in the 1990s and 2000s sought to keep private international law on the agenda.[86] Both projects, however, failed to build momentum and the HCCH ceased its work on the topic. Meanwhile, increasing attention towards human rights litigation against corporations in domestic courts led commentators to conclude that private international law was 'beginning to be affected by human rights and access to justice concerns in novel and important ways that have implications for future environmental litigation'.[87]

The growing concern for the safeguard of human rights in private international law is cause for celebration. Interestingly, however, documents such as the OECD Recommendation and the Nordic Convention continue to appear in today's scholarship, more than 40 years after their adoption. One other recently proposed an approach based on non-discrimination in the aftermath of the *Pakootas* litigation and the allegedly extraterritorial application of American law to Teck Cominco in Canada.[88] Another explored a similar approach to deal with transboundary haze pollution in Southeast Asia.[89] Leading texts

[83] ILC Principles on the Allocation of Loss (n 25).

[84] OECD, Recommendation of the Council for the Implementation of a Regime of Equal Right of Access and Non-Discrimination in Relation to Transfrontier Pollution, OECD Doc C(77)28/FINAL (1977) 16 ILM 977 ('OECD Recommandation'), reprinted in Organisation for Economic Co-operation and Development, *Legal Aspects of Transfrontier Pollution* (Paris, OECD, 1977).

[85] Convention on the Protection of the Environment (19 February 1974, entered into force 5 October 1976) 1092 UNTS 279 ('Nordic Convention').

[86] For further discussion on the work of the HCCH and the ILA, see section 2.I below.

[87] Boyle and Redgewell (n 28) 354.

[88] T Kruger, 'Trail Smelter II: A Prudent Approach? From Extraterritoriality to Non-Discrimination' (2010) 43 *UBC Law Review* 109.

[89] P Listiningrum, 'Transboundary Civil Litigation for Victims of Southeast Asian Haze Pollution: Access to Justice and the Non-Discrimination Principle' (2019) 8 *Transnational Environmental Law* 119.

still mention non-discrimination as an important benchmark.[90] The ILC relied on this concept to craft its Principles on the Allocation of Loss, particularly the sixth principle on international and domestic remedies.[91] In Canada and elsewhere, scholars continue to discuss and criticise the rules that barred private action in *Trail Smelter* some 80 years ago.[92]

Early work on the private law of transboundary pollution has not lost all relevance to the transboundary issues we face today. For instance, climate change litigation has emerged as a regulatory mechanism to prevent, mitigate and compensate damage caused by the human production of greenhouse gas causing global warming.[93] Many lawsuits seek to hold governments accountable for regulatory inaction through public or administrative law, but tort claims have also been filed against greenhouse gas emitters themselves.[94] A Peruvian farmer and mountain guide, for instance, recently sued a major energy company in Germany, arguing that the company was partly responsible for the adverse impacts of climate change on his family, his land and his region, which is vulnerable to flooding. German courts agreed to hear the case.[95]

Despite academic controversies and debates,[96] climate change lawsuits will continue to appear on the dockets for the foreseeable future.[97] Jurisdiction and choice of law will have an important role to play in this context given the global implications of climate change,[98] and the literature is already catching up.[99] But we should not forget the efforts put into applying private law

[90] P Sands and J Peel with A Fabra and R MacKenzie, *Principles of International Environmental Law*, 4th edn (Cambridge, Cambridge University Press, 2018) 164–65; Boyle and Redgewell (n 28) 169–70, 324–30.

[91] ILC Principles on the Allocation of Loss (n 25) principle 6.

[92] For further discussion on the local action rule, see section 3.II.A.i.b below.

[93] See generally W Kahl and M-P Weller, *Climate Change Litigation: A Handbook* (Oxford, Hart, 2021); J Peel and HM Osofsky, *Climate Change Litigation: Regulatory Pathways to Cleaner Energy* (Cambridge, Cambridge University Press, 2017).

[94] In the United States, see eg *City of New York v Chevron Corporation* 993 F (3d) 81 (2nd Cir 2021).

[95] W Frank, C Bals and J Grimm, 'The Case of Huaraz: First Climate Lawsuit on Loss and Damage Against an Energy Company Before German Courts' in R Mechler et al (eds), *Loss and Damage from Climate Change: Concepts, Methods and Policy Options* (Cham, Springer, 2019).

[96] cf C Piñon Carlarne, 'The Essential Role of Climate Litigation and the Courts in Averting Climate Crisis' in B Mayer and A Zahar (eds), *Debating Climate Law* (Cambridge, Cambridge University Press, 2021); G Dwyer, 'Climate Litigation: A Red Herring Among Climate Mitigation Tools' in Mayer and Zahar (ibid).

[97] G Ganguly, J Setzer and V Heyvaert, 'If at First You Don't Succeed: Suing Corporations for Climate Change' (2018) 38 *Oxford Journal of Legal Studies* 841, 850. In Canada, see C Choquette, D Klaudt and L Shay Lyne, 'Climate Change Litigation in Canada' in F Sindico and MM Mbengue (eds), *Comparative Climate Change Litigation: Beyond the Usual Suspects* (Cham, Springer, 2021).

[98] eg *City of Oakland v BP plc* 2018 WL 3609055 (Westlaw) (ND Cal 2018). The issue of personal jurisdiction was left open on appeal: *City of Oakland v BP plc* 969 F (3d) 895, 911, fn 13 (9th Cir 2020).

[99] O Boskovic, 'Le contexte transnational en matière de responsabilité climatique' in M Hautereau-Boutonnet and S Porchy-Simon (eds), *Le changement climatique, quel rôle pour le droit privé?* (Paris, Dalloz, 2019); M Lehmann and F Eichel, 'Globaler Klimawandel und Internationales Privatrecht – Zuständigkeit und anzuwendendes Recht für transnationale Klagen wegen klimawandelbedingter Individualschäden' (2019) 83 *Rabel Journal of Comparative and International Private Law (RabelsZ)* 77; F Giansetto, 'Le droit international privé à l'épreuve des nouveaux contentieux en matière de responsabilité climatique' [2018] *Journal du droit international* 507.

(including private international law) to other transboundary issues that were on the agenda not so long ago, and the lessons they can teach us in dealing with contemporary issues. This book reassesses the relevance of early debates on transboundary pollution against the rise of the human rights discourse, the judicial fight against climate change and the attempts at elaborating international liability regimes for some of the greatest environmental challenges of our time.

V. STRUCTURE OF THE BOOK

This book is divided into two parts. The first part explores liability for transboundary pollution in international environmental law (chapter one), and the function of private international law in this context (chapter two). The second part relies on Canadian private international law as an illustration of the field's potential. It addresses jurisdiction and foreign judgments (chapter three) and choice of law (chapter four).

Chapter one argues that states have a duty to ensure prompt and adequate compensation for victims of transboundary pollution. It begins with a demonstration of the road taken from the first international liability regimes to the present day. It introduces the issue of liability in international environmental law, including notions of state responsibility, state liability and treaty-based state/civil liability. It then demonstrates the states' preference for regimes that rely on domestic laws to implement the polluter-pays principle, contrasting this preference with the failure of many treaty-based civil liability regimes to achieve consensus. Taking a step back, the first chapter returns to the primary objective of international liability regimes to argue that states now have a duty to ensure prompt and adequate compensation of environmental damage, as stated in the ILC Principles on the Allocation of Loss.[100]

Chapter two demonstrates the role of private international law in fulfilling the duty to ensure prompt and adequate compensation. The regulatory function of private international law has recently come under academic scrutiny in the literature on private international law and global governance, despite being somewhat intuitive to those accustomed to its methods and rules. This second chapter demonstrates that the attempts we have seen in international environmental law to improve civil liability through domestic law are not misguided. They are, however, based on a certain conception of private international law – a conception that accounts for its regulatory function, the erosion of the public/private distinction and domestic courts' involvement in global governance.

Chapters three and four build on the ILC Principles on the Allocation of Loss and assess how Canadian private international law regulates

[100] ILC Principles on the Allocation of Loss (n 25) principle 3.

transboundary pollution and helps ensure (or inhibit) prompt and adequate compensation. They also reexamine how Canadian private international law plays out in the context of transboundary pollution. These two chapters do not proceed to review all possible connecting factors, and their advantages and inconveniences for plaintiffs and defendants. Instead, and more importantly, they lay out the connections between the rules of private international law and the current state of international environmental law. It is from this novel perspective that the current legal landscape is reviewed – not for its own sake, but to better understand its relationship with international environmental law.

Chapter three examines jurisdictional obstacles that have stood in the way of civil litigation since the *Trail Smelter* arbitration, and the solutions proposed over the years. It argues that courts are now increasingly willing to assert jurisdiction over transboundary pollution, which helps ensure prompt and adequate compensation. This third chapter sets out the jurisdictional requirements associated with the duty to ensure prompt and adequate compensation and the solutions proposed in the ILC Principles on the Allocation of Loss. Against this backdrop, it reviews the reforms undertaken in North America and the general law of jurisdiction in Canada. It examines the possibility of suing at the place of acting or the place of injury, the location (or *situs*) of transboundary pollution for jurisdictional purposes and other issues such as the doctrine of *forum non conveniens* and the enforcement of foreign judgments. It concludes that Canadian jurisdictional rules are satisfactory in light of the duty to ensure prompt and compensation.

Chapter four addresses the implementation of environmental policy in choice of law rules. It argues that accounting for environmental policy in choice of law rules, including the polluter-pays principle, helps ensure prompt and adequate compensation. As in the third chapter, this fourth chapter sets out the choice of law requirements associated with the duty to ensure prompt and adequate compensation, the solutions proposed in the ILC Principles on the Allocation of Loss and the growing international consensus surrounding one particular approach: the ubiquity principle. Against this backdrop, it reviews Canadian choice of law rules. It concludes that Canadian choice of law rules fail to live up to the requirements of the duty to ensure prompt and adequate compensation.

The conclusion revisits the duty to ensure prompt and adequate compensation and the ILC Principles on the Allocation of Loss. It assesses the ability of private international law to deal with transboundary pollution and to help fulfill the duty to ensure prompt and adequate compensation. This assessment provides valuable lessons on the legitimacy and viability of a liability regime that relies primarily on domestic law (including private international law) to hold polluters accountable.

Part 1

Liability and the Intersection of Public and Private International Law

1

Liability for Transboundary Pollution in International Environmental Law

THIS FIRST CHAPTER argues that states have under international law a duty to ensure prompt and adequate compensation for victims of transboundary pollution. They can discharge their duty either by assuming liability themselves or ensuring the availability of civil remedies to victims. In the latter, more plausible scenario, states can fulfil a part of their duty by adopting rules of private international law which help victims bring claims against transboundary polluters. Private international law addresses the gaps and overlaps associated with transboundary pollution and eases the regulatory coordination of domestic laws. This approach moves away from treaty-based civil liability regimes (which have become extremely difficult to put in place because states have conflicting interests and are reluctant to change their own domestic laws) while maintaining their rationale and objective. This central proposition runs through all subsequent chapters and allows us to explore private international law from a new perspective.

This chapter first introduces the concepts of responsibility and liability in international environmental law, which paved the way for the proliferation of civil liability regimes and the development of the duty to ensure prompt and adequate compensation (section I). It then assesses the scope and contents of the duty itself (section II). A conclusion follows (section III).

This chapter does not deal exhaustively with either state responsibility, state liability or civil liability, nor does it provide a comprehensive account of their checkered history or status in customary international law. Scholars have produced staggering amounts of research on those topics and the ILC struggled with them for decades.[1] Grey areas subsist, but the true purpose of this book lies elsewhere: to study precisely how private international law and its regulatory function fit within the current landscape of international environmental law.

[1] For an overview, see C Voigt, 'International Responsibility and Liability' in L Rajamani and J Peel (eds), *The Oxford Handbook of International Environmental Law*, 2nd edn (Oxford, Oxford University Press, 2021).

I. STATE RESPONSIBILITY, STATE LIABILITY AND CIVIL LIABILITY

This section introduces the notions of state responsibility, state liability and civil liability in international environmental law. I deal with the fundamental distinctions (section I.A) and then turn to state responsibility (section I.B), state liability (section I.C) and civil liability (section I.D). This section demonstrates what is at stake in international liability regimes and contextualises the ILC's choice to focus on prompt and adequate compensation as the guiding principle of international liability regimes.

A. Introduction to the Distinction between Responsibility and Liability

Liability is accurately described as the 'Yeti of international environmental law – pursued for years, sometimes spotted in rough outlines, but remarkably elusive in practice'.[2] As an enforcement mechanism, its place in the arsenal of responses to non-compliance in international law leaves no doubt. As a result, 'few multilateral environmental agreements … can be negotiated today without running across the liability issue in one way or another'.[3] Yet the idea that polluters should be held liable for the harm that they cause (which generally carries an obligation to compensate victims of the harm) is fraught with difficulties in all its basic components: the identity of the polluter and the role of the state, the standard of care, the nature and threshold of the harm and the very assumption that the prospect of liability will lead to deterrence.

International lawyers approached the problem first by distinguishing state liability from state responsibility. The distinction became ubiquitous under the impulse of the ILC, which separated the two topics early on.[4] This approach led to controversy,[5] not the least because the distinction is unintelligible in some languages, including French, which uses *responsabilité* to describe both notions.[6]

State responsibility entails the violation of an obligation under international law – primary norms typically found in treaties, customary international

[2] N Sachs, 'Beyond the Liability Wall: Strengthening Tort Remedies in International Environmental Law' (2008) 55 *UCLA Law Review* 837, 839.

[3] J Brunnée, 'Of Sense and Sensibility: Reflections on International Liability Regimes as Tools for Environmental Protection' (2004) 53 *International and Comparative Law Quarterly* 351, 351.

[4] International Law Commission, 'Report of the Commission to the General Assembly on the work of its twenty-fifth session' UN Doc A/9010/Rev.1 (1973) in *Yearbook of the International Law Commission 1973*, vol 2, part 2 (New York, UN, 1975) 169 para 38.

[5] AE Boyle, 'State Responsibility and International Liability for Injurious Consequences of Acts Not Prohibited by International Law: A Necessary Distinction?' (1990) 39 *International and Comparative Law Quarterly* 1.

[6] G Hafner and I Buffart, 'The Work of the International Law Commission: From Liability to Damage Prevention' in Y Kerbrat and Sandrine Maljean-Dubois (eds), *The Transformation of International Environmental Law* (Paris, Pedone, 2011) 234–35.

law or general principles of international law.[7] State liability entails the compensation of damage in the absence of a wrongful act.[8] The latter is concerned with the transboundary risk associated with legitimate activities occurring in a state's territory (including activities carried out by private actors).[9] Transboundary pollution is a prime example because it occurs as a result of activities which may not be unlawful or inherently reprehensible (energy production, for instance).

B. State Responsibility

Under the regime of state responsibility codified by the ILC, parts of which are now thought to be part of customary international law[10] but which is still unincorporated into a treaty,[11] states can be held responsible for an internationally wrongful act, that is, the breach of an international obligation attributable to the state.[12] Environmental treaties may also contain specific rules to that effect – for instance, the 1982 United Nations Convention on the Law of the Sea (UNCLOS)[13] and the 2005 Antarctic Liability Annex (not yet in force).[14]

Identifying an internationally wrongful act is relatively easy when it relates to the breach of a treaty obligation. Obligations arising from customary international environmental law are, however, notoriously difficult to pinpoint and insufficiently developed. Their open-ended nature makes it difficult to identify exactly what states can and cannot do, let alone address complex environmental phenomena with the same precision as detailed regulation.[15]

[7] A Pellet, 'The Definition of Responsibility in International Law' in J Crawford, A Pellet and S Olleson with the assistance of K Parlett (eds), *The Law of International Responsibility* (Oxford, Oxford University Press, 2010).

[8] M Montjoie, 'The Concept of Liability in the Absence of an Internationally Wrongful Act' in Crawford, Pellet and Olleson (ibid).

[9] J Barboza, *The Environment, Risk and Liability in International Law* (Leiden, Martinus Nijhoff, 2011) 3.

[10] J Peel, 'Unpacking the Elements of a State Responsibility Claim for Transboundary Pollution' in S Jayakumar et al (eds), *Transboundary Pollution: Evolving Issues of Law and Policy* (Cheltenham, Edward Elgar, 2015) 51.

[11] Responsibility of States for internationally wrongful acts, UNGA Res 74/180 (18 December 2019) UN Doc A/RES/74/180, para 9.

[12] Responsibility of States for internationally wrongful acts, annexed to GA Res 56/83 (12 December 2001) UN Doc A/RES/56/83.

[13] United Nations Convention on the Law of the Sea (10 December 1982, entered into force 16 November 1994) 1833 UNTS 3 (UNCLOS), Arts 139(2), 235(1), 304.

[14] Liability Arising from Environmental Emergencies (14 June 2005, not yet in force) 45 ILM 5 ('Antarctic Liability Annex'), Art 10, Annex VI to the Protocol on Environmental Protection to the Antarctic Treaty (4 October 1991, entered into force 14 January 1998) 30 ILM 1461.

[15] On the texture and determinacy of primary rules in international environmental law, see J Brunnée, 'International Legal Accountability Through the Lens of the Law of State Responsibility' (2005) 36 *Netherlands Yearbook of International Law* 3, 9, 26; Brunnée, 'Sense and Sensibility' (2004) 353–54; D Bodansky, 'Customary (And Not So Customary) International Environmental Law' (1995) 3 *Indiana Journal of Global Legal Studies* 105, 118, reprinted in PM Pevato (ed), *International Environmental Law*, vol 1 (London, Routledge, 2018).

At a minimum, states have a duty to prevent and abate transboundary pollution. The International Court of Justice (ICJ) held that states must 'use all the means at [their] disposal in order to avoid activities which take place in [their] territory, or in any area under [their] jurisdiction, causing significant damage to the environment of another [s]tate'.[16] This is the prevention principle. This obligation of due diligence is the core component of customary international environmental law, but it is so open-ended that it is difficult to determine what it requires, and whether it has been breached. Its implementation depends on more concrete procedural norms such as the obligation to conduct an environmental impact assessment and to consult and notify potentially affected states when a project poses a risk of transboundary damage.[17] Procedural norms branch out of the substantive duty to prevent harm and participate in its maturation.[18] They are important, but they remain basic in scope and in substance even when they seem well-established.

Customary international environmental law – when it exists – is not easily nor frequently enforced through a judicial process.[19] Environmental disputes rarely result in litigation, and even less so in an interstate setting. An incident as dramatic as Chernobyl did not trigger claims from states against the Soviet Union.[20] Neither did Fukushima -although in this case, it may be because the catastrophe's transboundary impacts were not as severe.[21] As Springer explains:

> International environmental law is best developed when states recognize the value of creating rules and procedures that address environmental problems before they become sources of international dispute. [...] The good news is that law is applied, its limitations uncovered, and better law developed even in times of conflict.[22]

[16] *Case concerning Pulp Mills on the River Uruguay (Uruguay v Argentina)* [2010] ICJ Rep 14 (*Pulp Mills*) [101]. See also *Certain Activities Carried out by Nicaragua in the Border Area (Costa Rica v Nicaragua)* [2015] ICJ Rep 665 (*Nicaragua Border Area*) [104], [118], [168].

[17] *Nicaragua Border Area* (n 16) [104], [153], [161], [168]; *Pulp Mills* (n 16) [204]–[205].

[18] O McIntyre, 'The Role of Customary Rules and Principles of International Environmental Law in the Protection of Shared International Freshwater Resources' (2006) 46 *Natural Resources Journal* 157, 170.

[19] Bodansky (n 15) 117.

[20] Phoebe Okowa, *State Responsibility for Transboundary Air Pollution in International Law* (Oxford, Oxford University Press, 2000) 121–30.

[21] J Suttenberg, 'Who Pays? The Consequences of State Versus Operator Liability Within the Context of Transboundary Environmental Nuclear Damage' (2016) 24 *NYU Environmental Law Journal* 201, 222–23.

[22] As Springer explains, '[i]nternational environmental law is best developed when states recognize the value of creating rules and procedures that address environmental problems before they become sources of international dispute. Yet the record of state behaviour suggests that too often such proactive collaboration simply does not take place. The good news is that law is applied, its limitations uncovered, and better law developed even in times of conflict'. AL Springer, *Cases of Conflict: Transboundary Disputes and the Development of International Environmental Law* (Toronto, University of Toronto Press, 2016) 234.

A critical mass of cases would not only reinforce the law of state responsibility itself, but also help transform broad obligations such as the prevention principle into something more tangible. This is not yet the case.

Examples of state responsibility for environmental damage do exist, but they are peculiar, and their precedential value (in the general sense of a persuasive and replicable approach) is debatable. Resolution 687 of the UN Security Council (UNSC) can be seen as a precedent of state responsibility for environmental damage.[23] The UNSC held Iraq 'liable under international law for any direct loss, damage, including environmental damage and the depletion of natural resources, or injuries to foreign [g]overnments, nationals and corporations, as a result of Iraq's unlawful invasion and occupation of Kuwait'.[24] It established the United Nations Compensation Commission (UNCC), a subsidiary organ charged with administering compensation and assessing the value of damage suffered in Kuwait.[25] The panel of commissioners responsible for the adjudication of environmental claims noted that environmental protection and conservation were a common concern, and that states had obligations not only towards other states but also towards future generations and the international community.[26]

The implications of Resolution 687 for international environmental law, however, are unclear. On the one hand, the practice of the UNCC provides a precedent that may facilitate the invocation of state responsibility or help design specific compensation schemes in other cases.[27] On the other hand, judges cannot, unlike the UNSC, craft brand-new compensation mechanisms or create institutions such as the UNCC to implement their decisions.[28] The practice of the UNCC is notable, but not the harbinger of a radical evolution in international environmental law.[29]

Cases brought before international courts and tribunals are sparse and only occasionally result in a judgment on the merits that satisfactorily clarifies substantive obligations of customary international environmental law. In the *Gabčíkovo-Nagymaros* dispute over the construction of a dam on the Danube, for instance, the ICJ focused on the bilateral treaty obligations of the parties.[30] It did not address Hungary's claim that Slovakia had breached its obligations

[23] A Boyle and C Redgewell, *Birnie, Boyle and Redgewell's International Law and the Environment*, 4th edn (Oxford, Oxford University Press, 2021) 221.

[24] UNSC Res 687 (3 April 1991) UN Doc S/RES/687, para 16.

[25] UNSC Res 692 (20 May 1991) UN Doc S/RES/692, para 3.

[26] United Nations Compensation Commission, 'Report and Recommendations Made by the Panel of Commissioners Concerning the Third Installment of 'F4' Claims' UN Doc S/AC.26/2003/31 (2003), para 42 (cited in subsequent reports).

[27] P Sands and J Peel with A Fabra and R MacKenzie, *Principles of International Environmental Law*, 4th ed (Cambridge, Cambridge University Press, 2018) 743, 755, 803.

[28] Boyle and Redgewell, *International Law and the Environment* (2021) 242.

[29] J-C Martin, 'The United Nations Compensation Commission Practice with Regards to Environmental Claims' in Kerbrat and Maljean-Dubois (n 6) 267.

[30] *Case concerning the Gabčíkovo-Nagymaros Project (Hungary v Slovakia)* [1997] ICJ Rep 92.

to prevent environmental damage and to cooperate with affected states.[31] More recently, the ICJ held Nicaragua responsible for environmental damage caused by excavations and military activities in a disputed territory which it found belonged to Costa Rica.[32] But the ICJ did so only on the basis that Nicaragua had violated Costa Rica's sovereignty. It rejected the argument that Nicaragua had breached a procedural obligation to carry out an environmental impact assessment and to consult with Costa Rica, as well as a substantive obligation not to cause harm.[33] In another case between the same parties and decided in the same judgment, the ICJ found that Costa Rica ought to have carried out an environmental impact assessment when it built a road alongside the San Juan river,[34] but that the construction of the road itself had not caused significant transboundary harm.[35]

Other cases never reach the trial stage. Consider the *Aerial Spraying* case brought to the ICJ in 2008. The dispute involved Colombia's spraying of herbicides over coca plantations to eradicate drug production. The herbicides drifted into Ecuador and caused severe harm to the residents' health and their environment. This textbook example of transboundary pollution boosted observers' hopes of an authoritative and comprehensive ruling in an area of the law that has few of them. Unfortunately for them, parties settled their dispute on the eve of oral submissions on the merits.[36]

The settlement in *Aerial Spraying* proves that the prospect of interstate litigation can persuade the parties to find more durable arrangements and possibly even put an end to transboundary pollution.[37] It also reminds us that the scarcity of reported cases may not accurately reflect the practice of invoking state responsibility for transboundary pollution.[38] As Peel suggests:

> Even if rarely used in practice, a robust and effective regime of state responsibility for transboundary pollution can stimulate more concerted efforts to prevent environmental harm or to better mitigate damage through improved systems of risk management, risk transfer, rehabilitation and compensation mechanisms.[39]

Furthermore, as Boyle accurately observes, 'States litigate for a variety of reasons that may have little or nothing to do with developing international law', including for diplomatic or political purposes.[40] Litigation is not an alternative

[31] ibid, Memorial of the Republic of Hungary, paras 6.56–6.82.

[32] *Nicaragua Border Area* (n 16) [92].

[33] ibid [112], [120].

[34] ibid [162], [168], [173].

[35] ibid [217].

[36] *Case concerning Aerial Herbicide Spraying (Ecuador v Colombia)* (Order of 13 September 2013) [2013] ICJ Rep 278.

[37] A Boyle, 'Transboundary Air Pollution: A Tale of Two Paradigms' in Jayakumar et al (n 10) 255.

[38] Peel (n 10) 75, fn 105.

[39] ibid 78.

[40] A Boyle, 'Progressive Development of International Environmental Law: Legislate or Litigate? (2019) 62 *German Yearbook of International Law* 305, 321. See also Boyle and Redgewell (n 23) 261.

to diplomacy and political commitment.[41] But regardless of why states engage in litigation, and the obvious limitations of that process,[42] decisions by international courts and tribunals help shape international environmental law. They may not create new norms, but they affirm existing ones and give them coherence.[43] As such, states would clearly benefit from frequent judicial guidance, particularly with respect the nature of the measures required to discharge the duty to prevent harm.

Unfortunately, the 'great wave' of environmental cases brought before international courts and tribunals has now died down.[44] The law of state responsibility seems to be stuck in a vicious circle in which uncertain customary obligations impede the articulation of a claim while states maintain uncertainty to shield themselves from legal consequences.[45] The most optimistic scholars concede that it has evolved slowly in environmental matters,[46] while others describe shared responsibility in this area as a simple 'buck-passing' process from state to operator, from operator to insurer and so on, tolerated by states only – and precisely – because they are not part of it.[47] All signs point to a lack of political interest in the *consequences* of misconduct. States clearly have less difficulty agreeing on a vague obligation to conduct an environmental assessment, for instance, than on the actual consequences of a failure to do so,[48] and their inaction is made easier by the fact that the private sector is directly involved in most pollution incidents.

State responsibility will remain an insatisfactory means of obtaining reparation for transboundary pollution, unless customary international environmental law becomes more sophisticated[49] and the regime is applied more often through litigation.[50] There are signs of hope. Climate change, for

[41] ibid 331.

[42] ibid 321–30. See also Boyle and Redgewell (n 23) 246–47, 260–64.

[43] ibid 323.

[44] ibid 309.

[45] Brunnée (n 3) 354; N Craik, 'Transboundary Pollution, Unilateralism and the Limits of Extraterritorial Jurisdiction: The Second *Trail Smelter* Dispute' in RM Bratspies and RA Miller (eds), *Transboundary Harm in International Law: Lessons from the Trail Smelter Arbitration* (Cambridge, Cambridge University Press, 2006) 112.

[46] A Kiss and D Shelton, 'Strict Liability in International Environmental Law' in T Malick Ndiaye and R Wolfrum (eds), *Law of the Sea, Environmental Law and Settlement of Disputes: Liber Amicorum Judge Thomas A Mensah* (Leiden, Martinus Nijhoff, 2007) 1131.

[47] I Plakokefalos, 'Liability for Transboundary Harm' in A Nollkaemper and I Plakokefalos (eds), *The Practice of Shared Responsibility in International Law* (Cambridge, Cambridge University Press, 2017) 1064.

[48] Springer, *Cases of Conflict* (2016) 92 ('It is one thing to say that a state must conduct an environmental assessment of projects that pose significant transboundary risks. It is another to suggest that its failure to do so could have practical consequences').

[49] Secretary-General of the United Nations, 'Gaps in international environmental law and environment-related instruments: towards a global pact for the environment' UN Doc A/73/419 (2018) 40, para 96 ('The rules of State responsibility may need to be further developed if they are to play any significant role as a tool for redressing transboundary environmental harm').

[50] cf Boyle, 'Legislate or Litigate' (2019) (suggesting that political action, not more litigation or more legislation, is required to address the environmental crisis).

instance, is sparking new interest in the definition of primary obligations,[51] with implications for the law of state responsibility.[52] States threatened with the catastrophic consequences of global warming are pushing for a change. In 2002, Tuvalu threatened to sue Australia and the United States in the ICJ over greenhouse gas emissions.[53] In 2012, the Republic of Palau sought to secure the support of the UNGA to request an advisory opinion from the ICJ. Palau proposed to ask the ICJ to identify 'the obligations under international law of a [s]tate for ensuring that activities under its jurisdiction or control that emit greenhouse gas do not cause, or substantially contribute to, serious damage to another [s]tate or [s]tates'.[54] The International Union for Conservation of Nature (IUCN) later picked up on the same idea.[55] Neither initiative came to fruition, but scholars continue to discuss the possibility of an advisory opinion from the ICJ.[56] While this reflection should undoubtedly continue, it is difficult to see how a problem as complex and politically sensitive as climate change can push states to accept their own responsibility for environmental damage when they have been so reluctant to do so in the past. And even then, a clearer and more frequently applied doctrine of state responsibility for environmental damage would continue to focus on states themselves and their failure to act diligently, regardless of who directly causes the harm – in many cases, the private sector.

C. State Liability

Liability for environmental damage (without an internationally wrongful act) has developed much more rapidly than state responsibility, albeit again with mixed results. International liability regimes target either the state (state liability) or a private party, typically the operator of a facility (civil liability). They provide compensation, often by imposing strict liability on the defendant

[51] Global Justice Program at Yale University, 'Oslo Principles on Global Climate Change Obligations' (1 March 2015), available at globaljustice.yale.edu; International Law Association, 'Legal Principles Relating to Climate Change' in International Law Association Report of the Seventy-Sixth Conference (Washington DC, 2014).

[52] B Mayer, *The International Law of Climate Change* (Cambridge, Cambridge University Press, 2018) 78–82, 267–71.

[53] ibid 87.

[54] United Nations, 'Press Conference on Request for International Court of Justice Advisory Opinion on Climate Change' (United Nations Meetings Coverage and Press Releases, 3 February 2012), available at www.un.org/press/en.

[55] International Union for Conservation of Nature, 'Request for an Advisory Opinion of the International Court of Justice on the Principle of Sustainable Development in View of the Needs of Future Generations' (1–10 September 2016) IUCN Res WCC-2016-Res-079-EN.

[56] D Bodansky, 'The Role of the International Court of Justice in Addressing Climate Change: Some Preliminary Reflections' (2017) 49 *Arizona State Law Journal* 689; P Sands, 'Climate Change and the Rule of Law: Adjudicating the Future in International Law' (2016) 28 *Journal of Environmental Law* 19.

(in other words without requiring the proof of some wrongdoing) while capping the amount payable as a trade-off for a more stringent liability standard. They can also require the industry to set up compensation funds and obtain insurance coverage to ensure that victims get paid after an incident.[57]

The first comprehensive international liability regime appeared in 1960 to deal with the potentially disastrous consequences of the peaceful use of nuclear energy. The real urgency to develop international liability regimes came in the aftermath of the grounding and breakup of the Torrey Canyon supertanker in 1967.[58] The incident reminded the world that catastrophic damages could result from lawful but hazardous activities. It paved the way for the 1969 Convention on Civil Liability for Oil Pollution Damage (CLC)[59] and the 1971 Convention on the Establishment of an International Fund for Compensation for Oil Pollution Damage (Fund Convention).[60] The regime, still in place today, seeks to compensate victims of oil pollution using funds from the cargo industry.

Three years after the adoption of the CLC, the international community committed in Stockholm to develop international liability law.[61] Much insistence was initially placed on the liability of the state, as opposed to that of private parties. The ILC explored the idea that states could be held liable for transboundary pollution without having breached international law, but it became clear that states would not readily sacrifice economically beneficial activities in the name of compensation. After years of protracted work on the topic, the ILC special rapporteur described state liability as a case of 'misplaced emphasis'.[62] He admitted that '[s]tate liability and strict liability are not widely supported at the international level, nor is liability for any type of activity located within the territory of a [s]tate in the performance of which no [s]tate officials or agents are involved'.[63]

[57] MG Faure, 'In the Aftermath of Disaster: Liability and Compensation Mechanisms as Tools to Reduce Disaster Risks' (2016) 52 *Stanford Journal of International Law* 95, 122–25.

[58] J Peel, 'International Environmental Law and Climate Disasters' in R Lyster and RRM Verchick (eds), *Research Handbook on Climate Disaster Law: Barriers and Opportunities* (Cheltenham, Edward Elgar, 2018) 84–85.

[59] Convention on Civil Liability for Oil Pollution Damage (29 November 1969, entered into force 19 June 1975) 973 UNTS 3, superseded by the International Convention on Civil Liability for Oil Pollution Damage (27 November 1992, entered into force 30 May 1996) 1956 UNTS 255 (CLC).

[60] International Convention on the Establishment of an International Fund for Compensation for Oil Pollution Damage (18 December 1971, entered into force 16 October 1978) 1110 UNTS 57, superseded by the International Convention on the Establishment of an International Fund for Compensation for Oil Pollution Damage (27 November 1992, entered into force 30 May 1996) 1953 UNTS 373 ('Fund Convention').

[61] Declaration of the United Nations Conference on the Human Environment (16 June 1972) UN Doc A/CONF 48/14/Rev 1 ('Stockholm Declaration') principle 22.

[62] International Law Commission, 'First Report on the Legal Regime for the Allocation of Loss in Case of Transboundary Harm Arising out of Hazardous Activities, by Mr Pemmaraju Sreenivasa Rao, Special Rapporteur' UN Doc A/CN.4/531 (2003) in *Yearbook of the International Law Commission 2003*, vol 2, part 1 (New York, UN, 2010) ('First Report on the Allocation of Loss') 79.

[63] ibid 76, para 3.

Little has changed today. State responsibility now has a strong hold in customary international law even though its application in environmental disputes is not yet settled. State liability, on the other hand, is a project that is effectively relinquished. Commenting on the efforts of the ILC, the Seabed Disputes Chamber of the International Tribunal for the Law of the Sea (ITLOS) opined that 'such efforts have not yet resulted in provisions entailing [s]tate liability for lawful acts'.[64] States tend to compensate environmental damage through lump-sum settlements and voluntary payments,[65] but the pattern is not consistent enough to establish the liability of the state of origin as a matter of international law.[66]

In treaty law, the only clear example of state liability comes from the 1972 Convention on International Liability for Damage Caused by Space Objects. It provides that 'A launching [s]tate shall be absolutely liable to pay compensation for damage caused by its space object on the surface of the earth or to aircraft in flight'.[67] The Space Liability Convention led to a well-known compensation claim following the crash of a Soviet nuclear satellite in Canada.[68] Cosmos 954 crashed in January 1978, spreading radioactive fuel over a large area in the Northwest Territories, Alberta and Saskatchewan. Authorities proceeded to a two-phase cleanup process that lasted several months but managed to recover only a small fraction of the satellite's radioactive power source. Canada then claimed six million CAD to the Soviet Union under the Space Liability Convention and general principles of international law.[69] The Soviet Union replied that it would consider the issue of damage 'in strict accordance with the provisions [of the Space Liability Convention]'.[70] The dispute ended in a three-million CAD lump sum settlement with no admission of liability and consequently no reference to the Space Liability Convention or to international law.[71] It is said to have been motivated by past settlements, the desire to avoid prolonged negotiations and other political considerations.[72]

[64] *Responsibilities and Obligations of States Sponsoring Persons and Entities with Respect to Activities in the Area* (Advisory Opinion) [2011] ITLOS Rep 10 [209].

[65] For a survey of state practice, see Barboza, *The Environment, Risk and Liability* (2011) 45–72; R Lefeber, *Transboundary Environmental Interference and the Origin of State Liability* (The Hague, Kluwer Law International, 1996) 159–87.

[66] Boyle and Redgewell (n 23) 227–28; Plakokefalos, 'Liability' (2017) 1059; E Orlando, 'Public and Private in the International Law of Environmental Liability' in F Lenzerini and AF Vrdoljak (eds), *International Law for Common Goods: Normative Perspectives on Human Rights, Culture and Nature* (Oxford, Hart, 2014) 414–15.

[67] Convention on International Liability for Damage Caused by Space Objects (29 March 1972, entered into force 1 September 1972) 961 UNTS 187 ('Space Liability Convention'), Art II.

[68] Claim Against the USSR for Damage Caused by Soviet Cosmos 954 (23 January 1979) 18 ILM 899.

[69] A Brearley, 'Reflections upon the Notion of Liability: The Instances of *Kosmos 954* and Space Debris' (2008) 34 *Journal of Space Law* 291, 297–300, 310.

[70] Claim Against the USSR (n 68) 923.

[71] Protocol on Settlement of Canada's Claim for Damages Caused by "Cosmos 954" (Canada–Union of Soviet Socialist Republics) (2 April 1981) 20 ILM 689.

[72] EG Lee and DW Sproule, 'Liability for Damage Caused by Space Debris: The Cosmos 954 Claim' (1988) 26 *Canadian Yearbook of International Law* 273, 274, fn 4.

References to the Cosmos 954 incident are strangely ubiquitous in environmental literature, even today. Some suggest that the payment looks more like an admission of responsibility than a voluntary and non-prejudicial gesture.[73] Even if it were purely voluntary, they say, it would still imply that the state of origin has an 'inner conviction' about its liability.[74] But just as the *Trail Smelter* arbitration is a dubious foundation for the entire field of international environmental law, the Space Liability Convention is not particularly helpful to reflect on state liability for transboundary pollution generally. First, it was negotiated at a time when global environmental protection was only beginning to attract the world's attention. Today, the Space Liability Convention faces strong criticism for its failure to properly deal with contemporary problems such as space debris.[75] Second, it concerns a very specific form of transboundary pollution, with a high likelihood of transboundary impact. Third, space was primarily a military affair at the time. The parties to the Space Liability Convention did not contemplate that private parties would engage in outer space activities alongside governments as extensively as they do today.[76] The choice of state liability over other models must be understood in this context.

Meanwhile, civil liability regimes proliferated at a faster pace. Cynics will not be surprised. The same lack of political will that hampered the development of state-centric doctrines led the states to divert attention from themselves and target private operators instead.[77] Civil liability regimes are also a familiar concept for most lawyers. They closely mirror domestic law and provide an easy way out of the conceptual entanglements associated with state responsibility and liability. As we will see, there are more principled reasons to focus on civil liability besides mere opportunism. Paradoxically, however, civil liability regimes have resulted in little hard law. Most existing regimes remain a dead letter.

D. Civil Liability

Treaty-based civil liability regimes target private parties within the state of origin.[78] They have three main functions. First, they ensure non-discrimination

[73] Barboza (n 9) 63.

[74] ibid.

[75] E Kisiel, 'Law as an Instrument to Solve the Orbital Debris Problem' (2021) 51 *Environmental Law* 223, 229–32; B Kellman, 'Space: The Foulded Frontier. Adjudicating Space Debris as an International Environmental Nuisance' (2014) 39 *Journal of Space Law* 227, 255–58.

[76] RJ Lee, 'The Liability Convention and Private Space Launch Services: Domestic Regulatory Responses' (2006) 31 *Annals of Air and Space Law* 351, 352–53.

[77] E Rehbinder, 'Extra-Territoriality of Pollution Control Laws from a European Perspective' in G Handl, J Zekoll and P Zumbansen (eds), *Beyond Territoriality: Transnational Legal Authority in an Age of Globalization* (Leiden, Martinus Nijhoff, 2012) 145.

[78] Barboza (n 9) 31.

and equal access to foreign victims in the state of origin. Second, they address issues of jurisdiction, choice of law and enforcement of foreign judgments (their most relevant function for our purposes). Third, they harmonise substantive liability law on issues such as the standard of fault, damages, insurance and defences.[79]

Because of they purport to harmonise domestic law, civil liability treaties do not resemble typical norms of international environmental law. They are uniform tort law in disguise, 'amphibious' international instruments operating through domestic laws and institutions.[80] They may nonetheless impose direct obligations on states in relation to the operations of private actors under their jurisdiction. First, they may require states to offer private remedies in order to ensure the availability of prompt and adequate compensation for victims of transboundary pollution. Second, they may provide for the state's alternative, subsidiary or supplementary liability, for example when compensation exceeds the financial capacity of the liable party.[81] Polluters do not always have deep pockets: state liability becomes useful when a small private operator causes catastrophic damage while drilling off the coast or running a nuclear facility.[82] Finally, states may themselves act as operators, in which case civil liability treaties can also apply to them.[83]

Below, I introduce existing treaties (section I.D.i) and explain their fundamental assumptions (section I.D.ii) and their ultimate failure (section I.D.iii). I emphasise the need for a new vehicle going forward, one that derives from the duty to ensure prompt and adequate compensation but avoids mistakes of the past. This new vehicle, I argue, has one rather old and reliable component: private international law.

i. Civil Liability Regimes in International Environmental Law

The number of civil liability treaties increased from the 1980s to the 2000s through new standalone documents and declarations of interest for developing a liability counterpart to existing regimes.[84] More than a dozen treaties

[79] Sachs, 'Beyond the Liability Wall' (2008) 849–50.

[80] P-M Dupuy and JE Viñuales, *International Environmental Law*, 2nd edn (Cambridge, Cambridge University Press, 2018) 322.

[81] Principles on the allocation of loss in the case of transboundary harm arising out of hazardous activities, annexed to GA Res 61/36 (4 December 2006) UN Doc A/RES/61/36 ('ILC Principles on the Allocation of Loss') principle 4(5).

[82] A Boyle et al, 'International Law and the Liability for Catastrophic Environmental Damage' (2011) 105 *American Society of International Law Proceedings* 423, 429 (comments by G Handl).

[83] International Law Commission, 'Report of the Commission to the General Assembly on the work of its fifty-eight session' UN Doc A/61/10 (2006) in *Yearbook of the International Law Commission 2006*, vol 2, part 2 (New York, UN, 2013) ('Commentary to the ILC Principles on the Allocation of Loss') 72, para 33.

[84] Brunnée (n 3) 359.

currently exist. They are typically confined to a sector or activity although some have a broader scope.[85]

Four treaties address civil liability for marine oil pollution. The 1977 Seabed Mineral Resources Convention deals with oil pollution resulting from the exploration and exploitation of certain seabed mineral resources.[86] The 1992 CLC and Fund Convention deal with pollution resulting from oil tankers.[87] The 2001 Bunker Convention deals with pollution resulting from ships' bunker oil.[88] An intricate web of rules deals with civil liability for nuclear damage: the 1960 Paris Convention, the 1963 Brussels Supplementary Convention, the 1963 Vienna Convention, the 1988 Vienna Joint Protocol and the 1997 Convention on Supplementary Compensation (CSC).[89] In addition, the 1962 Nuclear Ships Convention deals with the liability of (non-existent) civil nuclear ships operators[90] and the 1971 Nuclear Material Convention deals with damage caused by a nuclear incident occurring in the course of the maritime carriage of nuclear material.[91]

Civil liability treaties also cover other forms of transboundary pollution. The 1989 CRTD Convention deals with damage caused during the carriage of dangerous goods by road, rail and inland navigation vessels[92] while the 1996 HNS Convention deals with damage resulting from the carriage of hazardous and noxious substances by sea.[93] The 1999 Basel Liability Protocol deals with

[85] Convention on Civil Liability for Damage Resulting from Activities Dangerous to the Environment (26 June 1993, not yet in force) 32 ILM 1228 ('Lugano Convention'); Convention on the Protection of the Environment (19 February 1974, entered into force 5 October 1976) 1092 UNTS 279 ('Nordic Convention').

[86] Convention on Civil Liability for Oil Pollution Damage Resulting from Exploration for and Exploitation of Seabed Mineral Resources (1 May 1977, not yet in force) 16 ILM 1450 ('Seabed Mineral Resources Convention').

[87] CLC (n 59); Fund Convention (n 60).

[88] Convention on Civil Liability for Bunker Oil Pollution Damage (23 March 2001, entered into force 21 November 2008) 40 ILM 1493 ('Bunker Convention').

[89] Convention on Supplementary Compensation for Nuclear Damage (12 September 1997, entered into force 15 April 2015) 36 ILM 1454 (CSC); Joint Protocol relating to the Application of the Vienna Convention and the Paris Convention (21 September 1988, entered into force 27 April 1992) 1672 UNTS 293 ('Vienna Joint Protocol'); Convention on Civil Liability for Nuclear Damage (21 May 1963, entered into force 12 November 1977) 1063 UNTS 265 ('Vienna Convention'); Convention Supplementary to the Paris Convention on Third Party Liability in the Field of Nuclear Energy (31 January 1963, entered into force 4 December 1974) 1041 UNTS 358 ('Brussels Supplementary Convention'); Convention on Third Party Liability in the Field of Nuclear Energy (29 July 1960, entered into force 1 April 1968) 956 UNTS 251 ('Paris Convention').

[90] Convention on the Liability of the Operators of Nuclear Ships (25 May 1962, not yet in force) 57 *American Journal of International Law* 268 ('Nuclear Ships Convention').

[91] Convention Related to Civil Liability in the Field of Maritime Carriage of Nuclear Material (17 December 1971, entered into force 15 July 1975) 974 UNTS 255 ('Nuclear Material Convention').

[92] Convention on Civil Liability for Damage Caused During Carriage of Dangerous Goods by Road, Rail and Inland Navigation Vessels (10 October 1989, not yet in force) UN Doc ECE/TRANS/79 ('CRTD Convention').

[93] International Convention on Liability and Compensation for the Carriage of Hazardous and Noxious Substances by Sea (3 May 1996, not yet in force) 35 ILM 1406 ('HNS Convention').

damage resulting from the transboundary movement and disposal of hazardous wastes.[94] The 2003 Kiev Liability Protocol deals with damage caused by the transboundary effects of industrial accidents on transboundary waters.[95] The 2005 Antarctic Liability Annex deals with environmental emergencies in the Antarctic.[96] Finally, the 2010 Nagoya–Kuala Lumpur Supplementary Protocol deals with liability for damage resulting from the transboundary movement of living modified organisms.[97]

Regardless of their practical impact (or lack thereof), the very existence of civil liability treaties is notable. Through them, states acknowledge that liability is essential to the enforcement of international environmental law, and that victims of transboundary pollution deserve compensation even though it may not come from states themselves. The language used in many treaties also signals some agreement over the standard of compensation for environmental damage: 'prompt and adequate'.[98] Civil liability treaties are therefore worth studying both as evidence of the path taken in international environmental law, and as an illustration of the function of civil liability in the resolution of transboundary environmental disputes.

ii. Assumptions of Civil Liability Regimes

Civil liability treaties rest on two fundamental assumptions: liability may be imposed on private parties rather than the states, and ex post liability is not entirely superfluous when compared to *ex ante* regulation of transboundary pollution. The question then becomes whether existing treaties succeed in conveying the benefits of an approach based on civil liability, or whether – as proposed in this book – a new vehicle is needed going forward.

Civil liability regimes for domestic or transboundary pollution are typically justified by four rationales. The first three are persuasive but should be carefully nuanced. The fourth one is plausible, but more often asserted than truly demonstrated.

First, civil liability directly assists victims of pollution regardless of whether public authorities choose to act against polluters.[99] This rationale does not

[94] Protocol on Civil Liability and Compensation for Damage Resulting from Transboundary Movements of Hazardous Waste (10 December 1999, not yet in force) UN Doc UNEP/CHW.5/29 Annex III ('Basel Liability Protocol').

[95] Protocol on Civil Liability and Compensation for Damage Caused by the Transboundary Effects of Industrial Accidents on Transboundary Waters (21 May 2003, not yet in force) Un Doc ECE/MP.WAT/11-ECE/CP.TEIA/9 ('Kiev Liability Protocol').

[96] Antarctic Liability Annex (n 14).

[97] Nagoya–Kuala Lumpur Supplementary Protocol on Liability and Redress to the Cartagena Protocol on Biosafety (15 October 2010, entered into force 5 March 2018) 50 ILM 108 ('Nagoya–Kuala Lumpur Supplementary Protocol').

[98] For further discussion on prompt and adequate compensation in civil liability treaties, see section 1.II.A.i below.

[99] Sachs (n 2) 845.

exclude the state as plaintiff, but assumes that it will not always act as such. This is particularly true for transboundary pollution Slaughter and Burke-White point out that 'Arresting criminals or terrorists, securing nuclear materials, and preventing pollution are within the traditional province of domestic law. The result is that the external security of many states depends on the ability of national governments to maintain internal security sufficient to establish and enforce national law'.[100] Paradoxically, however, those same national governments may not act as vigorously when foreign interests are at stake. As Wai explains, 'there are often severe practical impediments to effective extraterritorial regulation by national regulators. Local regulators may not pursue the case because of industry capture, inefficiency, shortage of resources, or restrictive ideological conditions'.[101] Similarly, Banda notes that 'Picking a fight with a foreign government is costly, and localized injuries to human health and the environment will often be dwarfed by the perceived need for bilateral cooperation on other issues, such as trade, defense, or border control'.[102] In the end, few governments will be willing to aggressively and unilaterally defend the environment (or its population's) beyond borders.

Citizen suits under environmental statutes reflect the idea that civil liability can bypass government inaction. Statutory provisions may allow individuals to enforce environmental laws in the public interest.[103] When the United States' Environmental Protection Agency (EPA) did not enforce its administrative orders against a Canadian company in the *Pakootas* case, members of the Confederated Tribes of the Colville Reservation in the state of Washington filed a citizen suit and asked for injunctive relief, penalties and recovery under CERCLA.[104] They effectively did what they considered the EPA should have done. This is an important function of civil liability, even though the informal coordination of private actors through litigation may appear less plausible or desirable than the action of politically accountable public authorities with a consistent agenda (that is, assuming public authorities do have a consistent agenda and are willing to take the legal, financial and political steps to implement it).

Second, civil liability reduces the complexity of environmental disputes. They de-escalate them to the neighbourhood level and avoid issues of state responsibility or liability. As mentioned earlier, the dynamics of transboundary pollution

[100] A-M Slaughter and W Burke-White, 'The Future of International Law Is Domestic (or, The European Way of Law)' (2006) 47 *Harvard International Law Journal* 327, 330–31.

[101] R Wai, 'Transnational Private Law and Private Ordering in a Contested Global Society' (2005) 46 *Harvard International Law Journal* 471, 479.

[102] ML Banda, 'Regime Congruence: Rethinking the Scope of State Responsibility for Transboundary Environmental Harm' (2019) 103 *Minnesota Law Review* 1879, 1881.

[103] See generally KS Coplan, 'Citizen Enforcement' in LC Paddock, RL Glicksman and NS Bryner (eds), *Elgar Encyclopedia of Environmental* Law, vol 2: Decision Making in Environmental Law (Cheltenham, Edward Elgar, 2016).

[104] Comprehensive Environmental Response, Compensation, and Liability Act of 1980, Pub L No 96-510, 94 Stat 2767 (1980) (codified as amended at 42 USC § 9601–9628) ('CERCLA'); *Pakootas v Teck Cominco Metals Ltd* 452 F (3d) 1066 (9th Cir 2006), *certiorari* denied 552 US 1095 (2008).

suggest a conflict between private parties. The Canadian government did not initially view the *Trail Smelter* dispute as having an interstate character. A closer look at its history shows 'that the actors most directly affected were not sovereign states but farmers, employees, businesspeople – in other words, members of the populations within the transboundary regions affected'.[105] If it were to happen today, *Trail Smelter* could well unfold in civil courts rather than through interstate arbitration, as it indeed did in *Pakootas* (albeit in the form of a citizen suit under a public regulatory statute rather than a 'pure' private law claim).[106]

Many would sympathise with the idea that civil litigation is a quicker, cheaper and more and efficient way of settling environmental disputes than lengthy and politically charged interstate dispute resolution mechanisms.[107] But it is not necessarily quick, cheap and efficient. Leaving states out of the equation streamlines the process when it involves a simple transboundary nuisance that affects the legally protected interests of private actors in one neighbouring state. The argument weakens, however, as the issue becomes more complex or involves actors in more than two states, which can easily be the case in environmental disputes. Civil litigation may then become as lengthy as interstate proceedings, with protracted proceedings, complex jurisdictional and evidentiary issues and, ultimately, enforcement difficulties abroad. The Amoco Cadiz oil spill off the French coast in 1978, for instance, led to 14 years of civil litigation.[108] The length of this saga matches the 13 years of litigation in *Trail Smelter* and exceeds the seven years of proceedings before the parties settled in *Aerial Spraying*.

Third, civil liability channels liability to the person responsible for the damage. This is important because transboundary environmental damage is very often the result of private conduct overseen by state regulation, rather than state conduct per se. International environmental law 'directs its rights and duties at the state and relies on the way in which the state in its national law controls corporations'.[109] International environmental law faces a pervasive

[105] J Ellis, 'Has International Law Outgrown *Trail Smelter*?' in Bratspies and Miller, *Transboundary Harm in International Law* (2006) 63.

[106] M van de Kerkhof, 'The Trail Smelter Case Re-Examined: Examining the Development of National Procedural Mechanisms to Resolve a Trail Smelter Type Dispute' (2011) 27 *Utrecht Journal of International and European Law* 68, 82; Boyle and Redgewell (n 23) 228. But see J Brunnée, 'The United States and International Environmental Law: Living with an Elephant' (2004) 15 *European Journal of International Law* 617, 633.

[107] JH Knox, 'The Flawed *Trail Smelter* Procedure: The Wrong Tribunal, the Wrong Parties, and the Wrong Law' in Bratspies and Miller (n 45) 70–71; MJ Robinson-Dorn, 'The Trail Smelter: Is What's Past Prologue? EPA Blazes a New Trail for CERCLA' (2006) 14 *NYU Environmental Law Journal* 233, 317–18.

[108] *Re Oil Spill by the Amoco Cadiz Off the Coast of France on March 16, 1978* 954 F (2d) 1279 (7th Cir 1992).

[109] A Nollkaemper, 'Responsibility of Transnational Corporations in International Environmental Law: Three Perspectives' in G Winter (ed), *Multilevel Governance of Global Environmental Change: Perspectives from Science, Sociology and the Law* (Cambridge, Cambridge University Press, 2006) 187. For a possible 'individualistic' reading of civil liability treaties, see A Peters, *Beyond Human Rights: The Legal Status of the Individual in International Law* (Cambridge, Cambridge University Press, 2016) 153–61.

challenge: it purports to address private conduct, yet speaks to states, essentially through obligations of prevention and due diligence. This framework works better for the prevention rather than the compensation of environmental damage. Civil liability avoids this structural limitation by targeting the polluter itself, the entity directly responsible for the harm – hence its significant importance for the regulation of transboundary pollution. Civil liability also strengthens the polluter-pays principle – a basic tenet of Canadian environmental law,[110] and a familiar (if controversial) concept on a global scale.[111] Circumstances may require that an insurer or an industry fund compensate the victims instead of the polluters themselves. Nonetheless, civil liability regimes internalise at least partly the costs of pollution and distribute the risk associated with activities susceptible of causing environmental damage.[112]

Fourth, it is suggested that civil liability can have a positive impact on environmental protection through deterrence.[113] While the first three rationales for civil liability are persuasive (with the nuances mentioned), the fourth one is more controversial. Little empirical evidence on the systemic implications of civil liability exists to either support or debunk the argument. This leaves us with intellectual postures rooted in so many assumptions regarding the behaviour of polluters and the role of the market that they become almost impossible to disentangle from their broader theoretical framework. One would celebrate the prospect of regulation through tort law or suggest that the threat of litigation provides an incentive for polluters to adjust their behaviour. Another would reply that this behaviour is always dictated by financial considerations, such that only the credible threat of crippling liability will alter the equation. Because financial considerations include reputation, image and the like, economic actors may align their conduct with socially beneficial ideals such as environmental protection, but that is purely coincidental. They will refrain from polluting only because they deem it financially beneficial to obey the rules rather than to disregard them, not because of the inherent deterrent effect of previous condemnations and the threat of future liability. Yet another would point to the lack of uniformity in the adjudication of private environmental disputes and the potential for discord among neighbouring states to denounce civil liability as a mechanism to protect the environment.

[110] *Orphan Well Association v Grant Thornton Ltd* 2019 SCC 5 [29]; *Imperial Oil Ltd v Quebec (Minister of the Environment)* 2003 SCC 58 [23]–[24].

[111] Rio Declaration on Environment and Development (13 June 1992) UN Doc A/CONF.151/26/Rev.1 (Vol 1) ('Rio Declaration') principle 16. See generally Boyle and Redgewell (n 23) 341–45.

[112] But see L Bergkamp, *Liability and Environment: Private and Public Law Aspects of Civil Liability for Environmental Harm in an International Context* (The Hague, Kluwer Law International, 2001).

[113] M Anderson, 'Transnational Corporations and Environmental Damage: Is Tort Law the Answer?' (2002) 41 *Washburn Law Journal* 399, 408–09. For a detailed examination of this rationale, see MG Faure, 'Regulatory Strategies in Environmental Liability' in H Muir Watt and F Cafaggi (eds), *The Regulatory Function of European Private Law* (Cheltenham, Edward Elgar, 2009).

Deterrence and better environmental protection do not inevitably flow from imposing liability on polluters. It is true that we often perceive the 'behavioural effects of tort law' on corporate actors who consciously assess their litigation exposure around the world.[114] But as Boyle explains, 'Liability, and liability treaties, are not a panacea …, and sceptics rightly question whether they have had much impact on industry or contribute to improving standards'.[115] Furthermore, 'the principal purpose of liability is to secure redress for victims, not necessarily to influence the behaviour of defendants'.[116]

From the limited but important perspective of compensation, the effectiveness of civil liability varies depending on the circumstances. Legal concepts such as standing, harm and causation do not fare well in relation to complex ecological problems involving diffuse sources of pollution, unidentifiable victims and long-term consequences. Biosafety, climate change and toxic chemicals come to mind here. The EU legislature was surprisingly candid about this in its Environmental Liability Directive, noting in the preamble that 'Liability is … not a suitable instrument for dealing with pollution of a widespread, diffuse character, where it is impossible to link the negative environmental effects with acts or failure to act of certain individual actors'.[117] The sheer complexity of litigating such issues may create a perception of injustice in the eyes of the victims, as a result of what Weaver and Kysar describe as judicial nihilism in the face of catastrophic harm – the fundamental mistake of 'refus[ing] responsibility over the extraordinary and the indeterminate' using procedural and jurisdictional grounds.[118]

At the opposite end of the spectrum, simple forms of pollution such as the *Trail Smelter* dispute are more amenable to civil liability claims. Their consequences extend to large, but identifiable environments and groups of people. They can be traced back to a complex, but again identifiable chain of events. To be sure, procedural hurdles and financial constraints may delay the judicial process immensely. But claims of this kind do not question the relevance of civil liability as a fundamental legal institution. They strain the system, but they do not break it.[119]

[114] R Wai, 'Private v Private: Transnational Private Law and Contestation in Global Economic Governance' in H Muir Watt and DP Fernández Arroyo (eds), *Private International Law and Global Governance* (Oxford, Oxford University Press, 2014) 48. See also JA Zerk, *Multinationals and Corporate Social Responsibility: Limitations and Opportunities in International Law* (Cambridge, Cambridge University Press, 2006) 236–37.

[115] AE Boyle, 'Globalising Environmental Liability: The Interplay of National and International Law' (2005) 17 *Journal of Environmental Law* 3, 9.

[116] ibid.

[117] Directive 2004/35/EC of the European Parliament and of the Council of 21 April 2004 on environmental liability with regard to the prevention and remedying of environmental damage [2004] OJ L143/56 ('Environmental Liability Directive') preamble, para 13.

[118] RH Weaver and DA Kyser, 'Courting Disaster: Climate Change and the Adjudication of Catastrophe' (2017) 93 *Notre Dame Law Review* 295, 354.

[119] For a similar point, see M Latham, VE Schwartz and CE Appel, 'The Intersection of Tort and Environmental Law: Where the Twains Should Meet and Depart' (2011) 80 *Fordham Law Review* 737, 753–54.

Civil liability teaches significant lessons for environmental law despite its inherent limitations. Catastrophes monopolise public attention for a time. They cause national governments to pay attention to the transboundary consequences of the activities that they allow on their territory. Through civil liability, private actors can exert additional pressure to set legal reforms in motion. Courthouses become a beacon for them to assert their rights, expose misconduct, maintain an issue on the public agenda, or promote good governance and environmental justice.[120] Liability does not replace other forms of regulation, but it acts as an important fail-safe and a forum for the disempowered to be heard, provided they have the means to go to court (which, of course, is not always a given). It is telling, for instance, that a number of victims brought private claims after the nuclear catastrophes in Chernobyl[121] and Fukushima[122] even though no state made a claim against the Soviet Union or Japan.

The systemic implications of tort law may be debatable, but liability regimes for transboundary pollution are legitimate and not entirely superfluous when compared to *ex ante* regulation of transboundary pollution. Convincing justifications and copious treaty-making aside, however, civil liability treaties rarely achieve their purpose because many of them are simply not in force.

iii. Treaty Failure

Noah Sachs' research points to a 'yawning gap' in the coverage of civil liability treaties.[123] At the time of the publication of Sachs' extensive survey of civil liability treaties in 2008, six of the 14 major treaties had entered into force.[124] Three treaties concern maritime oil pollution: the CLC; the Fund Convention; and the Bunker Convention.[125] The other three concern nuclear damage: the Paris Convention; the Brussels Supplementary Convention; and the Vienna Convention.[126] Since Sachs' survey, the CSC (nuclear damage) and the Nagoya–Kuala Lumpur Supplementary Protocol (biosafety) entered into force, respectively in 2015 and 2018.[127]

[120] R Wai, 'The Interlegality of Transnational Private Law' (2008) 71 *Law and Contemporary Problems* 107, 117–18; Wai, 'Transnational Private Law and Private Ordering' (2005) 481–82.

[121] For a survey, see A Rest, 'International Environmental Law in German Courts' (1997) 27 *Environmental Policy and Law* 409, 415–16; A Rest, 'Need for an International Court for the Environment? Underdeveloped Legal Protection for the Individual in Transnational Litigation' (1994) 24 *Environmental Policy and Law* 173, 175–79.

[122] For a survey, see EA Feldman, 'Compensating the Victims of Japan's 3-11 Fukushima Disaster' (2015) 16 *Asian-Pacific Law and Policy Journal* 127, 144–52.

[123] Sachs (n 2) 853.

[124] ibid 839.

[125] Bunker Convention (n 88); CLC (n 59); Fund Convention (n 60).

[126] Vienna Convention (n 89); Brussels Supplementary Convention (n 89); Paris Convention (n 89).

[127] Nagoya–Kuala Lumpur Supplementary Protocol (n 97); CSC (n 89).

Even if a 50/50 rate were considered a success, the numbers are deceptive. The treaties in force cover only two areas (marine oil pollution and nuclear damage) and, even then, the membership of the nuclear liability regime remains limited. For example, no major nuclear state ratified the 1997 Protocol amending the Vienna Convention to strengthen the nuclear liability regime after Chernobyl.[128] Parties to the Protocol either have minimal nuclear power production or none, qualifying them primarily (or only) as potential victims of a nuclear incident.[129]

The nuclear liability regime purports to regulate an activity that comes with exceptional hazards but few occurrences. Few treaties, however, cover activities with a less remarkable impact on the environment (with the exception of maritime transport). The Antarctic Liability Annex, the Kiev Liability Protocol, the Basel Liability Protocol, the HNS Convention and the CRTD Convention all have yet to come into force,[130] sometimes decades after their adoption, 'cast[ing] serious doubt on their acceptability or relevance, and on the wisdom of negotiating any more of them'.[131]

States show no enthusiasm for developing new civil liability treaties. The ILA was already skeptical when it developed the 1996 Helsinki Articles on Private Law Remedies for Transboundary Damage in International Watercourses, noting that 'there was not yet a sufficiently widespread international consensus' on the use of a strict liability standard and the harmonisation of liability rules.[132] A look at two recent environmental instruments – the 2010 Nagoya–Kuala Lumpur Supplementary Protocol on biosafety and the 2016 Paris Agreement on climate change – reveals continuing reluctance to enter into any meaningful and binding commitment on liability.

The Nagoya–Kuala Lumpur Supplementary Protocol purports to establish a liability regime for damage resulting from the transboundary movement of living modified organisms. States must provide for response measures in case of damage to biodiversity. They must also 'aim to provide' compensation for material or personal damage associated with damage to biodiversity (a more relaxed formulation). To accomplish this, they can either apply their existing domestic law, apply/develop specific civil liability rules or apply/develop a

[128] Protocol to Amend the Vienna Convention on Civil Liability for Nuclear Damage (12 September 1997, entered into force 4 October 2003) 2241 UNTS 270.

[129] JA Schwartz, 'International Nuclear Third Party Liability Law: The Response to Chernobyl' in International Atomic Energy Agency and OECD Nuclear Energy Agency, *International Nuclear Law in the Post-Chernobyl Period* (Paris, OECD, 2006) 48–49.

[130] Antarctic Liability Annex (n 14); Kiev Liability Protocol (n 95); Basel Liability Protocol (n 94); HNS Convention (n 93); CRTD Convention (n 92).

[131] Boyle and Redgewell (n 23) 337. See also Boyle, 'Globalising Environmental Liability' (2005) 16; Brunnée (n 3) 365; RR Churchill, 'Facilitating (Transnational) Civil Liability Litigation for Environmental Damage by Means of Treaties: Progress, Problems, and Prospects' (2001) 12 *Yearbook of International Environmental Law* 3, 32, 40–41.

[132] Water Resources Committee, 'Interim Report' in International Law Association Report of the Sixty-Seventh Conference (Helsinki, 1996) 407 ('ILA Helsinki Articles on Private Law Remedies').

combination of both.[133] This is a convoluted way of saying that states have full discretion in this regard.

The Nagoya–Kuala Lumpur Supplementary Protocol could have been more ambitious on this point. Developing countries pushed for a detailed provision on liability,[134] and negotiators discussed several detailed proposals.[135] The final text, however, is an exceedingly vague provision imposing little more than the status quo in a regime precisely designed to deal with liability. A Malaysian negotiator even described the Nagoya–Kuala Lumpur Supplementary Protocol as 'spectacularly deficient in providing for an effective civil liability regime'.[136] Others are more nuanced, but nonetheless point to the vagueness of the compromise reached in the end.[137]

Liability also interfered with the negotiations leading up to the Paris Agreement. Parties recognised in the Paris Agreement the importance of 'averting, minimizing and addressing loss and damage' resulting from climate change,[138] but made sure to specify in its final decision that the provision did not 'involve or provide a basis for any liability or compensation'.[139] Developed countries, particularly the United States,[140] appeared unwilling to incorporate any concept of state responsibility/state liability or civil liability into the Agreement. On the other hand, the Cook Islands, Nauru, Niue, Micronesia, the Philippines, Tuvalu, the Solomon Islands and Vanuatu – immensely vulnerable to the effects of climate change on water levels – ratified the Paris Agreement but declared that it could not affect the existing regime of state responsibility for climate change nor impede its future development.[141]

The divergent views on liability expressed during the negotiation of the Paris Agreement are nothing new. They are consistent with the history of previous climate negotiations, 'where concepts of wrongdoing, injustice and liability complicate, if not completely bring to a standstill, efforts to engage the

[133] Nagoya–Kuala Lumpur Supplementary Protocol (n 97), Art 12.

[134] E Thomas and MT Kebede, 'One Legally Binding Provision on Civil Liability: Why It Was So Important from the African Negotiators' Perspective' in A Shibata (ed), *International Liability Regime for Biodiversity Damage: The Nagoya–Kuala Lumpur Supplementary Protocol* (Abingdon, Routledge, 2014).

[135] R Lefeber, 'The Legal Significance of the Supplementary Protocol: The Result of a Paradigm Evolution' in Shibata (ibid) 83.

[136] G Singh Nijar, 'Civil Liability in the Supplementary Protocol' in Shibata, *International Liability Regime for Biodiversity Damage* (2014) 113. cf Lefeber, 'Supplementary Protocol' (ibid) 83.

[137] E Orlando, 'From Domestic to Global? Recent Trends in Environmental Liability from a Multi-Level Perspective and Comparative Law Perspective' (2015) 24 *Review of European, Comparative and International Environmental Law* 290, 300.

[138] Paris Agreement (12 December 2015, entered into force 4 November 2016) 55:4 ILM 743, Art 8(1).

[139] Adoption of the Paris Agreement, COP21 Dec 1/CP.21 in 'Report of the Conference of the Parties on its twenty-first session' UN Doc FCCC/CP/2015/10/Add.1 (2016) 2, para 51.

[140] E Calliari, S Surminski and J Mysiak, 'The Politics of (and Behind) the UNFCCC's Loss and Damage Mechanism' in R Mechler et al (eds), *Loss and Damage from Climate Change: Concepts, Methods and Policy Options* (Cham, Springer, 2019) 162.

[141] 'Status of the Paris Agreement' (19 May 2021), available at www.treaties.un.org.

biggest emitters in ongoing processes of international cooperation'.[142] Drafters therefore show extreme caution before using words that are even remotely connected to responsibility or liability. The 1979 Convention on Long-Range Transboundary Air Pollution, for instance, contains a provision in which states undertake to exchange scientific data on the effects of pollution and 'the extent of the damage which these data indicate can be attributed to long-range transboundary air pollution'.[143] At the time, the word 'damage' caused so much concern that the drafters added a footnote to let the reader know that the text did 'not contain a rule on [s]tate liability as to damage'.[144] Ironically, the footnote itself created confusion among scholars because it left unaddressed the possibility of a claim based on customary international law.[145]

It is easy to see how international liability regimes dealing with issues such as living modified organisms or climate change would be controversial. Those are diffuse and complex problems, with no single, readily identifiable perpetrator causing the damage.[146] But how to explain the failure of most international liability regimes, regardless of the problem? Sachs identifies three causes.[147] First, the conflicting interests of developed and developing countries push negotiating parties to adopt substantive provisions and to postpone indefinitely their discussions on liability. By contrast, marine oil pollution and nuclear liability regimes succeeded because of the nature of the underlying activities, which developed states perceived as beneficial. They were also (in the case of marine shipping) already subject to international rules and their risks threatened states indiscriminately – states of origin could become victims and vice versa. Second, negotiating and implementing liability agreements has low benefits (uncertain future events) and high transaction costs (high number of parties). Finally, current treaties impose overly high liability ceilings and require substantial changes in domestic law. Their content, Sachs says, is simply too demanding for states to agree. The conclusion of his study is alarming: 'The lack of viable legal remedies for victims of transboundary pollution is a glaring and longstanding hole in international environmental law, and private law solutions, which can address transboundary problems without resort to dispute resolution among governments, are urgently needed'.[148]

Sachs assumes – and indeed argues – that existing treaties fail when they are not widely ratified. This is a sound assumption. Ratification is obviously

[142] C Carlarne and JD Colavecchio, 'Balancing Equity and Effectiveness: The Paris Agreement and the Future of International Climate Change Law' (2019) 27 *NYU Environmental Law Journal* 107, 124.

[143] Convention on Long-Range Transboundary Air Pollution (13 November 1979, entered into force 16 March 1983) 1302 UNTS 217, Art 8(f).

[144] ibid, Art 8(f), fn 1.

[145] On the interpretation of the footnote, see PH Sand, 'Transboundary Air Pollution' in Nollkaemper and Plakokefalos, *Shared Responsibility* (2017) 977–78; Okowa, *State Responsibility for Transboundary Air Pollution* (2000) 32–33.

[146] Churchill, 'Facilitating (Transnational) Civil Liability Litigation' (2001) 41.

[147] Sachs (n 2) 867–90.

[148] ibid 890.

not the only measure of success in international environmental law. Scholars have gone beyond beyond state-based conceptions of treaty performance to demonstrate that private parties can channel environmental treaties as a source of private standards even if those treaties do not directly bind them, thereby attenuating the constraints of public international law and participating in a form of private governance.[149] Likewise, private actors could voluntarily comply with the spirit of unratified civil liability treaties by settling claims and providing prompt and adequate compensation for the damage that they cause. But there is no evidence of a large-scale channelling effect of unratified civil liability treaties by private actors. Ratification remains, for now, the most reliable indication of their success. And from this perspective, most civil liability treaties fail.

Whether treaty failure results from 'genuine disagreement' or bad faith 'free-riding' by polluting states,[150] the reality is implacable: major sources of pollution such as air and water-related industrial activities, handling and disposal of hazardous waste, transboundary movement of living modified organisms, deep-water drilling and other risky endeavours fail to be captured by an international liability regime. Repeated failures have caused another vicious circle in which the failure of existing civil liability treaties makes it increasingly difficult to negotiate new ones.[151]

The prospect of a broader international liability regime for transboundary pollution (customary or treaty-based) is remote. States show little interest in going beyond their aspirational statements. Yet we continue to discuss liability, because it 'cut[s] to the core question of whether international environmental law should involve only governmental obligations to monitor and to prevent ecological damage, or whether it should broaden to provide a viable remedy to citizens when ecological damage does occur'.[152] If the latter is correct, and in the absence of successful treaties, domestic law can offer an alternative mechanism to implement liability standards in relation to transboundary pollution.[153] But first, we must identify what international environmental law expects from states in this area. The answer lies in the duty to ensure prompt and adequate compensation.

II. THE DUTY TO ENSURE PROMPT AND ADEQUATE COMPENSATION

Civil liability treaties pursue a common objective: to compensate environmental damage. In this section, it is argued that states must ensure the availability of

[149] N Affolder, 'The Market for Treaties' (2010) 11 *Chicago Journal of International Law* 160.

[150] U Grušić, 'International Environmental Litigation in EU Courts: A Regulatory Perspective' (2016) 35 *Yearbook of European Law* 180, 188.

[151] Lefeber (n 135) 83.

[152] Sachs (n 2) 904.

[153] RV Percival, 'International Responsibility and Liability for Environmental Harm' in S Alam et al (eds) *Routledge Handbook of International Environmental Law* (London, Routledge, 2013) 689.

prompt and adequate compensation for victims of transboundary pollution. States do not have an obligation to pay compensation themselves (which is what state liability would entail), but if they do not voluntarily do so, they must at least enact procedural standards to ensure that victims can bring claims before domestic courts. This includes appropriate rules on jurisdiction, choice of law and the enforcement of foreign judgments. Lefeber expresses the theory as follows:

> [T]his obligation confers on the source state the *right* to choose between the assumption of liability *sine delicto* and the provision of effective civil law remedies to victims … In order to be effective, civil law remedies will have to meet certain procedural and substantive minimum standards. As for the procedural minimum standards, it has been found that effective civil law remedies must be made available to victims in the source state on a non-discriminatory basis.[154]

Framed this way, the duty to ensure prompt and adequate compensation reveals the role of private international law in strengthening civil liability regimes outside the treaty process (without excluding solutions inside the treaty process as well).[155] In the next sections, I elaborate on the duty itself, its origins and implications (section II.A) as well as its future development (section II.B).

A. Prompt and Adequate Compensation in International Law

Many civil liability treaties mention in their preamble or provisions the need to ensure prompt, adequate or effective compensation for victims of transboundary pollution. These words are neither new, nor environment-specific. They echo the famous Hull Formula in international investment law, a benchmark used to assess compensation for the lawful expropriation of foreign property by a state. In this section, I summarise the most notable environmental treaties alluding to prompt, adequate or effective compensation (section II.A.i). I then delve into the meaning of those words, by exploring their origins in international investment law (section II.A.ii) and their current status in international environmental law (section II.A.iii).

A few terminological notes are in order. This book refers to the 'duty to ensure prompt and adequate compensation' (equivalent for stylistic purposes to the 'duty to ensure *the availability of* prompt and adequate compensation'). This is because the book's focus is on the states' obligation to adopt certain procedural rules designed to facilitate civil lawsuits – in other words to *ensure* rather than to *provide* compensation. The terminology used in this book also leaves out the requirement of 'effective' compensation. As we will see, effectiveness seems to refer to the currency of the payment, which is generally

[154] Lefeber, *Transboundary Environmental Interference* (1996) 320.
[155] Sachs (n 2) 896–903.

not a problem. The ILC Principles on the Allocation of Loss themselves mention effectiveness sporadically: one principle refers to prompt, adequate and effective remedies and two other principles refer to prompt and adequate compensation.[156] Effectiveness also has a different meaning when it is used to describe the measures required to minimise environmental damage after it occurs, which obviously has nothing to do with currency.[157] The terminology chosen for this book should not be interpreted, however, as suggesting that effectiveness has a lesser status than promptness and adequacy in defining the standard of compensation required under international environmental law.

i. Prompt and Adequate Compensation in Environmental Treaties

The need to ensure prompt and adequate compensation has become a common feature in civil liability treaties. The wording varies but the premise – most often expressed in the preamble of the instrument – is remarkably consistent. The Paris Convention seeks to 'ensure adequate and equitable compensation' for victims of nuclear damage.[158] The Seabed Mineral Resources Convention, the CLC and the Fund Convention each seek to provide 'adequate compensation' for victims of damage caused by certain forms of oil pollution.[159] The more recent Bunker Convention aims to 'ensure the payment of adequate, prompt and effective compensation' for pollution caused by ships' bunker oil.[160] The HNS Convention recognises 'the need to ensure that adequate, prompt and effective compensation is available' for victims of pollution associated with the carriage of hazardous and noxious substances by sea.[161] The CRTD Convention seeks to ensure 'adequate and speedy compensation' for victims of damage caused during the carriage of dangerous goods by road, rail and inland navigation vessels.[162] The Basel Liability Protocol and the Kiev Liability Protocol both recognise 'the need to provide for third party liability and environmental liability in order to ensure that adequate and prompt compensation is available' in relation respectively to the transboundary movement and disposal of hazardous waste and industrial accidents on transboundary waters.[163] The Antarctic Liability Annex seeks to 'provide for prompt and effective response action to environmental emergencies' in the Antarctic.[164] Finally, the Nagoya–Kuala

[156] ILC Principles on the Allocation of Loss (n 81) principles 3(a), 4(1), 6(1)–6(2).
[157] Antarctic Liability Annex (n 14), Arts 5–6.
[158] Paris Convention (n 89) preamble, para 3.
[159] CLC (n 59) preamble, para 3; Fund Convention (n 60) preamble, para 4; Seabed Mineral Resources Convention (n 86) preamble, para 3.
[160] Bunker Convention (n 88) preamble, para 4.
[161] HNS Convention (n 93) preamble, para 2.
[162] CRTD Convention (n 92) preamble, para 3.
[163] Kiev Liability Protocol (n 95) preamble, para 5; Basel Liability Protocol (n 94) preamble, para 5.
[164] Antarctic Liability Annex (n 14) preamble, para 3, referring to the Protocol on Environmental Protection to the Antarctic Treaty (ibid), Art 15.

Lumpur Supplementary Protocol recognises 'the need to provide for appropriate response measures' in case of damage or likelihood of damage caused by the transboundary movement of living modified organisms.[165]

Prompt and adequate compensation also resonates beyond civil liability treaties. The 1981 Convention for Co-operation in the Protection and Development of the Marine and Coastal Environment of the West and Central African Region,[166] the 1990 Protocol for the Protection of the Marine Environment,[167] the 1992 Convention on the Protection of the Black Sea Against Pollution[168] and the 1994 Protocol for the Protection of the Mediterranean Sea[169] all use those words. The 2007 Nairobi International Convention on the Removal of Wrecks is premised on 'the need to adopt uniform international rules and procedures to ensure the prompt and effective removal of wrecks and payment of compensation for the costs therein involved'.[170] The 1982 UNCLOS provides that states must 'ensure that recourse is available in accordance with their legal systems for prompt and adequate compensation or other relief in respect of damage caused by pollution of the marine environment by natural or juridical persons under their jurisdiction'.[171] The Bunker Convention refers to this provision in its own preamble.[172] ITLOS took it as a 'direct obligation … to establish procedures, and, if necessary, substantive rules governing claims for damages before its domestic courts'.[173] According to ITLOS, to ensure means 'to deploy adequate means, to exercise best possible efforts, to do the utmost, to obtain this result'.[174]

Other references to prompt and adequate compensation abound. The 1998 Aarhus Convention requires states to ensure access to justice in environmental

[165] Nagoya–Kuala Lumpur Supplementary Protocol (n 97) preamble, para 4.

[166] Convention for Co-operation in the Protection and Development of the Marine and Coastal Environment of the West and Central African Region (23 March 1981, entered into force 5 August 1984) 20 ILM 746, Art 15.

[167] Protocol for the Protection of the Marine Environment Against Pollution from Land-Based Sources (21 February 1990, entered into force 1 February 1993) 2399 UNTS 3 ('Protocol for the Protection of the Marine Environment'), Art XIII(1).

[168] Convention on the Protection of the Black Sea Against Pollution (21 April 1992, entered into force 15 January 1994) 1764 UNTS 3, Art XVI(3).

[169] Protocol for the Protection of the Mediterranean Sea Against Pollution Resulting from Exploration and Exploitation of the Continental Shelf and the Seabed and its Subsoil (14 October 1994, entered into force 24 March 2011) [2013] OJ L4/15 ('Protocol for the Protection of the Mediterranean Sea'), Art 27(2)(a). cf Guidelines for the Determination of Liability and Compensation for Damage Resulting from Pollution of the Marine Environment in the Mediterranean Sea Area, COP15 Dec IG 17/4 in 'Report of the 15th Ordinary Meeting of the Contracting Parties to the Convention for the Protection of the Marine Environment and the Coastal Region of the Mediterranean and its Protocols' UN Doc UNEP(DEPI)/MED IG.17/10 (2008) 135, paras 31–32.

[170] Nairobi International Convention on the Removal of Wrecks (18 May 2007, entered into force 14 April 2005) 46 ILM 697 preamble, para 2.

[171] UNCLOS (n 13), Art 235(2).

[172] Bunker Convention (n 88) preamble, para 2.

[173] Responsibilities and Obligations of States (n 64) [140].

[174] ibid [110] (referring to the obligations of sponsoring states in relation to the seabed and ocean floor under UNCLOS).

matters, including through procedures that 'provide adequate and effective remedies, including injunctive relief as appropriate, and [are] fair, equitable, timely and not prohibitively expensive'.[175] The Compliance Committee of the Aarhus Convention held that private nuisance proceedings in English law are judicial procedures within the meaning of the convention,[176] such that they must offer prompt, adequate and effective remedies when the nuisance complained of affects the environment.[177] The ILA relied on prompt, adequate and effective compensation in the Helsinki Articles on Private Law Remedies[178] and the commentary to the 2004 Berlin Rules on Water Resources,[179] suggesting it was consistent with the aspirations of the international community expressed in the tenth principle of the Rio Declaration.[180] Similar wording appears in soft law instruments such as the 2006 ILA Toronto Rules on Transnational Enforcement of Environmental Law,[181] the 2010 UNEP Guidelines on Access to Justice[182] and the 2015 IUCN Draft International Covenant on Environment and Development (the latter emphasising that the duty to ensure prompt and adequate compensation amounts to a due diligence obligation).[183] The 2017 Draft Global Pact for the Environment, conceived by legal experts as the basis of a new all-encompassing international agreement,[184] conveys the same idea, requiring effective and affordable access to justice and the adequate remediation of environmental damage.[185]

[175] Convention on Access to Information, Public Participation in Decision-Making and Access to Justice in Environmental Matters (25 June 1998, entered into force 30 October 2001) 2161 UNTS 447 ('Aarhus Convention'), Art 9(4).

[176] *United Kingdom of Great Britain and Northern Ireland* ACCC/C/2013/85 and ACCC/C/2013/86, UN Doc ECE/MP.PP/C.1/2016/10 (2016), paras 68–73; *United Kingdom of Great Britain and Northern Ireland* ACCC/C/2008/23, UN Doc ECE/MP.PP/C.1/2010/6/Add.1 (2010), paras 43–47.

[177] Aarhus Convention (n 175), Art 9(4).

[178] ILA Helsinki Articles on Private Law Remedies (n 132), Arts 2(1), 3(1)(d).

[179] Water Resources Committee, 'Fourth Report' in International Law Association Report of the Seventy-First Conference (Berlin, 2004) ('ILA Berlin Rules on Water Resources') 371–72.

[180] Rio Declaration (n 111) principle 10.

[181] International Law Association, 'Resolution No 6/2006: Transnational Enforcement of Environmental Law' in International Law Association Report of the Seventy-Second Conference (Toronto, 2006) ('ILA Toronto Rules on Transnational Enforcement of Environmental Law') 48, rule 3(3).

[182] Guidelines for the development of national legislation on access to information, public participation and access to justice in environmental matters, UNEPGC Dec SS.XI/5 A in UNEP Governing Council, 'Report of the Governing Council/Global Ministerial Environment Forum on the work of its eleventh special session' UN Doc A/65/25 (2010) ('UNEP Guidelines on Access to Justice') 12, guideline 21.

[183] International Union for Conservation of Nature, *Draft International Covenant on Environment and Development: Implementing Sustainability*, 5th edn (Gland, IUCN, 2015) ('IUCN Draft International Covenant on Environment and Development') 21–22 Arts 59, 61–62), 154–63.

[184] Global Pact for the Environment, 'Draft Global Pact for the Environment' (2017), available at globalpactenvironment.org. The UNGA later established a working group to discuss options for a new international instrument: Towards a Global Pact for the Environment, UNGA Res 72/277 (10 May 2018) UN Doc A/RES/72/277.

[185] ibid, Arts 7, 11. cf World Charter for Nature, annexed to GA Res 37/7 (28 October 1982) UN Doc A/RES/37/7, para 23. For a criticism, see L Kotzé, 'A Global Environmental Constitution for the Anthropocene?' (2019) 8 *Transnational Environmental Law* 11, 26–27.

The UNGA itself has requested on 14 occasions since 2006 that Israel 'assume responsibility for prompt and adequate compensation' for environmental damage after the Israeli Air Force bombed storage tanks in Lebanon, causing massive oil spills on the Lebanese and Syrian coastlines.[186] One hundred and sixty-two states voted in favour of the most recent version of the resolution. Seven voted against (Australia, Canada, Israel, Marshall Islands, Micronesia, Nauru and the United States) and seven abstained.[187] Resolutions from the UNGA have no binding effect, but the vote indicates a wide consensus on the standard of compensation for environmental damage.[188]

Finally, the duty to ensure prompt and adequate compensation echoes similar principles found in soft law instruments which promote access to remedies against private parties for human rights violations. For instance, the 2018 Framework Principles on Human Rights and the Environment require states to 'provide for access to effective remedies for violations of human rights and domestic laws relating to the environment'.[189] UN Special Rapporteur John H Knox emphasised that states should provide individuals with effective remedies against private parties and governments, and ensure the availability of meaningful judicial and administrative procedures to address past, current and future violations of domestic environmental laws.[190] The 2011 Guiding Principles on Business and Human Rights, endorsed by the UN Human Rights Council,[191] require states to 'take appropriate steps to ensure, through judicial, administrative, legislative or other appropriate means, that when [business-related human rights abuses] occur within their territory and/or jurisdiction those affected have access to effective remedy', including through state-based judicial mechanisms.[192] Ongoing negotiations to adopt a binding UN treaty on business and human rights also hinge on a possible state obligation to provide 'fair, adequate, effective, prompt and non-discriminatory access to justice and

[186] Oil slick on Lebanese shores, GA Res 75/209 (21 December 2020) UN Doc A/RES/75/209, para 5 (and previous resolutions cited in the preamble).

[187] UNGA 52nd Plenary Meeting (74th Session) (19 December 2019) UN Doc A/74/PV.52, 9/58–9/59.

[188] *Legality of the Threat or Use of Nuclear Weapons* (Advisory Opinion) [1996] ICJ Rep 226 [70]; *Case concerning Military and Paramilitary Activities in and Against Nicaragua (Nicaragua v United States)* [1986] ICJ Rep 14 [188].

[189] Framework Principles on Human rights and the Environment, annexed to United Nations Human Rights Council, 'Report of the Special Rapporteur on the issue of human rights obligations relating to the enjoyment of a safe, clean, healthy and sustainable environment' UN Doc A/HRC/37/59 (2018) framework principle 10.

[190] ibid 13, paras 28–29.

[191] Human rights and transnational corporations and other business enterprises, HRC Res 17/4 (16 June 2011) UN Doc A/HRC/RES/17/4, para 1.

[192] Guiding Principles on Business and Human Rights, annexed to United Nations Human Rights Council, 'Report of the Special Representative of the Secretary General on the issue of human rights and transnational corporations and other business enterprises' UN Doc A/HRC/17/31 (2011) principles 25–26, Office of the United Nations High Commissioner for Human Rights, *Guiding Principles for Business and Human Rights: Implementing the United Nations 'Protect, Respect and Remedy' Framework* (New York, UN, 2011).

effective remedy' for human rights abuses committed in the course of business activities.[193] The duty to ensure prompt and adequate compensation of transboundary environmental damage remains the primary focus of this book – it has its own history and development, including as a distinct project of the ILC – but resembles and often parallels the duties developed under international human rights law.

ii. Prompt and Adequate Compensation in International Investment Law

The origins of the duty to ensure prompt and adequate compensation in international environmental law are unclear. The ILC traces it back to the *Trail Smelter* and *Corfu Channel* cases,[194] but they have more to say on the prevention principle than on any given standard of compensation. In fact, the duty to ensure prompt and adequate compensation comes from international investment law. It echoes a standard of compensation known as the Hull Formula – prompt, adequate and effective compensation for lawful expropriation of foreign property by a state.[195] Debates over the standard of compensation for lawful expropriation in international law have a long and checkered history which goes beyond the scope of this book, but a glance at this history helps us understand how the same language became so pervasive in international environmental law.

The Hull Formula came in response to the nationalisation of American-owned properties by the Mexican state in the 1920s. The nationalisation was part of a major land reform in the wake of the Mexican Revolution and the promulgation of the 1917 Constitution.[196] Years of discussions followed in order to determine the amount of compensation owed by Mexico to American nationals. Secretary of State Cordell Hull eventually exchanged letters with Mexican officials to resolve the matter. In 1938, Hull wrote in a letter to the Mexican ambassador in Washington that 'no government is entitled to expropriate private property, for whatever purpose, without provision for *prompt, adequate, and effective* payment therefor'.[197] This became known as the Hull Formula.

[193] Second Revised Draft of a Legally Binding Instrument to Regulate, in International Human Rights Law, the Activities of Transnational Corporations and Other Business Enterprises (6 September 2020) (UN Draft Treaty on Business and Human Rights), Art 4(2)(c). On the progress made so far, see I Bantekas, 'The Emerging UN Business and Human Rights Treaty and Its Codification of International Norms' (2021) 12 *George Mason Journal of International Commercial Law* 1.

[194] Commentary to the ILC Principles on the Allocation of Loss (n 83) 72, para 3, citing *Trail Smelter (United States v Canada)* (1941) 3 RIAA 1905, 1965; *Corfu Channel Case (United Kingdom v Albania)* [1949] ICJ Rep 4, 22.

[195] Compensation for unlawful expropriation, by contrast, engages the rules on state responsibility.

[196] T Levy, 'NAFTA's Provision for Compensation in the Event of Expropriation: A Reassessment of the "Prompt, Adequate and Effective" Standard' (1995) 31 *Stanford Journal of International Law* 423, 424–29; FG Dawson and BH Weston, '"Prompt, Adequate and Effective": A Universal Standard of Compensation?' (1962) 30 *Fordham Law Review* 727, 740–41.

[197] United States Department of State, *Compensation for American-owned Lands Expropriated in Mexico: Full Text of Official Notes, July 21, 1938 to November 12, 1938* (Washington DC, United States Government Printing Office, 1939) 18 (emphasis added).

Today, promptness is typically defined as a payment made 'without undue delay' and effectiveness as a payment 'made in realizable and readily transferable currency'.[198] Adequacy is more difficult to define, but commonly refers to the market value of the property before the taking occurred.[199]

The Hull Formula became the default American position in the post-war period.[200] Today, the United States' Model Bilateral Investment Treaty equates prompt, adequate and effective compensation with the payment without delay (promptness) of the fair market value of the expropriated investment (adequacy) in realisable and transferable currency (effectiveness).[201] Canada's standard Foreign Investment Protection Agreement also incorporates the Hull Formula.[202]

In the 1960s and 1970s, newly independent and developing states began to question the legitimacy of a customary minimum standard of compensation, claiming that the domestic law of the nationalising state should prevail.[203] The debate culminated at the UN with the 1974 Charter of Economic Rights and Duties of States,[204] The resolution – adopted without the support of some major capital exporting states – indicated that the domestic law of the nationalising state would govern disputes over compensation,[205] effectively rejecting the Hull Formula.[206]

Despite its demise at the UN, the Hull Formula has made its way into the 'overwhelming majority' of recent bilateral investment treaties.[207] Multilateral treaties[208] and guidelines from the OECD[209] and the World Bank[210] have used similar words. The debate over its status in customary international law

[198] JW Salacuse, *The Law of Investment Treaties*, 3rd edn (Oxford, Oxford University Press, 2021) 428. See also Dawson and Weston, 'Prompt, Adequate and Effective' (1962) 736–40.

[199] Salacuse (ibid) 428.

[200] ibid 76; P Dumberry, *The Formation and Identification of Rules of Customary International Law in International Investment Law* (Cambridge, Cambridge University Press, 2016) 68–69.

[201] 2012 US Model Bilateral Investment Treaty, Arts 6(1)(c), 6(2)(a), (b), (d), reprinted in LM Caplan and JK Sharpe, 'United States' in C Brown (ed), *Commentaries on Selected Model Investment Treaties* (Oxford, Oxford University Press, 2013) 763–850.

[202] 2004 Model Foreign Investment Protection Agreement, Art 13(1), reprinted in C Lévesque and A Newcombe, 'Canada' in Brown (ibid) 62.

[203] See generally Salacuse, *The Law of Investment Treaties* (2021) 85–93; Dumberry, *Customary International Law in International Investment Law* (2016) 70–74.

[204] Charter of Economic Rights and Duties of States, GA Res 3281 (XXIX) (12 December 1974) UN Doc A/9631.

[205] ibid, Art 2(c)

[206] Dumberry (n 200) 73–74.

[207] ibid 113–14; B Sabahi, *Compensation and Restitution in Investor-State Arbitration* (Oxford, Oxford University Press, 2011) 93.

[208] Energy Charter Treaty (21 November 1990, entered into force 16 April 1998) 2080 UNTS 95, Art 12(2); ASEAN Comprehensive Investment Agreement (26 February 2009, entered into force 29 March 2012), Art 14(1)(c). See also Comprehensive Economic and Trade Agreement, Canada and European Union (30 October 2016, provisionally entered into force 21 September 2017) [2017] OJ L11/23, Art 8.12(1)(d).

[209] OECD, Multilateral Agreement on Investment: Draft Consolidated Text, OECD Doc DAFFE/MAI(98)7/REV1 (1998), Art 3.2.

[210] World Bank, 'Guidelines on the Treatment of Foreign Direct Investment' in World Bank, *Legal Framework for the Treatment of Foreign Direct Investment*, vol 2 (Washington DC, World Bank, 1992) 33, guideline IV(2), reprinted in (1992) 31 *International Legal Materials* 1379 and (1992) 7 *ICSID Review* 297.

continues,[211] but the Hull Formula has undeniably become prevalent in investment treaties. At a minimum, this consistency in treaty language indicates that 'the members of the international community share the view that foreigners cannot be deprived of their property for domestic policy reasons without being effectively compensated for the current value of their investment'.[212]

Compensation for lawful expropriation remains a controversial area of international law, shaped by stark disagreement between capital-importing and capital-exporting states. It is perhaps no coincidence, then, that the Hull Formula has crossed into international environmental law, which features equally strong tension between developed and developing states. Just how and when it did, however, is unclear. Transplantation is likely to have occurred incrementally through various political statements, negotiating positions and anecdotal occurrences. For instance, when a Liberian tanker discharged 12,000 gallons of crude oil while unloading at a refinery in Cherry Point (Washington State), causing severe damage to Canadian coasts in 1972, Canadian Secretary of State for External Affairs Mitchell Sharp declared in Parliament that 'the Canadian government expect[ed] full and prompt compensation of all damages suffered in Canada, as well as full [clean-up] costs, to be paid by those responsible'.[213]

There are parallels between expropriation and transboundary pollution. Just like expropriation, transboundary pollution involves an interference with property and the deprivation of its economic benefits, an 'obvious analogy' according to Boyle.[214] This analogy makes sense conceptually and historically. The debate over expropriation at the UN was anchored in the principle of national sovereignty over natural resources.[215] The same principle was critical in the development of modern international environmental law. Even as a new environmental consciousness arose, states consistently reasserted their sovereign right to exploit natural resources under their own terms as long as they did not cause damage to other states.[216] Broadly framed, every rule of international environmental law is the product of a loose compromise and permanent tug-of-war between state sovereignty, environmental protection and the prevention principle.[217] The transplantation of the Hull Formula into international

[211] Dumberry (n 200) 203–05.

[212] G Sacerdoti, 'Bilateral Treaties and Multilateral Instruments on Investment Protection' (1997) 269 *Recueil des cours de l'Académie de droit international* 251, 397.

[213] 'Statement on Cherry Point Oil Spill and Representations to United States Government Arising Therefrom', *House of Commons Debates*, 28th Parl, 4th sess, vol 4 (8 June 1972) 2955 (Mitchell Sharp), reprinted in ALC de Mestral, 'Practice in International Law During 1972 as Reflected in Resolutions of the House of Commons and in Government Statements in the House of Commons' (1973) 11 *Canadian Yearbook of International Law* 314, 333–34.

[214] Boyle (n 115) 18. See also Boyle and Redgewell (n 23) 339.

[215] Charter of Economic Rights and Duties of States (n 204), Art 2.

[216] Rio Declaration (n 111) principle 2; Stockholm Declaration (n 61) principle 21.

[217] L-A Duvic-Paoli and JE Viñuales, 'Principle 2: Prevention' in JE Viñuales (ed), *The Rio Declaration on Environment and Development: A Commentary* (Oxford, Oxford University Press, 2015) 108–10. cf Banda, 'Regime Congruence' (2019) 1896–97; J Brunnée and SJ Toope, 'The Sovereignty of International Law?' (2017) 67 *University of Toronto Law Journal* 496, 506 (both describing a shift in the

environmental law may have been coincidental, but a shared conceptual and historical background facilitated it.

iii. Status of the Duty to Ensure Prompt and Adequate Compensation

Arguably, the duty to ensure prompt and adequate compensation can be viewed as an emerging principle of international environmental law. As we will see in the next section, the ILC took it up as the foundation for the Principles on the Allocation of Loss. The ILC recommended that states ensure prompt and adequate compensation[218] and suggested that such a duty had the support of the international community.[219] The ILA was bolder, declaring in the commentary to the Berlin Rules on Water Resources that 'there [was] a right under international law to prompt, adequate, and effective compensation or other appropriate remedies for injuries arising from activities in a [s]tate relating to an international drainage basin'.[220] The formula varies (much like the thousands of bilateral investment treaties that are in place today) but the notion of prompt and adequate compensation is increasingly well established in international environmental law.

Grey areas obviously remain. The duty to ensure prompt and adequate compensation is not part of customary international law yet and has not reached the level of fine-tuning seen in international investment jurisprudence and scholarship. The ILC Principles on the Allocation of Loss do not stick to any rigid interpretation of the Hull Formula or any other standard. It may be that the standard of compensation is less stringent than the Hull Formula or that it deviates from it in some respects. For now, the duty to ensure prompt and adequate compensation refers more broadly to the availability of compensation for environmental damage. It could morph into a more precise standard of compensation as time passes and its precise meaning is judicially tested.[221]

Scholarship confirms that prompt and adequate compensation has an increasingly important place in international environmental law. Anderson, for instance, hints at a general obligation in international law to provide remedies for transboundary pollution but concludes that this obligation is more of a soft law principle than a binding norm, notably because treaty practice is insufficiently

focus of international environmental law, from sovereign rights and resource allocation to environmental damage itself).

[218] ILC Principles on the Allocation of Loss (n 81) principle 4(1).

[219] Commentary to the ILC Principles on the Allocation of Loss (n 83) 72–73, paras 4–5; International Law Commission, 'Third Report on the Legal Regime for the Allocation of Loss in Case of Transboundary Harm Arising out of Hazardous Activities, by Mr Pemmaraju Sreenivasa Rao, Special Rapporteur' UN Doc A/CN.4/566 in *Yearbook of the International Law Commission 2006*, vol 2, part 1 (New York, UN, 2013) 85, para 36.

[220] ILA Berlin Rules on Water Resources (n 179) 371.

[221] Expropriation precedents could be useful in this regard, as was the case in *In the Matter of the People of Enewetak* (2000) 39 ILM 1214, 1215 (Marshall Islands Nuclear Claims Tribunal).

developed.[222] Barboza, who acted as Special Rapporteur in the ILC's project on liability, thinks it is conceivable to deduce a perceived obligation to ensure prompt and adequate compensation from the states' willingness to deal with transboundary damage in one way or another.[223]

Others are more assertive. For Boyle, primary materials reveal the existence of a principle of compensation that is more than just soft law, even though it is not easily definable.[224] Orlando underscores a growing international consensus surrounding the duty to ensure prompt and adequate compensation.[225] Foster notes that it is possible to argue that the duty to ensure prompt and adequate compensation already exists in international law.[226] Plakokefalos hints at the very least at a *de lege ferenda* obligation:

> [I]t is safe to conclude that there is no liability rule that would oblige states to pay compensation in international law. What might be inferred, however, is that there is a *de lege ferenda obligation* of states to ensure that compensation is provided in cases of transboundary harm. The [ILC Principles on the Allocation of Loss] and the number of civil liability conventions, in combination with the general obligation to prevent transboundary harm, lead to this conclusion.
>
> The fact that there is no customary rule on state liability does not mean that states do not bear obligations, beyond those on prevention of transboundary harm, whenever damage to the environment occurs. According to the [ILC Principles on the Allocation of Loss], the state has the obligation to ensure that the victims of the harm are compensated. Similar obligations are to be found, explicitly or implicitly, in a number of civil liability conventions and protocols.[227]

The strongest doctrinal support for this proposition comes from René Lefeber. In a monograph published in 1996, Lefeber points out that unlike state responsibility/liability, the obligation to ensure prompt and adequate compensation has wide support in international law. This support includes the state practice of settling claims with lump-sum agreements and voluntary payments (even though it does not persuasively establish a principle of state liability in customary international law), in treaties obliging states to provide civil remedies and in the above-mentioned civil liability treaties.[228]

Lefeber also defines the words prompt, adequate and effective, an exercise later endorsed by the ILC. Lefeber argues that victims obtain prompt compensation (the time component) when they do not face lengthy procedural obstacles to

[222] Anderson, 'Transnational Corporations and Environmental Damage' (2002) 414.
[223] Barboza (n 9) 157.
[224] Boyle (n 115) 18–19. See also Boyle and Redgewell (n 23) 338–39.
[225] Orlando, 'From Domestic to Global' (2015) 303.
[226] C Foster, 'The ILC Draft Principles on the Allocation of Loss in the Case of Transboundary Harm Arising out of Hazardous Activities: Privatizing Risk?' (2005) 14 *Review of European, Comparative and International Environmental Law* 265, 280–81.
[227] Plakokefalos (n 47) 1059–60.
[228] Lefeber (n 65).

bring their claim.[229] At a minimum, they should have access to interim relief to make up for unavoidable delays in legal proceedings.[230] Victims obtain adequate compensation (the quantitative component) when the amount covers at least a portion of the claim.[231] Victims finally obtain effective compensation (the qualitative component) when the funds are provided in a convertible currency and without conditions.[232] Lefeber does not refer to the Hull Formula and its interpretation, but his conclusion aligns with the state of the law as described in the previous section. Another author recently interpreted the components of the duty to ensure prompt and adequate compensation in similar fashion.[233]

For Lefeber, the duty to ensure prompt, adequate and effective compensation requires states to provide civil remedies that meet certain minimum procedural standards unless they choose to assume their own liability. These standards, he says, are found in the rules governing jurisdiction, choice of law and the recognition and enforcement of foreign judgments.[234] Lefeber explicitly hints here at a connection between the duty to ensure prompt and adequate compensation and the rules of private international law.

Lefeber's analysis does not add much flesh to the bones of the duty to ensure prompt and adequate compensation. It seems obvious that prompt and adequate compensation entails a certain amount of money paid in a certain time and in a certain currency, but the details are harder to pin down. Nonetheless, Lefeber successfully demonstrates that private international law plays a key role in turning the duty to ensure prompt and adequate compensation into a meaningful concept. This is particularly obvious in the ILC Principles on the Allocation of Loss.

In 1996, Lefeber identified prompt and adequate *compensation* as the basis for the future development of international liability law. Recent liability regimes, however, adopt a different approach. The Antarctic Liability Annex and the Nagoya–Kuala Lumpur Supplementary Protocol contain detailed provisions on response measures designed to prevent environmental damage, avoid further damage or restore the damage already caused.[235] For Lefeber, 'regulatory liability' imposed on the polluter (and subsidiarily on the state) is an alternative to civil liability, which focuses solely on the compensation of environmental

[229] ibid 323. cf Commentary to the ILC Principles on the Allocation of Loss (n 83) 77, para 7.
[230] ibid 323.
[231] ibid 323–24. cf Commentary to the ILC Principles on the Allocation of Loss (n 83) 78, para 8.
[232] ibid 324.
[233] M Piri Damagh, *Prevention and Compensation of Trans-Boundary Damage in Relation to Cross-Border Oil and Gas Pipelines* (Cambridge, Intersentia, 2015) 343–44.
[234] ibid.
[235] Nagoya–Kuala Lumpur Supplementary Protocol (n 97), Art 5; Antarctic Liability Annex (n 14), Arts 3–6. See also ILC Principles on the Allocation of Loss (n 81) principle 5; Articles on prevention of transboundary harm from hazardous activities, annexed to GA Res 62/68 (6 December 2007) UN Doc A/RES/62/68 ('ILC Articles on the Prevention of Transboundary Harm'), Arts 16–17.

damage and does not work particularly well to protect the environment itself as a public good.[236] This is an 'administrative approach to liability' which, Lefeber says, represents a major shift in international liability law.[237] Some older civil liability treaties required the operator to take all necessary response measures after environmental damage occurs, in addition to providing financial compensation.[238] Others referred to environmental damage as including the cost of preventive measures taken *after* an accident has occurred to prevent or minimise further damage.[239] But those provisions were often vague and did not delve into the nature and implementation of specific response measures. Compensation for damage to the environment itself as a public good was also problematic. The Antarctic Liability Annex and the Nagoya–Kuala Lumpur Supplementary Protocol, by contrast, contain more sophisticated arrangements and a clearer role for states and private parties. A duty to ensure prompt, adequate and effective *response measures* is now emerging.[240]

It is too early to tell whether the increase in the sophistication of response obligations will have any lasting impact on international liability law. The Nagoya–Kuala Lumpur Supplementary Protocol entered into force in 2018, but the Antarctic Liability Annex is not yet in force. Lukewarm response may not suffice for these instruments to avoid the fate of so many civil liability treaties – once promising, now headed for textbook oblivion. In any event, this book focuses on the compensation of environmental damage in domestic courts, and therefore on the duty to ensure prompt and adequate compensation as developed in Lefeber's earlier work – bearing in mind that civil and regulatory liability are not mutually exclusive and that the emergence of a duty to ensure prompt and adequate response measures is a welcome development, particularly with respect to the global commons.

As explained above, the notion of prompt and adequate compensation runs through international environmental law and underlies many of the international liability regimes crafted over the years. The next section examines the ILC Principles on the Allocation of Loss – the latest synthesis of the law in this area, the clearest illustration of the role of private international law in ensuring prompt and adequate compensation, and an anchor for its future development.

[236] Lefeber (n 135) 84–87.

[237] ibid.

[238] Kiev Liability Protocol (n 95), Art 6; Basel Liability Protocol (n 94), Art 6.

[239] Bunker Convention (n 88), Arts 1(7), 1(9)(b); CSC (n 89), Arts I(f)(vi), I(h); HNS Convention (n 93), Arts 1(6)(d), 1(7); CLC (n 59), Art I(6)(b), I(7); Fund Convention (n 59), Arts 1(2), 3(b); CRTD Convention (n 92) Arts 1(10)(d), 1(11); Seabed Mineral Resources Convention (n 86), Arts 1(6)–1(7).

[240] But see CE Foster, 'Diminished Ambitions? Public International Legal Authority in the Transnational Economic Era' (2014) 17 *Journal of International Economic Law* 355, 369, fn 78 (questioning whether Lefeber's account of regulatory liability 'amounts to any form of liability on the public international plane').

B. Future Development of the Duty to Ensure Prompt and Adequate Compensation

The ILC blazed a trail for the future development of the duty to ensure prompt and adequate compensation when it adopted the Principles on the Allocation of Loss, which marked the end of its tremendously long and protracted journey into the depths of liability.[241] The ILC submitted eight principles to the UNGA, which in turn commended them to the attention of governments.[242] While the law is not entirely settled, the very existence of the ILC Principles on the Allocation of Loss and its consideration by the UNGA strengthens the place of the duty to ensure prompt and adequate compensation in international law.

The ILC Principles on the Allocation of Loss provide a roadmap to allocate losses after transboundary environmental damage occurs. Their preamble reaffirms the commitment to develop international liability law and recalls existing civil liability treaties.[243] The ILC made it clear that it did not attempt to define the precise status of each principle in customary international law. It simply sought to contribute to the development of international law without prejudice to existing and future treaties, or other doctrines such as state responsibility.[244]

The ILC Principles on the Allocation of Loss have two purposes: to ensure prompt and adequate compensation for victims of transboundary damage[245] and to protect the environment.[246] To comply with the ILC Principles on the Allocation of Loss, states must adopt appropriate response measures in the event of transboundary damage and ensure that compensation is available for victims who choose to sue the person responsible in civil courts.[247] States do not have to pay compensation themselves[248] except if they are acting as the operator.[249] The document assumes that the state of origin acted with due diligence in preventing damage such that its responsibility/liability is not engaged in that regard.[250]

The ILC Principles on the Allocation of Loss possess the basic features of civil liability treaties, including the concern for prompt and adequate compensation. There are two types of rules: ones that set out the substantive conditions of

[241] ILC Principles on the Allocation of Loss (n 81). For an overview of the project, see Barboza (n 9) chs 6–7.

[242] Allocation of loss in the case of transboundary harm arising out of hazardous activities, GA Res 61/36 (4 December 2006) UN Doc A/RES/61/36, para 2.

[243] ILC Principles on the Allocation of Loss (n 81) preamble, paras 1, 8.

[244] Commentary to the ILC Principles on the Allocation of Loss (n 83) 60–61, para 13.

[245] ILC Principles on the Allocation of Loss (n 81) principle 3(a).

[246] ibid principle 3(b).

[247] ibid principle 5.

[248] Commentary to the ILC Principles on the Allocation of Loss (n 83) 77, para 3.

[249] ibid 72, para 33.

[250] ibid 77, para 2.

the operator's liability (standard of liability, financial limits, compensation funds, etc) and ones that set out the procedural requirements needed to effectively impose liability on the operator. They define the operator as the person in control of the activity when damage occurs.[251]

The fourth principle entitled 'prompt and adequate compensation' goes to the substantive conditions of the operator's liability. It requires each state to take necessary measures to ensure prompt and adequate compensation, including the imposition of no-fault liability on the operator, the requirement to establish and maintain insurance coverage and, in appropriate cases, industry funds and other financial resources.[252]

The sixth principle, by contrast, lists the procedural means to ensure prompt and adequate compensation. It is the most important for our purposes:

> **Principle 6: International and Domestic Remedies**
>
> 1. States shall provide their domestic judicial and administrative bodies with the necessary jurisdiction and competence and ensure that these bodies have prompt, adequate and effective remedies available in the event of transboundary damage caused by hazardous activities located within their territory or otherwise under their jurisdiction or control.
> 2. Victims of transboundary damage should have access to remedies in the State of origin that are no less prompt, adequate and effective than those available to victims that suffer damage, from the same incident, within the territory of that State.
> 3. Paragraphs 1 and 2 are without prejudice to the right of the victims to seek remedies other than those available in the State of origin.
> 4. States may provide for recourse to international claims settlement procedures that are expeditious and involve minimal expenses.
> 5. States should guarantee appropriate access to information relevant for the pursuance of remedies, including claims for compensation.[253]

The ILC gave further substance to the words prompt and adequate in its commentary of the fourth principle. It is said that promptness refers to the time and duration of procedures, while adequacy refers to an amount of compensation that is not arbitrary or grossly disproportionate, even if it is not sufficient.[254] The ILC's take echoes the work of Lefeber[255] and international investment law.[256]

Interestingly, the United Nations Environment Programme (UNEP) interpreted the same words quite differently in its implementation guide to the UNEP Guidelines on Access to Justice. UNEP defined adequacy as the full

[251] ILC Principles on the Allocation of Loss (n 81) principle 2(g).
[252] ibid principle 4.
[253] ibid principle 6.
[254] Commentary to the ILC Principles on the Allocation of Loss (n 83) 77–78, paras 7–8.
[255] ibid 85, para 1, fn 462, citing Lefeber (n 65) 234–36.
[256] For further discussion on international investment law, see section 1.II.A.ii above.

compensation of past damage, the prevention of future damage and the restoration of the status quo *ante*.[257] It referred to effectiveness in terms of how well states prevent or rectify environmental damage, and how efficiently remedies can be enforced.[258] Finally, it associated promptness with the provision of injunctive relief before environmental damage becomes irreversible.[259] The United Nations Economic Commission for Europe (UNECE) used similar concepts in its implementation guide to the Aarhus Convention.[260] These definitions are all plausible, and should also help shape the duty to ensure prompt and adequate compensation.

The fourth and the sixth ILC Principles on the Allocation of Loss confirm that the duty to ensure prompt and adequate compensation is now the focal point of international liability law, both substantively and procedurally. As Boyle argues, 'it is not new, and builds on existing law, but it is the first occasion on which such a core principle has been articulated in such general terms'.[261] Such general statements admittedly have a precarious status in international environmental law, but the ILC's choice to frame its principles as a 'semi-non-binding' declaration of a residual nature could paradoxically spare them from past failures. Expecting that total harmonisation would prove impossible, the ILC had initially designed a pure soft law instrument, a decision met by heavy criticism.[262] The ILC then made certain provisions mandatory.[263] It identified prompt and adequate compensation as the overarching principle and gave states leeway to implement it as they saw fit.[264] Domestic laws could therefore keep distinctive features while still reflecting global goals such as access to justice, public participation and compensation.[265] This is sensible, even though the combination of *shoulds* and *shalls* throughout the ILC Principles on the Allocation of Loss makes for mystifying reading.[266]

There are reasons to be optimistic towards the potential impact of the ILC Principles on the Allocation of Loss – it is the point of this book. At the same time, the apparent lack of interest in the ILC's work cannot be overlooked. Only

[257] United Nations Environment Programme, *Putting Rio Principle 10 into Action: An Implementation Guide* (Nairobi, United Nations Environment Programme, 2015) 119, commenting on UNEP Guidelines on Access to Justice (n 182) guideline 21.

[258] ibid.

[259] ibid 120.

[260] United Nations Economic Commission for Europe, *The Aarhus Convention: An Implementation Guide*, 2nd edn (Geneva, United Nations, 2014) 199–200, commenting on the Aarhus Convention (n 175), Art 9(4).

[261] Boyle (n 115) 18.

[262] ibid, 18–20, 26.

[263] ILC Principles on the Allocation of Loss (n 81) principles 5(a)–5(b), 5(d), 6(1), 8(2) (all using the word 'shall' as opposed to 'should').

[264] Commentary to the ILC Principles on the Allocation of Loss (n 83) 60, paras 11–12.

[265] Rio Declaration (n 111) principles 10, 13.

[266] Barboza (n 9) 150–51. See also Piri Damagh, *Prevention and Compensation* (2015) 376.

a few states gave feedback to the ILC throughout the process.[267] Some welcomed the ILC Principles on the Allocation of Loss with well-deserved scepticism.[268] Others were more optimistic,[269] but there was no unbridled celebration. The ILC itself chose not to reopen the Pandora's box of liability in its subsequent work on the protection of the atmosphere.[270] The UNGA, however, has continued to bring the ILC Principles on the Allocation of Loss to the attention of governments every three years since then.[271]

The ILC Principles on the Allocation of Loss 'exist in the legal-political space of normative desiderata'.[272] Realistically, they will not lead to a global liability regime,[273] but they could lead to meaningful procedural changes in domestic law. The adoption of prompt and adequate compensation as a governing principle of environmental liability would then turn out to be the most important legacy left by the ILC in this area, even in the absence of a single new civil liability treaty.[274] The next chapters of this book explore whether this legacy can leave traces in Canadian private international law.

III. CONCLUSION

The authors of a leading work of international environmental law write that civil liability 'is an area in which some serious thinking is overdue'.[275] In this

[267] Prior to the adoption of the ILC Principles on the Allocation of Loss, see International Law Commission, 'Comments and observations received from Governments' UN Doc A/CN.4/562 and Add.1 in *Yearbook of the International Law Commission 2006*, vol 2, part 1 (New York, UN, 2013). More states, however, gave feedback after the adoption of the ILC Principles on the Allocation of Loss and their consideration at the UNGA: see eg Secretary-General of the United Nations, 'Consideration of prevention of transboundary harm from hazardous activities and allocation of loss in the case of such harm' UN Doc A/74/131 and Add.1 (2019) (also citing previous reports).

[268] eg Hafner and Buffart, 'International Law Commission' (2011) 248–49; G Haibo, 'ILC Proposal on the Role of Origin State in Transboundary Damage' in MG Faure and S Ying (eds), *China and International Environmental Liability: Legal Remedies for Transboundary Pollution* (Cheltenham, Edward Elgar, 2008) 125.

[269] eg M Wilde, *Civil Liability for Environmental Damage: Comparative Analysis of Law and Policy in Europe and the US*, 2nd edn (Alphen on the Rhine, Kluwer Law International, 2013) 204; Sands and Peel, *International Environmental Law* (2018) 770; Barboza (n 9) 159.

[270] International Law Commission, 'Report of the Commission to the General Assembly on the work of its sixty-fifth session' UN Doc A/68/10 (2013) in *Yearbook of the International Law Commission 2013*, vol 2, part 2 (New York, UN, 2018) 78, para 168(a).

[271] Consideration of prevention of transboundary harm from hazardous activities and allocation of loss in the case of such harm, GA Res 74/189 (18 December 2019) UN Doc A/RES/74/189 (also citing previous resolutions).

[272] D French and LJ Kotzé, '"Towards a Global Pact for the Environment": International Environmental Law's Factual, Technical and (Unmentionable) Normative Gaps' (2019) 28 *Review of European, Comparative and International Environmental Law* 25, 28.

[273] But see P Listiningrum, 'Transboundary Civil Litigation for Victims of Southeast Asian Haze Pollution: Access to Justice and the Non-Discrimination Principle' (2019) 8 *Transnational Environmental Law* 119, 132; Piri Damagh (n 233) 179.

[274] Boyle and Redgewell (n 23) 339; Boyle (n 115) 18.

[275] Boyle and Redgewell (n 23) 337.

chapter, I have indicated the direction in which our thinking should go as far as victims' right to compensation is concerned. I isolated the notion of prompt and adequate compensation as an overarching and emerging principle of international environmental law. I argued that states have a duty to ensure its availability, not necessarily by assuming liability themselves but by laying out the necessary conditions for civil proceedings.

International law's shift towards civil liability as the dominant approach to deal with compensation for transboundary pollution is conceptually sound. Existing treaties, however, fail to attract consensus and political will is lacking. This is a major problem. Now that the ILC's project is over, the message needs a new messenger. It also needs a new package.

The most promising option outside treaty negotiation is to strengthen domestic liability regimes in order to make them a viable threat. But domestic liability regimes can only play a role if appropriate rules of private international law are in place, ones that successfully bring transboundary polluters within the purview of domestic law. Non-treaty solutions therefore rest on the development of underlying norms governing access to justice and jurisdiction. As Sachs explains, these norms might be meagre when compared to a comprehensive treaty-based liability regime, but they 'would have the advantages of flexibility and the ability to take root across diverse legal cultures "transform[ing], mutat[ing], and percolat[ing] up and down, from the public to the private, from the domestic to the international level and back down again"'.[276] The ILC Principles on the Allocation of Loss (particularly the sixth principle) contain the seeds of these norms. This book defines them further and explores how they translate into private international law.

[276] Sachs (n 2) 898, citing HH Koh, 'Transnational Legal Process' (1996) 75 *Nebraska Law Review* 181, 184.

2

Private International Law as Environmental Regulation

THIS CHAPTER ENGAGES with the idea that private international law is a legitimate form of governance in a globalised world. With respect to transboundary pollution, private international law can perform a regulatory function by coordinating domestic environmental regimes and eventually achieving the standard to which international environmental law strives (and which the ILC Principles on the Allocation of Loss clearly express): the availability of prompt and adequate compensation for victims of transboundary pollution.

I begin this chapter by briefly emphasising the relationship between private international law and the duty to ensure prompt and adequate compensation, while also reviewing the work already undertaken by international organisations at the intersection of private international law and environmental law (section I). Drawing from recent scholarship on private international law and global governance, I then recast private international law as a regulatory device to deal with transboundary pollution through domestic courts (section II). A conclusion follows (section III).

I. PREVIOUS WORK ON PRIVATE INTERNATIONAL LAW IN ENVIRONMENTAL MATTERS

The duty to ensure prompt and adequate compensation implies *some* role for private international law. The sixth ILC Principle on the Allocation of Loss explicitly bears on jurisdiction and choice of law. In a previous report, the Special Rapporteur of the ILC stated that 'the duty [to compensate] could equally well be discharged, if it is considered appropriate, … by allowing forum shopping and letting the plaintiff sue in the most favourable jurisdiction'.[1]

[1] International Law Commission, 'First Report on the Legal Regime for the Allocation of Loss in Case of Transboundary Harm Arising out of Hazardous Activities, by Mr Pemmaraju Sreenivasa Rao, Special Rapporteur' UN Doc A/CN.4/531 (2003) in *Yearbook of the International Law Commission 2003*, vol 2, part 1 (New York, UN, 2010) ('First Report on the Allocation of Loss') 102.

This statement suggests that minimum procedural standards exist within the duty to ensure prompt and adequate compensation.[2] This stands to reason. Clearly, the availability of prompt and adequate compensation rests on the ability of domestic bodies to assert jurisdiction over instances of transboundary pollution.[3] Similarly, enabling foreign victims to seek remedies in the state of origin under the same conditions as local victims requires jurisdictional rules to that effect. But promptness and adequacy involve something more than the mere non-discrimination of local and foreign victims – a subtler but equally important connection with private international law. How to reconcile, for example, promptness with lengthy proceedings to debate jurisdiction over foreign land or *forum non conveniens*? These doctrines can force victims to sue abroad, in an unknown legal system, or to embark on a long quest to enforce their judgment against foreign polluters. How to reconcile access to justice – a cornerstone of international environmental law – with a denial of jurisdiction? How to reconcile adequate compensation with choice of law rules that lead to a denial of compensation in substantive law? How should a court factor a state's international obligations into a decision on choice of law? Is choice of law inherently discriminatory towards foreign plaintiffs?

These are difficult questions. They are partially answered through the study of the relationship between private international law and human rights law,[4] but they remain hard to grasp in the context of international environmental law. They may even appear foreign to international lawyers, in part due to the prevailing conception of private international law as a separate field of study.[5] They are not. Private international law can participate in a form of environmental justice, in the sense that it can help reduce 'unpredictability, complexity and cost, balancing the interests of plaintiffs in the widest choice of law and jurisdiction against the interests of defendants in ordering their affairs in an environmentally responsible manner'.[6] Of course, the language of the two disciplines may differ.

[2] R Lefeber, *Transboundary Environmental Interference and the Origin of State Liability* (The Hague, Kluwer Law International, 1996) 260–69.

[3] F Giansetto, 'Le droit international privé à l'épreuve des nouveaux contentieux en matière de responsabilité climatique' [2018] *Journal du droit international* 507, 513.

[4] See generally J Fawcett, M Ní Shúilleabháin and S Shah, *Human Rights and Private International Law* (Oxford, Oxford University Press, 2016); P Kinsch, 'Droits de l'homme, droits fondamentaux et droit international privé' (2014) 318 *Recueil des cours de l'Académie de droit international* 9. See also the ongoing work of the Institute of International Law, 'Draft Resolution on Human Rights and Private International Law' (27 January 2021); Institute of International Law, 'Human Rights and Private International Law' in *Yearbook of the Institute of International Law. Session of The Hague, 2019*, vol 79: Preparatory Work (Paris, Pedone, 2020); Institute of International Law, 'Human Rights and Private International Law' in *Yearbook of the Institute of International Law. Session of The Hague, 2019*, vol 80: Deliberations (Paris, Pedone, 2019).

[5] JR Paul, 'The Isolation of Private International Law' (1988) 7 *Wisconsin International Law Journal* 149.

[6] A Boyle and C Redgewell, *Birnie, Boyle and Redgewell's International Law and the Environment*, 4th edn (Oxford, Oxford University Press, 2021) 335 (referring, however, to the harmonisation of environmental liability as a way to mitigate private international law problems).

There are experts in each, with only a small portion of them working within both. This is precisely why this book seeks to provides a framework that is intelligible in both private international law *and* international environmental law.

The literature occasionally mentions the connections between private international law and international environmental law. Some, for instance, questioned whether the commitment made in Stockholm to develop international liability law included the promotion of private remedies.[7] Yet most connections are largely unexplored in legal scholarship.

International organisations have issued a wide array of recommendations at the intersection of private international law and environmental law. The ILC identified overarching principles and other organisations filled in the gaps, chiefly the HCCH, the ILA and UNEP. In their own way and within their own mandate, they all contributed to the development of international environmental law by identifying desirable rules of private international law that align with the ILC's final proposal. Their work has noticeable common threads. This is unsurprising as each project occurred while civil liability treaties were being negotiated and the ILC was crafting the ILC Principles on the Allocation of Loss. Representatives from those organisations also met throughout the years. For instance, the ILA met with Special Rapporteur Rao of the ILC, while Christophe Bernasconi of the HCCH acted as co-rapporteur for the ILA's project.[8]

The bulk of the substantive work comes from the HCCH, which began working on civil liability for transboundary pollution in the early 1990s.[9] The Permanent Bureau of the HCCH issued three background research papers to structure the negotiation of a potential Hague convention on environmental liability that would have harmonised choice of law and jurisdiction for transboundary environmental damage and filled the gaps left by existing civil liability treaties.[10] Christophe Bernasconi (the Secretary of the Permanent

[7] PH Sand, 'The Role of Domestic Procedures in Transnational Environmental Disputes' in Organisation for Economic Co-operation and Development, *Legal Aspects of Transfrontier Pollution* (Paris, OECD, 1977) 190, reprinted in PH Sand (ed), *Transnational Environmental Law: Lessons in Global Change* (The Hague, Kluwer Law International, 1999).

[8] Committee on Transnational Enforcement of Environmental Law, 'Final Report' in International Law Association Report of the Seventy-Second Conference (Toronto, 2006) ('Final Report on Transnational Enforcement of Environmental Law') 656. Many aspects of the HCCH's background research, authored by Bernasconi, made its way into the ILA's reports.

[9] On the origins of the project, see C Bernasconi, 'Civil Liability Resulting from Transfrontier Environmental Damage: A Case for the Hague Conference?' (1999) 12 *Hague Yearbook of International Law* 35, 35–37, reprinted in Hague Conference on Private International Law, *Proceedings of the Nineteenth Session: 6 to 22 June 2001*, vol 1: Miscellaneous Matters (Leiden, Koninklijke Brill, 2008) 320; PR Beaumont, 'Private International Law of the Environment' [1995] *Juridical Review* 28, 28–31.

[10] Bernasconi, 'Civil Liability Resulting from Transfrontier Environmental Damage' (1999); Hague Conference on Private International Law, 'Note on the Law Applicable to Civil Liability for Environmental Damage' HCCH Prel Doc 3 (April 1995) in Hague Conference on Private International Law, *Proceedings of the Eighteenth Session: 30 September to 19 October 1996*, vol 1: Miscellaneous Matters (The Hague, SDU, 1999); Hague Conference on Private International Law, 'Note on the Law Applicable to Civil Liability for Environmental Damage' HCCH Prel Doc 9 (May 1992)

Bureau at the time) noted that 'if environmental law ha[d] remained the exclusive preserve of *public* international law, it [was] because *private* international law did not offer a sufficiently relevant regime'.[11]

The idea seemed controversial at the outset. Some experts who attended preliminary meetings doubted that the HCCH could ever produce a comprehensive and widely ratified instrument in this complex and politically sensitive area.[12] Scepticism won the day and the project was aborted in the early 2000s. The Permanent Bureau reported the following debates and decision:

> Whilst recognising the importance of this area, the experts drew attention to the risk of overlap which might occur between various existing instruments. Attention was drawn to the work previously done by the Council of Europe and the European Union in this domain, and work that might be undertaken by the Organization of American States. A number of experts pointed to the problems raised by issues of public international law and indicated that the time was not ripe for a Hague Convention on this subject. While further study was welcome, these experts were not in favour of a governmental experts meeting on this topic. Other experts, however, felt that the topic was important and promising and spoke in favour of giving priority to the topic. No delegation recommended that the issue should be deleted from the agenda and it was decided to maintain the topic on the agenda of the [HCCH], but without priority.[13]

The HCCH did indeed leave the topic on its agenda for some time without priority.[14] It officially removed it in 2010,[15] despite the Permanent Bureau's invitation to focus on a non-binding choice of law instrument as an alternative.[16] The former Secretary General of the HCCH, Hans van Loon, sought to revitalise the project in a recent lecture, expressing optimism that rising concern about environmental protection and corporate social responsibility would encourage the harmonisation of private international law in environmental

in Hague Conference on Private International Law, *Proceedings of the Seventeenth Session: 10 to 29 May 1993*, vol 1: Miscellaneous Matters and Centenary (The Hague, SDU, 1995). The term 'HCCH' is used to refer to the research conducted by the Permanent Bureau and the successive decisions of the Council on General Affairs and Policy to maintain the topic on its agenda. The Council did not adopt a formal instrument in this area, nor did it formally approve the research findings of the Permanent Bureau.

[11] Bernasconi (n 9) 143 (emphasis in the original).

[12] As described by Beaumont, 'Private International Law of the Environment' [1995] 37–39. For a nuanced overview of the challenges and hopes of the project at the time, see SC McCaffrey, 'Liability for Transfrontier Environmental Harm: The Relationship Between Public and Private International Law' in C von Bar (ed), *Internationales umwelthaftungsrecht*, vol 1 (Köln, Heymann, 1995).

[13] Hague Conference on Private International Law, 'Conclusions of the Special Commission of May 2000 on General Affairs and Policy of the Conference' HCCH Prel Doc 10 (June 2000) 13.

[14] Hague Conference on Private International Law, 'Final Act of the Nineteenth Session' in Hague Conference on Private International Law, *Proceedings of the Nineteenth Session* (n 9) 46.

[15] Hague Conference on Private International Law, 'Conclusions and Recommendations Adopted by the Council on General Affairs and Policy of the Conference' (7–9 April 2010) 4.

[16] Hague Conference on Private International Law, 'Should the Hague Conference Revisit the Scope and Nature of Possible Work in the Field of Civil Liability for Environmental Damage?' HCCH Prel Doc 12 (February 2010).

matters.[17] The Permanent Bureau also insisted, in a recent information document, on the normative opportunities arising out of the UN's 2030 Sustainable Development Goals.[18]

Meanwhile, as the HCCH project faltered, the ILA established a committee to study the transnational enforcement of environmental law by private parties and non-governmental organisations in domestic courts.[19] The Committee, chaired by Alan Boyle, produced three reports which led to the adoption of the ILA Toronto Rules on Transnational Enforcement of Environmental Law, a set of six rules (and one draft rule) dealing with issues such as access to justice, jurisdiction and choice of law.[20] The rules reflect the contents of civil liability treaties and other instruments such as the Aarhus Convention on access to justice.[21] They also overlap with the ILC Principles on the Allocation of Loss. The Boyle Committee did not claim that its work reflected customary international law in its entirety but sought to influence the future development of international law.[22] The ILA commended the final product to the attention of the ILC and other international organisations.[23]

Finally, UNEP (the UN's leading international environmental body) proposed a set of guidelines on liability.[24] The 2010 UNEP Guidelines on Liability focus on key issues which states should pay attention to when they design domestic liability regimes for environmental damage.[25] The UNEP Guidelines on Liability include a choice of law provision discussed in chapter four.[26]

[17] H van Loon, 'The Global Horizon of Private International Law' (2016) 380 *Recueil des cours de l'Académie de droit international* 9, 105.

[18] Hague Conference on Private International Law, 'The HCCH and the United Nations Sustainable Development Goals' HCCH Info Doc 3 (January 2020).

[19] Committee on Transnational Enforcement of Environmental Law, 'First Report' in International Law Association Report of the Seventieth Conference (New Delhi 2002) ('First Report on Transnational Enforcement of Environmental Law') 825–26. On the origins of the project, see ILA, 'Final Report on Transnational Enforcement of Environmental Law' (n 8) 655–57.

[20] International Law Association, 'Resolution No 6/2006: Transnational Enforcement of Environmental Law' in International Law Association Report of the Seventy-Second Conference (Toronto 2006) ('ILA Toronto Rules on Transnational Enforcement of Environmental Law') 48.

[21] Convention on Access to Information, Public Participation in Decision-Making and Access to Justice in Environmental Matters (25 June 1998, entered into force 30 October 2001) 2161 UNTS 447 ('Aarhus Convention').

[22] Committee on Transnational Enforcement of Environmental Law, 'Working Session' in International Law Association Report of the Seventy-Second Conference (Toronto, 2006) 684–85 (comments by J Brunnée and C Bernasconi).

[23] International Law Association, 'Resolution No 6/2006: Transnational Enforcement of Environmental Law' in International Law Association Report of the Seventy-Second Conference (Toronto, 2006) 48.

[24] Guidelines for the development of domestic legislation on liability, response action and compensation for damage caused by activities dangerous to the environment, UNEPGC Dec SS.XI/5 B in UNEP Governing Council, 'Report of the Governing Council/Global Ministerial Environment Forum on the work of its eleventh special session' UN Doc A/65/25 (2010) ('UNEP Guidelines on Liability') 16.

[25] ibid preamble.

[26] ibid guideline 13.

Efforts to harmonise private international law in environmental matters have attracted uneven attention and support.[27] The HCCH's work may have been influential, if only because of the organisation's membership and stature, but the same cannot be said of the ILA Toronto Rules on Transnational Enforcement of Environmental Law or the UNEP Guidelines on Liability. Negotiators of the Nagoya–Kuala Lumpur Supplementary Protocol seem to have considered the UNEP Guidelines on Liability,[28] but it is difficult to know for sure whether (and to what extent) states have relied on them to reform domestic law. The lack of echo is unfortunate, not only because the work is significant but also because it fills the gaps left by the ILC Principles on the Allocation of Loss and provides more precise guidelines than the ILC could ever have offered in the area of private international law (the ILC being primarily concerned with public international law, albeit not prohibited from studying private international law[29]).

The ILC, the HCCH, the ILA, UNEP and other bodies whose work is relied upon in this book have disparate roles, structures and degrees of influence. Not all of them are state-sanctioned – the ILA, for instance, is entirely private – and their work does not always turn into hard law. Yet each of these organisations has contributed to the progressive development of many areas of international law and it is entirely realistic that they will exert the same influence in international environmental law. Taken as a whole, their policy work can alleviate the academic and doctrinal separation of public and private international law and ensure that private international law responds to the environmental challenges of our time. As Paul argues, 'Our rhetoric, our conceptual categories and scholarly framework, actually shape our perception of, and our response to, reality'.[30] On this view, the ILC Principles on the Allocation of Loss could spearhead a new era in the liability discourse. They provide a new opportunity to achieve a real connection between public and private international law in environmental matters.[31]

[27] O Boskovic, 'Droit international privé et environnement' in *Juris-classeur environnement et développement durable*, fasc 2030 (1 September 2014) para 1; O Boskovic, 'Le contexte transnational en matière de responsabilité climatique' in M Hautereau-Boutonnet and S Porchy-Simon (eds), *Le changement climatique, quel rôle pour le droit privé?* (Paris, Dalloz, 2019) 194–95.

[28] F Perron-Welch and O Rukundo, 'Biosafety, Liability and Sustainable Development' in M-C Cordonier Segger, F Perron-Welch and C Frison (eds), *Legal Aspects of Implementing the Cartagena Protocol on Biosafety* (Cambridge, Cambridge University Press, 2013) 200.

[29] Statute of the International Law Commission, GA Res 174 (II) (21 November 1947) UN Doc A/519 ('Statute of the ILC'), Art 1(2).

[30] Paul, 'Isolation' (1988) 172.

[31] cf C Scott and R Wai, 'Transnational Governance of Corporate Conduct Through the Migration of Human Rights Norms: The Potential Contribution of Transnational "Private" Litigation' in C Joerges, I-J Sand and G Teubner (eds), *Transnational Governance and Constitutionalism: International Studies in the Theory of Private Law* (Oxford, Hart, 2004) 316.

II. THE REGULATORY FUNCTION OF PRIVATE INTERNATIONAL LAW

The development of the duty to ensure prompt and adequate compensation rests on our ability to 'translate' the ILC Principles on the Allocation of Loss into private international law. This would contribute to the domestic interpretation and enforcement of international environmental law in subtler ways than direct legislative implementation or judicial applications. This translation process is entirely realistic. Domestic litigation against corporations for human rights abuses abroad, for instance, may involve the 'translation' of customary international law into domestic tort law, which, despite inherent imperfections, can protect and enforce human rights through domestic courts.[32] Translation tends to be easier when the priorities are clear: international norms prohibiting torture or slavery, to name a few, have a long history that contrasts with the uneven legal treatment of transboundary pollution.[33] Translation from international environmental law will be difficult if the source material is controversial or in flux. Nonetheless, some carefully delineated principles – including equal access and remedy, discussed in the second part of this book – attract wide support.

The possibility of translating principles of international environmental law into private international law rests on a certain conception of the discipline, which transcends its dominant characterisation as an obstacle to justice (section II.A) and embraces instead its regulatory potential (section II.B).

A. Private International Law as Obstacle?

Private international law has historically been treated as an obstacle to compensation in environmental disputes.[34] As Benidickson noted decades ago,

> [f]or whatever reason, the impression appears to be widespread that courts in Canada have not to this point played a very significant role in resolving environmental disputes. Obstacles to litigation have received a good deal of discussion, and awareness of courts' limitations as decision-makers in the environmental context has no doubt discouraged their use.[35]

The depiction of private international law as a roadblock for victims of transboundary pollution dates back to the *Trail Smelter* saga itself[36] and the plaintiffs'

[32] G Holly, 'Transnational Tort and Access to Remedy Under the *UN Guiding Principles on Business and Human Rights*: *Kamasaee v Commonwealth*' (2018) 19 *Melbourne Journal of International Law* 52, 80. In Canada, see *Nevsun Resources Ltd v Araya* 2020 SCC 5.

[33] N Sachs, 'Beyond the Liability Wall: Strengthening Tort Remedies in International Environmental Law' (2008) 55 *UCLA Law Review* 837, 902.

[34] Boskovic, 'Droit international privé et environnement' (2014) paras 1–2.

[35] J Benidickson, Book Review of *The Price of Pollution: Environmental Litigation in Canada* by E Swanson and EL Hughes, (1991) 23 *Ottawa Law Review* 475, 475.

[36] *Trail Smelter (United States v Canada)* (1941) 3 RIAA 1905.

stillborn attempt to sue the polluter. Lawyers had advised them that Canadian provincial courts would not accept jurisdiction over a dispute related to foreign land (the local action rule) and Washington courts did not have long-arm jurisdiction over absent defendants.[37] Like so many other aspects of the dispute, this anecdote durably altered legal imagination. Ever since, the literature has consistently pointed to the existence of liability walls that add up to unpopular civil liability treaties and form a 'defensive bulwark' that favours risk externalisation by polluters.[38] Sachs, for example, warns that 'Without specific treaties setting the ground rules for tort suits, individuals harmed by transboundary pollution have few viable avenues for redress because of … "liability walls" – procedural hurdles to bringing transnational tort suits'.[39]

The obstacle theory presents jurisdiction and choice of law as procedural impediments to a meaningful trial on the merits. They exhaust plaintiffs' limited financial resources on lengthy preliminary issues. They offer escape devices to polluters who are then free to settle on their own terms. Combined with other obstacles such as the cost of bringing proceedings and the practicalities of doing so in a foreign country, they deny access to justice and accountability.[40] This line of argument recalls the rhetoric of human rights litigation, in which jurisdictional rules are often presented as a tool for defendants to evade liability rather than a legitimate way of allocating regulatory authority or ensuring fairness. If we accept that civil procedure is about the power to assert substantive rights and to claim meaningful remedies,[41] summary dismissals on jurisdictional grounds symbolise the ability of powerful private actors to deny those rights to weaker parties and ultimately evade liability through regulatory arbitrage. This is obvious in the famous reasons of Judge Doggett, concurring in the American case of *Alfaro*, in which he wrote that the doctrine of *forum non conveniens* was 'obsolete in a world in which markets are global and in which ecologists have documented the delicate balance of all life on this planet' and 'enable[d] corporations to evade legal control merely because they are transnational'.[42]

[37] JE Read, 'The *Trail Smelter* Dispute' (1963) 1 *Canadian Yearbook of International Law* 213, 222. For further discussion on the local action rule, see section 3.II.A.i.b below.

[38] Sachs, 'Beyond the Liability Wall' (2008) 865.

[39] ibid 839.

[40] This is especially prevalent in the early literature on private remedies for transboundary pollution: SM Siros, 'Borders, Barriers, and Other Obstacles to a Holistic Environment' (1992) 13 *Northern Illinois University Law Review* 633; HS Fairley, 'Private Remedies for Transboundary Injury in Canada and the United States: Constraints Upon Having to Sue Where You Can Collect' (1978) 10 *Ottawa Law Review* 253; SC McCaffrey, 'Trans-Boundary Pollution Injuries: Jurisdictional Considerations in Private Litigation Between Canada and the United States' (1973) 3 *California Western International Law Journal* 191.

[41] TCW Farrow, 'Globalization, International Human Rights and Civil Procedure' (2003) 41 *Alberta Law Review* 671, 673.

[42] *Dow Chemical Co v Alfaro* 786 SW (2d) 674, 689 (Tex Sup Ct 1990) (Doggett J, concurring), *certiorari* denied 498 US 1024 (1991).

The obstacle theory relates to the idea that private international law is dreary, jargon-filled and unintelligible to all but a few technicians whose 'tunnel-vision'[43] reflects a lack of interest in broader regulatory challenges.[44] At best, it is indifferent to the 'communities of misfortune' suffering at the hand of mass tortfeasors and lacks a valuable social agenda.[45] At worst, its pursuit of so-called adjudicative efficiency turns it into a vehicle for the promotion of free trade as the default value of the international order,[46] and actually *favours* a few privileged actors (generally corporations) over masses of disempowered individuals.

In fact, the obstacle theory is not so much a theory as it is a way to advocate reforms of private international law or to dismiss it altogether in favour of other approaches to deal with regulatory conflicts. With respect to liability for transboundary pollution, alternative approaches include universal civil jurisdiction,[47] substantive harmonisation of domestic laws[48] or a general international instrument that would fill the gaps left by existing treaties. In its most drastic iterations, the obstacle theory suggests that private international law plays no role in the regulation of transboundary pollution or the compensation of victims. Like the rest of private law, its shortcomings merely illustrate the need for an approach based on public or administrative law.

The obstacle theory is not necessarily misconceived. In some cases, rules of private international law have indeed led to results which shake our instinctive sense of substantive justice regardless of the particular legal doctrines at stake, particularly in high-profile cases where innocent victims of egregious misconduct were denied access to courts on jurisdictional grounds.[49] But there is more to private international law than the obstacle theory and its narrative acknowledge, at least with respect to transboundary pollution. As long as regulatory conflicts persist and substantive harmonisation of liability regimes remains unlikely, part of the solution comes from

[43] H Muir Watt, 'Private International Law Beyond the Schism'' (2011) 2 *Transnational Legal Theory* 347, 374.

[44] FK Juenger, 'Mass Disasters and the Conflict of Laws' [1989] *University of Illinois Law Review* 105, 106 (an idea debunked by Juenger).

[45] U Baxi, 'Mass Torts, Multinational Enterprise Liability and Private International Law' (1999) 276 *Recueil des cours de l'Académie de droit international* 297, 317.

[46] V Black, J Blom and J Walker, 'Current Jurisdictional and Recognitial Issues in the Conflict of Laws' (2011) 50 *Canadian Business Law Journal* 499, 505–06 (comments by V Black); V Black, 'Commodifying Justice for Global Free Trade: The Proposed Hague Judgments Convention' (2000) 38 *Osgoode Hall Law Journal* 237, 249–50, fn 45.

[47] J Colón-Ríos, 'Constituent Power, the Rights of Nature, and Universal Jurisdiction' (2014) 60 *McGill Law Journal* 127, 151–71.

[48] F Munari and L Schiano Di Pepe, 'Liability for Environmental Torts in Europe: Choice of Law and the Case for Pursuing Effective Legal Uniformity' (2005) 41 *Rivista di diritto internazionale privato e processuale* 607, 631–32.

[49] eg *Anvil Mining Ltd c Association canadienne contre l'impunité* 2012 QCCA 117, leave to appeal to SCC refused [2012] 3 SCR v (where the Quebec Court of Appeal refused to rely on the forum of necessity doctrine to hear the claim of victims of human rights violations in the Democratic Republic of Congo).

a bottom-up approach that relies precisely on private international law to coordinate domestic liability regimes and ensure prompt and adequate compensation. In other words, reform must come from within private international law. This is what OECD countries attempted to do in the 1970s when they worked on private remedies for transboundary pollution.[50] The ILC's project was wider in scope, but it too relied on private international law to ensure prompt and adequate compensation of environmental damage. Today, private international law is an important part of the work towards a binding UN treaty on business and human rights, which might require states to 'provide their courts … with the necessary jurisdiction … to enable victims access to adequate, timely and effective remedy' and include detailed jurisdictional and choice of law rules to that effect.[51] In all these examples, private international law is not sidelined or ignored: it is part of a larger effort to *regulate* through domestic courts.

B. Private International Law as Regulation?

The regulation theory embraces discrepancies in domestic laws and casts private international law as an important device to prevent regulatory arbitrage by powerful actors. As Riles explains in the context of financial regulation, 'Unlike the harmonization paradigm, which pursues legal uniformity, the [conflict of laws] approach accepts that regulatory nationalism is a fact of life, and sets for itself the more modest goal of achieving coordination among different national regimes'.[52] The regulation theory is especially relevant when states cannot effectively or fully enforce their regulations, when harmonisation of substantive laws is politically unlikely or when states engage in regulatory competition[53] – all too familiar challenges in environmental law.[54]

The extent of private international law's contribution to global governance hinges on the proper conceptualisation of its regulatory function. Wai's theories

[50] OECD, Recommendation of the Council for the Implementation of a Regime of Equal Right of Access and Non-Discrimination in Relation to Transfrontier Pollution, OECD Doc C(77)28/FINAL (1977) 16 ILM 977 ('OECD Recommandation'), reprinted in OECD, *Transfrontier Pollution* (1977). For further discussion on the work of the OECD, see section 3.I.B.ii below.

[51] Second Revised Draft of a Legally Binding Instrument to Regulate, in International Human Rights Law, the Activities of Transnational Corporations and Other Business Enterprises (6 September 2020) ('UN Draft Treaty on Business and Human Rights'), Arts 7(1), 9, 11.

[52] A Riles, 'Managing Regulatory Arbitrage: A Conflict of Laws Approach' (2014) 47 *Cornell International Law Journal* 63, 66–67.

[53] H Muir Watt, 'Choice of Law in Integrated and Interconnected Markets: A Matter of Political Economy' (2003) 9 *Columbia Journal of European Law* 383, 400; R Wai, 'Transnational Liftoff and Juridical Touchdown: The Regulatory Function of Private International Law in a Global Age' (2002) 40 *Columbia Journal of Transnational Law* 209, 250.

[54] K Kreuzer, 'Environmental Disturbance and Damage in the Context of Private International Law' (1992) 44 *Revista española de derecho internacional* 57, 72–73.

on the existence of touchdown points are particularly useful here. He explains that the 'major regulatory concern' of private law is to protect third parties from the negative externalities of private transactions.[55] Victims harness civil liability to get compensation from the tortfeasor, which potentially contributes (at least in theory) to deterrence and social stigma.[56] If the tortfeasor has 'lifted-off' from national legal systems (because the actor or the problem transcends borders), private international law can correct the course by leading victims to touchdown points.[57]

The regulation theory assumes a major role for domestic courts as participants in the international legal order[58] or, as the Supreme Court of Canada described them, 'institutions of public norm generation and legitimation'.[59] It also suggests that seemingly procedural rules of private international law have substantive implications:

> The question of whether a court is willing to grant or deny jurisdiction over a given cause of action or litigant becomes, in the end, a question of power. Because different justice will be dispensed in different jurisdictions, the decision to afford or deny jurisdiction is a threshold decision that ultimately may mean the difference between meaningful justice gained and meaningful justice denied. As Berman has argued, '[a]n assertion of jurisdiction, therefore, is never simply a legal judgment, but a socially embedded, meaning-producing act'.[60]

Simply put, asserting jurisdiction over a transnational actor allows its regulatory oversight in domestic courts through the proxy of domestic law. Declining to assert jurisdiction makes that oversight more difficult and therefore less likely.[61] The same goes for the application of a more or less stringent substantive law to govern a dispute in domestic courts by virtue of choice of law rules.[62] On this view, private international law impacts the level of regulation and the perpetuation/reduction of gaps and overlaps between domestic regimes because it determines 'whether state-based regulation will occur'.[63]

The regulation theory can be harnessed to promote a greater role for private international law in global governance, but the claims in this regard often begin

[55] Wai, 'Transnational Liftoff and Juridical Touchdown' (2002) 233.
[56] ibid 235–36.
[57] ibid 266.
[58] CA Whytock, 'Domestic Courts and Global Governance' (2009) 84 *Tulane Law Review* 67.
[59] *Douez v Facebook Inc* 2017 SCC 33 [25], citing TCW Farrow, *Civil Justice, Privatization and Democracy* (Toronto, University of Toronto Press, 2014) 41.
[60] Farrow, 'Globalization' (2003) 691, citing P Schiff Berman, 'The Globalization of Jurisdiction' (2002) 151 *University of Pennsylvania Law Review* 311, 544.
[61] Wai (n 53) 253.
[62] ibid.
[63] ibid 253. See also U Grušić, 'International Environmental Litigation in EU Courts: A Regulatory Perspective' (2016) 35 *Yearbook of European Law* 180, 189–90; JA Zerk, *Multinationals and Corporate Social Responsibility: Limitations and Opportunities in International Law* (Cambridge, Cambridge University Press, 2006) 114–15.

with bold assessments of the discipline's shortcomings.[64] Such assessments tend to imply that private international law has consistently or systematically turned a blind eye to substantive justice and matters of public interest more generally, as a result of inherent defects in its neutral and process-based methodology which have obscured its regulatory function, prevented it from addressing injustices and ultimately made it irrelevant in the twenty-first century.

This idea that the regulatory function of private international law is somehow less discernable than the regulatory function of substantive private law, and that private international law has failed to fulfil that function so far, should not be overstated. Private international law is not completely neutral, blind or apolitical. For one thing, most conflict rules come from domestic law. This means that 'Even though conflict rules can hardly be reduced to shadow projections of the forum country's substantive law, it is reasonable to expect that they take into account the basic substantive policies underlying the particular field of substantive *lex fori*'.[65] Furthermore, modern private international law has moved beyond process-based methodology and towards substantive justice in many areas and jurisdictions. Scholars refer to this shift as the materialisation of private international law.[66] Symeonides, in particular, studied extensively the distinction between 'conflicts justice' (applying the law that is the most closely related to a situation no matter the substantive result) and 'material justice' (achieving the right substantive outcome) and demonstrated that private international law regimes around the world regularly strive for the latter.[67] Substantive objectives appear not only in specific mechanisms designed to supplant conflict rules (a public policy exception overriding the designation of a particularly offensive foreign law, for instance), but in the fabric of conflict rules themselves. It does not make just any substance-oriented rule acceptable. We might question, for instance, the legitimacy of an outcome-oriented unilateral choice

[64] eg H Muir Watt, 'Theorizing Private International Law' in A Orford and F Hoffmann (eds), *The Oxford Handbook of the Theory of International Law* (Oxford, Oxford University Press, 2016); Muir Watt, 'Beyond the Schism' (2011). Lehmann speaks of a 'violent attack' on private international law: M Lehmann, 'Regulation, Global Governance and Private International Law: Squaring the Triangle' (2020) 16 *Journal of Private International Law* 1, 1.

[65] M Bogdan, 'On the So-Called Deficit of Social Values in Private International Law' in C Pampoukis (ed), *In Search for Justice: Essays in Honour of Professor Emeritus Spyridon Vrellis* (Athens, Nomiki, 2014) 32. See also SC Symeonides, 'Private International Law: Idealism, Pragmatism, Eclecticism' (2017) 384 *Recueil des cours de l'Académie de droit international* 9, 128–30; M Bogdan, 'Private International Law as Component of the Law of the Forum: General Course on Private International Law' (2011) 348 *Recueil des cours de l'Académie de droit international* 9, 61.

[66] Y Lequette, 'Les mutations du droit international privé: vers un changement de paradigme? Cours général de droit international privé' (2017) 387 *Recueil des cours de l'Académie de droit international* 9, 240–55; JD González Campos, 'Diversification, spécialisation, flexibilisation et matérialisation des règles de droit international privé' (2000) 287 *Recueil des cours de l'Académie de droit international* 9, 309–411.

[67] Symeonides, 'Idealism, Pragmatism, Eclecticism' (2017) 195–255; SC Symeonides, *Codifying Choice of Law Around the World: An International Comparative Analysis* (Oxford, Oxford University Press, 2014) ch 6; SC Symeonides, 'Result-Selectivism in Conflicts Laws' (2009) 46 *Willamette Law Review* 1.

of law provision which unreservedly promotes the interests of the forum and offends basic comity between nations.[68] But the materialisation of private international is incompatible with a blanket claim that the discipline has isolated itself from the rest of the law (public and private) by being oblivious to policy considerations and completely neutral.[69]

The treatment of international consumer contracts offers a good example of private international law's alignment with legitimate and widely accepted substantive concerns – in this case, the curtailing of party autonomy to protect the weaker party in an era of globalised commerce. The protection of consumers is indeed a common concern in many private international law regimes.[70] In Quebec, Article 3117 CCQ lists circumstances in which the mandatory rules of the consumer's place of residence override the choice of a less protective law by the parties.[71] Article 3149 CCQ also provides that Quebec courts always have jurisdiction when the consumer has its domicile or residence in the province – merchants cannot oppose a forum selection clause designating a foreign court.[72] The latter provision exists precisely to protect consumers who, despite having signed a contract containing a forum selection clause, cannot be expected to spend thousands of dollars to vindicate their rights abroad, and would otherwise be left without a remedy, contrary to the forum's domestic policy.[73] Canadian common law similarly accounts for 'public policy considerations relating to the gross inequality of bargaining power between the parties' in determining whether to enforce forum selection clauses in consumer contracts.[74] There are many other examples of sensitive areas in which conflict rules operate differently in order to protect the weaker party (employment,[75] insurance[76] and product liability,[77] for instance) or to favour a certain outcome (the establishment of filiation as opposed to its absence, for instance[78]).

[68] In Quebec, see eg Civil Code of Quebec, CQLR c CCQ-1991 (CCQ), Arts 3129, 3151, 3165(1°) and the comments of HP Glenn, 'La guerre de l'amiante' (1991) 80 *Revue critique de droit international privé* 41.

[69] For challenges to the ideal of substantive neutrality in European private international law, see Bogdan, 'Social Values in Private International Law' (2014); TM de Boer, 'Forum Preferences in Contemporary European Conflicts Law: The Myth of a "Neutral Choice"' in H-P Mansel (ed), *Festschrift für Erik Jayme*, vol 1 (Munich, Sellier, 2004).

[70] G Rühl, 'Consumer Protection in Choice of Law' (2011) 44 *Cornell International Law Journal* 569, 570.

[71] CCQ (n 68), Art 3117, para 1.

[72] CCQ (n 68), Art 3149. See generally M Wilderspin, 'Consumer Contracts' in J Basedow et al (eds), *Encyclopedia of Private International Law*, vol 1 (Cheltenham, Edward Elgar, 2017).

[73] *Douez* (n 59) [101]–[103] (Abella J, concurring); *Dell Computer Corp v Union des consommateurs* 2007 SCC 34 [64]–[65].

[74] *Douez* (n 59) [38].

[75] In Quebec, see CCQ (n 68), Arts 3118, 3149. See generally M Fornasier, 'Employment Contracts, Applicable Law' in Basedow et al, *Encyclopedia of Private International Law*, vol 1 (2017); M Fornasier 'Employment Contracts, Jurisdiction' in Basedow et al, vol 1 (ibid).

[76] In Quebec, see CCQ (n 68), Art 3119, 3150. See generally H Heiss, 'Insurance Contracts' in Basedow et al, vol 2 (n 72).

[77] In Quebec, see CCQ (n 68), Art 3128. See generally T Kadner Graziano, 'Products Liability' in Basedow et al, vol 2 (n 72).

[78] In Quebec, see CCQ (n 68), Art 3091, para 1.

The point here is not, of course, to discuss whether private international law pursues the right substantive objectives or achieves them in all cases. The point is simply to show that conflict rules come with substantive considerations which are more visible than the critics of its neutrality would suggest. Typically, substance-oriented rules will attempt to protect a vulnerable party or favour a certain outcome. Whether private international law performs a regulatory function in a broader, more systemic sense akin to a form of governance – for instance, by correcting market distortions instead of simply protecting the victim in any given case[79] – remains open for debate. In our context, this question harks back to the debate over the systemic impact of tort law on environmental protection. It was argued above that a systemic impact is plausible but cannot be demonstrated in all cases.[80]

This brief incursion into substance-oriented conflict rules shows that the methodological intricacies of private international law are not the root of all injustices created by globalisation. In its current form, private international law has frequently shown concern for substantive outcomes and will continue to do so, either by protecting individual rights or seeking to achieve more systemic goals. What is striking, however, is the lack of a similar reflection with respect to environmental damage specifically. Scholars have only begun to apply the regulation theory to improve environmental protection or to secure the rights of the victims of transboundary pollution through conflict rules.[81] Before the EU adopted the Rome II Regulation in 2007,[82] few states had applied the technique of substance-oriented conflict rules to environmental damage.[83] Private international law is, of course, not a complete solution to the many challenges of globalisation[84] (the allocation of regulatory authority being one thing, the exercise of that authority by legislators and judges being another), but it has great untapped potential in environmental law. The regulation theory, particularly Wai's foundational work, reveals that potential.

[79] eg H Muir Watt, 'European Integration, Legal Diversity and the Conflict of Laws' (2005) 9 *Edinburgh Law Review* 6; H Muir Watt, 'Aspects économiques du droit international privé: réflexions sur l'impact de la globalisation économique sur les fondements des conflits de lois et de juridictions' (2004) 307 *Recueil des cours de l'Académie de droit international* 25; Muir Watt, 'Political Economy' (2003).

[80] For further discussion on the assumptions of civil liability regimes, see section 1.I.D.ii above.

[81] Grušić, 'International Environmental Litigation' (2016); I Kunda, 'Policies Underlying Conflict of Law Choices in Environmental Law' in V Sancin (ed), *International Environmental Law: Contemporary Concerns and Challenges* (Ljubljana, Založba, 2012); O Boskovic, 'L'efficacité du droit international privé en matière environnementale' in O Boskovic (ed), *L'efficacité du droit de l'environnement: mise en œuvre et sanctions* (Paris, Dalloz, 2010); O Boskovic, 'The Law Applicable to Violations of the Environment – Regulatory Strategies' in H Muir Watt and F Cafaggi (eds), *The Regulatory Function of European Private Law* (Cheltenham, Edward Elgar, 2009); J Ebbesson, 'Piercing the State Veil in Pursuit of Environmental Justice' in J Ebbesson and P Okowa (eds), *Environmental Law and Justice in Context* (Cambridge, Cambridge University Press, 2009).

[82] Regulation (EC) 864/2007 of the European Parliament and of the Council of 11 July 2007 on the law applicable to non-contractual obligations (Rome II) [2007] OJ L199/40 ('Rome II Regulation').

[83] For further discussion on the Rome II Regulation, see section 4.I.D.ii.c below.

[84] Lehmann, 'Squaring the Triangle' (2020) 2.

Conceptualising private international law as a form of regulation does not mean that it must systematically or aggressively match the substantive orientations of the forum. Wai persuasively argues that we should not associate the regulatory function of private international law with parochialism or unilateralism, as opposed to the more 'internationalist' concerns of modern private international law such as the facilitation of free trade. We should instead expand our definition of what internationalism means in order to include other important objectives such as the effective regulation of transnational actors in a globalised world.[85] On this view, private international law is not limited to being the mouthpiece of some unilateral state policy (parochial) or the promoter of an unbridled liberalist discourse seeking to facilitate international commerce above all things (narrowly defined internationalism). It can, and should, address other legitimate concerns (broadly defined internationalism) which are no less valuable than the ones typically promoted in recent internationalist reforms.[86]

Traditional deference to the regulatory policy of other states in private international law does not prevent the adoption of substance-oriented conflict rules[87] as long as the substance attracts some degree of consensus. Documents such as the ILC Principles on the Allocation of Loss were drafted with the aim of reaching consensus on a global concern – to hold transboundary polluters liable and to provide compensation to the victims. They avoid the parochial stigma associated with regulatory accounts of private international law. They are a better point of reference than any given domestic environmental policy, no matter how desirable it may be. They are prime candidates for translation into private international law and do not make it more parochial or unilateral as a result.

This book's theoretical stance is therefore a cautious one. Private international law has not failed to rise to the challenge of globalisation in all areas, but it has stayed on the sidelines with respect to transboundary pollution. More can be done. The regulation theory has the crucial advantage of maintaining private international law in the conversation instead of casting it aside as unhelpful. We can then determine whether it contributes to environmental protection or at least helps translate the duty to ensure prompt and adequate compensation into domestic law. This is what the second part of this book aims to do. This is more productive than trying to avoid private international law in an area where private actors are everywhere, international harmonisation has proven so difficult, and domestic state law retains so much importance – three features that engage rather than disengage private international law.

[85] Wai (n 53) 239, 268, 273.
[86] ibid.
[87] As argued by Van Loon, 'Global Horizon' (2016) 31–32.

III. CONCLUSION

In this chapter, I explained how private international law can, beyond the obstacle theory and under certain conditions, help ensure prompt and adequate compensation of environmental damage through a better understanding of its regulatory function. Scholars and international organisations have already given considerable thought to how environmental damage fits within the traditional methods of private international law. The HCCH, in particular, undertook an important initiative in the early 1990s. With hindsight, the HCCH may have discarded its environmental project too quickly. Now more than ever, as climate change threatens humankind, an instrument governing the transboundary aspects of environmental disputes would prove useful to litigants around the world. Ten years have passed since the HCCH officially removed environmental liability from its agenda. Reviving the project would certainly stir controversy, as it did in the 1990s. On the other hand, the ongoing environmental crisis and a new wave of political support might create the impetus for a legislative project on climate change – an option which seems far-fetched, but deserves to be taken seriously.

With or without the HCCH, however, the time is now ripe to consider whether private international law can do more, and openly favour victims of pollution as it already does with other groups such as consumers or employees. Private international law has never been entirely value-neutral, nor should it always strive to be. We may have good reasons to hold on to private international law's perceived neutrality in environmental matters, but we may also have good reasons to leave it aside in order to fulfil the (admittedly ambitious) promises of private litigation. The second part of the book makes the case for this proposition.

This first part of the book showed that the journey from early work on state responsibility to increased treaty-making in the area of civil liability has not been entirely successful. But it has provided the ILC with enough precedents to settle on a promising way forward. Instruments such as the ILC Principles on the Allocation of Loss and the UNEP Guidelines on Liability have helped reach a point where 'The web of responsibility for environmental harm seems today less inextricable than it did before'.[88] They offer an authoritative basis for future work, if we take seriously the regulatory function of private international law in environmental matters. It is on this basis that jurisdiction and choice of law are approached in part two of this book. The chapters three and four refer primarily to the ILC Principles on the Allocation of Loss and other soft law instruments in international environmental law, to explain what the duty to ensure prompt and adequate compensation entails in private international law and how Canadian law responds to its requirements.

[88] T Scovazzi, 'The Mediterranean Guidelines for the Determination of Environmental Liability and Compensation: The Negotiations for the Instrument and the Question of Damage That Can Be Compensated' (2009) 13 *Max Planck Yearbook of United Nations Law* 183, 210.

The intersection of international environmental law and private international law offers a unique site to study transboundary environmental disputes, particularly as they unfold in domestic courts. But the authorities relied upon in the first part of this book reveal a critical disconnect between how vigorously we discuss liability for transboundary pollution in legal scholarship, and how rarely the victims of transboundary pollution sue polluters and actually obtain a judgment on the merits. There is also a disconnect in how enthusiastically writers promise deterrence in the wake of private litigation and how little empirical evidence exists to support such a broad claim. Thus the literature tends to feed on itself rather than on actual cases.[89] We must pay close attention to those disconnects: to be mindful of the law's fundamental struggle to grasp complex ecological problems, to question how neutral or blind private international law really is, to identify the real obstacles to litigation, and not to take for granted that their removal will inevitably lead to a brave new world of enforcement by like-minded individuals who have converging views on how to protect the environment through domestic courts. The difficulties and controversies accounted for in this book have inhibited the full potential of private law to address transboundary pollution, but other socio-legal phenomena are also at play. They cannot be neglected.

[89] HW Baade, 'Codes of Conduct for Multinational Enterprises: An Introductory Survey' in N Horn (ed), *Legal Problems of Codes of Conduct for Multinational Enterprises* (Deventer, Kluwer, 1980) 413, cited in D Bodansky, 'Customary (And Not So Customary) International Environmental Law' (1995) 3 *Indiana Journal of Global Legal Studies* 105, 1[illegible]7, fn 65.

Part 2

Transboundary Pollution in Canadian Private International Law

3

Jurisdiction Over Transboundary Pollution

THIS THIRD CHAPTER focuses on the jurisdictional aspects of the duty to ensure prompt and adequate compensation, as well as the recognition and enforcement of foreign judgments. If the pollution originates in state *x* but damage is suffered in state *y*, the court seised by the plaintiff (in one of those states or elsewhere) has to decide first whether it can hear the dispute, pursuant to jurisdictional rules. In this chapter, I argue that the Canadian law of jurisdiction meets the requirements associated with the duty to ensure prompt and adequate compensation. So does the law of foreign judgments, subject to a few exceptions analysed below.[1]

This chapter debunks the common assumption that victims face strong or insurmountable jurisdictional obstacles if they wish to litigate. In all Canadian provinces, courts can hear actions by foreign plaintiffs against local polluters at the place of acting, as well as actions by local plaintiffs against foreign polluters at the place of injury. Foreign plaintiffs have access to courts on no less disadvantageous terms than local plaintiffs. Courts will also enforce most foreign judgments rendered against a local polluter. Overall, rules of jurisdiction and foreign judgments do not significantly hinder the availability of prompt and adequate compensation. They provide the necessary touchdown points to prevent the lift-off of transboundary polluters and contribute to their regulatory oversight through private litigation,[2] as long as there remains no evidence of a widespread resort to declinatory strategies such as *forum non conveniens*.

Private international law has changed significantly since the *Trail Smelter* dispute (when it was believed that a private lawsuit in Canada would be difficult). The recent history of Canada-United States environmental litigation shows a greater willingness from both sides to assert jurisdiction and to enforce foreign judgments.[3] As early as 1986, a research project on cross-border environmental litigation led by the Canadian Environmental Law Research Foundation concluded that 'residents of the Great Lake Basin [were] in a reasonably better

[1] For the purposes of this book, 'local' refers to Canada, unless the analysis is generic.

[2] R Wai, 'Transnational Liftoff and Juridical Touchdown: The Regulatory Function of Private International Law in a Global Age' (2002) 40 *Columbia Journal of Transnational Law* 209.

[3] See the sources cited below n 358.

position to involve themselves in cross-border legal proceedings than expected'.[4] An even more positive conclusion is reached in this chapter, after careful examination of the modern jurisdictional framework for torts in Canada.

Jurisdiction remains worthy of our attention for two reasons. First, it intersects with important principles of international environmental law, chiefly access to justice and public participation. Second, the law does not always clearly locate where transboundary pollution occurs for jurisdictional purposes. Victims face real challenges if they sue outside their home jurisdiction – unfamiliarity with the foreign legal system and the costs of bringing a lawsuit abroad, to name a few.[5]

The jurisdictional implications of transboundary pollution are real, but the obstacles faced by victims today should not be overstated. Jurisdiction is only the first building block. Thorny issues also arise after a court finds that it has jurisdiction, when it seeks to determine the law applicable to the dispute. Choice of law is indeed fundamental in the articulation of substantive liability standards for transboundary pollution. This issue will be discussed in chapter four.

This chapter identifies the jurisdictional aspects of the duty to ensure prompt and adequate compensation, their origins in international environmental law and their limits. It provides a standard to assess whether and how the Canadian law of jurisdiction helps ensure prompt and adequate compensation (and where it can go from there). First, I analyse the relationship between jurisdiction and prompt and adequate compensation through the fundamental concepts set out in the ILC Principles on the Allocation of Loss, chiefly non-discrimination and equal access (section I). Taking a step back, I review the current jurisdictional framework against the duty to ensure prompt and adequate compensation, arguing that the law of jurisdiction and foreign judgments contributes to prompt and adequate compensation even though specific legislative reforms are nowhere in sight (section II). I conclude with final remarks (section III).

I. INTERNATIONAL ENVIRONMENTAL LAW AND THE APPROACH OF THE ILC

This section identifies what the duty to ensure prompt and adequate compensation entails in terms of jurisdiction. I begin with an overview of the ILC's position expressed in the sixth principle of the ILC Principles on the Allocation of Loss (section I.A). I explore non-discrimination and equal access, transitioning from the Nordic Convention and the work of the OECD, which many

[4] PR Muldoon, DA Scriven and JM Olson, *Cross-Border Litigation: Environmental Rights in the Great Lakes Ecosystem* (Toronto, Carswell, 1986) 349.

[5] EA Purcell Jr, 'Geography as a Litigation Weapon: Consumers, Forum-Selection Clauses, and the Rehnquist Court' (1992) 40 *UCLA Law Review* 423, 446–49.

consider to be the first milestones in this area, to subsequent manifestations of the same logic (section I.B). I explain how Canada has formally incorporated these notions into domestic law (section I.C). As we will see, equal access is a feature of Canada-United States relations, but it remains limited even in that setting, and the general law of jurisdiction will apply in most cases. With this conclusion in mind, I return to the ILC Principles on the Allocation of Loss and identify a preferable approach to jurisdiction beyond the minimal requirements of equal access (section I.D). Note that equal *access* is related to but differs from equal *remedy*. As explained below, the first has implications for jurisdiction and the second has implications for choice of law, hence their separate treatment in chapters three and four.

A. Jurisdiction in the ILC Principles on the Allocation of Loss

The sixth principle of the ILC Principles on the Allocation of Loss[6] puts forward three jurisdictional provisions designed to operationalise and implement the duty to ensure prompt and adequate compensation.[7] First, it requires states to 'provide their domestic judicial and administrative bodies with the necessary jurisdiction and competence and ensure that these bodies have prompt, adequate and effective remedies available' to deal with transboundary pollution originating in their territory.[8] Second, it recommends that 'Victims of transboundary damage ... have access to remedies in the [s]tate of origin that are no less prompt, adequate and effective than those available to victims that suffer damage, from the same incident, within the territory of that [s]tate'.[9] Third, it reiterates 'the right of the victims to seek remedies other than those available in the [s]tate of origin'.[10] These provisions are the core jurisdictional components of prompt and adequate compensation. The first is jurisdictional on its face, while the other two also touch on the substantive law applied by the competent body.

The sixth principle of the ILC Principles on the Allocation of Loss expands on equal or non-discriminatory access,[11] which the earlier ILC Articles on the

[6] Principles on the allocation of loss in the case of transboundary harm arising out of hazardous activities, annexed to GA Res 61/36 (4 December 2006) UN Doc A/RES/61/36 ('ILC Principles on the Allocation of Loss').

[7] International Law Commission, 'Report of the Commission to the General Assembly on the work of its fifty-eight session' UN Doc A/61/10 (2006) in *Yearbook of the International Law Commission 2006*, vol 2, part 2 (New York, UN, 2013) ('Commentary to the ILC Principles on the Allocation of Loss') 85, para 1.

[8] ILC Principles on the Allocation of Loss (n 6) principle 6(1).

[9] ibid principle 6(2).

[10] ibid principle 6(3).

[11] Commentary to the ILC Principles on the Allocation of Loss (n 7) 86, para 2.

Prevention of Transboundary Harm also contained.[12] The ILC sought to make it easier for victims to directly seek compensation of transboundary damage in the courts of the state of origin, as an alternative to the creation of interstate claim-settlement mechanisms such as the UNCC.[13] It proceeded on the assumption that non-discrimination in the state of origin could replace an international liability regime and ensure that victims could deal with transboundary pollution in a domestic court. This approach

> reflect[s] a very different strategy for dealing with transboundary pollution – one that eschews a universal standard of conduct in favor of norms embedded in the practices of the affected parties, and designed to promote a spirit of reciprocity rather than an abstract environmental ideal.[14]

Other organisations have taken the same path. The ILA Toronto Rules on Transnational Enforcement of Environmental Law, for instance, guarantee the right of access to courts, extend the requirement of a prompt, adequate and effective remedy to all transboundary plaintiffs and secure the jurisdiction of the courts at the place of acting and at the place of injury.[15] The work of a commission of the Institute of International Law on responsibility and liability for environmental damage, led by Francisco Orrego Vicuña,[16] and the background

[12] ILC Principles on the Allocation of Loss (n 6) principle 5; Articles on prevention of transboundary harm from hazardous activities, annexed to GA Res 62/68 (6 December 2007) UN Doc A/RES/62/68 ('ILC Articles on the Prevention of Transboundary Harm'), Art 15; International Law Commission, 'Report of the Commission to the General Assembly on the work of its fifty-third session' UN Doc A/56/10 (2001) in *Yearbook of the International Law Commission 2001*, vol 2, part 2 (New York, UN, 2007) ('Commentary to the ILC Articles on the Prevention of Transboundary Harm') 167–68, paras 1–6.

[13] Commentary to the ILC Principles on the Allocation of Loss (n 7) 88, para 12.

[14] TW Merrill, 'Golden Rules for Transboundary Pollution' (1997) 46 *Duke Law Journal* 931, 954.

[15] International Law Association, 'Resolution No 6/2006: Transnational Enforcement of Environmental Law' in International Law Association Report of the Seventy-Second Conference (Toronto, 2006) ('ILA Toronto Rules on Transnational Enforcement of Environmental Law') 48, rules 1, 3–4; Committee on Transnational Enforcement of Environmental Law, 'Final Report' in International Law Association Report of the Seventy-Second Conference (Toronto, 2006) ('Final Report on Transnational Enforcement of Environmental Law') 657–59, 661–68; Committee on Transnational Enforcement of Environmental Law, 'First Report' in International Law Association Report of the Seventieth Conference (New Delhi, 2002) ('First Report on Transnational Enforcement of Environmental Law') 838–41. See also Water Resources Committee, 'Fourth Report' in International Law Association Report of the Seventy-First Conference (Berlin, 2004) ('ILA Berlin Rules on Water Resources'), Art 71(1); International Law Association, 'Resolution No 3/2002: Sustainable Development. New Delhi Declaration of Principles of International Law Relating to Sustainable Development' in International Law Association Report of the Seventieth Conference (New Delhi, 2002) ('ILA New Delhi Declaration') para 5.3, reprinted in (2002) 2 *International Environmental Agreements: Politics, Law and Economics* 211.

[16] Institute of International Law, 'Resolution on Responsibility and Liability under International Law for Environmental Damage' in *Yearbook of the Institute of International Law. Session of Strasbourg, 1997*, vol 67, part II: Deliberations of the Institute (Paris, Pedone, 1998) ('IIL Resolution on Responsibility and Liability') 487, Art 30, reprinted in (1998) 37 *International Legal Materials* 1474 and (1998) 10 *Georgetown International Environmental Law Review* 269; Institute of International Law, 'Final Report' in *Yearbook of the Institute of International Law. Session of Strasbourg, 1997*, vol 67, part I: Preparatory Works (Paris, Pedone, 1998) 342, reprinted in (1998) 10 *Georgetown International Environmental Law Review* 279.

research conducted by the Permanent Bureau of the HCCH also put strong emphasis on non-discrimination (the latter in the context of the participation of non-residents in administrative proceedings in the state of origin).[17]

B. Non-Discrimination and Equal Access

Non-discrimination suggests that foreign victims of transboudary pollution (or the persons exposed to a risk thereof) should receive the same treatment as victims of pollution in the state of origin. They should equally be able to access information, participate in proceedings, claim remedies or avail themselves of any other right under foreign environmental laws and regulations.[18]

Non-discrimination has a long history in trade law and human rights law, as well as EU law. It crossed over to international environmental law in the 1970s[19] and gradually became prevalent in legal reasoning and state practice. Non-discrimination found fertile ground in developed areas with similar laws, intermingled economies and a strong interest in reciprocity such as North America or Western Europe,[20] and is now commonplace in international law.[21] The Industrial Accidents Convention even recognises non-discrimination as a principle of 'international law and custom'.[22] The ILC Principles on

[17] C Bernasconi, 'Civil Liability Resulting from Transfrontier Environmental Damage: A Case for the Hague Conference?' (1999) 12 *Hague Yearbook of International Law* 35, 94–95, reprinted in Hague Conference on Private International Law, *Proceedings of the Nineteenth Session: 6 to 22 June 2001*, vol 1: Miscellaneous Matters (Leiden, Koninklijke Brill, 2008) 320.

[18] See generally A Boyle and C Redgewell, *Birnie, Boyle and Redgewell's International Law and the Environment*, 4th edn (Oxford, Oxford University Press, 2021) 324–30; T Kruger, 'Trail Smelter II: A Prudent Approach? From Extraterritoriality to Non-Discrimination' (2010) 43 *UBC Law Review* 109, 122–29; H Smets, 'Le principe de non-discrimination en matière de protection de l'environnement' (2000) 4 *Revue européenne de droit de l'environnement* 3; P-M Dupuy, 'La contribution du principe de non-discrimination à l'élaboration du droit international de l'environnement' (1991) 7 *Revue québécoise de droit international* 135.

[19] Smets, 'Le principe de non-discrimination' (ibid) 3; P-M Dupuy, 'Sur des tendances récentes dans le droit international de l'environnement' (1974) 20 *Annuaire français de droit international* 815.

[20] P Okowa, *State Responsibility for Transboundary Air Pollution in International Law* (Oxford, Oxford University Press, 2000) 225; SC McCaffrey, 'Liability for Transfrontier Environmental Harm: The Relationship Between Public and Private International Law' in C von Bar (ed), *Internationales umwelthaftungsrecht*, vol 1 (Köln, Heymann, 1995) 96; A Caputo, 'Equal Right of Access in Matters of Transboundary Pollution: Its Prospects in Industrial and Developing Countries' (1984) 14 *California Western International Law Journal* 192, 217–18.

[21] R Kinna, 'Non-Discrimination and Liability for Transboundary Acid Mine Drainage Pollution of South Africa's Rivers: Could the UN Watercourses Convention Open Pandora's Mine?' (2016) 41 *Water International* 371, 378–79; A Boyle, 'Human Rights and the Environment: Where Next?' (2012) 23 *European Journal of International Law* 613, 635, 639; J Ebbesson, 'Piercing the State Veil in Pursuit of Environmental Justice' in J Ebbesson and P Okowa (eds), *Environmental Law and Justice in Context* (Cambridge, Cambridge University Press, 2009) 284–85; Smets (n 18) 3, 33.

[22] Convention on the Transboundary Effects of Industrial Accidents (17 March 1992, entered into force 19 April 2000) 2105 UNTS 457 ('Industrial Accidents Convention') preamble, para 10. See also Boyle and Redgewell, *International Law and the Environment* (2021) 325.

the Allocation of Loss add another layer of authority to the principle of non-discrimination, even though its formal status in international law remains controversial,[23] as evidenced by the debates on the non-discrimination provision in the 1997 UN Watercourses Convention.[24]

Despite the ubiquitousness of non-discrimination in legal discourse, the words used to describe the notion often muddle its contents. The Commentary to the ILC Principles on the Allocation of Loss amalgamates 'non-discrimination' and 'equal access'.[25] It seems clear, however, that non-discrimination operates on two different levels, only one of which encompasses equal access. Dupuy demonstrates this distinction in the clearest terms.[26] First, non-discrimination operates at the *state* level, when a state treats transboundary damage the same way it would treat local damage.[27] This is the substantive aspect of non-discrimination. Second, it operates at the *individual* level, when a state treats a foreign plaintiff the same way it would treat a local plaintiff in legal proceedings.[28] This is the procedural aspect of non-discrimination, also called equal access.

The literature distinguishes between the substantive and procedural aspects of non-discrimination but shows little consistency in describing what falls in each category. The distinction can easily become artificial if applied too rigidly. For instance, the participation of foreigners in decision-making processes and administrative proceedings such as environmental impact assessments counts not only as procedural non-discrimination, but also as substantive non-discrimination. This is because the process involves consideration by the state of potential transboundary environmental damage originating in its territory – a decidedly substantive inquiry. In the end, describing non-discrimination as procedural or substantive is a terminological divergence with little consequence in principle.

[23] M Mason, 'Citizenship Entitlements Beyond Borders? Identifying Mechanisms of Access and Redress for Affected Publics in International Environmental Law' (2006) 12 *Global Governance* 283, 292; H Xue, *Transboundary Damage in International Law* (Cambridge, Cambridge University Press, 2003) 105–08; Okowa, *State Responsibility for Transboundary Air Pollution* (2000) 225.

[24] Convention on the Law of the Non-Navigational Uses of International Watercourses (21 May 1997, entered into force 17 August 2014) 36 ILM 703 ('UN Watercourses Convention'), Art 32. See generally SC McCaffrey, *The Law of International Watercourses*, 3rd edn (Oxford, Oxford University Press, 2019) 573–74; R Greco, 'Access to Procedures and the Principle of Non-Discrimination (Article 32)' in L Boisson de Chazournes et al (eds), *The UN Convention on the Law of the Non-Navigational Uses of International Watercourses: A Commentary* (Oxford, Oxford University Press, 2018) 338–40; SV Vinogradov, 'Observations on the International Law Commission's Draft Rules on the Non-Navigational Uses of International Watercourses: Management and Domestic Remedies' (1992) 3 *Colorado Journal of International Law and Policy* 235, 254–55.

[25] Commentary to the ILC Principles on the Allocation of Loss (n 7) 86, para 2.

[26] Dupuy, 'La contribution du principe de non-discrimination' (1991).

[27] ibid 136–40.

[28] ibid 140–43.

This book refers to equal access as the procedural arm of non-discrimination and one of the ways to achieve it.[29] The plaintiff-centric approach taken in the sixth principle of the ILC Principles on the Allocation of Loss makes it clear that the ILC understood non-discrimination primarily in this sense.[30] The terminology also aligns with the OECD's.[31] This book further distinguishes equal *access* from equal *remedy*.[32] The first concept refers to access to courts by foreign plaintiffs. The obvious effect of equal access is to remove procedural obstacles specifically aimed at foreign plaintiffs. It also has an effect on jurisdictional rules, as explained below. The second concept refers to the remedies available to foreign plaintiffs. Existing instruments do not clearly explain how equal remedy differs from equal access. As explained in the fourth chapter, equal remedy is indeed a different concept that affects the substantive law designated by choice of law rules. For now, let us focus on on equal access, and more specifically on equal access to *judicial* proceedings (civil actions against polluters, as opposed to administrative proceedings such as environmental impact assessments).

As far as private international law is concerned, the most important question is whether equal access has any implications for jurisdiction. In a very strict sense, the answer is no. Equal access does not mandate any particular rule of jurisdiction. It simply requires a state to treat plaintiffs equally as a matter of civil procedure, regardless of their nationality and *assuming* that the courts of that state have jurisdiction over the dispute. Understood in this limited sense, only certain procedural measures qualify as barriers to equal access in transboundary environmental disputes litigated in Canada. For instance, certain provinces and territories prohibit foreign plaintiffs from acting as class representatives.[33] Certain environmental statutes also limit the availability of injunctions to local plaintiffs.[34] Foreign plaintiffs may also have to post security for the costs of proceedings.[35]

[29] For a similar understanding of equal access, see Muldoon, Scriven and Olson, *Environmental Rights in the Great Lakes Ecosystem* (1986) 16. See also Caputo, 'Equal Right of Access in Matters of Transboundary Pollution' (1984) 197–98.

[30] Commentary to the ILC Principles on the Allocation of Loss (n 7) 85–89, paras 1–16.

[31] OECD, Recommendation of the Council for the Implementation of a Regime of Equal Right of Access and Non-Discrimination in Relation to Transfrontier Pollution, OECD Doc C(77)28/FINAL (1977) 16 ILM 977 ('OECD Recommandation') s 4(b), reprinted in Organisation for Economic Co-operation and Development, *Legal Aspects of Transfrontier Pollution* (Paris, OECD, 1977).

[32] F Ferrand-Desmars, 'La non-discrimination dans le traitement des dommages causés aux personnes privées par les pollutions transfrontières' (doctoral thesis, Université Paris-II Panthéon-Assas, 1998), para 143.

[33] Class Proceedings Act, RSBC 1996 c 50 ('British Columbia Class Proceedings Act'), s 2(1); The Class Actions Act, SS 2001 c C-12.01 ('Saskatchewan Class Actions Act'), s 4(1); Class Proceedings Act, RSNB 2011 c 125 ('New Brunswick Class Proceedings Act'), s 3(1); Class Actions Act, SNL 2001 c C-18.1 ('Newfoundland and Labrador Class Actions Act'), s 3(1).

[34] Environmental Bill of Rights 1993, SO 1993 c 28 (Ontario), s 84(1); Environment Quality Act, CQLR c Q-2 (Quebec), s 19.3, para 1; Environmental Rights Act, SNWT 2019 c 19 (Northwest Territories), s 8(1); Environmental Rights Act, RSNWT (Nu) 1988 c 83 (Supp) (Nunavut), s 6(1); Environment Act, RSY 2002 c 76 (Yukon), s 8(1).

[35] eg Code of Civil Procedure, CQLR c C-25.01 (CCP), Art 492; Ontario Rules of Civil Procedure, RRO 1990 Reg 194, s 56.01(1)(a).

Security for costs warrants further discussion. Canadian courts have held that security for costs does not constitute unlawful discrimination towards foreign plaintiffs[36] and the ILC declared that it was not prohibited by the non-discrimination provisions contained in the ILC Articles on the Prevention of Transboundary Harm[37] and in the draft Articles that inspired the UN Watercourses Convention.[38] But it seems clear that security for costs affects foreign plaintiffs' ability to sue, even though it may not be discriminatory per se. The correlation is apparent in the HCCH's 1980 Convention on International Access to Justice, which prohibits the requirement of 'security, bond or deposit of any kind' for the sole reason that a plaintiff is a foreign national or resides elsewhere.[39] The American Law Institute's and UNIDROIT's Principles of Transnational Civil Procedure similarly discourage the imposition of security for costs on the sole basis of nationality or residence.[40] Likewise, the OECD Secretary General advocated for the attenuation of the obligation to post security for costs in transboundary environmental disputes through reciprocal agreements, in the course of the OECD's work on equal access and transboundary pollution in the 1970s.[41] There is at least one example of such reciprocal agreement in Canada. In *Pembina County Water Resource District*, the Federal Court exempted North Dakota plaintiffs from posting security for costs in their lawsuit against Manitoba authorities over the flooding of lands in North Dakota due to a road allowance built in Southern Manitoba, near the United States border.[42] The Court held that the equal access provision of the International Boundary Waters Treaty Act,[43] a statute which incorporates into Canadian law the 1909 Boundary Waters Treaty signed by Great Britain (for the Dominion of Canada) and the United States,[44] prevailed over usual rules of procedure which

[36] *Lapierre c Barrette* [1988] RJQ 2374, 2381–82 (Qc CA); *Crothers v Simpson Sears Ltd* 1988 ABCA 155 [37]–[50]. For a similar issue in England and in the EU, see *Nasser v United Bank of Kuwait* [2001] EWCA Civ 556; Case 323/95 *Hayes v Kronenberger GmBH* [1997] ECR I-1711.

[37] Commentary to the ILC Articles on the Prevention of Transboundary Harm (n 12) 167, para 2, commenting on ILC Articles on the Prevention of Transboundary Harm (n 12), Art 15.

[38] International Law Commission, 'Report of the Commission to the General Assembly on the work of its forty-sixth Session' UN Doc A/49/10 (1994) in *Yearbook of the International Law Commission 1994*, vol 2, part 2 (New York: UN, 1997) 132, para 2.

[39] Convention on International Access to Justice (25 October 1980, entered into force 1 May 1988) 1510 UNTS 375, Art 14. See also Convention on the Recognition and Enforcement of Foreign Judgments in Civil or Commercial Matters (2 July 2019, not yet in force), Art 14; M Dotta Salgueiro, 'Article 14 of the Judgments Convention: The Essential Reaffirmation of the Non-Discrimination Principle in a Globalized Twenty-First Century' (2020) 67 *Netherlands International Law Review* 113.

[40] American Law Institute and UNIDROIT, *Principles of Transnational Civil Procedure* (Cambridge, Cambridge University Press, 2006) 20–21.

[41] OECD Secretary General, 'Report on the Implementation of a Regime of Equal Right of Access and Non-Discrimination in Relation to Transfrontier Pollution' in OECD, *Transfrontier Pollution* (1977) 46.

[42] *Pembina County Water Resource District v Manitoba* 2005 FC 1226 [17].

[43] International Boundary Waters Treaty Act, RSC 1985 c I-17, s 4(1).

[44] Treaty Relating to the Boundary Waters and Questions Arising Along the Border Between the United States and Canada (Boundary Waters Treaty) (United Kingdom–United States) (11 January 1909, entered into force 5 May 1910) UKTS 1910 No 23, Art II, para 1.

would have permitted the imposition of security for costs on non-residents. The bottom line is that security for costs has significant implications for the notion of equal access, even when that notion is narrowly interpreted.

Equal access, however, is not concerned only with the procedural obstacles that are specifically aimed at foreign plaintiffs, such as the procedural measures mentioned above. If it were, the ILC would have set the bar quite low. Equal access understood in this sense is already well implanted in many legal systems. For instance, anyone can sue in Canadian courts,[45] except in peculiar cases such as lawsuits brought by enemy aliens[46] or unregistered foreign corporations in certain circumstances.[47] The procedural obstacles that do exist in Canada are a cause for concern, but they do not prevent foreign victims from suing in Canada altogether. For instance, the fact that they cannot act as class representatives does not prevent them from being class members if the court authorises the appointment of a non-member as class representative.[48] The fact that they cannot claim statutory injunctive relief does not prevent them from suing in Canadian courts and claiming a similar remedy under general civil or common law. And while security for costs may be a financial obstacle for foreign plaintiffs, courts have wide discretionary powers and usually consider all relevant circumstances before making the order and setting an appropriate amount.[49] The law of jurisdiction, on the other hand, is a significant obstacle to justice if it prohibits foreign victims of pollution from filing a claim in the state of origin (particularly if their own court will not assert jurisdiction over an out-of-state defendant).

It would be incoherent to focus only on open discrimination and maintain jurisdictional obstacles that produce the same result for foreign victims of transboundary pollution. The issue is not necessarily whether certain jurisdictional rules treat foreign plaintiffs differently than local plaintiffs, or whether that differential treatment amounts to discrimination in the sense of human rights or constitutional standards. The issue is whether jurisdictional rules prevent access to environmental justice to a significant portion of the people affected by transboundary pollution. Equal access, understood in a wider sense, therefore has something to say about jurisdiction. This is evident in the ILA's commentary to the 1982 Articles on Water Pollution in an International Drainage Bassin

[45] CCP, Art 489, para 2; *Montana v Les développements du Saguenay Ltée* [1977] 1 SCR 32, 36–37.

[46] *International Association of Science and Technology for Development v Hamza* 1995 ABCA 9 [22]; *Porter v Freudenberg* [1915] 1 KB 857, 867–74.

[47] eg *Success International Inc v Environmental Export International of Canada Inc* (1995) 23 OR (3d) 137, 146 (Ont Gen Div); *International Association of Science and Technology for Development* (n 46) [23]–[29].

[48] British Columbia Class Proceedings Act (n 33), s 2(4); Saskatchewan Class Actions Act (n 33), s 4(4); New Brunswick Class Proceedings Act (n 33), s 3(5); Newfoundland and Labrador Class Actions Act (n 33), s 3(4).

[49] *Yaiguaje v Chevron Corporation* 2017 ONCA 827 [24]–[26]; *Iraq (Republic of) c Instrubel nv* 2014 QCCA 1183 [3].

(Montreal Rules on Water Pollution), in which the ILA praised the jurisdictional rule articulated by the European Court of Justice in *Bier* as a sign that the law was evolving towards equal access.[50] This is also evident the ILA's commentary to the Helsinki Articles on Private Law Remedies, in which the ILA explains that equal access

> requires elimination of jurisdictional or other procedural obstacles for transboundary claimants, including such requirements as security for costs from foreign plaintiffs, the denial of legal aid to such plaintiffs, *and the rule found in various forms in certain jurisdictions that deny jurisdiction over actions involving foreign land.*[51]

From this perspective, it seems clear that equal access requires at a minimum that courts in the state of origin have jurisdiction over transboundary pollution. Consider a polluting facility in state *x* that affects only the residents of state *x*. Being a local matter, courts of state *x* will undoubtedly have jurisdiction to hear the residents' claim. Consider then a polluting facility in state *x* that affects both the residents of state *x* and *y* (or even only the residents of state *y*). To secure equal treatment for residents of state *y*, courts of state *x* must have jurisdiction to hear their claim, if only because residents of state *x* could have sued there in a local scenario. This will not be a problem in most situations because the place of acting often aligns with the domicile or place of business of the polluter, two common grounds of jurisdiction.

Of course, equal access has its limits. It does not alleviate non-jurisdictional obstacles faced by foreign victims who sue at the place of acting, notably their unfamiliarity with a foreign legal system and the costs of bringing a lawsuit abroad.[52] It does not help them sue at the place of injury either (even though it does not exclude it). Finally, it does not eliminate substantive obstacles to prompt and adequate compensation in the state of origin if those obstacles apply equally to local and foreign plaintiffs. Equal access only marks the beginning of the discussion on jurisdiction over transboundary pollution. It is not an end in itself – more can be done, as we will see later on.

Many states and international organisations have sought to implement equal access into domestic law. The Nordic Convention and the OECD Recommendation are among the best-known instruments. They inspired the ILC and helped shape early Canada-United States environmental relations. The literature often exaggerates their significance, but they remain important

[50] International Water Resources Law Committee, 'Report of the Committee' in International Law Association Report of the Sixtieth Conference (Montreal, 1982) ('ILA Montreal Rules on Water Pollution') 545.

[51] Water Resources Committee, 'Interim Report' in International Law Association Report of the Sixty-Seventh Conference (Helsinki, 1996) ('ILA Helsinki Articles on Private Law Remedies') 408, cited in Commentary to the ILC Principles on the Allocation of Loss (n 7) 86, para 5, fn 468 (emphasis added). See also Boyle and Redgewell (n 18) 326.

[52] Boyle and Redgewell (n 18) 330; ML Banda, 'Regime Congruence: Rethinking the Scope of State Responsibility for Transboundary Environmental Harm' (2019) 103 *Minnesota Law Review* 1879, 1883.

to understand the ILC's position on jurisdiction and identify any potential shortcoming in Canadian private international law.

I address each of them below, beginning with the Nordic Convention (section I.B.i) and then turning to the OECD Recommendation (section I.B.ii). The two instruments are intertwined: the OECD began its work the year the Nordic Convention was adopted, and the latter provided a basis for the final OECD Recommendation three years later.[53] In turn, the OECD Recommendation publicised the Nordic Convention to a broader audience. It is therefore advisable to read them together.

i. The 1974 Nordic Convention

Equal access truly appeared on the radar with the adoption of the Nordic Convention by Denmark, Finland, Norway and Sweden in 1974,[54] in the wake of the Stockholm Declaration and an earlier agreement on cooperation between Nordic countries.[55] Some form of non-discrimination had already been seen in environmental instruments prior to 1974, in peculiar contexts or under strict conditions. This included the Boundary Waters Treaty between Canada and the United States,[56] American statutes such as the Clean Air Act[57] and the National Environmental Policy Act[58] (and later CERCLA[59]), a bilateral treaty between Austria and Germany regarding an Austrian airport at the border[60] and a resolution from the Council of Europe.[61] The Nordic Convention, however, broke new ground. It promoted equal access in wide terms, applied to all environmentally

[53] TM Shoesmith, 'Transfrontier Pollution – *OECD Council Recommendation on Implementing a Regime of Equal Right of Access and Non-Discrimination in Relation to Transfrontier Pollution*' (1978) 19 *Harvard International Law Journal* 407, 408, fn 8; RE Stein, 'The OECD Guiding Principles on Transfrontier Pollution' (1976) 6 *Georgia Journal of International and Comparative Law* 245, 250–51.

[54] Convention on the Protection of the Environment (19 February 1974, entered into force 5 October 1976) 1092 UNTS 279 ('Nordic Convention').

[55] Agreement Concerning Co-operation (23 March 1962, entered into force 1 July 1962) 434 UNTS 145.

[56] Boundary Waters Treaty (n 44), Art II, para 1.

[57] Clean Air Act, Pub L No 88-206, 77 Stat 392 §115 (1963) (codified as amended at 42 USC § 7415).

[58] National Environmental Policy Act of 1969, Pub L No 91-190, 83 Stat 852 (1970) (codified as amended at 42 USC § 4321–4370); Council on Environmental Quality, 'Memorandum to U.S. Agencies on Applying the Environmental Impact Statement Requirement to Environmental Impacts Abroad' (24 September 1976) 15 ILM 1426; Executive Order 12114 – Environmental Effects Abroad of Major Federal Actions, 44 Fed Reg 1957 (1979), 3 CFR 356 (1980).

[59] Comprehensive Environmental Response, Compensation, and Liability Act of 1980, Pub L No 96-510, 94 Stat 2767 (1980) (codified as amended at 42 USC § 9601–9628) (CERCLA) § 111(l).

[60] Agreement Concerning the Effects on the Territory of the Federal Republic of Germany of Construction and Operation of the Salzburg Airport (Germany–Austria) (19 December 1967, entered into force 17 May 1974) 945 UNTS 87, Art 4(3).

[61] Council of Europe, Resolution 71(5) on Air Pollution in Frontier Areas, Doc 2934, Appendix VIII (1971), 19 *European Yearbook* 262.

harmful activities and defined them very broadly.[62] This was an unusual approach at the time of its adoption, as global environmental problems were beginning to attract legal and political attention.[63]

The Nordic Convention represents a strong stance in favour of environmental cooperation, both in terms of prevention and compensation.[64] It is procedural in nature. Its central provision requires that all persons affected by an environmentally harmful activity benefit from the same compensation standards and have equal access to courts and administrative bodies in the four countries.[65] It also institutes a regime of administrative approval to deal with the transboundary effects of activities in the area.[66]

The Nordic Convention seeks to consolidate the rights of victims and facilitate private litigation.[67] Curiously, however, it seems to have had little discernible impact in practice.[68] The similarity of the four states' environmental laws and an already sufficiently broad jurisdictional basis may explain the paucity of cases that require resorting to the Nordic Convention. Nonetheless, the Nordic Convention is still consistently hailed as one of the most innovative models for environmental protection. Scandinavian countries carried it into treaty negotiations.[69] It has left a durable mark on subsequent efforts to achieve equal access and also inspired the ILC Principles on the Allocation of Loss.[70] Scholars routinely refer to it when discussing the possibility of litigating transboundary pollution in domestic courts, and few dare to admit that its practical significance has been somewhat exaggerated in the literature.[71] The Nordic Convention seems to have earned its place in the Pantheon of unlikely milestones of international environmental law.

[62] PH Sand, 'The Evolution of Transnational Environmental Law: Four Cases in Historical Perspective' (2012) 1 *Transnational Environmental Law* 183, 189, fn 5.

[63] PJ Sands, 'Environment, Community and International Law' (1989) 30 *Harvard International Law Journal* 393, 413.

[64] But see R Klocker Larsen, 'Foreign Direct Liability Claims in Sweden: Learning from *Arica Victims KB v Boliden Mineral AB*' (2014) 83 *Nordic Journal of International Law* 404, 413 (noting a decline in regional cooperation in private law between Scandinavian countries since the 1970s).

[65] Nordic Convention (n 54), Art 3.

[66] ibid, Arts 4–12.

[67] B Broms, 'The Nordic Convention on the Protection of the Environment' in C Flinterman, B Kwiatkowska and JG Lammers (eds), *Transboundary Air Pollution: International Legal Aspects of the Co-operation of States* (Dordrecht, Martinus Nijhoff, 1986) 149–50; C Phillips, 'Nordic Co-operation for the Protection of the Environment Against Air Pollution and the Possibility of Transboundary Private Litigation' in C Flinterman, B Kwiatkowska and JG Lammers (ibid) 169–70.

[68] T Koivurova, 'The Future of the Nordic Environment Protection Convention' (1997) 66 *Nordic Journal of International Law* 505, 505.

[69] N Glickman, 'Keep Your Pollution to Yourself: Institutions for Regulating Transboundary Pollution and the United States-Mexico Approach' (1984) 25 *Virginia Journal of International Law* 693, 714.

[70] Commentary to the ILC Principles on the Allocation of Loss (n 7) 86, para 2.

[71] But see PW Birnie and AE Boyle, *International Law and the Environment* (Oxford, Clarendon Press, 1992) 198.

ii. The 1977 OECD Recommendation

The OECD Recommendation is a non-binding recommendation that followed in the footsteps of the Nordic Convention. After issuing two preliminary recommendations,[72] the OECD Council chose to promote equal access on similar terms as the Nordic Convention. It recommended that OECD countries adjust their domestic law and treat foreign victims of transboundary pollution in a manner equivalent to local victims in a purely domestic case, including by preserving the right of all persons to participate in administrative and judicial proceedings in the state of origin.[73]

The OECD did not insist on a jurisdictional rule – only on the absence of discrimination in procedural law.[74] But its prior statements went further on this point. They made it clear that the exclusive jurisdiction of the courts at the place of injury offends the principle of non-discrimination and should be avoided.[75] In other words, non-discrimination *requires* jurisdiction at the place of acting. It can also accommodate complementary jurisdiction at the place of injury. The OECD was criticised for focusing on the place of acting (to the disadvantage of foreign victims),[76] but equal access obviously does not prevent victims from suing elsewhere. The ILC Principles on the Allocation of Loss are clearer on this point in any event.[77]

The non-binding OECD Recommendation comes from a small group of states (24 at the time) and would have needed further elaboration in order to have an impact on domestic laws.[78] But the document remains an important landmark of its time, and helped turn non-discrimination into a workable and widely recognised principle of international environmental law. In the years that followed, provisions on non-discrimination or equal access appeared in environmental treaties,[79]

[72] OECD, Recommendation of the Council on Equal Right of Access in Relation to Transfrontier Pollution, OECD Doc C(76)55/FINAL (1976) 15 ILM 1218, reprinted in OECD (n 31); OECD, Recommendation of the Council on Principles Concerning Transfrontier Pollution, OECD Doc C(74)224 (1974) 15 ILM 242, reprinted in OECD (n 31).

[73] OECD Recommendation (n 31), s 4.

[74] OECD Secretary General (n 41) 46.

[75] OECD Council, Environment Committee, 'Report on Equal Right of Access' in OECD (n 31) 26; OECD Secretariat, 'Equal Right of Access in Matters of Transfrontier Pollution in OECD Member Countries' in OECD (n 31) 126.

[76] E Willheim, 'Private Remedies for Transfrontier Environmental Damage: A Critique of OECD's Doctrine of Equal Right of Access' (1976) 7 *Australian Yearbook of International Law* 174, 180, 198–99; I Seidl-Hohenveldern, 'Alternative Approaches to Transfrontier Environmental Injuries' (1976) 2 *Environmental Policy and Law* 6, 8; SC McCaffrey, 'The OECD Principles Concerning Transfrontier Pollution: A Commentary' (1975) 1 *Environmental Policy and Law* 2, 7.

[77] ILC Principles on the Allocation of Loss (n 6) principle 6(3).

[78] M Anderson, 'Transnational Corporations and Environmental Damage: Is Tort Law the Answer?' (2002) 41 *Washburn Law Journal* 399, 414.

[79] eg African Convention on the Conservation of Nature and Natural Resources (revised) (11 July 2003, entered into force 23 July 2016), Art XVI(2); Revised Protocol on Shared Watercourses of the Southern African Development Community (7 August 2000, entered into force 22 September 2003) 40 ILM 321 ('Revised Protocol on Shared Watercourses'), Art 3(10)(c); Convention on Access to Information, Public Participation in Decision-Making and Access to Justice in Environmental

guidelines,[80] resolutions and reports from the ILA[81] and the IIL,[82] and model laws drafted by various organisations and research groups.[83] The experts who worked on the 1988 Brundtland Report also included non-discrimination and equal access as two of the 22 foundational principles of environmental protection and sustainable development that strongly influenced the negotiation of the Rio Declaration a few years later.[84]

Several important multilateral instruments entrench non-discrimination and equal access. The Aarhus Convention expressly requires that the public have access to justice in environmental matters without discrimination based on citizenship, nationality or domicile.[85] The UNECE declared that under that provision, states must ensure that foreign members of the public have access to justice under the same conditions as locals.[86] The UN Watercourses Convention prohibits discrimination on the basis of nationality, residence or place of injury when a state grants access to justice or a right to claim compensation to victims.[87] The 1991 Espoo Convention gives the public a right to participate

Matters (25 June 1998, entered into force 30 October 2001) 2161 UNTS 447 ('Aarhus Convention'), Art 3(9); UN Watercourses Convention (n 24), Art 32; Protocol for the Protection of the Mediterranean Sea Against Pollution Resulting from Exploration and Exploitation of the Continental Shelf and the Seabed and its Subsoil (14 October 1994, entered into force 24 March 2011) [2013] OJ L4/15 ('Protocol for the Protection of the Mediterranean Sea'), Art 26(4) (administrative proceedings); Industrial Accidents Convention (n 22), Art 9; Convention on Environmental Impact Assessment in a Transboundary Context (25 February 1991, entered into force 27 June 1997) 1989 UNTS 309 ('Espoo Convention'), Art 2(6).

[80] eg Intergovernmental Working Group of Experts on Natural Resources Shared by Two or More States, 'Draft principles of conduct in the field of the environment for the guidance of states in the conservation and harmonious utilisation of natural resources shared by two or more states' UN Doc UNEP/GC.6/17, 17 ILM 1097 (1978) principle 14.

[81] ILA Toronto Rules on Transnational Enforcement of Environmental Law (n 15), rule 3(3); ILA Berlin Rules on Water Resources (n 15), Art 71(1); ILA New Delhi Declaration (n 15) para 5.3; ILA Helsinki Articles on Private Law Remedies (n 51), Art 3(1); ILA Montreal Rules on Water Pollution (n 50), Art 8.

[82] IIL Resolution on Responsibility and Liability (n 16), Art 30; International Law Institute, 'Final Report' (n 16) 342.

[83] International Union for Conservation of Nature, *Draft International Covenant on Environment and Development: Implementing Sustainability*, 5th edn (Gland, IUCN, 2015) ('IUCN Draft International Covenant on Environment and Development') 22, Art 62; Société française pour le droit de l'environnement and Gesellschaft für Umweltrecht, 'Projet de convention entre la République française et la République fédérale d'Allemagne pour la limitation et la prévention des pollutions transfrontières' [1997] 1 *Revue juridique de l'environnement* 99, 103 (Art 5), 108 (Art 23); Muldoon, Scriven and Olson (n 4) 358, s 4.

[84] Summary of Proposed Legal Principles for Environmental Protection and Sustainable Development Adopted by the WCED Experts Group on Environmental Law, Arts 13, 20, annexed to World Commission on Environment and Development, 'Report of the World Commission on Environment and Development' UN Doc A/42/427 (1987) 339, reprinted in Experts Group on Environmental Law of the World Commission on Environment and Development, *Environmental Protection and Sustainable Development: Legal Principles and Recommendations* (London, Graham & Trotman, 1987).

[85] See Aarhus Convention (n 79), Art 3(9).

[86] United Nations Economic Commission for Europe, *The Aarhus Convention: An Implementation Guide*, 2nd edn (Geneva, United Nations, 2014) 189. See also *Ukraine* ACCC/C/2004/03, UN Doc ECE/MP.PP/C.1/2005/2/Add.3 (2005) para 26.

[87] UN Watercourses Convention (n 24), Art 32.

in environmental impact assessments.[88] In the United States, the Restatement (Third) of Foreign Relations promotes equal access to foreign victims of transboundary pollution.[89] Recently, the Inter-American Court of Human Rights issued a voluminous advisory opinion in which it declared that American states must guarantee non-discriminatory access to justice to all victims of pollution originating in their territory, including foreign victims.[90] This growing corpus of domestic and international law reflects broader commitments to increase public participation and access to justice in environmental matters.[91]

C. Implementation of Equal Access in Canada

Four documents promote equal access specifically in relation to Canada. The 1909 Boundary Waters Treaty marked the introduction of the concept in Canada (section I.C.i). The 1979 Draft Treaty on a Regime of Equal Access and Remedy in Cases of Transfrontier Pollution (section I.C.ii) and the 1982 Transboundary Pollution Reciprocal Access Act (section I.C.iii) later expanded equal access to all transboundary environmental disputes. They were not entirely successful but led to special legislation that overrides the general law of jurisdiction in four provinces. Finally, North American states put equal access at the heart of their trade policy with the 1994 North American Agreement on Environmental Cooperation, now superseded by a new free-trade regime (section I.C.iv). Each of those four documents reflect the approach of the ILC in the Principles on the Allocation of Loss. They also share many of the features of earlier documents such as the Nordic Convention and the OECD Recommendation.

In addition, the Nuclear Liability and Compensation Act requires the Nuclear Claims Tribunal to treat claims equitably and without discrimination on the basis of nationality or residence.[92] This administrative tribunal is

[88] Espoo Convention (n 79), Art 2(6).

[89] American Law Institute, *Restatement of the Law, Third: Foreign Relations Law of the United States*, vol 2 (St Paul: American Law Institute, 1987) § 602(2). American courts held that the equal access provision of the *Restatement (Third) of Foreign Relations Law* did not reflect a 'universally recognized principl[e] of international law' but only 'iterate[d] the existing *U.S.* view of the law of nations regarding global environmental protection'. *Amlon Metals Inc v FMC Corp* 775 F Supp 668, 671 (SD NY 1991) (emphasis in the original).

[90] *Environment and Human Rights (Colombia)* (2017) IACHR (Ser A) No 23 [238]–[240].

[91] Guidelines for the development of national legislation on access to information, public participation and access to justice in environmental matters, UNEPGC Dec SS.XI/5 A in UNEP Governing Council, 'Report of the Governing Council/Global Ministerial Environment Forum on the work of its eleventh special session' UN Doc A/65/25 (2010) ('UNEP Guidelines on Access to Justice') 12; Rio Declaration on Environment and Development (13 June 1992) UN Doc A/CONF.151/26/Rev.1(Vol 1) ('Rio Declaration') principle 10.

[92] Nuclear Liability and Compensation Act, SC 2015 c 4 s 120, s 41(3). See generally N Pelzer, 'Facing the Challenge of Nuclear Mass Tort Proceedings' (2017) 99 *Nuclear Law Bulletin* 45, 53–57.

established by the Governor in Council if deemed necessary in order to process claims after a nuclear incident.[93] If such tribunal is not established, the Act gives jurisdiction to the courts of the province where the incident occurred (or the Federal Court when the incident spanned two provinces or Canada's exclusive economic zone).[94] The Act, however, provides that no court in Canada has jurisdiction over a claim for damage suffered outside Canada or its exclusive economic zone.[95] Foreign victims therefore do not have access to Canadian courts in this scenario.

i. The 1909 Boundary Waters Treaty

The International Boundary Waters Treaty Act was the first to introduce the concept of equal access in Canada.[96] The Act incorporates into domestic law the 1909 Boundary Waters Treaty signed by Great Britain (for the Dominion of Canada) and the United States to govern certain aspects of water management in the Great Lakes area.[97] The treaty itself is an important milestone for environmental cooperation in North America. It created the bilateral International Joint Commission (IJC) to prevent and manage disputes over the use of transboundary watercourses.[98] The details of the regime go beyond the scope of this book, but its equal access provision warrants attention.

Section 4(1) of the International Boundary Waters Treaty Act reflects the first paragraph of Article II of the Boundary Waters Treaty. The Treaty grants each state exclusive jurisdiction over the use or diversion of a watercourse partially located on their territory and flowing into the other state's territory, and requires each state to provide equal rights and remedies to victims of a water diversion on the other side:

> **Boundary Waters Treaty, Article II, paragraph 1**
>
> II. Each of the High Contracting Parties reserves to itself … the exclusive jurisdiction and control over the use and diversion, whether temporary or permanent, of all waters on its own side of the line which in their natural channels would flow across the boundary or into boundary waters; but it is agreed that any interference with or diversion from their natural channel of such waters on either side of the boundary, resulting in any injury on the other side of the boundary, shall give rise to the same

[93] ibid, s 36(1).
[94] ibid, s 34(1)–(2). cf Nuclear Liability Act, RSC 1985 c N-28, s 14 (now repealed – jurisdiction of courts at the place of injury, or where the facility is located, if an injury was suffered in more than one place).
[95] ibid, s 34(6).
[96] International Boundary Waters Treaty Act (n 43).
[97] Boundary Waters Treaty (n 44).
[98] ibid.

> rights and entitle the injured parties to the same legal remedies as if such injury took place in the country where such diversion or interference occurs[99]
>
> **International Boundary Waters Treaty Act, section 4(1)**
>
> **4(1)** Any interference with or diversion from their natural channel of any waters in Canada, which in their natural channels would flow across the boundary between Canada and the United States or into boundary waters, as defined in the treaty, resulting in any injury on the United States side of the boundary, gives the same rights and entitles the injured parties to the same legal remedies as if the injury took place in that part of Canada where the interference or diversion occurs.[100]

The International Boundary Waters Treaty Act also gives the Federal Court jurisdiction over any dispute brought by an American victim under the Act.[101]

Section 4(1) of the International Boundary Waters Treaty Act essentially creates a special right of action.[102] The interference with or the diversion of a watercourse flowing from Canada into the United States can give rise to a remedy in Federal Court if it causes damage (including environmental damage) to American victims. This right of action, however, applies only to water interference or diversion, not pollution. The wording of the provision, and that of Article II, paragraph 1 of the Boundary Waters Treaty which it incorporates, leave no doubt on this point ('any interference with or diversion from').[103] By contrast, Article IV, paragraph 2 of the Boundary Waters Treaty explicitly prohibits pollution on either side of the border, but unlike Article II, it does not mention the legal remedies attached to the obligation nor the beneficiaries of those remedies:

> IV. The High Contracting Parties agree that, except in cases provided for by special agreement between them, they will not permit the construction or maintenance on their respective sides of the boundary of any remedial or protective works or any dams or other obstructions in waters flowing from boundary waters or in waters at a lower level than the boundary in rivers flowing across the boundary, the effect of which is to raise the natural level of waters on the other side of the boundary unless the construction or maintenance thereof is approved by the aforesaid International Joint Commission.

[99] Boundary Waters Treaty (n 44), Art II, para 1. On Article II of the Boundary Waters Treaty, see TA Kalavrouziotis, 'U.S.-Canadian Relations Regarding Diversions from an International Basin: An Analysis of Article II of the Boundary Waters Treaty' (1989) 12 *Fordham International Law Journal* 658; SC McCaffrey, 'Trans-Boundary Pollution Injuries: Jurisdictional Considerations in Private Litigation Between Canada and the United States' (1973) 3 *California Western International Law Journal* 191, 203–17; R Day Scott, 'The Canadian-American Boundary Waters Treaty: Why Article II?' (1958) 36 *Canadian Bar Review* 511.

[100] International Boundary Waters Treaty Act (n 43), s 4(1).

[101] ibid, s 5.

[102] *Pembina County Water Resource District v Manitoba* 2011 FC 1118 [18].

[103] International Boundary Waters Treaty Act (n 43), s 4(1); Boundary Waters Treaty (n 44), Art II, para 1.

> *It is further agreed that the waters herein defined as boundary waters and waters flowing across the boundary shall not be polluted on either side to the injury of health or property on the other.*[104]

Victims cannot, under the International Boundary Waters Treaty Act, claim a remedy in Canadian courts for pollution of a transboundary watercourse. In *Pembina County Water Resource District*, the Federal Court of Appeal held that section 4(1) of the International Boundary Waters Treaty Act extends only to the acts covered by Article II of the Boundary Waters Treaty, not those covered by Article IV. It also held that Article IV does not grant any private right of action or remedies to persons who suffer an injury as a result of the acts contemplated in Article IV (including pollution).[105]

Section 4(1) of the International Boundary Waters Treaty Act was invoked twice in Canadian courts. The first case involved a Canadian victim of flooding who sued the IJC for its manipulation of water levels in the St Lawrence River. The Federal Court ruled in 1976 that the equal access provision could not apply because the injury had occurred in Ontario, not the United States.[106] The rest of the claim was struck down because the IJC did not have a legal personality and therefore could not be sued.[107]

The second case took longer to unfold. In 2004, North Dakota authorities and private landowners sued the Government of Manitoba and the rural municipality of Rhineland in nuisance and negligence. The dispute involved a road allowance in Manitoba, near the North Dakota border. Embankments on the road allowance blocked the natural dispersion of the Pembina River from North Dakota into Manitoba and caused floods in North Dakota. Plaintiffs sought injunctive relief and damages from the Federal Court under section 4(1) of the International Boundary Waters Treaty Act.

Thirteen years of preliminary procedures followed. In 2017, the Federal Court of Appeal concluded that it did not have jurisdiction to hear the claim and the Supreme Court of Canada refused to hear the case.[108] In the Federal Court of Appeal's view, Article II of the Boundary Waters Treaty referred only to Canada's diversion or interference in Canada with the flow of a river flowing *into* the United States and vice versa. The Pembina River, by contrast, flowed *from* the United States into Canada, where the alleged interference had occurred.[109] While this reasoning may appear overly formal, it is important to

[104] Boundary Waters Treaty (n 44), Art IV, para 2 (emphasis added).

[105] *Pembina County Water Resource District v Manitoba (Government)* 2017 FCA 92 [65]–[66], [69]–[73], leave to appeal to SCC refused [2017] 2 SCR ix. cf AT Carter, 'The Boundary Waters Treaty of 1909: Does It Provide an Environmental Cause of Action?' (1975) 20 *South Dakota Law Review* 147 (discussing a possible cause of action for Canadian victims in the United States under the Boundary Waters Treaty).

[106] *Burnell v International Joint Commission* [1977] 1 FC 269, 273.

[107] ibid 276–77.

[108] *Pembina County Water Resource District* (n 105).

[109] ibid [62].

note that the Federal Court derives its powers from statute only.[110] It cannot exceed the statutory grant of jurisdiction contained in the International Boundary Waters Treaty Act. The wording of the Act is therefore determinative. The Federal Court of Appeal nonetheless left the door open to a lawsuit before provincial courts (the courts of general jurisdiction in Canada).[111]

Plaintiffs publicly expressed their intention to file a claim in the Manitoba Court of Queen's Bench after the Supreme Court of Canada refused to hear their appeal.[112] The limitations periods in force in the province, however, could limit the amounts recoverable.[113] The case illustrates once again the hardship faced by foreign plaintiffs in environmental litigation. Thirteen years after filing their claim, plaintiffs were still at the starting gates. But if the case ever gets to trial in Manitoba, it may provide important insights on cross-border environmental disputes in North America.

Overall, the Boundary Waters Treaty remains a significant example of the implementation of equal access in Canada because there are parallels to be made between water diversion and pollution, but it has a very limited scope and does not leave a role of the private enforcement of the anti-pollution rule it contains.[114] We must look elsewhere for more comprehensive initiatives.

ii. The 1979 Draft Treaty on Equal Access and Remedy

In 1979, the American Bar Association (ABA) and the Canadian Bar Association (CBA) endorsed and commended to the attention of their governments an instrument drafted by a joint working group and designed to implement equal access between Canada and the United States.[115] The 1979 Draft Treaty on Equal Access and Remedy guaranteed equal access to procedures and remedies for victims of pollution on both sides of the border.[116] The co-chairman of the ABA/CBA Working Group explained that the text did not propose 'a new legal system, but the adjustment of the two countries' existing municipal legal

[110] Federal Courts Act, RSC 1985 c F-7; *Windsor (City) v Canadian Transit Co* 2016 SCC 54 [33].

[111] *Pembina County Water Resource District* (n 105) [76]–[77].

[112] D Robertson, 'Court No Closer to Fording International Flood Dispute: U.S. Trying to Change Flow of Flooding Water' *Winnipeg Free Press* (31 January 2018) 4.

[113] ibid.

[114] An 'inherent weakness' of the Treaty according to ND Hall, 'Transboundary Pollution: Harmonizing International and Domestic Law' (2007) 40 *University of Michigan Journal of Law Reform* 681, 723.

[115] American Bar Association and Canadian Bar Association, 'Draft Treaty on a Regime of Equal Access and Remedy in Cases of Transfrontier Pollution' in American Bar Association and Canadian Bar Association, *Settlement of International Disputes Between Canada and the USA* (Chicago, Section of International Law of the American Bar Association, 1979) xiii, reprinted in (2011) 35 *Canada–United States Law Journal* 9, 16–20 and Muldoon, Scriven and Olson (n 4) 365–67 ('Draft Treaty on Equal Access and Remedy'). See generally JA Gallob, 'Birth of the North American Transboundary Environmental Plaintiff: Transboundary Pollution and the 1979 Draft Treaty for Equal Access and Remedy' (1991) 15 *Harvard Environmental Law Review* 85.

[116] Draft Treaty on Equal Access and Remedy (ibid), Art 2.

systems' in order to facilitate the private settlement of environmental disputes.[117] The project began in the midst of extensive academic debate on the viability of private remedies for acid rain damage, a pressing environmental preoccupation at the time.[118] Interestingly, the ABA/CBA Working Group took the view that governmental intervention in transboundary environmental disputes was neither necessary nor desirable.[119] This is in stark contrast with the approach taken in the *Trail Smelter* arbitration. It also contracts with the approach that British Columbia and Canadian governments would later take as *amicus curiae* in *Pakootas*, where they argued that private litigation was not the proper means of addressing transboundary environmental problems.[120]

The ABA/CBA Working Group's focus on individual action over governmental intervention led to heavy reliance on procedural equal access: the main provisions of the proposed treaty are in fact very similar to those of the OECD Recommendation.[121] The ABA/CBA Working Group also confined its proposal to transboundary pollution instead of covering all Canada-United States litigation. They hoped that the inherently bilateral nature of the pollution problem and a growing environmental consciousness would cause the populations of each country and their governments to support a targeted reform inspired by the experience of the Nordic countries, which, if successful, could lead to broader reforms in other bilateral matters.[122] The Draft Treaty on Equal Access and Remedy initially gathered some attention, but the two governments never formally endorsed it.[123]

iii. The 1982 Reciprocal Access Act

After the release of the Draft Treaty on Equal Access and Remedy, lawyers on both sides of the border were apparently displeased with the unwillingness of their governments to secure equal access through a bilateral treaty.[124]

[117] T Bradbrooke Smith, 'Report to the Executive and to the 1979 Annual Meeting of the Canadian Bar Association' in American Bar Association and Canadian Bar Association (n 115) xxxv, reprinted in (2011) 35 *Canada–United States Law Journal* 9, 30–35.

[118] eg M Pallemaerts, 'Judicial Recourse Against Foreign Air Polluters: A Case Study of Acid Rain in Europe" (1985) 9 *Harvard Environmental Law Review* 143; JM Fischer, 'The Availability of Private Remedies for Acid Rain Damage' (1981) 9 *Ecology Law Quarterly* 429.

[119] Smith (n 117) xxxvi–xxxvii.

[120] J Ellis, 'Extraterritorial Exercise of Jurisdiction for Environmental Protection: Addressing Fairness Concerns' (2012) 25 *Leiden Journal of International Law* 397, 412–13.

[121] Draft Treaty on Equal Access and Remedy (n 115), Art 2.

[122] American Bar Association and Canadian Bar Association Working Group, 'Report and Recommendations of the American and Canadian Bar Associations Joint Working Group on the Settlement of International Disputes' in American Bar Association and Canadian Bar Association (n 115) 42–43, reprinted in (2011) 35 *Canada–United States Law Journal* 9, 40–121.

[123] S-L Hsu and AL Parrish, 'Litigating Canada-U.S. Transboundary Harm: International Environmental Lawmaking and the Threat of Extraterritorial Reciprocity' (2007) 48 *Virgnia Journal of International Law* 1, 37.

[124] Gallob, 'Transboundary Pollution and the 1979 Draft Treaty for Equal Access and Remedy' (1991) 131; GF Fitzgerald, 'The Proposed Canada-United States Transboundary Air Pollution Agreement: The Legal Background' (1982) 20 *Canadian Yearbook of International Law* 219, 239.

The ABA/CBA Working Group decided to turn its attention to a more flexible instrument.[125] It established a liaison group with the Uniform Law Conference of Canada (ULCC), a century-old intergovernmental body that promotes legislative harmonisation between provinces and territories, and its counterpart the United States National Conference of Commissioners on Uniform State Laws. This process led to the 1982 Transboundary Pollution Reciprocal Access Act, a model law for states, provinces and territories to adopt.[126]

The Reciprocal Access Act resembles the Draft Treaty on Equal Access and Remedy but expands its scope to interprovincial and interstate pollution.[127] It implements equal access to courts at the place of acting for all persons (including corporations and public authorities) as well as equal right of relief.[128] The Reciprocal Access Act rests on reciprocity. For it to apply, the state of origin and the affected state must enact its provisions or provide substantially equivalent access to their courts.[129] Canadian provinces can also designate reciprocating jurisdictions by regulation.[130] This mechanism is less flexible than non-discrimination per se: nothing would normally prevent a state from granting equal access to foreign plaintiffs even if its own residents do not have the same advantage abroad. The logic of the Reciprocal Access Act, however, is different.

The Reciprocal Access Act could have facilitated litigation over transboundary pollution if it had been widely adopted.[131] The problem lies in who enacted it: Ontario, Manitoba, Nova Scotia, Prince Edward Island (in Canada), and Michigan, New Jersey, Wisconsin, Colorado, Oregon, Connecticut and Montana (in the United States).[132] Most of these jurisdictions do not share a border.[133]

[125] JN Mulvaney, 'Participation by Ontario in U.S. Administrative and Judicial Proceedings' (1983) 4 *New York Law School Journal of International and Comparative Law* 553, 566–67.

[126] Uniform Law Conference of Canada, 'Uniform Transboundary Pollution Reciprocal Access Act' in Uniform Law Conference of Canada Proceedings of the Sixty-Fourth Annual Meeting (Montebello, 1982) 504, reprinted in Muldoon, Scriven and Olson (n 4) 369 ('Reciprocal Access Act').

[127] Reciprocal Access Act (ibid), s 1(1); Uniform Law Conference of Canada, 'Uniform Transboundary Pollution Reciprocal Access Act: Prefatory Note' in Uniform Law Conference of Canada Proceedings of the Sixty-Fourth Annual Meeting (Montebello, 1982) 504.

[128] Reciprocal Access Act (n 126), ss 2–3.

[129] ibid, s 1(1).

[130] ibid, s 7(b).

[131] But see G Wetstone and A Rosencranz, 'Transboundary Air Pollution Between Canada and the United States' (1982) 1 *UCLA Pacific Basin Law Journal* 197, 217 ('Even if [the Reciprocal Access Act] led to the enactment of uniform state and provincial laws, a court would have to be bold indeed to entertain a suit involving acid rain damages').

[132] In Canada: Transboundary Pollution Reciprocal Access Act, RSO 1990 c T.18 (Ontario); The Transboundary Pollution Reciprocal Access Act, CCSM c T145 (Manitoba); Environment Act, SNS 1994–95 c 1 (Nova Scotia), ss 145–55; Transboundary Pollution (Reciprocal Access) Act, RSPEI 1988 c T-5 (Prince Edward Island). In the United States: Mich Comp Laws § 324.1801–324.1807 (2019); NJ Rev Stat § 2A:58A-1 to 2A:58A-8 (2019); Wis Stat § 299.33 (2019); Colo Rev Stat § 13-1.5-101–13.1.5-109 (2019); Or Rev Stat § 468.076–468.089 (2019); Conn Gen Stat § 51-351b (2019); Mont Code § 75-16-101–75-16-109 (2019).

[133] In addition, Ontario expressly designated the bordering state of Minnesota as a reciprocating jurisdiction: Reciprocating Jurisdictions, RRO 1990 Reg 1084, s 2.

The Reciprocal Access Act would not cover instances of pollution between British Columbia and Washington (the *Trail Smelter* case[134]) or Manitoba and North Dakota (the *Pembina County Water Resource District* case[135]) unless those jurisdictions mutually provided substantially equivalent access to their courts. This creates an inconsistent patchwork of private international law that excludes obvious instances of transboundary pollution (a shared watercourse, for instance) but includes some longer-range ones. The Reciprocal Access Act has had little discernible impact on transboundary environmental litigation, and no court has ever decided a case based on its provisions.

It would be difficult to raise the decades-old Draft Treaty on Equal Access and Remedy and Reciprocal Access Act from their state of latency. Scholars still advocate for their wider implementation,[136] but the indifference of governments and the lack of a single judicial precedent make it improbable. At the very least, the Reciprocal Access Act made its way into four provinces, which should not be neglected as a matter of positive law. More fundamentally, the Reciprocal Access Act shows how environmental policy – in this case equal access – percolates into private international law to help ensure prompt and adequate compensation. It emphasises the regulatory function of private international law and the idea that substantive justice can affect the fabric of conflict rules, as recalled in the second chapter. This is a worthwhile pursuit, again as a back-up to regulatory oversight by public authorities.

iv. The 1994 North American Agreement on Environmental Cooperation

The last initiative to implement equal access in Canada came with the adoption of the 1994 North American Agreement on Environmental Cooperation (NAAEC) as an environmental companion to the North American Free Trade Agreement (NAFTA) between Canada, the United States and Mexico.[137] The NAAEC created an independent Commission for Environmental Cooperation (CEC) to support environmental cooperation between NAFTA partners.[138] NAFTA was superseded by the 2018 Canada–United States–Mexico Agreement (CUSMA), which contains a full chapter on environmental matters.[139] The CEC

[134] *Trail Smelter (United States v Canada)* (1941) 3 RIAA 1905.

[135] *Pembina County Water Resource District* (n 105).

[136] Kruger, 'Trail Smelter II' (2010) 139, fn 102; ND Hall, 'Political Externalities, Federalism, and a Proposal for an Interstate Environmental Impact Assessment Policy' (2008) 32 *Harvard Environmental Law Review* 49, 89–90; Hall (n 114) 744–45.

[137] North American Agreement on Environmental Cooperation (Canada, United States and Mexico) (14 September 1993, entered into force 1 January 1994) 32 ILM 1480 (NAAEC); North American Free Trade Agreement (Canada, United States and Mexico) 17 December 1992, entered into force 1 January 1994) 32 ILM 289 (NAFTA).

[138] NAAEC (n 137), Art 10.

[139] Canada–United States–Mexico Agreement (30 November 2018, entered into force 1 July 2020) (CUSMA), Arts 24.1–24.32.

has survived the transition but will operate in accordance with a new parallel agreement, the 2018 Agreement on Environmental Cooperation.[140]

The success of the NAAEC in ensuring prompt and adequate damage for victims of transboundary pollution is minimal at best. It has had little practical impact in transboundary environmental disputes so far. It did issue important policy recommendations which could have been harnessed by lawmakers to promote broader reforms of civil procedure, environmental law and private international law, but were not.

From a practical perspective, the NAAEC did not significantly impact the rights of private parties in Canada-United States environmental litigation. The NAAEC required parties to ensure that all interested persons had access to private remedies for the enforcement of environmental laws.[141] The NAAEC also enabled the Secretariat of the CEC to receive submissions from individuals and non-governmental organisations who complain that a state failed to enforce its environmental laws, and to prepare a factual record of the situation if needed.[142]

The CEC received several complaints concerning private remedies or access to environmental justice in the past.[143] The NAAEC, however, did not provide much help in a transboundary context. First, the words 'interested persons' said nothing per se about the rights of transboundary plaintiffs – domestic law determined standing.[144] Second, the NAAEC did not seem to cover situations in which a lawful activity in state *x* caused environmental damage in state *y* if it did not involve the violation of state *x*'s own environmental laws.[145] Finally, the CEC is not an administrative tribunal. It has no enforcement powers of its own and it only disseminates information about specific environmental issues. Its functions make it an unlikely avenue for transboundary plaintiffs who seek compensation.[146]

[140] ibid, Art 24.25(3); Agreement on Environmental Cooperation Among the Governments of Canada, the United States of America, and the United Mexican States (18 December 2018, entered into force 1 July 2020) Can TS 2020 No 7 (AEC).

[141] NAAEC (n 137), Art 6(2). cf CUSMA (n 139), Art 24.6(2). Several of Canada's bilateral environmental agreements contain similar provisions: see eg Agreement on Environmental Cooperation Between Canada and the Republic of Honduras (Canada–Honduras) (5 November 2013, entered into force 1 October 2014) Can TS 2014 No 24, Art 8(2); Agreement on the Environment Between Canada and the Republic of Panama (Canada–Panama) (13 May 2010, entered into force 1 April 2013) Can TS 2013 No 10, Art 8(2).

[142] NAAEC (n 137) Arts 14–15. cf CUSMA (n 139), Arts 24.27–24.28.

[143] *Tarahumara* SEM-00-006, CEC Doc A14/SEM00-006/09/14(1)(2) (2001), reprinted in Commission for Environmental Cooperation, *North American Environmental Law and Policy*, vol 9 (Cowansville, Yvon Blais, 2002); *Dermet SEM-01-003*, CEC Doc A14/SEM/01-003/05/14(1) (2001), reprinted in Commission for Environmental Cooperation, *North American Environmental Law and Policy*, vol 9 (Cowansville, Yvon Blais, 2002); *Logging Rider* SEM-95-002, CEC Doc A14/SEM/95-002/03/14(1) (1995), reprinted in Commission for Environmental Cooperation, *North American Environmental Law and Policy*, vol 1 (Cowansville, Yvon Blais, 1998).

[144] NAAEC (n 137), Art 6(2). cf CUSMA (n 139), Art 24.6(2) (similar rule).

[145] MJ Robinson-Dorn, 'The Trail Smelter: Is What's Past Prologue? EPA Blazes a New Trail for CERCLA' (2006) 14 *NYU Environmental Law Journal* 233, 307.

[146] ibid.

The NAAEC had more potential from a policy perspective as it required that the CEC consider and develop recommendations regarding equal access and remedies for victims of transboundary pollution.[147] This policy mission aligns, in retrospect, with the recommendations of the ILC Principles on the Allocation of Loss and eventually follow up on earlier efforts to implement equal access between Canada and the United States. To fulfill its mission under the NAAEC, the Secretariat of the CEC issued a detailed report providing background information on the current state of equal access in North America. The report recalled previous North American initiatives, including the Draft Treaty on Equal Access and Remedy and the Reciprocal Access Act,[148] and took the typical stance in favour of private litigation over governmental intervention to resolve transboundary environmental disputes.[149] Following that logic, the Secretariat of the CEC identified several barriers to equal access: the absence of jurisdiction over foreign land (the so-called local action rule addressed later in this chapter), the residency requirements in environmental statutes and their territorial scope (addressed in chapter four).[150]

The CEC, however, never acted in response to the report of its secretariat. Nor did the NAAEC push Canada and the United States to revisit the Draft Treaty on Equal Access and Remedy or the Reciprocal Access Act.[151] Knox explains the CEC's inaction by the inherent challenge of addressing bilateral issues between Canada and the United States (or the United States and Mexico) within a trilateral institution such as the CEC.[152] At the same time, bilateral solutions did not have much more success,[153] as the fate of the Draft Treaty on Equal Access and Remedy demonstrates. This casts doubt on whether the CEC would fare better in a smaller setting, particularly with its limited budget.[154]

[147] NAAEC (n 137), Art 10(9). But see JF DiMento and PM Doughman, 'Soft Teeth in the Back of the Mouth: The NAFTA Environmental Side Agreement Implemented' (1998) 10 *Georgetown International Environmental Law Review* 651, 737, fn 445 (criticising the NAAEC for being 'overly cautious in addressing judicial remedies for transborder disputes' compared to the 'more substantive' provisions of the Nordic Convention).

[148] Secretariat of the Commission for Environmental Cooperation, 'Access to Courts and Administrative Agencies in Transboundary Pollution Matters' in Commission for Environmental Cooperation, *North American Environmental Law and Policy*, vol 4 (Cowansville, Yvon Blais, 2000) 299–309.

[149] ibid 215.

[150] Secretariat of the Commission for Environmental Cooperation (n 148) 217.

[151] As speculated by PN Hanson, PE Hagen and K Rogers, 'The Application of the United States Hazardous Waste Cleanup Laws in the Canada-U.S. Context' (1992) 18 *Canada–United States Law Journal* 137, 170–71.

[152] JH Knox, 'The Neglected Lessons of the NAFTA Environmental Regime' (2010) 45 *Wake Forest Law Review* 391, 408; JH Knox, 'The CEC and Transboundary Pollution' in DL Merkell and JH Knox (eds), *Greening NAFTA: The North American Commission for Environmental Cooperation* (Stanford, Stanford University Press, 2003) 89–93.

[153] N Collins, 'On the Borderline: *Pakootas*, NAFTA and the Problem of Transboundary Pollution' (2020) 47 *Ecology Law Quarterly* 251, 285–88.

[154] On the CEC's budget, see Knox, 'The Neglected Lessons of the NAFTA Environmental Regime' (2010) 412.

The NAAEC is a sharp reminder of North American states' commitment to equal access and the reforms they could have achieved in that area. Practical results, however, have been meagre and targeted efforts such as those seen in the 1970s and 1980s have run out of gas. The CEC's report quietly marked the end of more than two decades of discussion over equal access. No major initiative has appeared on the agenda since then. The new CUSMA uses similar language as the NAAEC regarding private remedies,[155] but the new work programme of the CEC may not include the promotion of equal access specifically.[156] The future of a North American concept of equal access remains unclear in the meantime.[157]

D. Going beyond the ILC Principles on the Allocation of Loss

We have seen that the ILC Principles on the Allocation of Loss require equal access, but that Canada lacks a comprehensive instrument in this sense. But this is not the end of the matter: the general law of jurisdiction may effectively ensure equal access even when no specific framework such as the Reciprocal Access Act is in place. As Knox suggests, the lack of political pressure to implement equal access may in fact result from a perception that private international law *already* provides a sufficient jurisdictional basis.[158] In other words, legal reform may not be needed if local and foreign victims of transboundary pollution both have access to Canadian courts under general jurisdictional rules. The question then becomes which jurisdictional rule aligns best with the ILC Principles on the Allocation of Loss. Given the logic of equal access, jurisdiction must, at a minimum, allow domestic courts in the state of origin to hear claims and grant remedies.[159] Jurisdiction at the place of injury is not excluded. Equal access also requires that the jurisdictional threshold be the same for all plaintiffs (no discrimination).

The ILC admitted that the lack of consensus on an appropriate jurisdictional rule could impair the availability of prompt and adequate compensation.[160] Interestingly, it mentioned only a single example of a possible jurisdictional rule, which it seemed to view favourably: the possibility for plaintiffs to sue at the place of acting or at the place of injury.[161] Several civil liability treaties adopt

[155] CUSMA (n 139), Art 24.6(2).

[156] AEC (n 140), Art 10(2)(c).

[157] On NAFTA, CUSMA and equal access, see Collins (n 153) 284–85, 295–98.

[158] Knox, 'The CEC and Transboundary Pollution' (2010) 89, fn 40.

[159] ILC Principles on the Allocation of Loss (n 6) principle 6(1); Commentary to the ILC Principles on the Allocation of Loss (n 7) 86, para 4.

[160] Commentary to the ILC Principles on the Allocation of Loss (n 7) 87, para 7.

[161] ibid 87, para 8.

this dual solution as the default rule.[162] The IIL did not take a firm stance,[163] but the ILA[164] and the IUCN[165] endorsed the idea. The Permanent Bureau of the HCCH also seemed in favour of this solution in its exploratory work on the subject.[166]

The EU has followed that approach for decades. The Brussels I Recast Regulation (and its predecessors) allow plaintiffs to sue a tortfeasor in the courts of the place where the harmful event occurred or may occur,[167] in addition to other places such as the domicile of the defendant or the location of its branches.[168] In the *Bier* case involving transboundary pollution of the Rhine, the European Court of Justice (ECJ) held that plaintiffs have 'an option to commence proceedings either at the place where the damage occurred or the place of the event giving rise to it'.[169] The damage, however, must be direct.[170] The ECJ has reiterated the possibility of an option to this day,[171] but its jurisprudence makes it clear that the rule is justified by proximity and the sound administration of justice rather than sheer generosity towards plaintiffs.

[162] Protocol on Civil Liability and Compensation for Damage Caused by the Transboundary Effects of Industrial Accidents on Transboundary Waters (21 May 2003, not yet in force) Un Doc ECE/MP.WAT/11-ECE/CP.TEIA/9 (Kiev Liability Protocol), Art 13(1); Protocol on Civil Liability and Compensation for Damage Resulting from Transboundary Movements of Hazardous Waste (10 December 1999, not yet in force) UN Doc UNEP/CHW.5/29 Annex III (Basel Liability Protocol), Art 17(1); Convention on Civil Liability for Damage Resulting from Activities Dangerous to the Environment (26 June 1993, not yet in force) 32 ILM 1228 (Lugano Convention), Art 19(1); Convention on Civil Liability for Damage Caused During Carriage of Dangerous Goods by Road, Rail and Inland Navigation Vessels (10 October 1989, not yet in force) UN Doc ECE/TRANS/79 (CRTD Convention), Art 19(1). See also Convention on Civil Liability for Oil Pollution Damage Resulting from Exploration for and Exploitation of Seabed Mineral Resources (1 May 1977, not yet in force) 16 ILM 1450 (Seabed Mineral Resources Convention), Art 11(1); Convention on the Liability of the Operators of Nuclear Ships (25 May 1962, not yet in force) 57 *American Journal of International Law* 268 (Nuclear Ships Convention), Art X(1).

[163] IIL Resolution on Responsibility and Liability (n 16), Art 32; Institute of International Law, 'Final Report' (n 16) 343–44.

[164] ILA Toronto Rules on Transnational Enforcement of Environmental Law (n 15), rule 4(1); ILA, 'Final Report on Transnational Enforcement of Environmental Law' (n 15) 664–66; Committee on Transnational Enforcement of Environmental Law, 'Second Report' in International Law Association Report of the Seventy-First Conference (Berlin 2004) ('Second Report on Transnational Enforcement of Environmental Law') 898–900.

[165] IUCN Draft International Covenant on Environment and Development (n 83) 23 (Art 66), 165–66.

[166] Bernasconi, 'Civil Liability Resulting from Transfrontier Environmental Damage' (1999) 96–97, 141; PR Beaumont, 'Private International Law of the Environment' [1995] *Juridical Review* 28, 36–37.

[167] Regulation (EC) 1215/2012 of the European Parliament and of the Council of 12 December 2012 on jurisdiction and the recognition and enforcement of judgments in civil and commercial matters (recast) [2012] OJ L351/1 ('Brussels I Recast Regulation'), Art 7(2).

[168] ibid, Arts 4(1), 7(5).

[169] Case 21/76 *Handelskwekeriz GJ Bier BV v Mines de potasse d'Alsace* [1976] ECR I-1735 [19], [24]–[25].

[170] Case 364/93 *Marinari v Lloyds Bank plc* [1995] ECR 1-2719 [14]–[15].

[171] eg Case 343/19 *Verein für Konsumenteninformation v Volkswagen AG* ECLI:EU:C:2020:534 [23]; C-27/17 *AB FlyLAL-Lithuanian Airlines v Starptautiskā lidosta Rīga VAS* ECLI:EU:C:2018:533 [28].

The ruling in *Bier* itself, albeit a case of transboundary pollution, does not attach any particular weight to environmental considerations.[172] Fundamentally, the place of acting and the place of injury are acceptable because they both have a sufficient connection with the dispute (particularly given the requirement of a direct injury), not because they maximise the plaintiff's ability to engage in forum shopping.[173] The result, however, ultimately benefits victims of transboundary pollution. They can, depending on the circumstances, choose to sue in their own courts (as damage usually occurs where they reside) or in the courts of the place where the polluter operates.

The assumption that a choice between the place of acting or the place of injury is inherently desirable to advance victims' rights must be weighed against other considerations such as uncertainty and fairness to defendants who must anticipate where damage might occur. Nonetheless, the rule has more upsides than downsides. Crucially, it recognises the difficulties of isolating a single element of the tort for jurisdictional purposes, particularly when the behaviour in dispute is in fact an omission. Moreover, the place of acting and the place of injury each have strategic advantages and disadvantages in transboundary environmental litigation. Suing at the place of injury may lead to difficulties in obtaining evidence or enforcing a judgment against the assets of foreign polluters. Conversely, suing at the place of acting may be daunting for foreign residents with limited financial means. Each forum also has its own procedural and choice of law rules which impact the course of litigation. The European rule lets plaintiffs weigh those factors and decide for themselves what works in their best interest. Disqualifying indirect damage at the outset also has the effect of alleviating some of the uncertainty faced by defendants, as there may be a point where the effects of pollution are simply too remote to create a jurisdictional connection with the place of injury.

It is therefore no coincidence that the European rule is mentioned in the work of the ILC and other organisations, given that it favours access to justice in cases involving transboundary pollution and other complex torts.[174] As the ILA put it, 'mandatory jurisdiction at the claimant's option is more in keeping with the overall objective of adequate and prompt compensation for or prevention of environmental damage'.[175] The rule fits neatly with the objectives of the ILC Principles on the Allocation of Loss and goes in fact further than basic equal access because it also guarantees jurisdiction at the place of injury. This favours

[172] F Giansetto, 'Le droit international privé à l'épreuve des nouveaux contentieux en matière de responsabilité climatique' [2018] *Journal du droit international* 507, 512.

[173] *Bier* (n 169) [11].

[174] CO García-Castrillón, 'International Litigation Trends in Environmental Liability: A European Union-United States Comparative Perspective' (2011) 7 *Journal of Private International Law* 551, 561. But see E Álvares Armas, '(Lack of) International Jurisdiction over Third-Country Polluters: A Trojan Horse to the EU's Environmental Policy?' in J-S Bergé, S Francq and M Gardenez Santiago (eds), *Boundaries of European Private International Law* (Brussels, Bruylant, 2015)

[175] ILA, 'Final Report on Transnational Enforcement of Environmental Law' (n 15 665–66.

the legal oversight of transboundary polluters through domestic courts, which, as we have seen, is a legitimate objective for private international law conceived as a regulatory device.

As the next section demonstrates, Quebec civil law offers a similar option between the place of acting and the place of injury in tortious disputes. Canadian common law takes a different path but reaches a similar result in most cases. This leads to the conclusion that the jurisdictional aspects of the duty to ensure prompt and adequate compensation do not cause significant difficulties in Canada, and in fact align with the spirit of the ILC Principles on the Allocation of Loss. Certain difficulties, however, may arise in relation to the enforcement of foreign judgments against a local polluter, particularly in Quebec.

II. JURISDICTION OVER TRANSBOUNDARY POLLUTION IN CANADIAN PRIVATE INTERNATIONAL LAW

In this section, I argue that Canadian law meets the jurisdictional requirements associated with the duty to ensure prompt and adequate compensation, even though equal access initiatives have not yielded significant results. This is because the courts in each Canadian province have the necessary jurisdiction to hear claims against transboundary polluters, even where specific legislation such as the International Boundary Waters Treaty Act or the Reciprocal Access Act does not apply.

In the next sections, I analyse jurisdiction over transboundary pollution originating in Canada or affecting its population (section II.A). I also comment on the possibility of declining jurisdiction once it has been established (section II.B), and the possibility of enforcing foreign judgments against domestic polluters in the country (section II.C). Recall that the words 'Canadian courts' refer to the courts of a province in relation to those of another province or foreign state, as provinces are considered distinct states in private international law.[176]

A. Asserting Jurisdiction Over Transboundary Pollution

This section examines the treatment of two types of plaintiffs against the ILC's views on jurisdiction: foreign victims suing in Canada for pollution originating in Canada (section II.A.i) and local victims suing in Canada for pollution originating abroad (section II.A.ii). The two scenarios cover the bulk of private lawsuits which victims of transboundary pollution could conceivably bring in Canada.

[176] See the text accompanying nn 68–69 (introduction) above. The same is true for ch 4 on choice of law.

Plaintiffs in the first scenario will rely on the polluters' operations in the province or locate the tort at the place of acting in order to establish jurisdiction. The result may then depend on the nature of the claim (specifically whether it involves foreign land), but contrary to common belief, this is unlikely to be a determining factor. Conversely, plaintiffs in the second scenario will locate the tort at the place of injury in order to establish jurisdiction there (assuming the defendant is not present in the province and does not consent to have the claim tried there). In both scenarios, courts have the necessary jurisdiction to hear tort claims against local or foreign polluters. This undermines the obstacle theory outlined in the second chapter and suggests that perceived difficulties should not be exaggerated.

i. Foreign Plaintiffs in Canada

The first jurisdictional question question is whether foreign plaintiffs can sue Canadian polluters in Canada over transboundary pollution originating in Canada. I examine the relevant grounds of jurisdiction available to foreign plaintiffs (section II.A.i.a) and deconstruct the most contentious issue in this scenario – claims involving damage to foreign land (section II.A.i.b). Nuclear damage is excluded from this analysis: as mentioned above, courts have no jurisdiction to hear an action for this kind of damage when suffered abroad.[177] This effectively closes the door to foreign victims of nuclear damage.

a. Presence in the Jurisdiction

Can foreign plaintiffs sue Canadian polluters for transboundary pollution originating in Canada? This question has important implications for climate change litigation against greenhouse gas emitters in their home state, among other scenarios.

In the narrow set of circumstances contemplated in the Reciprocal Access Act, the answer is yes because the Act explicitly guarantees jurisdiction at the place of acting.[178] In Quebec, the answer is also yes. Quebec courts have jurisdiction when the defendant has its domicile or residence in Quebec,[179] the defendant is a legal person not domiciled in Quebec but it has an establishment

[177] Nuclear Liability and Compensation Act (n 92), s 34(6) and the text accompanying nn 92–95 above.

[178] Reciprocal Access Act (n 126), s 2.

[179] Civil Code of Quebec, CQLR c CCQ-1991 (CCQ), Arts 3134, 3148, para 1(1°). Residence-based jurisdiction is only relevant for natural persons, as legal persons and other business entities do not possess a residence separate from their domicile (their head office under Art 307 CCQ). Case law, however, treats the establishment of a legal person under Art 3148, para 1(2°) CCQ as roughly equivalent to the residence of a physical person under Art 3148, para 1(1°) CCQ: *Spar Aerospace Ltd c American Mobile Satellite Corporation* [1998] RJQ 2802, 2806 (Qc Sup Ct).

in the province and the dispute relates to the defendant's activities in the province,[180] or a fault, injury or injurious act or omission occurred in the province.[181] In the latter case, any single element suffices.[182] This 'broad basis for jurisdiction', as the Supreme Court of Canada described it,[183] clearly covers pollution originating in the province. Additionally, Quebec courts have exclusive jurisdiction over civil liability claims for injuries suffered anywhere in relation to raw materials originating in the province.[184]

Neighbourhood disturbance and civil liability claims (two potential causes of action in case of environmental damage[185]) have conceptual differences in domestic law but they fall under the same jurisdictional rule for private international law purposes. Civil liability claims are grounded in Article 1457 CCQ whereby 'Every person has a duty to abide by the rules of conduct incumbent on him, according to the circumstances, usage or law, so as not to cause injury to another'. This provision is found in Book Five of the CCQ on obligations. Neighbourhood disturbance claims, by contrast, are grounded in Article 976 CCQ whereby neighbours must suffer only 'the normal neighbourhood annoyances that are not beyond the limit of tolerance they owe each other, according to the nature or location of their land or local usage'. This provision is found in Book Four of the CCQ on property.[186] It is often presented as a limitation to private property, but it has strong conceptual connections with civil liability[187] because the right belongs to a person who exercises it against another person.[188] Importantly, neighbourhood disturbance can lead to injunctive relief *and* damages, and is often invoked alongside civil liability.[189]

[180] ibid, Art 3148, para 1(2°). While the defendant must have an establishment in Quebec and the dispute must relate to the defendant's activities in Quebec, courts do not require that the Quebec establishment itself undertake the defendant's activities in Quebec. The two conditions should therefore be read disjunctively: *Interinvest (Bermuda) Ltd c Herzog* 2009 QCCA 1428 [41].

[181] ibid, Art 3148, para 1(3°).

[182] *Infineon Technologies AG v Option consommateurs* 2013 SCC 59 [45]; *Spar Aerospace Ltd v American Mobile Satellite Corp*, 2002 SCC 78 [56].

[183] *Infineon Technologies* (n 182) [47], citing *Spar Aerospace* (n 182) [58].

[184] CCQ (n 179), Art 3151.

[185] M-E Arbour, 'Liability Law and Nuisance in the Civil Law Tradition' in L Paddock, DL Markell and NS Bryner (eds), *Elgar Encyclopedia of Environmental Law*, vol 4: Compliance and Enforcement of Environmental Law (Cheltenham, Edward Elgar, 2017).

[186] Article 982 CCQ, also in Book Four, provides that 'Unless it is contrary to the general interest, a person having a right to use a spring, lake, sheet of water, underground stream or any running water may, to prevent the water from being polluted or depleted, require the destruction or modification of any works by which the water is being polluted or depleted'. This property law recourse has obvious relevance for our purposes, but it has rarely been invoked, and never in a transboundary context: see eg *Association des résidents du lac Mercier Inc c Paradis, ès qualités de ministre de l'Environnement* [1996] RJQ 2370, 2379–83 (Qc Sup Ct).

[187] Y Emerich, *Conceptualising Property Law: Integrating Common Law and Civil Law Traditions* (Cheltenham, Edward Elgar, 2018) 141–45.

[188] *St Lawrence Cement Inc v Barrette* 2008 SCC 64 [82].

[189] *Spieser c Procureur général du Canada* 2020 QCCA 42 [442]–[458], leave to appeal to SCC refused 39097 (23 December 2020).

The characterisation of neighbourhood disturbance for jurisdictional purposes arose in the *Uashaunnuat* case.[190] In that case, two Innus First Nations sued mining companies engaged in iron ore extraction in the Labrador Trough. Relying on Aboriginal rights over land, they claimed that the defendants' extraction projects had adversely impacted their traditional activities in the Nitassinan, a territory overlapping the provinces of Quebec and Newfoundland and Labrador. They sought injunctive relief and damages on the basis of civil liability (Article 1457 CCQ), neighbourhood disturbance (Article 976 CCQ) and the violation of their fundamental rights. The defendants sought to strike plaintiffs' allegations concerning Labrador because they involved the recognition of Aboriginal rights (including title) in Labrador. The defendants reasoned that Aboriginal rights over land in Labrador were property rights over which Quebec courts had no jurisdiction, as Article 3152 CCQ provides that Quebec courts have jurisdiction to hear a real action only when the property is located in the province.

The Supreme Court of Canada rejected the argument and held that Aboriginal rights were *sui generis* rights, not typical property rights. The plaintiffs' claim was properly characterised as having a *sui generis* aspect (claim based on Aboriginal rights) and a personal aspect (claims in civil liability and neighbourhood disturbance). The Supreme Court found that the action was a 'non-classical' mixed action because it did not seek to enforce real and personal rights (as most mixed actions subject to Article 3152 CCQ), but rather personal and *sui generis* rights. As such, it fell under Articles 3134 (residual jurisdictional rule based on the domicile of the defendant) and 3148 CCQ (jurisdictional rule for personal actions), not Article 3152 CCQ.[191] Quebec courts ultimately had jurisdiction over the entirety of the claim because the defendants had their domicile in Quebec. For our purposes, and Aboriginal rights aside, *Uashaunnuat* supports the proposition that neighbourhood disturbance claims fall under Article 3148 CCQ alongside civil liability claims.[192]

Courts outside Quebec would assert jurisdiction over a local polluter on a similar basis, insofar as the litigation involves the impact of an operation on Canadian soil (for instance, generating greenhouse gas or polluting a transboundary watercourse). Presence-based jurisdiction is indeed a traditional base of jurisdiction in Canadian common law.[193] The situation differs

[190] *Newfoundland and Labrador (Attorney General) v Uashaunnuat (Innu of Uashat and of Mani-Utenam)* 2020 SCC 4.

[191] ibid [53]–[60]. The decision was strongly divided, with four of the nine judges dissenting. Justices Brown and Rowe (also writing for Justices Moldaver and Côté) preferred to characterise the claim as mixed (and therefore subject to Art 3152 CCQ), on the basis that Aboriginal title and other Aboriginal rights were sufficiently close to real rights for the specific purposes of private international law: ibid [126]–[206] (Brown and Rowe JJ, dissenting).

[192] ibid [58].

[193] *Chevron Corp v Yaiguaje* 2015 SCC 42 [82]–[87]; *Club Resorts Ltd v Van Breda* 2012 SCC 17 [79].

slightly in the four provinces and territories that enacted the Court Jurisdiction and Proceedings Transfer Act (CJPTA) drafted by the ULCC.[194] The CJPTA supplants entirely the common law framework[195] and introduces the notion of ordinary residence as the primary basis for personal jurisdiction over a corporation or partnership.[196] Ordinary residence takes several forms in the CJPTA, including having a place of business in the province.[197] This is a large jurisdictional basis that effectively encompasses traditional presence-based jurisdiction, 'in substance if not in name'.[198] The CJPTA also presumes the existence of a 'real and substantial connection' with the forum when the dispute concerns a business carried on in the province, thus offering another ground of jurisdiction.[199]

Summing up, courts can easily assert jurisdiction over local polluters based on their presence or activities in a province, at common law and under the CJPTA or CCQ. Any injunction or damage award will be readily enforceable in that province.

b. Foreign Land and the Local Action Rule

The only jurisdictional obstacle standing in foreign plaintiffs' way in the first scenario seems to be the local action rule, also known as the *Moçambique* rule. This artefact of English law provides that courts have no jurisdiction to hear a claim concerning land and other immovable property located abroad,[200] even if the claim lies solely in tort.[201] The ILC suggests that the rule

[194] Uniform Law Conference of Canada, 'Court Jurisdiction and Proceedings Transfer Act' in Uniform Law Conference of Canada Proceedings of the Seventy-Sixth Annual Meeting (Charlottetown, 1994) 140, reprinted in J Basedow et al (eds), *Encyclopedia of Private International Law*, vol 4 (Cheltenham, Edward Elgar, 2017) 3046 and V Black, SGA Pitel and M Sobkin, *Statutory Jurisdiction: An Analysis of the Court Jurisdiction and Proceedings Transfer Act* (Toronto, Carswell, 2012) 264–287 (CJPTA). The four provinces and territories are British Columbia, Saskatchewan, Nova Scotia and Yukon: Court Jurisdiction and Proceedings Transfer Act, SBC 2003 c 28 (British Columbia); The Court Jurisdiction and Proceedings Transfer Act, SS 1997 c C-41.1 (Saskatchewan); Court Jurisdiction and Proceedings Transfer Act, SNS 2003 (2nd Sess) c 2; Court Jurisdiction and Proceedings Transfer Act SY 2000, c C-7 (Yukon). Prince Edward Island has adopted the CJPTA, but it has yet to come into force: Court Jurisdiction and Proceedings Transfer Act, SPEI 1997 c 61 (Prince Edward Island).

[195] CJPTA (n 194), s 2(2).

[196] ibid, s 3(d).

[197] ibid, ss 7(c), 8(b).

[198] C Walsh, 'General Jurisdiction over Corporate Defendants under the *CJPTA*: Consistent with International Standards?' (2018) 55 *Osgoode Hall Law Journal* 163, 180. cf SGA Pitel, 'Six of One, Half a Dozen of the Other? Jurisdiction in Common Law Canada' (2018) 55 *Osgoode Hall Law Journal* 63, 69–72.

[199] CJPTA (n 194), ss 3(e), 10(h).

[200] This section uses the terms 'land', 'real property' and 'immovable' depending on the context and the language used in the cases examined. As Emerich explains, real and personal property represent the *summa divisio* of common law property. Real property includes land, but also some of the things attached or affixed to it. The term 'immovable' recalls the *summa divisio* of civil law property and generally (although not perfectly) aligns with the common law notion of real property: Emerich (n 187) 179–80.

[201] *Lucasfilm Ltd v Ainsworth* [2011] UKSC 39 [54]–[60]; *Hesperides Hotels v Aegean Holidays Ltd* [1979] AC 508, 541 (HL); *British South Africa Co v Companhia de Moçambique* [1893] AC 602, 628–29 (HL).

is incompatible with prompt and adequate compensation because it prohibits jurisdiction at the place of acting when local polluters cause transboundary damage elsewhere.[202]

In Canada, the problem arises only in common law provinces since the contentious aspects of the local action rule have no equivalent in Quebec civil law. Article 3152 CCQ provides that courts have jurisdiction to hear a 'real action' when the property is located in Quebec, but the notion of a 'real action' is confined to pure property disputes such as those involving title.[203] Claims for damages related to foreign land are considered personal actions under Article 3148 CCQ, not real actions under Article 3152 CCQ. They fall under the jurisdiction of Quebec courts in the circumstances enumerated above. The situation is not so simple in common law provinces due to the local action rule, even though courts would normally have jurisdiction based on the polluter's presence in the province.

This section focuses on the extension of the *Moçambique* rule to tort claims in common law Canada, leaving aside its application to other disputes involving real property.[204] Arguably, the local action rule no longer applies to tort claims in Canada. Judicial authorities supporting the opposite view are ancient. They have been superseded by subsequent cases and an overwhelming academic consensus. The rule, as traditionally interpreted, no longer prevents Canadian courts in one province from asserting jurisdiction over a local polluter in a case brought by foreign victims. The rest of this section makes the case for this proposition, by examining the origins of the local action rule and the cases as they stand today.

The local action rule originated in England at a time when courts had to summon juries from the place where the cause of action had arisen. Faced with increasingly sophisticated transactions, English courts started dealing with jury requirements by distinguishing between transitory actions (which could arise anywhere, such as damage to personal property) and local actions (which could only arise in one place, such as damage to real property). Only local actions required plaintiffs to specify a venue for the purposes of summoning witnesses.[205]

The local action rule disappeared from civil procedure in the nineteenth century but withstood scrutiny as a jurisdictional rule in *Moçambique* (1893).[206] The case concerned a company whose agents had allegedly broken into the plaintiff's premises in South Africa to take possession of its mines and mining

[202] Commentary to the ILC Principles on the Allocation of Loss (n 7) 86, para 5, fn 468.

[203] *Uashaunnuat* (n 190) [54]; *Bern v Bern* [1995] RDJ 510, 515–16 (Qc CA).

[204] On the same topic, with a focus on climate change litigation, see G Laganière, 'Local Polluters, Foreign Land and Climate Change: The Myth of the Local Action Rule in Canada' (2020) 16 *Journal of Private International Law* 390.

[205] See generally S Lee, 'Title to Foreign Real Property in Transnational Money Claims' (1995) 32 *Columbia Journal of Transnational Law* 607, 613–32.

[206] *Moçambique* (n 201).

rights, while assaulting and imprisoning some of its employees. The House of Lords held that English courts did not have jurisdiction because the claim involved trespass and title to foreign land. According to the House of Lords, the fact that the rules of civil procedure no longer required plaintiffs to specify a venue had no impact on the courts' inability to hear claims over foreign land. This was a substantive jurisdictional rule which had always existed, and technical changes to civil procedure could not have altered it.[207] As the Supreme Court of the United Kingdom later put it:

> The essence of [*Moçambique*] is that jurisdiction in relation to land is local (that is, the claim has a necessary connection with a particular locality) as opposed to transitory (where such a connection is not necessary) and that it is contrary to international law, or comity, for one state to exercise jurisdiction in relation to land in another state.[208]

Moçambique eventually became a leading authority in Canada.[209] The scope of the rule, however, has been fraught with uncertainty. Canadian scholars have discussed whether it covers all disputes involving foreign land (including property torts such as trespass or nuisance, but also other torts such as negligence) or only those involving issues of title to foreign land (and if so, whether only primarily or also incidentally).[210] Most transboundary environmental disputes do not raise issues of title (with the notable exception of Aboriginal title in cases brought by First Nations[211]) but involve damage to foreign land. An expansive interpretation of the local action rule in the state of origin would bar foreign plaintiffs from invoking trespass or nuisance as a result of transboundary pollution. American victims faced that very problem in *Trail Smelter*.[212] As early as 1584, Lord Coke carved out an exception to the local action rule in *Bulwer's Case* where an act in one state had caused injury in another,[213] but English courts continued to apply the rule rigidly.[214]

The House of Lords reaffirmed the local action rule in 1978, in the landmark case of *Hesperides Hotels*.[215] The legislature abolished the tort aspects of the local action rule altogether in 1982, after the United Kingdom joined the European Economic Community in 1973 and acceded to the 1968 Brussels Convention on Jurisdiction and the Enforcement of Judgments.[216] Today, English

[207] ibid 629.
[208] *Lucasfilm* (n 201) [57].
[209] *Khan Resources Inc v WM Mining Company* (2006) 79 OR (3d) 411, 415 (Ont CA); *Tezcan v Tezcan* (1987) 46 DLR (4th) 176, 179 (BC CA); *Duke v Andler* [1932] SCR 734, 738–41. But see *Lanfer v Eilers* 2021 BCCA 241 (holding that the common law no longer prohibits the enforcement of a foreign order for specific performance which affects title to immovable property in Canada).
[210] SGA Pitel and NS Rafferty, *Conflict of Laws*, 2nd edn (Toronto, Irwin Law, 2016) 330–36.
[211] *Uashaunnuat* (n 190).
[212] See the text accompanying nn 11 (introduction), 37 (ch 2) above.
[213] *Bulwer's Case* (1584) 7 Co Rep 1a, 77 ER 411 (KB).
[214] *Doulson v Matthews* (1792) 4 TR 53, 100 ER 1143 (KB).
[215] *Hesperides Hotels* (n 200).
[216] Convention on Jurisdiction and the Enforcement of Judgments in Civil and Commercial Matters (27 September 1968, entered into force 1 February 1973) 1262 UNTS 153.

courts have statutory jurisdiction to hear claims for damages involving foreign immovable property if title to property is not primarily at stake.[217] In the EU, the Brussels I Recast Regulation provides for exclusive jurisdiction based on the situs of immovable property, but only over 'proceedings which have as their object rights *in rem* in immovable property or tenancies of immovable property'.[218] The ECJ held that that the rule did not extend to a nuisance claim brought in Austrian courts by an Austrian landowner against the operator of a Czech nuclear power plant, in connection with excessive levels of ionising radiation.[219]

Canadian provinces have occasionally applied the local action rule in tort disputes, regardless of whether title was at stake. *Brereton* (1898)[220] and *Boslund* (1925)[221] both involved out-of-province plaintiffs who claimed that the defendants had negligently allowed a fire to spread across the border and destroy their movable and immovable property. In both cases, the judges applied *Moçambique* and held that the plaintiffs could not recover damages related to foreign land.[222] The two cases treated the rest of the claims differently. In *Brereton*, Chancellor Boyd of the Ontario High Court of Justice noted that the furniture-related portion of the claim could proceed in Ontario only if the plaintiff abandoned the land-related portion of his claim,[223] whereas in *Boslund*, Justice McDonald of the British Columbia Supreme Court simply allowed the claims related to crops (treated personal property) and personal injuries, subject to the assessment of damages.[224]

Albert v Fraser Companies Ltd (1936) remains the most notorious case on the application of the local action rule to tort claims in Canada – possibly because it comes from an appellate court but also because of the strong disagreement of one magistrate over that very issue.[225] The case involved a Quebec plaintiff who had brought an action in New Brunswick against a company operating there. The plaintiff claimed that the defendant had accumulated excessive amounts of wood in the Madawaska River flowing from Quebec to New Brunswick. The accumulation had flooded the plaintiff's land in Quebec, resulting in the loss of a building and the property inside, and a loss of revenues derived from that building. The plaintiff sought injunctive relief and compensation. He argued

[217] Civil Jurisdiction and Judgments Act 1982, s 30(1); *Hamed v Stevens* [2013] EWCA Civ 911 [11]–[16]; *Lucasfilm* (n 201) [72]–[76]; *Re Polly Peck International plc (No 2)* [1998] 3 All ER 812, 829–30 (CA).

[218] Brussels I Recast Regulation (n 167), Art 24(1).

[219] Case 343/04 *Land Oberösterreich v ČEZ as* [2006] ECR I–4557 [40].

[220] *Brereton v Canadian Pacific Railway Co* (1898) 29 OR 57 (Ont H Ct J).

[221] *Boslund v Abbotsford Lumber, Mining and Development Co* [1925] 1 DLR 978 (BC SC), affd (1925) [1927] 1 DLR 279 (BC CA).

[222] *Boslund* (n 221) 981; *Brereton* (n 220) 61–62.

[223] *Brereton* (n 220) 62–63.

[224] *Boslund* (n 221) 981.

[225] *Albert v Fraser Companies Ltd* (1936) [1937] 1 DLR 39, 40 (NB SC (AD)).

that New Brunswick courts had jurisdiction because the claim did not concern title to land. Furthermore, the defendant carried on business in the province and had committed the tort there.[226]

Before the appellate division of the New Brunswick Supreme Court, the debate focused on the local action rule. Chief Justice Baxter, also writing for Justice Grimmer, held that the *Moçambique* rule applied regardless of whether title to the land was disputed.[227] The Court held that the claim concerned damage to foreign land. The defendant had also caused damage to personal property, but only indirectly through the initial damage to real property (contrary, the Court said, to *Brereton* in which the alleged negligence had directly caused the destruction of personal property).[228] The Court therefore dismissed the action for lack of jurisdiction.[229]

Justice Harrison, dissenting, noted that the claim did not involve any question of title.[230] He opined that *Moçambique* did not cover the facts of the case (damage to land in one province caused by a tortious act committed in another province) and chose to follow the logic of *Bulwer's Case* instead.[231] In his view, New Brunswick courts should have exercised their jurisdiction as the defendant was domiciled in the forum and only the courts of that province could enforce a potential injunction.[232]

Scholars strongly criticised the generous interpretation of *Moçambique* which led the courts in Brereton, Boslund and Albert to refuse to assert jurisdiction over a tort claim. They referred to a case 'wrongly decided' and 'dead wrong' (referring to the *Brereton*),[233] a rule 'unnecessary and unjust',[234] a rule with a 'dubious foundation and foreseeably objectionable consequences',[235] and an 'extreme formulation' of the local action rule which 'exhibits no practical values where issues of title are secondary'.[236] An American commentator suggested that stretching the American declination of the local action rule as Canadian courts did in *Brereton* and *Albert* would 'produce at worst a total denial of justice and at best some glaring anomalies'.[237]

[226] ibid 40–42.

[227] ibid 45.

[228] ibid 46–47. On this point, see also *Hesperides Hotels* (n 200) 538 (Wilberforce LJ), 546 (Fraser of Tullybelton LJ).

[229] ibid 48.

[230] ibid 50 (Harrison J, dissenting).

[231] ibid 51–52 (Harrison J, dissenting).

[232] ibid 55–56 (Harrison J, dissenting)

[233] B Welling and EA Heakes, 'Torts and Foreign Immovables Jurisdiction in Conflict of Laws' (1979) 18 *University of Western Ontario Law Review* 295, 309–10.

[234] J Willis, 'Jurisdiction of Courts – Action to Recover Damages for Injury to Foreign Land' (1937) 15 *Canadian Bar Review* 112, 114.

[235] McCaffrey, 'Trans-Boundary Pollution Injuries' (1973) 227.

[236] HS Fairley, 'Private Remedies for Transboundary Injury in Canada and the United States: Constraints Upon Having to Sue Where You Can Collect' (1978) 10 *Ottawa Law Review* 253, 264.

[237] RB Looper, 'Jurisdiction over Immovables: The Little Case Revisited After Sixty Years' (1956) 40 *Minnesota Law Review* 191, 202.

More contemporaneously, the authors of a leading study of Canadian private international law noted the 'excellent points' made by Justice Harrison in *Albert* and expressed the hope that 'the *Moçambique* rule will soon be discarded at least insofar as it precludes an action for tortious damage to foreign land'.[238]

Albert (and its predecessors by implication) is puzzling indeed. The majority applied the local action rule even though the facts of the case were easily distinguishable from those of *Moçambique* (where the event had occurred in a single place) and *Bulwer's Case* could have applied. The majority also failed to explain how foreign land affected the enforcement of an injunction and a monetary award against a defendant operating in the province. Some orders involving foreign land cannot be enforced by Canadian courts (indeed one of the concerns behind the local action rule[239]), but this is obviously not the case for a tort claim resulting in a monetary award or an injunction against a local defendant, as was the case in *Albert*.[240]

More alarming is the fact that a strict application of the local action rule could deprive victims of all judicial recourse if their home state does not accept jurisdiction based on damage suffered there and no other state has jurisdiction.[241] The forum of necessity doctrine could possibily intervene if it is legally impossible to sue in either place, but the conditions are stringent.[242] Beyond this doctrine, victims would have no hope for relief. One could say that this is simply not a relevant consideration, or that an unbridled interpretation of *Moçambique* exists precisely to protect local defendants. As Whincop explains,

> the most likely case of litigation involving foreign land will involve foreign plaintiffs bringing suit against a defendant with substantial forum connections. ... If the forum exercised jurisdiction, it would most likely benefit out-of-state plaintiffs at the expense of in-state defendants.[243]

From an environmental perspective, however, Justice Harrison had the better view in *Albert*. The local action rule has no justification when a polluter operates in the forum and cause transboundary damage to a foreign victim who then seeks remedies in tort. The undesirability of the local action rule in this context is especially obvious in light of international environmental law's inclination towards equal access and the availability of private remedies.

[238] Pitel and Rafferty, *Conflict of Laws* (2016) 333, 336.

[239] *Duke* (n 209) 739; Pitel and Rafferty (n 210) 330–31.

[240] Welling and Heakes, 'Torts and Foreign Immovables Jurisdiction' (1979) 309–10.

[241] McCaffrey (n 99) 219; Willis, 'Injury to Foreign Land' (1937) 114.

[242] In Quebec, see CCQ (n 179), Art 3136; *Anvil Mining Ltd c Association canadienne contre l'impunité* 2012 QCCA 117 [96]–[103], leave to appeal to SCC refused [2012] 3 SCR v. At common law, see *West Van Inc v Daisley* 2014 ONCA 232 [17]–[38], leave to appeal to SCC refused [2014] 2 SCR x. See also CJPTA (n 194) s 6. The Sakstachewan CJPTA (n 194), however, does note provide for necessity jurisdiction.

[243] MJ Whincop, 'Conflicts in the Cathedral: Towards a Theory of Property Rights in Private International Law' (2000) 50 *University of Toronto Law Journal* 41, 60.

Nowhere is this policy more apparent than in the ILC Principles on the Allocation of Loss, which require that the courts of the state of origin have the necessary jurisdiction to ensure access to prompt and adequate compensation for all victims of transboundary pollution.[244] The local action rule, as applied in a transboundary environmental dispute in which title is not disputed, does the exact opposite, by making compensation impossible to claim in the state of origin – hence the ILC's apparent inclination towards the abolition of the local action rule in this context.[245]

Criticism of the local action rule is nothing new, but as sound as it may be, it misses a more fundamental point – one rarely mentioned in the Canadian literature and which this section emphasises. The local action rule simply does not have the status it is assumed to have in relation to transboundary environmental litigation.

Many commentators continue to describe the local action rule as a major obstacle in transboundary environmental litigation in common law provinces. One suggests it is still 'alive and well' in British Columbia, where the *Trail Smelter* dispute unfolded.[246] Another examines what a modern *Trail Smelter* dispute would look like and concludes that 'In light of Canada's strict adherence to the local action rule it would be difficult to succeed in having a Canadian court exercise jurisdiction over a Trail Smelter type dispute'.[247] Yet another examines the viability of climate change litigation in Canada and concludes that the local action rule would favour lawsuits at the place of injury.[248] Many others limit themselves to *Moçambique* and *Albert* when assessing the viability of a transboundary environmental lawsuit in Canada, generally with dire consequences for foreign victims.[249]

[244] ILC Principles on the Allocation of Loss (n 6) principle 6(1).

[245] Commentary to the ILC Principles on the Allocation of Loss (n 7) 86, para 5, fn 468. The Permanent Bureau of the HCCH also doubted the validity of the local action rule in the context of transboundary pollution: Bernasconi (n 17) 104.

[246] SC McCaffrey, 'Of Paradoxes, Precedents and Progeny: The *Trail Smelter* Arbitration 65 Years Later' in RM Bratspies and RA Miller (eds), *Transboundary Harm in International Law: Lessons from the Trail Smelter Arbitration* (Cambridge, Cambridge University Press, 2006) 35.

[247] M van de Kerkhof, 'The Trail Smelter Case Re-Examined: Examining the Development of National Procedural Mechanisms to Resolve a Trail Smelter Type Dispute' (2011) 27 *Utrecht Journal of International and European Law* 68, 80.

[248] K Péloffy, '*Kivalina v Exxonmobil*: A Comparative Case Comment' (2013) 9 *McGill Journal of Sustainable Development and the Law* 121, 136.

[249] Boyle and Redgewell (n 18) 328 (citing *Albert* to suggest that the local action rule covers in some states the 'extraterritorial effects of activities within the territory of the forum'); Kruger (n 18) 129 (citing *Brereton* and *Albert* to suggest that 'Canadian courts have no subject matter jurisdiction to entertain proceedings for the determination of rights or interests in foreign real property, including actions concerning trespass, strict liability, or other environmental torts'); Knox, 'The CEC and Transboundary Pollution' (n 152) 88 (explaining that 'most Canadian provinces continue to apply a strict version of the local action rule, which would prevent transboundary suits based in nuisance'); MI Jeffery, 'Transboundary Pollution and Cross-Border Remedies' (1992) 18 *Canada–United States Law Journal* 173, 175 (citing *Albert* and suggesting, in reference to a nuisance lawsuit brought by Canadian victims in American Courts, that 'There is little doubt that the Canadian courts would have declined jurisdiction had the facts been reversed'); SM Siros, 'Borders, Barriers, and Other

The work of several organisations which delved into the issue reflects a similar pessimism. The Permanent Bureau of the HCCH mentioned only *Albert* in its account of the law in Canada.[250] The ULCC[251] and the Secretariat of the CEC[252] also relied on *Albert* to conclude that the local action rule would raise a significant obstacle to a claim made by foreign victims against a Canadian polluter.

The obstacle raised by the local action rule is often asserted but rarely demonstrated. Current assertions are misleading. Even if Canadian courts might not disregard the local action rule altogether, they could easily reject its application to a climate change lawsuit or other environmental claim, and in fact, they likely would. Substantive arguments make a strong case in this sense, but even as a matter of strict precedent, *Albert* does not have significant judicial weight. First, the New Brunswick Court of Appeal could overrule its own precedent[253] and appellate courts in other provinces could dismiss it as non-binding.[254] Second, there is support for the proposition that the local action rule ought not apply in an interprovincial setting – precisely the fact

Obstacles to a Holistic Environment' (1992) 13 *Northern Illinois University Law Review* 633, 649–50 (citing *Albert* and explaining that 'The Canadian courts follow a more confining interpretation of the local action rule, applying it to all types of trespass to foreign land, as well as nuisance actions, negligence and strict liability. Thus, if a United States citizen were to bring a nuisance action in Canada for damages caused to property located in the United States, the Canadian courts would probably decline jurisdiction based on this local action rule'); A Morriss, 'Supporting Structures for Resolving Environmental Disputes Among Friendly Neighbors' in J Schmandt, J Clarkson and H Roderick (eds), *Acid Rain and Friendly Neighbors: The Policy Dispute Between Canada and the United States*, revised edn (Durham, Duke University Press, 1988) 221, fn 13 (suggesting that *Albert* settled the law in Canada); CA Cooper, 'The Management of International Environmental Disputes in the Context of Canada-United States Relations: A Survey and Evaluation of Techniques and Mechanisms' (1986) 24 *Canadian Yearbook of International Law* 247, 273–74 (citing *Albert* and explaining that 'Canadian courts … have broadly applied the rule as expressed in [*Moçambique*] thereby declining jurisdiction in any case of injury to foreign land'); DC Arbitblit, 'The Plight of American Citizens Injured by Transboundary River Pollution' (1979) 8 *Ecology Law Quarterly* 339, 342 (citing *Albert* and suggesting that 'A suit by American plaintiffs in Canadian court for damages to American property would fail because Canadian courts adhere to the rule that they have no power to hear cases involving injury to foreign land … The rule, which appears to be applied uniformly in Canadian courts, would preclude Canadian jurisdiction over a suit by an American plaintiff for transboundary pollution injuries to American land due to wrongful or negligent acts of a Canadian corporation'); McCaffrey (n 99) 217 (noting, albeit with no jurisprudential support post-*Albert*, that '[*Albert*] has been uniformly accepted in Canada as standing for the sweeping proposition that Canadian courts lack jurisdiction to entertain actions to recover damages for injuries'); RW Ianni, 'International and Private Actions in Transboundary Pollution' (1973) 11 *Canadian Yearbook of International Law* 258, 269 (citing *Moçambique* and *Albert* to conclude that 'the courts lack jurisdiction to entertain actions for the recovery of damages for injuries to foreign land').

[250] Bernasconi (n 17) 104–05.

[251] Uniform Law Conference of Canada (n 127) 501–02.

[252] Secretariat of the Commission for Environmental Cooperation (n 148) 227.

[253] *R v Lee* 2012 ABCA 17 [44]–[54]; *David Polowin Real Estate Ltd v Dominion of Canada General Insurance Co* (2005) 76 OR (3d) 161, 190–97 (Ont CA), leave to appeal to SCC refused [2006] 1 SCR vii.

[254] *Wolf v The Queen* (1974) [1975] 2 SCR 107, 109.

pattern in *Albert*.[255] Third, no court has ever applied *Albert* to a transboundary pollution case and few cases have squarely applied the local action rule to tort claims generally, the primary instances being *Brereton*, *Boslund* and *Albert*. Taken together, these cases form a weak line of authority.

By contrast, courts have ignored or declined to apply *Albert* and *Moçambique* on several, more recent occasions. In *Pembina County Water Resource District* (2017), the Federal Court of Appeal dealt with a lawsuit in nuisance and negligence brought by North Dakota authorities and private landowners against the Government of Manitoba and the rural municipality of Rhineland, over a road allowance in the Canadian province of Manitoba, which blocked the natural dispersion of the Pembina River and flooded lands on the American side of the border, in North Dakota. The Federal Court of Appeal dismissed the foreign plaintiffs' claim for lack of subject matter jurisdiction under the International Boundary Waters Treaty Act.[256] The Court noted, however, that 'the appellants allege[d] to have suffered damages as a result of torts committed in Manitoba by the respondents' and that 'At first glance, there [did] not appear to be anything preventing the appellants from bringing an action before the Manitoba Court of Queen's Bench'.[257] The Federal Court of Appeal made no mention of the local action rule even though the claim clearly involved foreign land.

This omission is significant. Plaintiffs had expressly argued that a dismissal in Federal Court would leave them without a remedy because Manitoba's provincial courts would not hear a claim that involved foreign land.[258] Simply put, the International Boundary Waters Treaty Act was their only chance. One of the defendants replied that Manitoba courts had jurisdiction over the dispute, hence the plaintiffs did have a remedy outside the Federal Court.[259] The Federal Court of Appeal accepted Rhineland's argument but made no reference to the local action rule.[260]

Other courts have questioned the local action rule more explicitly. In the seminal case of *Interprovincial Co-operatives* (1972), Justice Matas expressed doubt about the majority's decision in *Albert*.[261] The dispute involved a Manitoba environmental statute, the Fishermen's Assistance and Polluters' Liability Act.[262] The statute created liability for damage caused to Manitoba

[255] J Walker, *Castel & Walker: Canadian Conflict of Laws*, vol 2, 6th edn (Markham, LexisNexis, 2005) (loose-leaf updated 2021) § 23.1(a), fn 15; DA Crerar, 'A Proposal for a Principled Public Policy Doctrine Post-*Tolofson*' (1998) 8 *Windsor Review of Legal and Social Issues* 23, 52, fn 83. But see *Welsh v Welsh* 2011 ABQB 686 [14].

[256] International Boundary Waters Treaty Act (n 43).

[257] *Pembina County Water Resource District* (n 105) [77].

[258] ibid (Memorandum of Fact and Law of the Appellant, paras 48–50, 77–78).

[259] ibid (Memorandum of Fact and Law of the Respondent Rural Municipality of Rhineland, paras 56–60).

[260] *Pembina County Water Resource District* (n 105) [77].

[261] *The Queen in Right of the Province of Manitoba v Interprovincial Co-operatives Ltd* (1972) 30 DLR (3d) 166 (Man QB), revd (1973) 38 DLR (3d) 367 (Man CA), restored (1975) [1976] 1 SCR 477.

[262] The Fishermen's Assistance and Polluters' Liability Act, SM 1970 c 32.

fisheries by contaminants discharged into provincial waters or carried from elsewhere into those waters, regardless of any foreign regulatory authorisation which the polluter may have had. It included a scheme whereby the province would make assistance payments to fishermen who had suffered financial loss, who in turn could assign to the province their right to sue the polluter for damages.[263] Manitoba relied on the Fishermen's Assistance and Polluters' Liability Act to sue Interprovincial Co-operatives and Dryden Chemicals on behalf of fishermen who had assigned their rights to the province after receiving financial assistance, claiming that the defendants' chlor-alkali plants in Saskatchewan and Ontario had contaminated Manitoba waters with mercury.[264]

Justice Matas held that the Act was constitutionally inapplicable and unenforceable against out-of-province defendants.[265] The Manitoba Court of Appeal reversed that decision[266] and the case went all to the way to the Supreme Court of Canada.[267] Four of the seven judges restored Justice Matas' decision. The majority held that the Fishermen Act exceeded the constitutional powers of the legislature,[268] such that Manitoba could rely only on common law causes of action and federal law to support its claims against out-of-province polluters.[269]

For our purposes, an important aspect of the restored trial judgment went unnoticed. Manitoba had argued that the impugned provision of the Fishermen Act concerned injury to real property, which fell squarely within the province's powers under the Constitution Act 1867 (property and civil rights in the province).[270] Relying on *Albert*, Manitoba pleaded that its courts had exclusive jurisdiction over claims concerning injury to real property. Justice Matas rejected Manitoba's position. He quoted Justice Harrison's dissent in *Albert* at length and noted widespread academic criticism of the majority's opinion.[271] He declined to artificially locate torts at the place of acting or the place of injury for all purposes.[272] He concluded that the province could legislate subject to constitutional constraints, and could sue in its own courts regardless of whether

[263] The Manitoba Court of Appeal explained the context of the Act as follows: 'Apparently when it was found that the waters of Lake Winnipeg were being polluted by mercury and other contaminants from the Saskatchewan River and other sources, the Government of Manitoba decided to prohibit fishing in Lake Winnipeg, commercial or otherwise, and to provide compensation to those people who had been deprived of their earning power because they were fishing in a commercial way'. *Hershfield v Amos* (1971) 21 DLR (3d) 597, 597–98 (Man CA).

[264] *Interprovincial Co-operatives Ltd v R* (1975), [1976] 1 SCR 477, 482 (Laskin CJC, dissenting).

[265] *Interprovincial Co-operatives* MBQB (n 261) 184.

[266] *R v Interprovincial Co-Operatives Limited* (1973) 38 DLR (3d) 367 (Man CA), revd (1975) [1976] 1 SCR 477.

[267] *Interprovincial Co-operatives* SCC (n 264).

[268] For further discussion on the grounds of the majority, see section 4.II.C.ii.b below.

[269] *Interprovincial Co-operatives* SCC (n 264) 516 (Pigeon J).

[270] *Interprovincial Co-operatives* MBQB (n 261) 178–79; Constitution Act 1867, 30 & 31 Vict c 3, s 92(13).

[271] *Interprovincial Co-operatives* MBQB (n 261) 179–80.

[272] ibid 182.

the tort involved an injury to real property.[273] This is not conclusive, of course: Justice Matas was sceptical of the local action rule but, ultimately, even the strictest observance of *Albert* could have led him to conclude that Manitoba courts had jurisdiction because lands in Manitoba were indeed affected. Furthermore, only one judge at the Supreme Court of Canada invalidated the Fishermen's Assistance and Polluters' Liability Act on the same ground as Justice Matas, namely its improper extraterritorial reach.[274] Nonetheless, Justice Matas' approach foreshadowed the rise of a more flexible approach to tort localisation,[275] and showed early signs of judicial disagreement with *Albert* in the context of transboundary pollution.

Malo (1943) is also instructive. Tenants brought a claim for damages in Ontario against the alleged owner and lessor of a building located in Quebec, after the roof had collapsed. The defendant denied that he was the owner or lessor. Justice Plaxton held that the Ontario courts had jurisdiction because title to foreign land only arose incidentally in the proceedings.[276] This reasoning is at odds with the wide interpretation of *Moçambique* favoured in *Albert*, but Justice Plaxton considered the claim to be based on a landlord-tenant contract rather than a tort.[277] *Malo* is therefore not determinative, but it suggests certain limits to the local action rule even when title is at stake.

Godley (1988), however, contradicts *Moçambique* and *Albert* more directly. The case dealt with an action for damages after a toilet in the condominium owned by the defendant leaked into the plaintiff's condominium located below.[278] The condominiums were in Florida. The defendant relied on *Moçambique* and *Brereton* and argued that Ontario courts had no jurisdiction to hear a claim involving damage to foreign immovable property. Justice Carnwath rejected this view and confined the local action rule to disputes involving title to foreign land, holding that *Moçambique*

> should not be taken for authority that wherever damage to land is included in the statement of claim, that an action for negligence to recover those damages should be precluded from being brought in the Province of Ontario where the land is situate[d] elsewhere.[279]

Godley supports the proposition that Canadian courts have jurisdiction to hear disputes involving damage to foreign land, when title is not disputed.[280] Nonetheless, the bulk of the literature on transboundary environmental disputes

[273] ibid.
[274] *Interprovincial Co-operatives* SCC (n 264) 525–26 (Ritchie J, concurring).
[275] GHL Fridman, 'Where is a Tort Committed?' (1974) 24 *University of Toronto Law Journal* 247, 272–73. For further discussion on the localisation of torts for jurisdictional purposes, see section 3.II.A.ii below.
[276] *Malo v Clement* [1943] 4 DLR 773, 776 (Ont H Ct J).
[277] ibid.
[278] *Godley v Coles* (1988) 39 CPC (2d) 162 (Ont Dist Ct), affd (1989) 40 CPC (2d) xlvi (Ont H Ct J).
[279] ibid 165–66.
[280] cf Walker, *Canadian Conflict of Laws*, vol 2 (2005) § 23.1(a).

continues to focus on *Albert*,[281] and only a few scholars mention *Godley*'s implications for the jurisdiction of Canadian courts in this context.[282] The minority is right: the case has a significant impact on the jurisdictional analysis in transboundary environmental disputes. *Godley* certainly has its own peculiarities: unlike *Albert*, a substantial proportion of the claim concerned damage to *movable* property inside the condominium. Read together, *Albert* and *Godley* could simply mean that courts will assess the proportion of the claim related to moveable and immovable property and decide accordingly whether it has jurisdiction (or else assess the degree of connection between damage to moveable and immovable property, as the Court did in *Albert* to distinguish *Brereton* and dismiss the entirety of the claim[283]). Yet *Godley* was a case in which all the events (acts and injury) had occurred in a foreign jurisdiction, and Justice Carnwath nonetheless declined to apply *Moçambique*. Justice Harrison (dissenting in *Albert*) did not go as far – he limited the exception to transboundary damage, a situation which, he said, the House of Lords could not have had in mind in *Moçambique* due to the 'geography of the British isles' but was highly relevant in the Canadian interprovincial context.[284] *Godley*, in other words, goes further in its repudiation of the local action rule than any other tort case reported in Canada.

Inconsistent if not inconclusive precedents and near-unanimous academic criticism cast a different light on the status of the local action rule in Canada, with significant inplications for cross-border environmental litigation. Decisions such as *Interprovincial Co-operatives*, *Godley* and *Malo* carry greater weight than generally acknowledged, particularly given the scarcity of authorities on point. By the same token, a controversial and divided 80-year-old case about log driving should not have the value it currently has in the literature. The continuing fame of *Albert* in the environmental literature (and, to a lesser extent, its single-judge predecessors *Brereton* and *Boslund*) is unwarranted.

Today, courts should not consider themselves bound to interpret the local action rule so widely.[285] In our context, a proper formulation of the rule would exclude its application in cases where foreign victims of transboundary pollution sue the wrongdoer in the state of origin and allege tortious damage to foreign land, at least when title is not at stake. It may be tempting for a defendant to strategically dispute title in order to trigger the local action rule. Disputed

[281] See the sources cited above nn 246–49.

[282] T Wood, 'Sticks and Carrots: *Rylands v Fletcher*, CSR, and Accountability for Environmental Harm in Common Law Jurisdictions' (2012) 91 *Canadian Bar Review* 275, 290–91; SL Seck, 'Environmental Harm in Developing Countries Caused by Subsidiaries of Canadian Mining Corporations: The Interface of Public and Private International Law' (1999) 37 *Canadian Yearbook of International Law* 139, 171; MI Jeffery, 'Seeking Redress for Environmental Harm in the Context of Transboundary Pollution: Remedies, Access, and Choice of Law Considerations' in SJ Rubin and DC Alexander (eds), *NAFTA and the Environment* (The Hague, Kluwer Law International, 1996) 481. See also Pitel and Rafferty (n 210) 335–36.

[283] *Albert* (n 225) 46–48 and the text accompanying n 228 above.

[284] ibid 51–52 (Harrison J, dissenting).

[285] Welling and Heakes (n 233) 314.

title was indeed a key consideration in *Brereton*,[286] before the majority in *Albert* made it irrelevant.[287] Yet it is hard to conceive a case in which a Canadian greenhouse-gas emitter, for instance, would persuasively attempt to challenge the title held by foreign victims in their own country.[288] Even if it did, the applicability of the local action rule in that context could be tied to the nature of the remedies sought (damages as opposed to an order affecting title, for instance)[289] or whether title arises incidentally or primarily in the proceedings (a distinction made in *Malo*[290]).

What are the prospects for legal reform? Provincial legislatures could conceivably abolish certain aspects of the local action rule by statute. Four provinces (Ontario, Manitoba, Nova Scotia and Prince Edward Island) already did so when they adopted the Reciprocal Access Act,[291] which effectively abolishes the local action rule[292] and guarantees equal access to the courts of the state of origin for local and foreign victims alike. Four provinces and territories (British Columbia, Nova Scotia, Saskatchewan and the Yukon) replaced the common law framework of jurisdiction with the CJPTA, which does not mention the local action rule and simply states that an immovable in the province amounts to a real and substantial connection with the province.[293] It is unlikely, however, that the CJPTA would be considered to have implicitly abolished the local action rule,[294] as only clear legislative intent can change the common law.[295] It would likely take more than the CJPTA to abolish the local action rule by statute, but the argument could be made.

Even if provinces do not abolish certain aspects of the local action rule, it is realistic and probable that an appellate court would favour today a strict interpretation of *Moçambique*. One author goes so far as to suggest that a jurisdictional challenge by the defendant in a lawsuit brought by foreign victims of transboundary pollution would be 'doomed to fail' because the *Moçambique* rule 'seemingly' no longer applies in Canada when title is not at stake.[296] While this may be overly optimistic, at the very least, we must acknowledge that 'The scope of [the *Moçambique*] rule and its numerous exceptions is complex and changing'.[297]

[286] *Brereton* (n 220) 58.
[287] *Albert* (n 225) 45.
[288] See by analogy Welling and Heakes (n 233) 309.
[289] ibid 308–10.
[290] *Malo* (n 276) 776.
[291] Reciprocal Access Act (n 126).
[292] Walker, vol 2 (n 255) § 23.3.
[293] CJPTA (n 194) s 10(a).
[294] Pitel, 'Jurisdiction in Common Law Canada' (2018) 77; Pitel and Rafferty (n 210) 332; Black, Pitel and Sobkin, *Statutory Jurisdiction* (2012) 46–48.
[295] *Canada (Attorney General) v Thouin* 2017 SCC 46 [19]; *Lizotte v Aviva Insurance Company of Canada* 2016 SCC 52 [56].
[296] Wood, 'Sticks and Carrots' (2012) 290–91.
[297] V Black and SGA Pitel, 'Reform of Ontario's Law of Jurisdiction' (2009) 47 *Canadian Business Law Journal* 469, 473.

Transboundary environmental disputes are a prime site for further change. The Supreme Court of Canada repeatedly emphasised the growing importance of environmental protection[298] and also suggested that private international law should remain 'in step with the dynamic and evolving fabric of our society'.[299] This fabric now includes more sophisticated environmental rights and greater emphasis on access to private remedies in international and soft law instruments. Disregarding *Albert* and opening the gates of Canadian courts respond to the preoccupations expressed in the ILC Principles on the Allocation of Loss regarding access to justice in the state of origin.[300] It also participates in a form of environmental justice sorely needed by foreign populations plagued by the effects of climate change, who might contemplate lawsuits against greenhouse gas emitters in Canada. In the absence of legislative reform, a judicial reassessment of the local action rule in climate change litigation (or in another type of transboundary environmental dispute) is realistic and highly desirable.

ii. Canadian Plaintiffs in Canada

The second jurisdictional question is whether Canadian plaintiffs can sue foreign polluters in Canada over transboundary pollution originating abroad. Certain states such as Singapore expressly allow courts to assert jurisdiction in such circumstances, regardless of where the pollution comes from, and as long as it affects Singaporeans.[301] Canadian law is not as explicit, and the Reciprocal Access Act only addresses jurisdiction at the place of acting.

Maintaining the possibility of suing at the place of injury is traditionally justified by the need to ensure fairness to plaintiffs who do not have the financial resources to sue abroad, but this may not always be the case. Canadian victims may prefer to sue in the United States if the pollution originates in the latter. Lawyers are accustomed to Canada-United States litigation,[302] and a judgment in the United States would also be readily enforceable against the polluter located there – an important factor if plaintiffs seek injunctive relief. Should victims nonetheless decide to sue in their home province, the question becomes whether environmental damage is enough for Canadian courts to assert jurisdiction over

[298] *British Columbia v Canadian Forest Products Ltd* 2004 SCC 38 [7]; *Imperial Oil Ltd v Quebec (Minister of the Environment)* 2003 SCC 58 [19]; *114957 Canada Ltée (Spraytech, Société d'arrosage) v Hudson (Town)* 2001 SCC 40 [1]; *R v Hydro-Québec* [1997] 3 SCR 213, 293–97; *Ontario v Canadian Pacific Ltd* [1995] 2 SCR 1031, 1075–76.

[299] *Douez v Facebook Inc* 2017 SCC 33 [36], citing *R v Salituro* [1991] 3 SCR 654, 670.

[300] For a similar point, see WK King, 'Transboundary Pollution: Canadian Jurisdiction' (1982) 1 *Canadian–American Law Journal* 1, 14.

[301] Transboundary Haze Pollution Act 2014 (Singapore), ss 4, 6; P Listiningrum, 'Transboundary Civil Litigation for Victims of Southeast Asian Haze Pollution: Access to Justice and the Non-Discrimination Principle' (2019) 8 *Transnational Environmental Law* 119, 139–40.

[302] Hsu and Parrish, 'Litigating Canada-U.S. Transboundary Harm' (2007) 37.

foreign polluters. This assumes that the polluting activities occurred elsewhere (at the place of acting), that the defendant has no presence in the province and that it does not consent to have the claim tried there.[303]

Again, the answer is yes in Quebec. The CCQ expressly contemplates injury suffered in the province as a jurisdictional basis for personal actions, including neighbourhood disturbance claims.[304] This includes neighbourhood disturbance claims.[305] Furthermore, unlike in the EU, an indirect injury suffices to establish jurisdiction.[306] The plaintiff ought to actually have suffered the injury in Quebec (as opposed to an injury recorded there based on the location of the plaintiff's patrimony),[307] but this is unlikely to be contentious in transboundary environmental disputes that involve damage other than pure economic loss.

The common law offers no such hard-and-fast rule, but it would likely lead to the same result. This is because the fact that the victim suffered an injury in the province suffices to create a presumption of jurisdiction for each of the relevant torts. To substantiate this claim, I explain the jurisdictional framework for torts at common law and under the CJPTA (section II.A.ii.a) and apply that framework to torts that are often seen in environmental litigation: negligence, nuisance, trespass, strict liability (also known as *Rylands v Fletcher*[308]) and breach of riparian rights (section II.A.ii.b).

a. Jurisdictional Framework for Torts

In 2012, the Supreme Court of Canada reviewed the common law of jurisdiction and established a list of tort-specific factors which indicate a real and substantial connection between the province and the dispute. The Court held in *Club Resorts* that a real and substantial connection presumptively exists when, among other things, the defendant is domiciled, resides or carries on business in the province, or when a tort occurred there.[309] These connecting factors supplement the traditional bases of jurisdiction (presence and consent),[310] and create a rebuttable presumption that the courts of that province have jurisdiction.[311] The list is not exhaustive. Lower courts can recognise more connecting factors in future cases based on considerations of order, fairness and comity.[312]

[303] The mere presence of the plaintiff in the forum does not alone suffice to establish jurisdiction: *Club Resorts* (n 193) [86].

[304] CCQ (n 179), Art 3148, para 1(3°).

[305] For further discussion on this point, see section 3.II.A.i.a above.

[306] *Spar Aerospace* (n 182) [36].

[307] *Infineon Technologies* (n 182) [46].

[308] *Rylands v Fletcher* (1868) LR 3 HL 330.

[309] *Club Resorts* (n 193) [90].

[310] ibid [79]. See also *Breeden v Black* 2012 SCC 19 [19].

[311] ibid [95]–[100].

[312] ibid [91]–[92].

The Supreme Court of Canada held in *Club Resorts* that the *situs* of the tort was clearly an appropriate connecting factor at common law.[313] The CJPTA similarly permits the assertion of jurisdiction when a tort was committed in the province.[314] Transboundary pollution, however, makes it difficult to localise the tort because the wrongful act and the injury occur in different states.

The Court, however, rejected damages sustained in the province as a presumptive connecting factor. Unreservedly accepting this factor would risk 'sweeping into that jurisdiction claims that have only a limited relationship with the forum'.[315] In other words, plaintiffs cannot rely merely on damages to sue in their home province. Absent other connections, claims for pain and inconvenience accumulating in the forum after an accident that occurred outside the province, for instance, do not provide a sufficient connection with the province.[316]

Importantly, the Court did not exclude the place of injury as a potential forum in all circumstances. It even acknowledged that some torts might occur at the place of injury.[317] In two companion cases, the Court did in fact locate the tort of defamation at the place of injury, where the defamatory statement had been published and caused reputational damage.[318] The Court later took the same view in *Haaretz.com*.[319] Admittedly, the localisation of the tort of defamation at the place of injury for jurisdictional purposes remains closely tied with the nature of the tort itself. Defamation is a tort of strict liability which crystallises upon the publication of defamatory material – a third party hears, reads or downloads the material, which causes damage to the plaintiff's reputation.[320] Environmental torts, by contrast, involve tangible injury to persons or property. But the point remains that damages sustained in the province – inappropriate as a standalone connecting factor – should not be confused with the *situs* of a tort, which may be located at the place of injury.

In the post-*Club Resorts* era, courts will seek to locate torts in order to decide whether to assume jurisdiction. No bright-line rule locates torts in one place or the other. The analysis should focus on where each tort crystallises, that is, where a cause of action exists.[321] Each tort has its own characteristics which

[313] ibid [88].

[314] CJPTA (n 194), s 10(g).

[315] *Club Resorts* (n 193) [89].

[316] cf *Brownlie v Four Seasons Holdings Incorporated* [2017] UKSC 80 [21], [67] (where Lord Sumption and Lord Wilson suggest that ongoing damage in the forum suffices to assert jurisdiction in common law Canada, without discussing *Club Resorts*).

[317] *Club Resorts* (n 193) [89].

[318] *Breeden* (n 310) [20]; *Éditions Écosociété Inc v Banro Corp* 2012 SCC 18 [38]–[39].

[319] *Haaretz.com v Goldhar* 2018 SCC 28 [36]–[38] (Côté J), [99] (Karakatsanis J, concurring), [147] (Wagner J, concurring), [166] (McLachlin CJ, Moldaver and Gascon JJ, dissenting). Only Justice Abella would have adopted a different jurisdictional rule for cross-border defamation: ibid [129] (Abella J, concurring).

[320] ibid [36]; *Éditions Écosociété* (n 318) [57]; *Crookes v Newton* 2011 SCC 47 [1], [16]; *Grant v Torstar Corp* 2009 SCC 61 [28].

[321] *Éditions Écosociété* (n 318) [3]; *Gulevich v Miller* 2015 ABCA 411 [37], [43].

could bear on this inquiry.[322] The same logic applies to statutory torts, particularly if they resemble common law torts,[323] but the relevance of *Van Breda* in this context is debatable.[324]

In this context, the question becomes whether torts that commonly arise in transboundary environmental disputes occur in the province for jurisdictional purposes if the victim suffered damage there. More accurately, the question is whether damage suffered in the province is sufficient for courts to assume jurisdiction rather than whether a tort *occurred* there, since courts reject the rigid localisation of torts at one place or the other. Arguably, the answer is yes, based on an application of the *Moran* case explained below.

Note that the analysis below applies not only to the *Club Resorts* framework of jurisdiction but also to the CJPTA. The CJPTA refers to the commission of a tort as indicative of a real and substantial connection with a province but does not explicitly address transboundary torts. Courts typically rely on CJPTA and common law authorities to deal with this issue.[325]

b. Jurisdiction over Environmental Torts

The *Moran* case, which concerns product liability, also provides the guiding principle to deal with jurisdiction over transboundary pollution when an injury is suffered in the forum.[326] Below, I examine *Moran* and its relevance in today's law of jurisdiction and apply its reasoning to transboundary pollution.

The *Moran* case

In *Moran*, the Supreme Court of Canada had to determine whether the Saskatchewan courts had jurisdiction to hear a statutory claim for negligent manufacture on the basis that the victim had suffered the injury in the province, even though the defendant had conducted its entire operation elsewhere. The Court found that Saskatchewan courts had jurisdiction and rejected earlier cases to the contrary.[327] Justice Dickson (as he then was) held that choosing

[322] eg *Ewert v Höegh Autoliners AS* 2020 BCCA 181 [77], leave to appeal to SCC refused 39403 (29 April 2021) (conspiracy); *Central Sun Mining Inc v Vector Engineering Inc* 2013 ONCA 601 [30]–[35], leave to appeal to SCC refused [2014] 1 SCR xiii (negligent misrepresentation).

[323] *Kaynes v BP plc* 2014 ONCA 580 [24]–[30]; *Ontario (Attorney General) v Rothmans Inc* 2013 ONCA 353 [44]–[45], leave to appeal to SCC refused [2013] 3 SCR vi; *British Columbia v Imperial Tobacco Canada Ltd* 2006 BCCA 398 [32]–[34], leave to appeal to SCC refused [2007] 1 SCR xiii.

[324] SGA Pitel and V Black, 'Assumed Jurisdiction in Canada: Identifying and Interpreting Presumptive Connecting Factors' (2018) 14 *Journal of Private International Law* 193, 209–19. On the localisation of statutory torts, see also SGA Pitel et al, *Private International Law in Common Law Canada: Cases, Text and Materials*, 4th edn (Toronto, Emond, 2016) 685–86.

[325] eg *Fairhurst v De Beers Canada Inc* 2012 BCCA 257 [35]–[46], leave to appeal to SCC refused [2013] 1 SCR vi; *Stanway v Wyeth Pharmaceuticals Inc* 2009 BCCA 592 [58]–[62], leave to appeal to SCC refused [2010] 1 SCR svi.

[326] *Moran v Pyle National (Canada) Ltd* (1973) [1975] SCR 393.

[327] *Abbott-Smith v Governors of University of Toronto* (1964) 45 DLR (2d) 672, 687 (NS SC); *George Monro Ltd v American Cyanamid and Chemical Corporation* [1944] KB 432, 439–40 (CA).

between the place of acting and the place of injury was too rigid.[328] Instead, torts occur 'in any country substantially affected by the defendant's activities or its consequences and the law of which is likely to have been in the reasonable contemplation of the parties'.[329] In the context of product liability, Justice Dickson concluded that

> where a foreign defendant carelessly manufactures a product in a foreign jurisdiction which enters into the normal channels of trade and he knows or ought to know both that as a result of his carelessness a consumer may well be injured and it is reasonably foreseeable that the product would be used or consumed where the plaintiff used or consumed it, then the forum in which the plaintiff suffered damage is entitled to exercise judicial jurisdiction over that foreign defendant.[330]

The test focuses on objective foreseeability rather than the defendant's subjective state of mind, even though reasonableness depends to some extent on what the defendant actually knew about its customers. Importantly, several courts may have jurisdiction over the dispute if the manufacturer could reasonably foresee that victims would use the product in several places.

The Supreme Court of Canada issued its judgment in 1973, but courts still rely on *Moran* to determine whether the place of injury has a real and substantial connection with the dispute. The case also extends beyond negligence. The British Columbia Court of Appeal, for instance, applied *Moran* to locate the tort of conspiracy at the place of injury under the CJPTA.[331]

Nothing in the CJPTA or *Club Resorts* contradicts *Moran*'s rationale.[332] Locating torts in the place most substantially affected by the defendant's activities or its consequences aligns with the presumptive factors set out in *Club Resorts*, which did not exclude jurisdiction at the place of injury in all cases.[333] Although the Court spoke of torts *committed* in the province rather than having *occurred* there,[334] it could hardly exclude the place of injury without explicitly overruling *Moran* or at least explain its place in the new framework for assumed jurisdiction.

Only the foreseeability caveat formulated in *Moran* has an uncertain status today (at least conceptually) because of a shift in the Supreme Court of Canada's jurisprudence. The Court explained in *Club Resorts* that defendants could rebut the presumption of assumed jurisdiction by showing that only a minor element of the tort had occurred in the province.[335] In such

[328] *Moran* (n 326) 408.

[329] ibid 409. See also *Distillers Co (Biochemicals) Ltd v Thompson* [1971] AC 458, 467–69 (PC) (cited by Justice Dickson in support of his approach).

[330] ibid.

[331] *Fairhurst* (n 325) [36]; *Imperial Tobacco* BCCA 2006 (n 323) [32].

[332] *SSAB Alabama Inc v Canadian National Railway Company* 2020 SKCA 74 [48]–[60], leave to appeal to SCC refused 39362 (11 February 2021).

[333] *Gulevich* (n 321) [44]–[48].

[334] Walker, vol 1 (n 255) § 11.5.

[335] *Club Resorts* (n 193) [96].

a case, the relationship between the dispute and the forum is so weak that 'it would ... not be reasonable to expect that the defendant would be called to answer proceedings in that jurisdiction'.[336] The Court mentioned reasonable expectations in a rather general fashion in *Club Resorts*: Justice LeBel used those words to describe what a weak connection with the forum generally looks like and did not refer to the defendant's expectations per se, but to the inherent reasonableness of assuming jurisdiction in these circumstances ('it would not be reasonable to expect').[337]

Six years after *Club Resorts*, *Haaretz.com* (2018) changed the meaning of those words slightly, but noticeably. There, the Supreme Court of Canada put considerably more emphasis on *the defendant's* reasonable expectations. Some courts had already done so after *Club Resorts*, but not consistently.[338] The shift in *Haaretz.com* is more striking. Justice Côté, also writing for Justices Brown and Rowe, held that the defendant could have reasonably expected to answer legal proceedings in Ontario, where the victim of its allegedly defamatory statement lived and conducted business.[339] Chief Justice McLachlin and Justices Moldaver and Gascon, dissenting, also identified reasonable foreseeability as a key criterion to rebut the presumption of jurisdiction.[340] Justice Abella, concurring, explained that from *Moran* to *Club Resorts*, courts had always asked whether it was inherently reasonable to assume jurisdiction, a question which, for her, meant asking whether the defendant had reasonably contemplated that scenario.[341] The analysis thus becomes more subjective and defendant-focused.

Perhaps the reasoning in *Haaretz.com* only applies to the tort of defamation, which has unique characteristics.[342] Conversely, it may be that reasonable foreseeability has become a formal test similar to the one used in *Moran* to locate complex torts. If that is the case, the shift is noteworthy but probably inconsequential in many cases. The defendant's expectations and the inherent reasonableness of assuming jurisdiction often converge. Conceptually, things are not so simple because the jurisdictional analysis now has two stages – locating the tort and rebutting the presumption. *Moran* uses foreseeability to locate the tort, and *Haaretz.com* uses foreseeability to rebut the presumption. But in reality, these are two sides of the same coin. Foreseeability helps establish jurisdiction when it indicates a strong connection with the forum.

[336] ibid [97].

[337] But see *Breeden* (n 310) [36] (where Justice LeBel agreed with the lower courts' finding that the appellants could have reasonably foreseen that their statements would cause damage to the reputation of the plaintiff in the province).

[338] *Geophysical Service Incorporated v Arcis Seismic Solutions Corp* 2015 ABQB 88 [44]; *Central Sun Mining* (n 322) [33]; *Sincies Chiementin SpA (Trustee of) v King* 2012 ONCA 653 [13], leave to appeal to SCC refused [2013] 2 SCR ix.

[339] *Haaretz.com* (n 319) [45] (Côté J).

[340] ibid [170]–[171] (McLachlin CJ, Moldaver and Gascon JJ, dissenting).

[341] ibid [125] (Abella J, concurring).

[342] See the text accompanying n 320 above.

Conversely, unforeseeability helps rebut the presumption of jurisdiction when it indicates a weak connection with the forum. The result is the same at either stage.

Moran and Transboundary Pollution

Combining *Moran* with the CJPTA or the *Club Resorts* framework as interpreted in *Haaretz.com*, the courts of the province where the injury was suffered have presumptive jurisdiction over foreign polluters when they could reasonably foresee that their operations would have an impact there. The diverse sets of reasons in *Interprovincial Co-operatives* – a lawsuit by the province of Manitoba against polluters operating in Ontario and Saskatchewan – already suggested that *Moran* was relevant in that context. In his concurring reasons, Justice Ritchie explicitly relied on *Moran* to note in conclusion that Manitoba courts would have jurisdiction to hear Manitoba's common law claims against foreign polluters, regardless of the constitutionality of the Fishermen's Assistance and Polluters' Liability Act.[343] At trial, Justice Matas had also relied on *Moran* at length, rejecting an all-or-nothing approach to the localisation of torts for jurisdictional purposes.[344] Chief Justice Laskin, dissenting with Justices Judson and Spence, approved *Moran*, but used it to determine the applicable law.[345] Justice Pigeon, also writing for Justices Martland and Beetz, preferred to confine *Moran* to the jurisdictional analysis and refused to apply that precedent 'to identify the legal system under which the rights and liabilities of the parties fall to be determined'.[346]

Applying the *Moran* principle of foreseeability to transboundary pollution (either to locate environmental torts or to rebut the presumption of jurisdiction) implies some limits to Canadian courts' jurisdictional reach. But the words are so open-ended that they make it difficult to assess exactly when and how those limits apply in practice. The foreseeability exception made sense in *Moran* because a manufacturer has some degree of control over its distribution chain and should answer to the courts of the states where its products end up. It also made sense in *Haaretz.com* because the defamatory statement targeted a specific individual who lived in Ontario. The environmental consequences of industrial operations have a different character. They are obviously not commercialised or put into the stream of commerce (except on carbon markets) and may remain unknown for decades. An American company operating near the Canadian border can contemplate that water or air pollution will have an impact across the border. But can a company operating thousands of kilometres away reasonably contemplate that its local operations will cause

[343] *Interprovincial Co-operatives* SCC (n 264) 526 (Ritchie J, concurring).

[344] *Interprovincial Co-operatives* MBQB (n 261) 180–82.

[345] *Interprovincial Co-operatives* SCC (n 264) 501 (Laskin CJC, dissenting).

[346] ibid 515 (Pigeon J). On the impact of *Moran* in *Interprovincial Co-operatives*, see Muldoon, Scriven and Olson (n 4) 49; A Popovici, 'Le « locus delicti » en droit international privé québécois' (1982–83) 17 *Revue juridique Thémis* 463, 467.

damage on Canadian territory? As the Ontario Court of Appeal recently recognised, 'the principal effect of GHG emissions – climate change – often bears no relationship to the location of the source of the emissions'.[347] This goes to the causal connection between the polluting activity and the damage suffered in the forum.[348] This is a notoriously difficult problem for plaintiffs in toxic torts and climate change litigation,[349] and it may arise early on as part of the jurisdictional analysis.[350] Even if plaintiffs successfully establish that the tort occurred in the forum, remote injuries could rebut the presumption of jurisdiction because they would amount to a very small portion of the tort and could not have been contemplated by the foreign defendant, even prima facie.[351] This said, neither unforeseeability nor remoteness alters the fact that applying *Moran* and *Club Resorts* (or the CJPTA) can, at least in principle, justify jurisdiction at the place of injury.

This becomes clearer when we look at each of the relevant common law torts. Most claims against polluters or public authorities involve negligence or property torts such as nuisance, trespass, strict liability (*Rylands v Fletcher*) and breach of riparian rights. In *Interprovincial Co-operatives*, for instance, Manitoba's common law claims against polluters operating in Ontario and Saskatchewan were based on negligence, nuisance and trespass.[352]

Negligence follows the *Moran* reasoning. Courts at the place of injury can assume jurisdiction because damage constitutes the tort.[353] Nuisance, trespass, strict liability (*Rylands v Fletcher*) and breach of riparian rights all involve interference with property. They have the most natural connections with the place of injury, that is, where the property is located.[354] Property in the forum in fact creates a presumption of jurisdiction in non-tort disputes.[355] The local action rule itself is premised on the fact that the courts where the land is located are best equipped to deal with the dispute. It is indefensible as a rule that denies

[347] *Reference re Greenhouse Gas Pollution Pricing Act* 2019 ONCA 544 [17], affd 2021 SCC 11.

[348] *Gariepy v Shell Oil Co* (2000) 51 OR (3d) 181, 190 (Ont Sup Ct).

[349] L Collins and H McLeod-Kilmurray, *The Canadian Law of Toxic Torts* (Toronto, Canada Law Book, 2014) ch 7.

[350] On causation, climate change and jurisdiction in European private international law, see Giansetto, 'Responsabilité climatique' [2018] 514–15, 518–25.

[351] *Club Resorts* (n 193) [96]. See also *SSAB Alabama* (n 332) [65]–[67].

[352] *Interprovincial Co-operatives* MBQB (n 261) 170. See generally L Collins and H McLeod Kilmurray, 'Common Law Tools to Protect the Environment' in Paddock, Markell and Bryner, *Elgar Encyclopedia* (2017); Collins and Kilmurray, *Toxic Torts* (2014) chs 4–6.

[353] *SSAB Alabama* (n 332) [61]–[63]; *Furlan v Shell Oil Co* 2000 BCCA 404 [21], leave to appeal to SCC refused [2001] 1 SCR xii; *GWL Properties Ltd v WR Grace & Co–Conn* (1990) 50 BCLR (2d) 260, 264 (BC CA); *Moran* (n 326) 409.

[354] *Peace River (Town) v British Columbia Hydro & Power Authority* (1972) 29 DLR (3d) 769, 773 (Johnson JA, concurring) (Alta SC (AD)), leave to appeal to SCC refused [1972] SCR ix; Pitel et al, *Private International Law* (2016) 680.

[355] *Knowles v Lindstrom* 2014 ONCA 116 [21]–[22], leave to appeal to SCC refused [2014] 2 SCR viii.

jurisdiction at the place of acting, but it does confirm that the place of injury is an acceptable basis for jurisdiction in tort disputes under the *Club Resorts* framework.

Scholars took the same view before *Club Resorts*. McCaffrey, in particular, suggested that environmental torts can be considered to occur at the place of injury for jurisdictional purposes.[356] This view remains persuasive today because *Moran* is still the primary authority on the localisation of torts for jurisdictional purposes. It is also suggested by certain commentators post-*Club Resorts*.[357]

Based on this analysis, it must be concluded that Canadian plaintiffs can sue foreign polluters in Canada for damages. Jurisdictional barriers have either fallen apart or become easier to overcome. They are no longer strong enough to preven litigation, and it is doubtful that courts would endorse them unreservedly.[358] Injunctions aimed at preventing damage, however, may still be ineffective. Courts can issue injunctions with extraterritorial effects,[359] but can only enforce them if the defendant is present in the jurisdiction in one way or another, such that conduct occurring elsewhere may lead to contempt proceedings in the province. Courts cannot otherwise compel foreign defendants or enforce orders against their property abroad.[360] If an injunction was granted against a foreign polluter, plaintiffs would have to seek its recognition and enforcement at the place of acting.

Summing up, both foreign and local plaintiffs can sue in Canada to seek compensation for transboundary pollution. Courts can assume jurisdiction against local polluters when they operate in the province. They can (and should) ignore the local action rule if foreign land is involved. Courts can also assume

[356] SC McCaffrey, 'Private Remedies for Transfrontier Environmental Disturbances', IUCN Environmental Policy and Law Paper 8 (Morges, International Union for Conservation of Nature and Natural Resources, 1975) 28; McCaffrey, 'Trans-Boundary Pollution Injuries' (n 99) 248. See also Jeffery, 'Transboundary Pollution' (1992) 178–79; Muldoon, Scriven and Olson (n 4) 49; P McNamara, *The Availability of Civil Remedies to Protect Persons and Property from Transfrontier Pollution* (Frankfurt, Alfred Metzner, 1981) 81–83.

[357] A Gage and M Byers, 'Payback Time? What the Internationalization of Climate Litigation Could Mean for Canadian Oil and Gas Companies' (West Coast Environmental Law, 1 October 2014) 16–19, available at www.wcel.org/sites/default/files/publications/Payback%20Time.pdf; Péloffy, '*Kivalina v Exxonmobil*' (2013) 136.

[358] For accounts of a greater willingness by domestic courts to assert jurisdiction in transboundary pollution cases, including in the Canada–United States context, see Kinna, 'Non-Discrimination and Liability' (2016) 378, citing Boyle, 'Human Rights and the Environment' (2012) 638; N Hall et al, 'Great Lakes Emerging Legal Issues Regarding the International Boundary Waters Treaty and the Great Lakes Water Quality Agreement' (2010) 34 *Canada–United States Law Journal* 193, 224 (comments by N Hall); S-L Hsu, 'A Realistic Evaluation of Climate Change Litigation Through the Lens of a Hypothetical Lawsuit' (2008) 79 *University of Colorado Law Review* 701, 760; Hsu and Parrish (n 123) 33–39; AL Parrish, 'Trail Smelter Déjà Vu: Extraterritoriality, International Environmental Law, and the Search for Solutions to Canada-U.S. Transboundary Water Pollution Disputes' (2005) 85 *Boston University Law Review* 363, 386–92.

[359] *Google Inc v Equustek Solutions Inc* 2017 SCC 34 [38]; *Impulsora Turistica de Occidente, SA de CV v Transat Tours Canada Inc* 2007 SCC 20 [6].

[360] *Chevron* SCC 2015 (n 193) [46].

jurisdiction against foreign polluters if local plaintiffs suffered damage in the province, because it indicates sufficient connections with the forum. In common law provinces, foreign polluters can rebut the presumption of jurisdiction by showing that they could not have reasonably contemplated the consequences of their activities in the province. This caveat may affect the availability of prompt and adequate compensation, but only on a case-by-case basis. It does not preclude the assumption of jurisdiction altogether. This casts new light on past efforts to implement equal access in North America: the Draft Treaty on Equal Access and Remedy, the Reciprocal Access Act and the NAAEC may not have achieved much, but the general law of jurisdiction matches the policies that inspired them in the first place and responds to the preoccupations expressed in the ILC Principles on the Allocation of Loss.

B. Declining Jurisdiction Over Transboundary Pollution

Even though Canadian courts should normally be able to assert jurisdiction over a transboundary environmental dispute, other aspects of the jurisdictional analysis appear to be less in tune with equal access and the duty to ensure prompt and adequate compensation. Once their jurisdiction is established (and only then), Canadian courts have the discretionary power to refuse to exercise their jurisdiction in certain circumstances under the doctrine of *forum non conveniens*. The doctrine originated in Scotland[361] and made its way to Canada through the common law (formally introduced in *Amchem Products*[362] and embedded into the *Club Resorts* framework of jurisdiction[363]), the CJPTA[364] and even the CCQ.[365] In broad outline, the doctrine allows the court to stay the proceedings if the defendant shows that it would be more appropriate to try the case in another forum for reasons of efficiency and fairness, even though the court seised has jurisdiction under its own rules. The discretionary power to refuse the exercise of jurisdiction keeps forum shopping in check, ensures proximity between the forum and the dispute, and avoids parallel proceedings.[366]

Difficulties arise, of course, when plaintiffs, defendants and the justice system have different perspectives on which forum is the most appropriate. Courts have developed over time a series of factors to determine whether to

[361] A Arzandeh, 'The Origins of the Scottish *Forum Non Conveniens* Doctrine' (2017) 13 *Journal of Private International Law* 130.

[362] *Amchem Products Incorporated v British Columbia (Workers' Compensation Board)* [1993] 1 SCR 897.

[363] *Club Resorts* (n 193) [101]–[112].

[364] CJPTA (n 194) s 11; *Teck Cominco Metals Ltd v Lloyd's Underwriters* 2009 SCC 11 [22].

[365] CCQ (n 179), Art 3135; *Stormbreaker Marketing and Productions Inc c Weinstock* 2013 QCCA 269 [74]–[119], leave to appeal to SCC refused [2013] 2 SCR xiv; *Spar Aerospace* (n 182) [65]–[82].

[366] Pitel and Rafferty (n 210) 117–19.

decline jurisdiction. In *Club Resorts*, the Supreme Court of Canada mentioned as examples the location of parties and witnesses, the costs of a transfer and its impact on litigation, the possibility of conflicting judgments, recognition and enforcement problems, and the strengths of the connections of the parties.[367] In *Haaretz.com*, the Court examined convenience and expenses for parties and witnesses, the loss of a legitimate juridical advantage, fairness, recognition and enforcement problems, applicable law and the avoidance of parallel proceedings.[368] The CJPTA and the CCQ operate in a similar way, but the list of factors varies.[369] All iterations of the test acknowledge that declining jurisdiction should remain exceptional. There must be more than just another forum where the case *could* be heard. That other forum must also be *clearly more appropriate* than the one chosen by the plaintiff,[370] who benefits from a presumption that his or her choice is acceptable as long as the court chosen has jurisdiction.

Forum non conveniens is a frequent target in the private international law and global governance discourse.[371] In the 'classic' scenario described by many, victims of gross corporate human rights violations who turn to civil courts cannot sue at the corporate domicile of the perpetrator (a well-developed legal system in which they can seise assets) and are forced instead to sue where the perpetrator operated and caused damage (possibly a developing country with weaker legal institutions and in which the defendant has minimal assets). This is a broad generalisation,[372] but one that illustrates the fundamental objection to *forum non conveniens* in the global governance discourse – that justice will not be achieved if plaintiffs are sent back to a country with weak legal institutions and no effective redress simply because it would be more appropriate to have their claim tried there. Injustices in this context include delays in trial, additional expenses and possibly outright denial of access to an effective remedy (even though, it must be recalled, the *forum non conveniens* analysis often explicitly accounts for those concerns by requiring the court to consider, for instance, the interests of justice and the interests of the parties).[373] A common line of argument blames injustices on the judicial overuse of a doctrine that

[367] *Club Resorts* (n 193) [110].

[368] *Haaretz.com* (n 319) [96] (Côté J), [192]–[193] (McLachlin CJ, Moldaver and Gascon JJ, dissenting).

[369] See the sources cited above nn 364 (CJPTA) and 365 (CCQ).

[370] *Club Resorts* (n 193) [108]–[109]; *Spar Aerospace* (n 182) [77].

[371] In Canada, see AM Manirabona, 'Toward Barrier Removal for Transnational Human Rights Litigation in Canadian Courts' in AM Manirabona and Y Vega-Cárdenas (eds), *Extractive Industrie and Human Rights in an Era of Global Justice: New Ways of Resolving and Preventing Conflicts* (Toronto, LexisNexis, 2019) 41–50.

[372] On this point, see L d'Avout, 'L'entreprise et les conflits internationaux de lois' (2018) 397 *Recueil des cours de l'Académie de droit international* 9, 448 (noting that a few 'spectacular' cases heavily discussed in the literature do not necessarily reflect the outcome of all litigation involving transnational corporations).

[373] J Fawcett, M Ní Shúilleabháin and S Shah, *Human Rights and Private International Law* (Oxford, Oxford University Press, 2016) paras 6.129–6.149.

should remain exceptional,[374] and possibly even completely unavailable when the defendant is domiciled in the jurisdiction.[375]

What are the doctrine's implications for the duty to ensure prompt and adequate compensation? In other words, does the existence of *forum non conveniens* in Canada prevent plaintiffs from obtaining prompt and adequate compensation in transboundary environmental disputes, given that courts would otherwise have the necessary jurisdiction to ensure its availability? This question has a theoretical and a practical side. Theoretically, the doctrine hardly aligns with the duty to ensure prompt and adequate compensation, even though the ILC Principles on the Allocation of Loss are silent on this point. Proceedings may last several more years if a court dismisses the case and forces plaintiffs to sue in another forum, not to mention the delays and costs associated with the debate itself and the risk that the limitation period expires. This judicial detour hardly favours prompt compensation. Nor is the compensation adequate if the plaintiffs never relitigate their case elsewhere. Historically, it seems that only a small portion of cases dismissed on the basis of *forum non conveniens* have reappeared on another court's docket.[376] Plaintiffs may have exhausted their financial resources or face corruption and coercion in the foreign state, forcing them to settle on disadvantageous terms with the defendants or drop their claim altogether. The *Cambior* case, for instance, was brought in Quebec after a major environmental disaster occurred on a gold mining operation in Guyana. Cambior, a Quebec company, owned 65 per cent of the Guyanese company which owned the mine.[377] The case was dismissed on grounds of *forum non conveniens* and reinstated in Guyana, but rejected on procedural grounds.[378]

From this perspective, *forum non conveniens* seems to contradict international commitments to foster access to justice in environmental matters.[379]

[374] eg J Talpis and SL Kath, 'The Exceptional as Commonplace in Quebec *Forum Non Conveniens* Law: *Cambior*, A Case in Point' (2000) 34 *Revue juridique Thémis* 731.

[375] International Law Association, 'Resolution No 2/2012: International Civil Litigation and the Interests of the Public' in International Law Association Report of the Seventy-Fifth Conference (Sofia 2012) ('Sofia Guidelines on Best Practices for International Civil Litigation for Human Human Rights Violations') 19, guideline 2.5(1). cf Committee on International Civil and Comercial Litigation, 'Third Interim Report – Declining and Referring Jurisdiction in International Litigation' in International Law Association Report of the Sixty-Ninth Conference (London, 2000) 161.

[376] CA Whytock and C Burke Robertson, 'Forum Non Conveniens and the Enforcement of Foreign Judgments' (2011) 111 *Columbia Law Review* 1444, 1448, fn 18; H Muir Watt, 'Aspects économiques du droit international privé: réflexions sur l'impact de la globalisation économique sur les fondements des conflits de lois et de juridictions' (2004) 307 *Recueil des cours de l'Académie de droit international* 25, 301.

[377] *Recherches internationales Québec c Cambior Inc* 1998 CanLII 9780 (Qc Sup Ct).

[378] S Imai, B Maheandiran and V Crystal, 'Access to Justice and Corporate Accountability: A Legal Case Study of Hudbay in Guatemala' (2014) 35 *Canadian Journal of Development Studies* 285, 297; C Scott and R Wai, 'Transnational Governance of Corporate Conduct Through the Migration of Human Rights Norms: The Potential Contribution of Transnational "Private" Litigation' in C Joerges, I-J Sand and G Teubner (eds), *Transnational Governance and Constitutionalism: International Studies in the Theory of Private Law* (Oxford, Hart, 2004) 302–03.

[379] Aarhus Convention (n 79), Arts 3(9), 9(4).

It also discriminates against foreign plaintiffs and threatens the right to a fair trial under human rights law when no such trial is available abroad. Practically, however, the abolition of *forum non conveniens* on the altar of prompt and adequate compensation is exaggerated and unrealistic. As Anderson observes, its rules 'have been framed over a period of many years without much reference to outside norms such as human rights, and have acquired their own kind of autonomy and self-referential processes of internal validation'.[380] Applying the doctrine only to the most obvious cases of reprehensible forum shopping is more feasible.[381] In any event, transboundary environmental disputes do not offer the best setting to highlight potential abuses of *forum non conveniens*. Those who advocate the doctrine's incompatibility with human rights standards primarily attack the idea of sending disempowered individuals back to the courts of a country that offers no meaningful prospect of redress. This would not be the case in a dispute involving pollution between Canada and the United States, or two EU states, for instance.

Other scenarios in which *forum non conveniens* could prevent prompt and adequate compensation of environmental damage are similarly narrow. Courts could conceivably dismiss a claim if it concerns extremely diffuse pollution with a remote connection to the forum (climate change comes to mind here), or even to avoid dealing with sensitive political issues, but there is no evidence of a widespread use of *forum non conveniens* that impedes prompt and adequate compensation of environmental damage in Canada. Legislatures and courts have kept the doctrine in check,[382] and defendants face a heavy burden in their attempts to have a claim dismissed – some claims against Canadian mining companies for wrongdoing committed abroad have survived *forum non conveniens* arguments in recent years.[383] When the issue has a bilateral or regional scope (as opposed to truly international), the connections between the dispute and each of the countries involved are typically strong enough that no single forum stands out as clearly more appropriate, and an attempt to invoke the doctrine will fail. Some even suggest that a 'global interest in the enforcement of laws which protect the global environment' might justify the denial of a *forum non conveniens* motion when a local polluter causes damage abroad.[384] While it is

[380] Anderson (n 78) 414.

[381] For attempts at a reformulation of the doctrine in Canada, see I Tchotourian and A Langenfeld, *Forum non conveniens: une impasse pour la responsabilité sociale des entreprises?* (Quebec, Presses de l'Université Laval, 2020) 138–45; C Nwapi, 'Re-Evaluating the Doctrine of *Forum Non Conveniens* in Canada' (2013) 34 *Windsor Review of Legal and Social Issues* 59.

[382] G Saumier, 'Le *forum non conveniens* au Québec: bilan d'une transplantation' in S Guillemard (ed), *Mélanges en l'honneur du professeur Alain Prujiner* (Cowansville, Yvon Blais, 2011) 349–50. But see Manirabona (n 371) 44–47.

[383] *Araya v Nevsun Resources Ltd* 2017 BCCA 401, affd 2020 SCC 5; *Garcia v Tahoe Resources Inc* 2017 BCCA 39, leave to appeal to SCC refused [2017] 1 SCR xviii. See generally G Saumier, 'L'ouverture récente des tribunaux canadiens aux poursuites dirigées contre les sociétés mères pour les préjudices causés par leurs filiales à l'étranger' (2018) 107 *Revue critique de droit international privé* 775.

[384] Talpis and Kath, *Cambior* (2000) 861–62.

difficult to speculate in the abstract on the application of a fact-specific doctrine that varies across jurisdictions, this suggests that *forum non conveniens* is not a systemic threat in transboundary environmental disputes.[385]

C. Enforcing Foreign Judgments against Local Polluters

The final question in this chapter concerns the recognition and enforcement in Canada of foreign judgments obtained by victims against Canadian polluters. The focus here is on enforcement,[386] which ensures that victims obtain payment – the *Chevron* saga being a striking illustration of the challenges faced by victims in this regard.[387] Enforcement can also ensure that pollution actually stops, as Canadian courts are prepared to enforce foreign injunctions and other non-monetary judgments in certain circumstances.[388]

International environmental law recognises the importance of facilitating the enforcement of foreign judgments in order to make sure that prompt and adequate compensation is not defeated after a judgment on the merits. Most civil liability treaties require the reciprocal recognition and enforcement of judgments by all parties, absent some exceptional and narrowly defined situations.[389] More surprisingly, neither the ILC Principles on the Allocation of Loss nor the HCCH, the ILA or the IIL gave detailed guidance on this point.

Here again, it is difficult to assess the implications of the rules governing the enforcement of foreign judgments in the abstract. For this reason, I do not examine every condition imposed by the common law or the CCQ, nor do I

[385] For a similar argument in the context of human rights litigation, see D'Avout, 'L'entreprise et les conflits internationaux de lois' (2018) 446–56.

[386] On the distinction between recognition and enforcement, see Pitel and Rafferty (n 210) 163.

[387] *Yaiguaje v Chevron Corporation* 2018 ONCA 472, leave to appeal to SCC refused 38183 (4 April 2019); MA Gómez, 'The Global Chase: Seeking the Recognition and Enforcement of the Lago Agrio Judgment Outside of Ecuador' (2013) 1 *Stanford Journal of Complex Litigation* 429.

[388] *United States of America v Yemec* 2010 ONCA 414 [43]–[53]; *Facebook Inc c Guerbuez* 2010 QCCS 4649 [37]–[41], affd 2011 QCCA 268; *Pro Swing Inc v Elta Golf Inc* 2006 SCC 52 [30]–[31].

[389] Kiev Liability Protocol (n 162), Art 18; Convention on Civil Liability for Bunker Oil Pollution Damage (23 March 2001, entered into force 21 November 2008) 40 ILM 1493 ('Bunker Convention'), Art 10; Basel Liability Protocol (n 162), Art 21; Convention on Supplementary Compensation for Nuclear Damage (12 September 1997, entered into force 15 April 2015) 36 ILM 1454 (CSC), Art XIII(5); International Convention on Liability and Compensation for the Carriage of Hazardous and Noxious Substances by Sea (3 May 1996, not yet in force) 35 ILM 1406 ('HNS Convention'), Art 40; Lugano Convention (n 162), Art 23; International Convention on Civil Liability for Oil Pollution Damage (27 November 1992, entered into force 30 May 1996) 1956 UNTS 255 (CLC), Art X; International Convention on the Establishment of an International Fund for Compensation for Oil Pollution Damage (27 November 1992, entered into force 30 May 1996) 1953 UNTS 373 ('Fund Convention'), Art 8; CRTD Convention (n 162), Art 20; Seabed Mineral Resources Convention (n 162), Art 12; Convention on Civil Liability for Nuclear Damage (21 May 1963, entered into force 12 November 1977) 1063 UNTS 265 ('Vienna Convention'), Art XII; Nuclear Ships Convention (n 162), Art XI(4); Convention on Third Party Liability in the Field of Nuclear Energy (29 July 1960, entered into force 1 April 1968) 956 UNTS 251 ('Paris Convention'), Art 13(d).

address reciprocity agreements with other provinces or foreign states. I focus instead on two issues that may become contentious in transboundary environmental disputes: the indirect jurisdiction of a foreign court (section II.C.i) and the public law/public policy exceptions to the enforcement of foreign judgments (section II.C.ii). The first issue may cause problems in Quebec and New Brunswick due to their restrictive approach to indirect jurisdiction in tort cases. The second issue is unlikely to raise an insurmountable obstacle in enforcement proceedings, except possibly in a small subset of cases which involve a widely different foreign legal regime and a sensitive issue in the state of origin. Other issues may arise depending on the contents of any given judgment and the context of each case, but they are not specific to transboundary pollution and will not be addressed below.

i. Indirect Jurisdiction of Foreign Courts

The first issue concerns indirect jurisdiction, or the assessment of foreign courts' jurisdiction before enforcing their judgments in the forum. Civil liability treaties typically require courts to assess indirect jurisdiction before enforcing foreign judgments.[390] In Canada, the courts of common law provinces will enforce foreign judgments only if the foreign court is considered to have jurisdiction under the law of the forum – in other words, if there was a real and substantial connection between that court and the dispute or the parties.[391] If a local polluter causes an injury to foreign victims without being present in the jurisdiction, the analysis will focus on whether the foreign court had jurisdiction following the approach established in *Moran* and *Club Resorts*. If the answer is yes, as was argued earlier, plaintiffs should have no difficulty enforcing their judgment in all common law provinces except New Brunswick. This is because New Brunswick has adopted a statute governing the enforcement of judgments issued outside Canada. The statute provides only two grounds of indirect jurisdiction: the ordinary residence of the defendant in the state of origin (which may be a problem if the plaintiffs sued at the place of injury) or its voluntary submission to the jurisdiction of the foreign court (a question of fact).[392]

[390] Kiev Liability Protocol (n 162), Art 18(1); Bunker Convention (n 389), Art 10(1); Basel Liability Protocol (n 162), Art 21(1); CSC (n 389), Art XIII(5); HNS Convention (n 389), Art 40(1); Lugano Convention (n 162), Art 23(1); CLC (n 389), Art X(1); Fund Convention (n 389), Art 8; CRTD Convention (n 162), Art 20(1); Seabed Mineral Resources Convention (n 162), Art 12(1); Vienna Convention (n 389), Art XII(1); Nuclear Ships Convention (n 162), Art XI(4)(a); Paris Convention (n 389), Art 13(d).

[391] *Beals v Saldanha* 2003 SCC 72 [24]–[38]; *Morguard Investments Ltd v De Savoye* [1990] 3 SCR 1077, 1106–1107.

[392] Foreign Judgments Act, RSNB 2011 c 162 ('New Brunswick Foreign Judgments Act'), s 2. Saskatchewan also has a statute on the enforcement of foreign judgments, but the grounds of indirect jurisdiction are closer to those of the common law: The Enforcement of Foreign Judgments Act, SS 2005 c E-9.121 ('Saskatchewan Foreign Judgments Act'), ss 4(a), 8–9.

The law is different in Quebec. Courts are unlikely to enforce foreign judgments against local polluters if the only basis of indirect jurisdiction available is the fact that plaintiffs suffered damage in the foreign state as a result of a fault committed elsewhere. Quebec courts assess the indirect jurisdiction of the foreign court using the grounds set out in Article 3168 CCQ when the underlying action is characterised as personal.[393] As with Article 3148 CCQ (direct jurisdiction), any single ground suffices.[394] Crucially, however, those grounds differ from those set out in Article 3148 CCQ to establish the direct jurisdiction of local courts. Article 3168(3°) CCQ provides that the foreign court has jurisdiction only if the fault, injurious act or omission *and* the injury occurred there.[395] Local courts, by contrast, have direct jurisdiction over a dispute even if only one element (injury, fault, injurious act or omission) is established.[396] Indirect jurisdiction is therefore significantly narrower than direct jurisdiction in this context.[397]

Why indirect jurisdiction is more limited than direct jurisdiction in this context remains unclear. When assessing indirect jurisdiction, Quebec courts cannot consider whether the foreign court should have applied the doctrine of *forum non conveniens* and declined to exercise its jurisdiction.[398] The unavailability of the 'important counterweight' provided by *forum non conveniens*[399] may then justify a restrictive approach to indirect jurisdiction, in order to avoid condoning overly broad assertions of jurisdictions by foreign courts.[400] This said, it was not clear at the time of the adoption of the CCQ that the doctrine of *forum non conveniens* did not apply in the context of indirect jurisdiction.[401] Another explanation, arguably more plausible, is that Article 3168 CCQ exists simply to protect Canadian judgment debtors.[402]

A few scholars noted Article 3168(3°) CCQ's overly restrictive approach of requiring that the entire cause of action had arisen in the foreign state,[403] but the provision did not spark major debates in the literature or the case law.

[393] CCQ (n 179), Arts 3155(1°), 3168; *Barer v Knight Brothers LLC* 2019 SCC 13 [23]–[35]; *Canada Post Corp v Lépine* 2009 SCC 16 [24]–[26].

[394] *Barer* (n 393) [34], [45].

[395] CCQ (n 179), Art 3168(3°).

[396] ibid, Art 3148, para 1(3°). For further discussion on the direct jurisdiction of Quebec courts under Art 3148, para 1(3°) CCQ, see section 2.II.A.i.a above.

[397] *Iraq (State of) c Heerema Zwijndrecht, bv* 2013 QCCA 1112 [18]–[20]; *Labs of Virginia Inc c Clintrials Bioresearch Ltd* [2003] RJQ 1876, 1879–81 (Qc Sup Ct).

[398] *Canada Post* (n 393) [28]–[37].

[399] *Spar Aerospace* (n 182) [57].

[400] G Goldstein, *Droit international privé*, vol 2: Compétence internationale des autorités québécoises et effets des décisions étrangères (Cowansville, Yvon Blais, 2013) para 3168.555.

[401] *Canada Post* (n 393) [30]–[33]; *Hocking c Haziza* 2008 QCCA 800 [174]–[178] (Bich JA, concurring).

[402] C Emanuelli, *Droit international privé québécois*, 3rd edn (Montreal, Wilson & Lafleur, 2011) para 290.

[403] G Goldstein and E Groffier, *Droit international privé*, vol 1: Théorie générale (Cowansville, Yvon Blais, 1998) para 181.

Its restrictive approach is not unprecedented. The 1971 Convention on the Recognition and Enforcement of Foreign Judgments in Civil and Commercial Matters established indirect jurisdiction when the facts leading to the injury had occurred in the foreign state *and* the author was there at the time.[404] The 2019 Convention on the Recognition and Enforcement of Foreign Judgments now takes a similar approach for non-contractual obligations.[405] The Convention frames indirect jurisdiction differently than in the CCQ, but like the latter, the Convention does not recognise jurisdiction at the place of injury alone, that is, when the defendant acted elsewhere (in cases involving product liability or transboundary pollution, for instance).[406] The Convention does not, however, displace the other grounds of indirect jurisdiction available in the domestic law of a member state, except when rights *in rem* in immovable property are at stake.[407] This means that a judgment rendered at the place of injury could be enforced elsewhere if the law of the enforcing court contemplates such possibility. At the time of writing, only a few states had signed the Convention, and its impact on the domestic law of foreign judgments around the world remains to be seen.

Quebec courts have developed innovative workarounds to enforce foreign judgments even if a tort is not easily located in a single place. In *Jules Jordan Video*, a California adult film production company and its sole shareholder sought to enforce in Quebec a judgment in damages for infringement of its intellectual property. The Quebec defendants had distributed counterfeited copies of the plaintiffs' work in California. Justice Gouin of the Quebec Superior Court found that California courts had jurisdiction over the dispute because the defendants ought to have been aware that the copies would end up in California, even though they had sold them through an intermediary. As a result, the fault (the sale of the copies) and the resulting injury (the harm to plaintiffs' intellectual property rights) had both occurred in California under Article 3168(3°) CCQ.[408] This is a creative interpretation of the fault, as the Court could have easily held that the fault had occurred in Quebec where all the defendants were located.

Glenn advocated a similar reasoning to circumvent the restrictive language of the CCQ, suggesting that plaintiffs frame their cause of action narrowly to make it fit entirely within the foreign jurisdiction.[409] The proposal is a throwback

[404] Convention on the Recognition and Enforcement of Foreign Judgments in Civil and Commercial Matters (1 February 1971, entered into force 20 August 1979) 1144 UNTS 249, Art 10(4).

[405] 2019 Convention on the Recognition and Enforcement of Foreign Judgments (n 39), Art 5(1)(j).

[406] P Arnt Nielsen, 'The Hague 2019 Judgments Convention: From Failure to Success?' (2020) 16 *Journal of Private International Law* 205, 220–21; J Blom, 'The *Court Jurisdiction and Proceedings Transfer Act* and the Hague Conference's Judgments and Jurisdiction Projects' (2018) 55 *Osgoode Hall Law Journal* 257, 283.

[407] 2019 Convention on the Recognition and Enforcement of Foreign Judgments (n 39), Art 15.

[408] *Jules Jordan Video Inc c 144942 Canada Inc* 2014 QCCS 3343 [54]–[71].

[409] HP Glenn, 'Recognition of Foreign Judgments in Quebec' (1997) 28 *Canadian Business Law Journal* 404, 410; HP Glenn, 'Droit international privé' in Barreau du Québec and Chambre des notaires (eds), *La réforme du Code civil*, vol 3 (Quebec, Presses de l'Université Laval, 1993) 777. See also *Cortas Canning & Refrigerating Company c Suidan Bros Inc* [1999] RJQ 1227, 1232–33 (Qc Sup Ct).

to a pre-CCQ era when Quebec courts could only assert jurisdiction if the whole cause of action had arisen there.[410] In this context, the Supreme Court of Canada held that the failure to warn about the dangers of a product occurred where the warning should have been given, such that the whole cause of action (fault and injury) could arise in a single place even if the product had been designed or sold elsewhere.[411] The explanatory report to the 2019 Convention on the Recognition and Enforcement of Foreign Judgments suggests a similar workaround.[412] The rapporteurs concede in their report that according to the Convention, a judgment emanating from the place of injury cannot be enforced, for instance, against a manufacturer in the place of acting. They do suggest, however, that it might be possible if the cause of action derived instead from a failure to warn the user of the dangers of a product. Courts at the place of injury would then have indirect jurisdiction because the faulty omission occurred in the forum, in addition to the injury itself.[413]

These methods were developed with the distribution of products in mind, but they can also help plaintiffs looking to enforce foreign judgments against local polluters. Quebec courts are not bound by a foreign court's findings on jurisdiction.[414] They might find that dumping harmful substances is a continuing fault that occurred in both jurisdictions, much like the United States Court of Appeals for the Ninth Circuit concluded in *Pakootas* that the release of substances from a facility had in fact occurred entirely on American soil for CERCLA purposes, even though the polluter was based in Canada.[415] Alternatively, they might find that the fault – framed as an omission to prevent pollution – occurred entirely in the foreign jurisdiction. Finally, they might find that an 'injurious act' occurred in the foreign jurisdiction, which is another ground of indirect jurisdiction under Article 3168(3°) CCQ. The Supreme Court of Canada defines an injurious act (a term also used in Article 3148, para 1(3°)) as a 'damage-causing event that attracts no-fault liability'.[416] This is especially relevant in product liability claims because the CCQ imposes a no-fault regime on the manufacturers, distributors and suppliers of a product.[417] The same reasoning applies in environmental claims involving no-fault neighbourhood disturbance under Article 976 CCQ. Pollution could thus be characterised as an injurious act that occurred in the foreign jurisdiction because it attracts a form of no-fault liability.

[410] *E Hofmann Plastics Inc v Tribec Metals Ltd* 2013 QCCA 2112 [13]; Code of Civil Procedure, 14–15 Eliz II 1965 c 80, Art 68, para 1(2) as it appeared before 1 January 1994 (repealed).

[411] *Air Canada v Mcdonnell Douglas Corp* [1989] 1 SCR 1554, 1568–70; *Wabasso Ltd v National Drying Machinery Co* [1981] 1 SCR 578, 591–92.

[412] F Garcimartín and G Saumier, *Explanatory Report on the Convention of 2 July 2019 on the Recognition and Enforcement of Foreign Judgments in Civil or Commercial Matters* (The Hague, Hague Conference on Private International Law, 2020) paras 197–98.

[413] ibid.

[414] *Zimmermann Inc c Barer* 2016 QCCA 260 [16]–[19]; *Iraq* (n 397) [15].

[415] *Pakootas v Teck Cominco Metals Ltd* 452 F (3d) 1066, 1075 (9th Cir 2006), *certiorari* denied 552 US 1095 (2008).

[416] *Spar Aerospace* (n 182) 42.

[417] CCQ (n 179), Art 1468.

Plaintiffs going after local polluters with a foreign judgment will no doubt ask courts to be inventive in the determination of indirect jurisdiction. On the other hand, the wording of Article 3168(3°) CCQ is clear, and creatively interpreting causes of action has its limits. A positive act in state *x* (discharging contaminants into a river, for instance) that causes damage in state *y* simply does not constitute a fault committed in state *y*. If it did, it would be because a statute says so. In *Pakootas*, CERCLA's wording and logic gave the Court enough leverage to conclude (somewhat artificially) that the dispute was purely domestic. In most cases, however, Quebec courts will have no choice but to conclude that the fault and the damage did not occur in the same place. Enforcement of foreign judgments against local polluters is therefore less likely in Quebec than in other provinces (except New Brunswick in an international context[418]).

Finally, it must be noted that Article 3168(3°) CCQ may be constitutionally impermissible in an interprovincial setting. The Supreme Court of Canada held in *Morguard Investments* and *Hunt* that courts are bound to give 'full faith and credit' to judgments from other provinces, so long as there exists a real and substantial connection between the dispute and the province in which the judgment was rendered.[419] In doing so, the Court explicitly referred to the facts of *Moran* (damage suffered in a place that the defendant could have reasonably contemplated) as an example of a real and substantial connection.[420] Justice La Forest noted that 'if this Court thinks it inherently reasonable for a court to exercise jurisdiction under circumstances like those described, it would be odd indeed if it did not also consider it reasonable for the courts of another province to recognize and enforce that court's judgment'.[421] Later, in *Spar Aerospace*, the Court found that that each of the grounds listed in Article 3148, para 1(3°) CCQ (fault, injurious act, injury and contract) seemed to be an example of a real and substantial connection.[422] It follows that any criterion more stringent than a real and substantial connection (including the requirement in Article 3168(3°) CCQ that the fault *and* the injury occurred in the same province) may offend the constitutionally mandated principle of full faith and credit between provinces.[423] It may remain permissible in an international setting (that is, when the judgment comes from the courts of another state rather than another province), but it nonetheless contradicts the principle of comity among sovereign nations, a princinple which the Supreme Court of Canada has insisted upon in the context of foreign judgments.[424]

[418] For further discussion on this point, see the text accompanying n 392 above.

[419] *Hunt v T&N plc*, [1993] 4 SCR 289, 324–26; *Morguard Investments* (n 391) 1100–03.

[420] *Hunt* (n 419) 315–16; *Morguard Investments* (n 391) 1105–06.

[421] *Morguard Investments* (n 391) 1107.

[422] *Spar Aerospace* (n 182) [56].

[423] On constitutional imperatives for provincial statutes governing the enforcement of judgments from other provinces, see generally *Worthington Corp c Atlas Turner Inc* [2004] RJQ 2376, 2383–85 (Qc CA), leave to appeal to SCC refused [2005] 1 SCR xvii; G Saumier, 'The Recognition of Foreign Judgments in Quebec – The Mirror Crack'd?' (2002) 81 *Canadian Bar Review* 677, 709–13.

[424] *Chevron* SCC 2015 (n 193) [51]–[52]; *Canada Post* (n 393) [36]; *Beals* (n 391) [28]–[29].

Aside from its uncertain constitutional validity, the restrictive approach to indirect jurisdiction in Article 3168(3°) CCQ hinders prompt and adequate compensation for victims of transboundary pollution. More fundamentally, it negates the regulatory function of private international law in relation to the enforcement of foreign judgments – an important way of ensuring that transboundary polluters do not escape the gravitational pull of domestic private law after a domestic court issued its judgment. This issue in Article 3168(3°) CCQ should be addressed, by mirroring the extensive approach to direct jurisdiction adopted in Article 3148, para 1(3°) CCQ.

ii. Public Law and Public Policy Exceptions to the Enforcement of Foreign Judgments

The second issue in the context of transboundary pollution comes from two related exceptions to the enforcement of foreign judgments: foreign public law (section II.C.ii.a) and public policy (section II.C.ii.b). I address each of them in turn, followed by observations on the current state of the law (section II.C.ii.c).

a. Public Law Exception to the Enforcement of Foreign Judgments

Canadian courts traditionally refuse to enforce judgments based on foreign public laws, believing those laws to be the product of the foreign state's sovereign power within its territory. As such, no other court should enforce them. This is the infamous 'public law taboo'[425] which is particularly strong in the areas of penal[426] and tax law.[427] As Blom explains, 'It is a virtually universal feature of systems of private international law that courts will not apply foreign laws whose purpose is to levy taxes or enforce penal sanctions'.[428] The rule prohibits direct application, that is, the application of foreign penal/tax laws by local courts as a result of choice of law rules.[429] It also prohibits indirect application, that is, the enforcement of judgments based on foreign penal/tax law (the focus of this section).[430]

[425] M Lehmann, 'Regulation, Global Governance and Private International Law: Squaring the Triangle' (2020) 16 *Journal of Private International Law* 1, 6. On public law in private international law, see generally C Wasserstein Fassberg, 'The Public in Private International Law' in Y Emerich (ed), *Le public en droit privé* (Montreal, Yvon Blais, 2019); H Muir Watt (ed), *Private International Law and Public Law* (Cheltenham, Edward Elgar, 2015); WS Dodge, 'The Public-Private Distinction in the Conflict of Laws' (2008) 18 *Duke Journal of Comparative and International Law* 371; William S Dodge, 'Breaking the Public Law Taboo' (2002) 43 *Harvard International Law Journal* 161.

[426] *Pro Swing* (n 388) [34]; *Laane & Baltser v Estonian SS Line* [1949] SCR 530, 542; *Huntington v Attrill* (1892) [1893] AC 150, 157 (PC).

[427] CCQ (n 179), Art 3155(6°); *United States of America v Harden* [1963] SCR 366, 369–71; *Government of India v Taylor*, [1955] AC 491, 503–504 (HL).

[428] J Blom, 'Public Policy in Private International Law and Its Evolution in Time' (2003) 50 *Netherlands International Law Review* 373, 378.

[429] On the public law exception in the choice of law context, see section 4.II.B.i.a below.

[430] See generally FD Strebel, 'The Enforcement of Foreign Judgments and Foreign Public Law' (1999) 21 *Loyola of Los Angeles International and Comparative Law Journal* 55.

Penal and tax laws are the two most commonly accepted categories within the public law exception. Some cases, however, suggest a third, residuary category of foreign public laws which cannot be enforced in local courts, either directly or indirectly.[431] This third category of 'other public laws' is less clearly established than the other two,[432] but leading English[433] and Anglo-Canadian[434] texts discuss it. The precise contents of the public law exception have attracted much debate over the years, including with respect to non-penal/tax laws. Is there a third category of unenforceable foreign public laws? Does it cover all public laws and if so, on what basis? The existence and scope of the public law exception have significant implications for transboundary environmental disputes because plaintiffs often rely on statutory causes of action to pursue their claims. Declaring all foreign public law unenforceable could lead to an outright denial of justice for plaintiffs who seek to rely on foreign public law or to enforce a judgment based on foreign public law against the defendant's assets elsewhere.

The Ontario Court of Appeal put an end to the uncertainty surrounding the public law exception in *Ivey*.[435] American authorities had obtained judgments in Michigan under CERCLA, a federal statute governing liability for sites contaminated with hazardous substances (and their cleanup).[436] The judgments ordered the reimbursement of the clean-up costs incurred by the EPA on a waste disposal site operated by Liquid Disposal. Authorities then sought to enforce those judgments in Ontario against Liquid Disposal's shareholders and officers domiciled in the province. The defendants resisted enforcement and argued that the basis of the Michigan judgments was a foreign public law.

In first instance, Justice Sharpe (then a trial judge, now sitting on the Ontario Court of Appeal) found that CERCLA was neither penal nor fiscal: it simply pertained to the reimbursement of costs already incurred and was therefore compensatory in nature.[437] Justice Sharpe recognised the existence of a third

[431] *United States of America v Inkley* (1988) [1989] QB 255, 264–65; *R v Governor of Pentonville Prison, ex parte Budlong* (1979) [1980] 1 All ER 701, 714 (QB); *Attorney-General of New Zealand v Ortiz* (1982) [1984] AC 1, 20–24 (CA) (Lord Denning), affd (1983) [1984] AC 1 HL 35. See also *Attorney-General (UK) v Heinemann Publishers Australia Pty Ltd* [1988] HCA 25.

[432] International Committee on Transnational Recognition and Enforcement of Foreign Public Laws, 'Report' in International Law Association Report of the Sixty-Third Conference (Warsaw, 1988) 755–56 (concluding that 'there probably is not, and certainly should not be, any rule of general application requiring rejection of so-called foreign public laws').

[433] eg P Torremans et al, *Cheshire, North & Fawcett: Private International Law*, 15th edn (Oxford, Oxford University Press, 2017) 123–25, 552–53; L Collins and J Harris (eds), *Dicey, Morris & Collins on the Conflict of Laws*, vol 1, 15th edn (London, Sweet & Maxwell, 2012) paras 5.032–42.

[434] Pitel and Rafferty (n 210) 39–41; Walker, vol 1 (n 255) § 8.5, 14.7.

[435] *United States of America v Ivey* (1996) 30 OR (3d) 370 (Ont CA), leave to appeal to SCC refused [1997] 2 SCR x.

[436] CERCLA (n 59).

[437] *United States of America v Ivey* (1995) 26 OR (3d) 533, 544–45 (Ont Gen Div), affd (1996) 30 OR (3d) 370 (Ont CA), leave to appeal to SCC refused, [1997] 2 SCR x.

category of other public laws but criticised its 'rather shaky foundation' and held that it did not preclude the enforcement of the Michigan judgments.[438] The enforcement of CERCLA judgments, he said, did not impinge on Canadian sovereignty. Public environmental statutes supplement the common law and help impose liability on polluters. Pecluding their enforcement beyond borders would defeat that purpose:

> Legislatures have determined that the complex issues of environmental protection and determination of liability for environmental harms require the positive intervention of the state. Common law actions brought by private parties who have suffered individual harm have been found wanting. The issues of liability for [cleanup] and remedial costs are dealt with awkwardly, if at all, in litigation between private parties, and most jurisdictions, including Ontario, have established regulatory regimes which encompass the imposition of civil liability for such costs. In this light, it is difficult to see the rationale for this court to refuse enforcement on the grounds that the efforts of the plaintiff to recover the costs it has incurred to remedy the environmental problems at the [Liquid Disposal] site represent an illegitimate attempt to assert sovereignty beyond its borders.[439]

The Ontario Court of Appeal upheld Justice Sharpe's judgment. The Court recalled that many jurisdictions had similar statutory regimes and that comity supported their mutual enforcement.[440]

The same should apply in Quebec, except that it is unclear whether the public law exception applies at all. The CCQ only expressly precludes the enforcement of foreign tax judgments coming from provinces and states that do not recognise Quebec tax laws.[441] It does not refer to a wider category of unenforceable foreign judgments based on public law.[442] If the public law exception does apply, *Ivey*'s logic should too.[443]

Overall, the *Ivey* case significantly reduced the scope of the public law exception in Canada, without closing the door to it completely.[444] Courts now refuse to enforce foreign public law only when it reflects the assertion of a true sovereign power, not simply because the plaintiff is a foreign state or related entity.[445] This is consistent with recent English authorities holding that not all foreign public laws are unenforceable, only those involving

[438] ibid 548.
[439] ibid 549.
[440] *Ivey* ONCA (n 435) 374.
[441] CCQ (n 179), Arts 3155(6°), 3162.
[442] Quebec courts, however, will not enforce penal judgments: *Groupe SNC-Lavalin Inc c Siegrist* 2020 QCCA 1004 [85]; C Emanuelli, 'Recognition and Enforcement of Foreign Judgments in Quebec' (2007) 9 *Yearbook of Private International Law* 343, 352.
[443] J Talpis, *'If I Am from Grand-Mère, Why Am I Being Sued in Texas?' Responding to Inappropriate Foreign Jurisdiction in Quebec-United States Crossborder Litigation* (Montreal, Thémis, 2001) 168–70.
[444] *Ivey* ONCA (n 435) 374.
[445] *Bienstock v Adenyo Inc* 2014 ONSC 4997 [12], affd 2015 ONCA 310.

sovereign rights.[446] It also aligns with the HCCH's Convention on the Recognition and Enforcement of Foreign Judgments, which specifically provides that a judgment is not excluded from the scope of the Convention simply because a state was party to the proceedings, as long as the judgment pertains to civil or commercial matters (and does not concern revenue, customs or administrative matters in particular).[447]

b. Public Policy Exception to the Enforcement of Foreign Judgments

Canadian courts can also refuse to enforce foreign judgments on the basis of public policy. The common law precludes the enforcement of foreign judgments that shock basic morality.[448] The CCQ precludes the enforcement of foreign judgments leading to a result manifestly inconsistent with 'public order as understood in international relations'.[449] The public policy exception seldom (if ever) applies in interprovincial cases,[450] and it is narrowly construed even in international cases, preserving only the most basic moral tenets of our society. As the Supreme Court of Canada put it, 'The public policy defence turns on whether the foreign law is contrary to our view of basic morality. … It would, for example, prohibit the enforcement of a foreign judgment that is founded on a law contrary to the fundamental morality of the Canadian legal system'.[451] Later, in a case involving the CCQ, the Court explained that 'a foreign decision will not be recognized if its outcome runs counter to the moral, social, economic or even political conceptions that underpin Quebec's legal order'.[452]

The public policy exception is distinct but closely related to the public law exception.[453] Both aim to protect the state against the enforcement of certain

[446] *United States Securities and Exchange Commission v Manterfield* [2009] EWCA Civ 27 [24]; *Islamic Republic of Iran v The Barakat Galleries Ltd* [2007] EWCA Civ 1374 [125]; *Mbasogo v Logo Ltd* [2006] EWCA Civ 1370 [50].

[447] 2019 Convention on the Recognition and Enforcement of Foreign Judgments (n 39), Arts 1(1), 2(4). See generally PR Beaumont, 'Judgments Convention: Application to Governments' (2020) 67 *Netherlands International Law Review* 121, 125–27.

[448] *Beals* (n 391) [71]–[77]. See also New Brunswick Foreign Judgments Act (n 392), ss 5(h)–5(i); Saskatchewan Foreign Judgments Act (n 392), s 4(g).

[449] CCQ (n 179), Art 3155(5°).

[450] *Tolofson v Jensen* [1994] 3 SCR 1022, 1055 (in the choice of law context). Some of the provincial statutes governing the enforcement of judgments within Canada do contain a public policy exception: see eg Enforcement of Canadian Judgments and Decrees Act, SBC 2003 c 29, s 6(2)(c)(iv).

[451] *Beals* (n 391) [71]–[72]. See also *Society of Lloyd's v Saunders* (2001) 55 OR (3d) 688, 718 (Ont CA), leave to appeal to SCC refused [2002] 2 SCR ix; *Boardwalk Regency Corp v Maalouf* (1992) 6 OR (3d) 737, 743 (Ont CA).

[452] *RS v PR* 2019 SCC 49 [53]. See also *AMBC Ventures Inc c Awanda* 2021 QCCS 543 [46]–[62], motion to dismiss the appeal dismissed 2021 QCCA 789; *Mutual Trust Co c St-Cyr* [1996] RDJ 623, 625 (Qc CA), leave to appeal to SCC refused [1997] 2 SCR xv; *Auerbach c Resorts International Hotel Inc* (1991) [1992] RJQ 302, 306 (Qc CA).

[453] *Gulf Oil Corporation v Gulf Canada Ltd* [1980] 2 SCR 39, 62.

foreign laws that are deemed incompatible with its own orientations. The public law exception simply focuses on certain categories of foreign laws while the public policy exception focuses on the result of their application.[454]

Litigants have invoked the public policy exception only on a few occasions in relation to foreign environmental statutes (all of which arose in common law provinces). In *Ivey*, the defendants pleaded that CERCLA offended public policy because it suffered from several substantive and procedural defects that Canadian courts should not condone. After having rejected the application of the public law exception, Justice Sharpe addressed the public policy exception. He recalled that mere inconsistencies between the law of the forum and the law applied by the foreign court do not suffice to prevent the enforcement of a foreign judgment. Fundamental values of the forum must be at stake. Justice Sharpe ultimately rejected the defendants' argument that CERCLA was too severe to be enforced in Canada. He found that 'While the measures chosen by our legislature do not correspond precisely with those chosen by the Congress of the United States, they are sufficiently similar in nature to defeat any possible application of the public policy defence'.[455] The Ontario Court of Appeal did not address the issue.[456]

In *Shield Development*, the Ontario Superior Court of Justice recognised another American judgment based on CERCLA, again rejecting the argument that it offended public policy.[457] Defendants pleaded among other things that the EPA had breached public policy when it chose not to sue the true perpetrator of environmental damage in the United States (an American company) and went after its Canadian shareholders and officers instead. Justice Herman adhered to *Ivey*. She reiterated that the differences between Canadian and American environmental laws were not significant enough to trigger the public policy exception.[458] She also held that the public policy exception was not concerned with the way in which the EPA enforced CERCLA.[459] The Ontario Court of Appeal upheld her findings in a brief judgment.[460]

Finally, in *Chevron*, the Ontario Superior Court of Justice held that Ecuador's retroactive environmental legislation did not offend Canadians' basic morality. Justice Hainey struck out Chevron's statement of defence on this point, partly prohibiting it from invoking public policy to resist the enforcement of an Ecuadorian judgment awarding billions of dollars in compensation for environmental damage.[461] Justice Hainey, however, refused to strike out many of

[454] Blom, 'Public Policy in Private International Law' (2003) 379.

[455] *Ivey* Ont Gen Div (n 437) 554.

[456] *Ivey* ONCA (n 435).

[457] *United States of America v Shield Development Co* (2004) 74 OR (3d) 583 (Ont Sup Ct), affd (2005) 74 OR (3d) 595 (Ont CA).

[458] ibid 593–94.

[459] ibid 594.

[460] *United States of America v Shield Development Co* (2005) 74 OR (3d) 595 (Ont CA).

[461] *Yaiguaje v Chevron Corporation* 2017 ONSC 135 [108]–[112], leave to appeal to Ont Div Ct refused 2017 ONSC 2251.

Chevron's other defences, and the Ontario Court of Appeal ultimately denied enforcement in the province on the basis of the corporate veil.[462]

One point remains unanswered in the above cases. Does an administrative authorisation issued under Canadian law suffice to preclude the enforcement of a foreign judgment on public policy grounds? The question did not arise in *Ivey*, *Shield Development* and *Chevron* because the defendants did not operate on Canadian soil. They were all somehow connected to the polluting activity in the foreign state, but only through their alleged corporate affiliations. *Pakootas*, by contrast, raises a different issue. Suppose that American courts seek to enforce a judgment against Teck Cominco in British Columbia: would Teck Cominco be able to invoke public policy on the basis that Canada allows the company to operate on its territory, and even has an economic interest in doing so?[463] Arguably, it would go against the duty to ensure prompt and adequate compensation for the courts of the state of origin to refuse to enforce a judgment from the courts of an affected state against a defendant operating in the forum under official authorisation. Such judgment does not offend basic morality, nor does it create unacceptable differences with Canadian law, which rarely shields a licensed polluter from all liability anyway.[464]

Overall, the public policy exception remains extremely narrow and is unlikely to have a major impact on environmental protection in one sense or the other. In the current state of the law, there is little room for defendants to frame public policy arguments when they are found liable under foreign environmental statutes and targeted for enforcement in Canada. A court could conceivably refuse to enforce a foreign judgment against a local polluter when the result is severe and particularly prejudicial to the economic interests of the forum, but it is unclear how this would fit within the current definition of the public law/public policy exceptions.[465] There seems to be no such precedent in Canadian law.

c. *Ivey*'s implications

Ivey and its progeny make it clear that judgments based on foreign environmental statutes which impose civil liability do not fall within the foreign public law exception to the enforcement of foreign judgments. Nor do they offend public

[462] *Chevron* ONCA 2018 (n 387).

[463] cf J Walker, '*Teck Cominco* and the Wisdom of Deferring to the Court First Seised, All Things Being Equal' (2009) 47 *Canadian Business Law Journal* 192, 202 (noting that 'In fact, to the extent that the Washington proceeding was understood as a claim that was initiated to give effect to a foreign public law, the resulting judgment might be regarded as unenforceable in Canada on that basis').

[464] C von Bar, 'Environmental Damage in Private International Law' (1997) 268 *Recueil des cours de l'Académie de droit international* 291, 353. On the relationship between civil liability and regulatory/statutory compliance in Canadian law, see the sources cited below n 302 (ch 4).

[465] But see Kruger (n 18) 117.

policy simply because they differ from Canadian law. Major divergences may lead to a different result, but this has yet to be seen in the case law.

Ivey represents an important judicial stance in favour of cross-border environmental cooperation. As the Supreme Court of Canada recalled in *Chevron*, 'Comity … militates in favour of recognition and enforcement. Legitimate judicial acts should be respected and enforced, not sidetracked or ignored'.[466] To be sure, the fact that the United States (and not some other state) were involved undoubtedly coloured the dispute in *Ivey*. Canadian courts stress the importance of facilitating commercial relationships with its neighbour.[467] Justice Sharpe himself declared that it was particularly appropriate for Canadian courts to recognise the environmental laws and judgments of their neighbours.[468] Cross-border environmental cooperation has particular importance in a closely integrated and interdependent region such as the Great Lakes. On the other hand, Ontario courts might not have praised cooperation so readily if the foreign judgment had come from a state with very different environmental laws, or if foreign authorities had targeted a company operating in Canada (such as Teck Cominco) as opposed to Canadian shareholders and officers of a company operating in the United States. Different circumstances could have led to a different result.

Despite this particular context, *Ivey* teaches important lessons. It shows that courts are aware of the problems associated with transboundary pollution and of the role of private international law – specifically, in this case, the rules governing the enforcement of foreign judgments – in ensuring compensation or protecting the environment. *Ivey* also illustrates how private international law achieves its regulatory function by acknowledging the public implications of private environmental disputes and rejecting an overly broad interpretation of the public law exception. In *Ivey*, a liberal interpretation of the rules governing the enforcement of foreign judgments, driven by the substantive objective of holding polluters liable for cleanup costs, contributed to a plaintiff-initiated form of transnational regulation. The regulation theory confirms this reading of *Ivey*, in particular Wai's assertion that a more permissive enforcement of foreign public law would help fill regulatory gaps by relying on domestic legal regimes.[469] It is possible that *Ivey* would have unfolded differently if the United States had not been involved, but there is no principled reason as to why it would have, unless public policy was at stake.

[466] *Chevron* SCC 2015 (n 193) [53].

[467] *Molson Coors Brewing Co v Miller Brewing Co* (2006) 83 OR (3d) 331, 340 (Ont Sup Ct).

[468] *Ivey* Ont Gen Div (n 437) 549.

[469] R Wai, 'Transnational Liftoff and Juridical Touchdown: The Regulatory Function of Private International Law in a Global Age' (2002) 40 *Columbia Journal of Transnational Law* 209, 270.

III. CONCLUSION

In this chapter, I identified the jurisdictional requirements associated with the duty to ensure prompt and adequate compensation and explained how they have been implemented in Canada. International environmental law has focused primarily on non-discrimination and equal access. The ILC viewed those notions as a palatable lifeline for its project and chose to sacrifice larger ambitions. Optimists will nonetheless celebrate their consecration in the ILC Principles on the Allocation of Loss after decades of efforts. Cynics, on the other hand, will observe that equal access is a low common denominator that works well in regional settings but fails to live up to the expectations on a larger scale. Both sides raise good points. On the one hand, the international recognition of equal access facilitates its dissemination and brings attention to the procedural challenges faced by victims of transboundary pollution. Equal access also gives concrete meaning to the duty to ensure prompt and adequate compensation. On the other hand, it is important to recognise the limited impact of equal access in practice. Legal reform has proven difficult even in a closely integrated area such as North America. Neither the International Boundary Waters Treaty Act, the Draft Treaty on Equal Access and Remedy, the Reciprocal Access Act nor the NAAEC made it significantly easier or faster for victims to obtain compensation through private litigation. They are a stark reminder that even the most enthusiastic legal projects can quickly fall into oblivion. And as the 13 years of preliminary procedures in the *Pembina County Water Resource District* show, equal access itself can lead to long judicial debates if the legal provision is ambiguous.

But this is not the point. We must go beyond the pros and cons of equal access and ask whether the general law of jurisdiction can respond to the same concerns that prompted Scandinavian countries and the OECD to act in the 1970s. This chapter shows that the Canadian law of jurisdiction generally aligns with the duty to ensure prompt and adequate compensation. Compelling arguments support the assertion of jurisdiction whether Canada is the state of origin or the affected state. This is equal access in its essence (jurisdiction in the state of origin for all victims) and beyond (jurisdiction in the affected state). The argument has particular strength in North America, but courts have no reason to react differently when other states are involved unless the connections with the forum are excessively remote. The law of foreign judgments is also generally compatible with the availability of prompt and adequate compensation from a Canadian polluter, except in Quebec and New Brunswick where statutory provisions may deny enforcement of a judgment issued by a court that asserted jurisdiction on the sole basis of an injury suffered in the forum.

Scholars often take for granted that transboundary pollution causes insoluble jurisdictional problems. There are several reasons for the prevalence of the obstacle theory: obsolete assessments of the law replicated in subsequent scholarship, old precedents repeated as mantras, scarcity of judgments on the merits upon which to extrapolate, etc. Together, they lead to a bleak conclusion: private international law deprives plaintiffs of a chance to try their case on the merits. The analysis in this chapter shows the contrary – not because of some specific environmental legal instrument, but by paying attention to the connections between international environmental law and our usual way of dealing with conflicts of jurisdiction.

Justice Sharpe's reasons in *Ivey* show that developing an environmental sensitivity in private international law is entirely feasible. His judgment is a concrete example of how the regulatory function of private international law plays out in practice, under the guise of seemingly technical rules of private international law. In the context of the recognition and enforcement of foreign judgments, *Ivey* might simply promote deference to the legitimate environmental policy of a foreign state – a common concern in modern private international law. But there is nothing illegitimate in seeking to align private international law with the *international* objective of ensuring prompt and adequate compensation of environmental damage if that is the choice we want to make. Ultimately, understanding how and why equal access and non-discrimination have become key aspects of international environmental law allows us to take a better and more informed look at private international law and its regulatory function. This is precisely what the ILC asked states to do in order to discharge their duty to ensure prompt and adequate compensation.

4

The Law Applicable to Transboundary Pollution

THIS FOURTH CHAPTER focuses on the choice of law aspects of the duty to ensure prompt and adequate compensation. After having established their jurisdiction over a transboundary environmental dispute, courts must identify the law (local or foreign) used to determine civil liability. If pollution originates in state *x* but victims suffered damage in state *y*, courts have to identify which law applies (the applicable law or *lex causae*): the law of the state of origin, the law of the affected state, or another law such as the law of the place where the defendant is domiciled. This chapter argues that Canadian law does not meet the choice of law requirements associated with the duty to ensure prompt and adequate compensation.

We have seen so far that appropriate jurisdictional rules can effectively achieve equal access to courts for local and foreign plaintiffs, a paramount concern in the ILC Principles on the Allocation of Loss. Jurisdictional rules have substantive implications because they are the first step towards a trial on the merits. They perform a regulatory function insofar as they allow for regulatory oversight by private parties in domestic courts.[1] Equal access (or its functional equivalent through the application of jurisdictional rules), however, does not determine whether to hold a polluter liable, nor does it affect the overall level of environmental protection. This comes down to the contents of the applicable law, selected through choice of law rules. Choice of law has an obvious regulatory impact because the promises of liability – including compensation, deterrence and environmental protection – hinge on the substantive law that governs a dispute.[2] Private international law goes some way to fulfilling these promises when it directs the application of a law that allows victims to obtain compensation or favours environmental protection. The regulation theory suggests that imbuing choice of law rules with this substantive orientation is not parochial (that is, serving only the interests of the forum), but internationalist in the sense that it responds to a global concern for the regulation of transnational actors.[3]

[1] R Wai, 'Transnational Liftoff and Juridical Touchdown: The Regulatory Function of Private International Law in a Global Age' (2002) 40 *Columbia Journal of Transnational Law* 209.

[2] J Ebbesson, 'Piercing the State Veil in Pursuit of Environmental Justice' in J Ebbesson and P Okowa (eds), *Environmental Law and Justice in Context* (Cambridge, Cambridge University Press, 2009) 282.

[3] ibid. In the context of environmental law, see U Grušić, 'International Environmental Litigation in EU Courts: A Regulatory Perspective' (2016) 35 *Yearbook of European Law* 180, 186–93.

Chapter three concluded that the Canadian law of jurisdiction meets the requirements of the ILC Principles on the Allocation of Loss and raises no significant obstacle to prompt and adequate compensation. The obstacle theory is unwarranted in that context because local and foreign victims of transboundary pollution both have satisfactory access to Canadian courts. Choice of law calls for a different conclusion.

As we will see, the duty to ensure prompt and adequate compensation entails equal remedy for all victims of transboundary pollution – in other words, that foreign victims of transboundary pollution receive at least the same treatment as victims in the state of origin. Choice of law rules play a fundamental role in this context because they determine which substantive law applies to the claims of foreign victims, and therefore whether they have the same rights as local victims. The duty to ensure prompt and adequate compensation also entails, evidently, that victims have a chance to obtain compensation. Again, choice of law rules play a fundamental role in this context.

Canadian courts apply in most cases the law of the place of the tort (*lex loci delicti*), understood as the law of the place where the wrongful activity occurred. This is an appropriate choice of law rule for torts, particularly when they occur in a single place, but its interpretation causes problems in relation to transboundary pollution because the fault and the injury occur in different states. This makes it difficult to locate environmental torts in one place or the other for choice of law purposes. Unlike jurisdictional rules, however, the *lex loci delicti* forces a determination because only a single law can apply to the dispute. The tort must occur at the place of acting *or* the place of injury, or else the *lex loci delicti* remains indeterminate.

There is considerable uncertainty in Canadian law over which of the two laws applies to transboundary pollution. More importantly, applying one or the other in all cases does not necessarily advance equal remedy nor prompt and adequate compensation. Applying the law of the place of injury in all cases is not satisfactory if foreign victims receive a lesser treatment than local victims because the law of the place of acting is more favourable than the law of the place of injury. Victims do not receive equal treatment unless they can all rely on the law of the place of acting. But applying the law of the place of acting in all cases is not satisfactory either if it prevents compensation for all victims.

The HCCH, the ILA and UNEP responded to concerns surrounding the rigid definition of the *lex loci delicti* and recommended the ubiquity principle as the preferred approach. The ubiquity principle posits that the law of the place of acting and the law of the place of injury can equally apply in transboundary environmental disputes. As we will see, the rule treats victims differently in certain scenarios, but it removes incentives for polluters to externalise the consequences of their activities to jurisdictions with low environmental standards. It can also increase the level of protection for some victims instead of lowering the bar for all. The ubiquity principle is increasingly accepted as an appropriate choice of law rule for transboundary pollution, including in EU law and in the Swiss statute that inspired Quebec private international law. UNEP recommends its adoption in domestic liability regimes.

For the reasons set out below, the ubiquity principle would significantly improve Canada's current approach to choice of law in transbounary environmental disputes, particularly in light of equal remedy and the duty to ensure prompt and adequate compensation. Its benefits outweigh its disadvantages. In an ideal scenario, an environment-specific statute would entrench the ubiquity principle into Canadian private international law (both in Quebec and in common law provinces). Courts in common law provinces could also rely on the inherent flexibility of choice of law rules to interpret them in a victim or environment-friendly way. In this alternative scenario, courts would find that transboundary environmental torts have sufficient connections with the place of acting and the place of injury. They would conclude that plaintiffs can elect the law of either place as the *lex loci delicti*.

This chapter proceeds in the same sequence as the previous chapter – distilling key concepts of international environmental law and identifying a standard to assess whether and how Canadian law helps ensure prompt and adequate compensation with respect to the choice of law process (and where it can go from there). I first explore the relationship between choice of law and prompt and adequate compensation through the fundamental concepts set out in the ILC Principles on the Allocation of Loss and other international projects, chiefly non-discrimination, equal remedy and the ubiquity principle (section I). Taking a step back, I review the current choice of law framework against the duty to ensure prompt and adequate compensation, arguing that Canadian choice of law rules cannot always ensure equal remedy and prompt and adequate compensation for victims of transboundary pollution. Specific legislative reforms or innovative judicial interpretations are required (section II). I conclude with final remarks (section III).

Note that this chapter focuses on the substantive aspects of transboundary environmental disputes such as the liability of polluters and the remedies available. These aspects are governed either by local law or foreign law, depending on the operation of the rules examined below. Other important aspects of transboundary environmental disputes, such as the availability of injunctive relief or the quantification of damages, may be characterised as procedural (although it may not always be possible to separate the substantive and procedural aspects of an environmental cause of action for choice of law purposes, when the same environmental statute provides for both). Procedural matters are invariably governed by local law[4] and are therefore not addressed here.

[4] Civil Code of Quebec CQLR c CCQ-1991 (CCQ), Art 3132; *Tolofson v Jensen* [1994] 3 SCR 1022, 1067.

I. INTERNATIONAL ENVIRONMENTAL LAW AND THE APPROACH OF THE ILC

This section identifies what the duty to ensure prompt and adequate compensation entails in terms of choice of law. Lefeber briefly made this connection when he suggested that choice of law had to 'offe[r] protection to victims, minimiz[e] uncertainty for the defendant, and discourag[e] forum shopping'.[5] The connection requires further investigation in light of the subsequent development of the duty to ensure prompt and adequate compensation.

I begin this section with an overview of the ILC's position expressed in the ILC Principles on the Allocation of Loss (section I.A). I investigate the notion of equal remedy (section I.B) and explain how Canada has formally incorporated that notion into domestic law (section I.C). Like equal access, equal remedy is a feature of Canada–United States relations, but it remains limited even in that setting, and general choice of law rules will apply in most cases. With this conclusion in mind, I return to the ILC Principles on the Allocation of Loss and identify a preferable choice of law rule beyond the minimal requirements of equal remedy (section I.D).

A. Choice of Law in the ILC Principles on the Allocation of Loss

The ILC Principles on the Allocation of Loss do not prescribe a particular approach for identifying the applicable law. Choice of law fills up only five lines and one footnote of the Commentary to the ILC Principles on the Allocation of Loss, in which the ILC simply acknowledges that 'State practice is not uniform: different jurisdictions have adopted either the law that is most favourable to the victim or the law of the place which has the most significant relationship with the event and the parties'.[6]

The treatment of cross-border torts indeed varies immensely among states. Current practice includes the law of the place of the tort (place of acting, place of injury or both), the most favourable law or the law with the closest relationship to the dispute.[7] This is a debate as old as private international law itself, nearly impossible to solve in the abstract. One could easily forgive the ILC for avoiding an issue that lies outside its primary area of expertise. At the same time, the ILC's laconism contrasts with its approach towards jurisdiction.

[5] R Lefeber, *Transboundary Environmental Interference and the Origin of State Liability* (The Hague, Kluwer Law International, 1996) 266.

[6] International Law Commission, 'Report of the Commission to the General Assembly on the work of its fifty-eight session' UN Doc A/61/10 (2006) in *Yearbook of the International Law Commission 2006*, vol 2, part 2 (New York, UN, 2013) ('Commentary to the ILC Principles on the Allocation of Loss') 87, para 9.

[7] See generally T Kadner Graziano, 'Torts' in J Basedow et al (eds), *Encyclopedia of Private International Law*, vol 2 (Cheltenham, Edward Elgar, 2017).

The ILC articulated the sixth principle on domestic remedies with a clear concern for access to justice and civil jurisdiction.[8] It did not take a clear stance in favour of the European approach of letting the victim choose between courts at the place of acting or at the place of injury, but it expressly noted the ILA's conclusion that this represented a 'firmly established' trend.[9] In this sense, the ILC took position and contributed to the development of private international law, which its peripheral mandate allows.[10] When it came to the choice of law problem, the ILC simply called for further harmonisation.

This restraint is unfortunate because choice of law is central to the philosophy underlying the ILC Principles on the Allocation of Loss. Some civil liability treaties provide that the law of the forum will govern any issue left unaddressed by the treaty itself.[11] This rule is understandable because the point of civil liability treaties is to comprehensively harmonise domestic law in order to avoid conflicts altogether. The same law applies wherever plaintiffs bring their case, and choice of law rules will only be useful to fill in any possible gaps in the treaty.[12] The ILC Principles on the Allocation of Loss, by contrast, emerged in the midst of treaty failure. The ILC understood that substantive harmonisation

[8] Principles on the allocation of loss in the case of transboundary harm arising out of hazardous activities, annexed to GA Res 61/36 (4 December 2006) UN Doc A/RES/61/36 ('ILC Principles on the Allocation of Loss') principle 6.

[9] Commentary to the ILC Principles on the Allocation of Loss (n 6) 87, para 8, citing Committee on Transnational Enforcement of Environmental Law, 'Second Report' in International Law Association Report of the Seventy-First Conference (Berlin, 2004) ('Second Report on Transnational Enforcement of Environmental Law') 899. See also Committee on Transnational Enforcement of Environmental Law, 'Final Report' in International Law Association Report of the Seventy-Second Conference (Toronto, 2006) ('Final Report on Transnational Enforcement of Environmental Law') 664–68.

[10] Statute of the International Law Commission, GA Res 174 (II) (21 November 1947) UN Doc A/519 ('Statute of the ILC'), Art 1(2). But see D French and LJ Kotzé, '"Towards a Global Pact for the Environment": International Environmental Law's Factual, Technical and (Unmentionable) Normative Gaps' (2019) 28 *Review of European, Comparative and International Environmental Law* 25, 29, fn 32 (noting that 'It is debatable how far [the allocation of loss in domestic regimes, ed] is a matter of international law (in contradistinction to domestic (or private international) law), and, more specifically, how far public international law can – or has so far provided detailed rules necessary to – prescribe the result').

[11] Protocol on Civil Liability and Compensation for Damage Resulting from Transboundary Movements of Hazardous Waste (10 December 1999, not yet in force) UN Doc UNEP/CHW.5/29 Annex III ('Basel Liability Protocol'), Art 19; Convention on Supplementary Compensation for Nuclear Damage (12 September 1997, entered into force 15 April 2015) 36 ILM 1454 (CSC), Arts I(k), XIV(2); Convention on Civil Liability for Nuclear Damage (21 May 1963, entered into force 12 November 1977) 1063 UNTS 265 ('Vienna Convention'), Arts I(e), VIII; Convention on the Liability of the Operators of Nuclear Ships (25 May 1962, not yet in force) 57 *American Journal of International Law* 268 ('Nuclear Ships Convention'), Art I(12); Convention on Third Party Liability in the Field of Nuclear Energy (29 July 1960, entered into force 1 April 1968) 956 UNTS 251 ('Paris Convention'), Art 14(b).

[12] CO García-Castrillón, 'International Litigation Trends in Environmental Liability: A European Union-United States Comparative Perspective' (2011) 7 *Journal of Private International Law* 551, 565–66. On the limits of uniform substantive law conventions and the persistence of forum shopping, see F Ferrari, 'Forum Shopping Despite Unification of Law' (2021) 413 *Recueil des cours de l'Académie de droit international* 13.

was unlikely. It gave the states much more latitude to implement the various aspects of the duty to ensure prompt and adequate compensation (including jurisdictional aspects) as they saw fit. It would have made sense for the ILC to offer more guidance on choice of law, precisely because it knew that regulatory diversity would persist and that the applicable law would have an impact on the availability of prompt and adequate compensation. Instead, the ILC settled for non-discrimination and equal remedy.

B. Non-Discrimination and Equal Remedy

The ILC Principles on the Allocation of Loss require that remedies available in the state of origin be at least as prompt, adequate and effective as those available in the affected state.[13] This requirement was referred to in chapter three as the equal remedy requirement, a subset of non-discrimination distinct from equal access. This language became a dominant trend in the 1970s when states were working on the law applicable to transboundary pollution from the angle of non-discrimination. The idea was to ensure that foreign victims of pollution could rely on all the remedies available in the state of origin as if they were local victims – in other words, that they were not disadvantaged when it came to the prevention and compensation of environmental damage.

The OECD, for instance, recommended that all victims be treated in a manner at least equivalent to how the state of origin treated local victims.[14] It went on to list a series of procedural requirements to achieve such equivalent treatment.[15] The Nordic Convention similarly provides that compensation should be assessed under rules that are no less favourable to victims than those of the state of origin.[16] Many of the environmental treaties,[17]

[13] ILC Principles on the Allocation of Loss (n 8) principle 6(2).

[14] OECD, Recommendation of the Council for the Implementation of a Regime of Equal Right of Access and Non-Discrimination in Relation to Transfrontier Pollution, OECD Doc C(77)28/FINAL (1977) 16 ILM 977 ('OECD Recommandation'), s 4(a), reprinted in Organisation for Economic Co-operation and Development, *Legal Aspects of Transfrontier Pollution* (Paris, OECD, 1977).

[15] ibid, s 4(b).

[16] Convention on the Protection of the Environment (19 February 1974, entered into force 5 October 1976) 1092 UNTS 279 ('Nordic Convention'), Art 3, para 2.

[17] Revised Protocol on Shared Watercourses of the Southern African Development Community (7 August 2000, entered into force 22 September 2003) 40 ILM 321 ('Revised Protocol on Shared Watercourses'), Art 3(10)(c); Convention on Access to Information, Public Participation in Decision-Making and Access to Justice in Environmental Matters (25 June 1998, entered into force 30 October 2001) 2161 UNTS 447 ('Aarhus Convention'), Art 3(9); Convention on the Law of the Non-Navigational Uses of International Watercourses (21 May 1997, entered into force 17 August 2014) 36 ILM 703 ('UN Watercourses Convention'), Art 32; Protocol for the Protection of the Mediterranean Sea Against Pollution Resulting from Exploration and Exploitation of the Continental Shelf and the Seabed and its Subsoil (14 October 1994, entered into force 24 March 2011) [2013] OJ L4/15 ('Protocol for the Protection of the Mediterranean Sea') (administrative proceedings); Treaty Relating to the Boundary Waters and Questions Arising Along the Border Between the United States and Canada ('Boundary Waters Treaty') (United Kingdom–United States) (11 January 1909, entered into force 5 May 1910) UKTS 1910 No 23, Art II, para 1.

guidelines,[18] resolutions and reports from the ILA[19] and the IIL,[20] and model laws[21] mentioned earlier in relation to equal access also speak of local remedies, treatment or standards.

It is difficult to say what the drafters had in mind with those provisions, as opposed to those providing for equal access. Is access to equal remedies in the state of origin the same as equal access to its courts? What about equivalent treatment, standards or rules? Like equal access and non-discrimination, equal remedy is a broad and shape-shifting notion, inconsistently used in different legal instruments and in academic writing. Semantics aside, the important question for our purposes is whether it means anything for the designation of the applicable law. Does it guarantee that a certain law (or parts thereof) will apply, just as equal access guarantees the jurisdiction of the courts in the state of origin, or is it strictly procedural? In other words, what is the relationship between equal remedy and choice of law?

At first blush, equal remedy is strictly procedural and has nothing to do with choice of law. It simply calls for the removal of procedural obstacles such as standing, security for costs, jurisdiction, etc. The logic is straightforward. Foreign plaintiffs who have no standing, for instance, cannot claim remedies available to local plaintiffs in the state of origin. A conflict between the law of the state of origin and the law of the affected state may still exist, but it is theoretical because local law invariably governs procedural issues in the

[18] Intergovernmental Working Group of Experts on Natural Resources Shared by Two or More States, 'Draft principles of conduct in the field of the environment for the guidance of states in the conservation and harmonious utilisation of natural resources shared by two or more states' UN Doc UNEP/GC.6/17, 17 ILM 1097 (1978) (Draft Principles of Conduct in the Field of the Environment) principle 14.

[19] International Law Association, 'Resolution No 6/2006: Transnational Enforcement of Environmental Law' in International Law Association Report of the Seventy-Second Conference (Toronto, 2006) ('ILA Toronto Rules on Transnational Enforcement of Environmental Law') 48, rule 3(3)–(4); Water Resources Committee, 'Fourth Report' in International Law Association Report of the Seventy-First Conference (Berlin, 2004) ('ILA Berlin Rules on Water Resources'), Art 71(1); Water Resources Committee, 'Interim Report' in International Law Association Report of the Sixty-Seventh Conference (Helsinki, 1996) ('ILA Helsinki Articles on Private Law Remedies'), Art 2(1); International Water Resources Law Committee, 'Report of the Committee' in International Law Association Report of the Sixtieth Conference (Montreal, 1982) ('ILA Montreal Rules on Water Pollution'), Art 8.

[20] Institute of International Law, 'Resolution on Responsibility and Liability under International Law for Environmental Damage' in *Yearbook of the Institute of International Law. Session of Strasbourg, 1997*, vol 67, part II: Deliberations of the Institute (Paris, Pedone, 1998) ('IIL Resolution on Responsibility and Liability') 487, Art 30, reprinted in (1998) 37 *International Legal Materials* 1474 and (1998) 10 *Georgetown International Environmental Law Review* 269.

[21] International Union for Conservation of Nature, *Draft International Covenant on Environment and Development: Implementing Sustainability*, 5th edn (Gland, IUCN, 2015) ('IUCN Draft International Covenant on Environment and Development') 22 (Art 62), 163; Société française pour le droit de l'environnement and Gesellschaft für Umweltrecht, 'Projet de convention entre la République française et la République fédérale d'Allemagne pour la limitation et la prévention des pollutions transfrontières' [1997] 1 *Revue juridique de l'environnement* 99, 103 (Art 5), 108 (Art 23); PR Muldoon, DA Scriven and JM Olson, *Cross-Border Litigation: Environmental Rights in the Great Lakes Ecosystem* (Toronto, Carswell, 1986) 358, s 5.

local court.[22] On this view, equal remedy has no bearing on the designation of the law applicable to liability itself, only the procedural steps prior to trial. It requires the state of origin to remove procedural obstacles aimed at foreign plaintiffs, such that they get an equal possibility of invoking *some remedy* in the state of origin, regardless of how it compares to the remedies available to local plaintiffs. In other words, the substantive remedies ultimately available to foreign victims when the case is tried on the merits (and applicable as a result of choice of law rules) may be less favourable than those available to local victims, without contradicting the idea of equal remedy.

This procedural interpretation of equal remedy, however, does not tell the whole story. Why speak of remedies at all if equal access already secures access to the courts of the state of origin in a transboundary context? The Reciprocal Access Act, for instance, contains different provisions for equal access and equal remedy.[23] This implies some difference between the two concepts (even though the Act further complicates things with a third separate provision on choice of law[24]).

The ILC's own interpretation of the Principles on the Allocation of Loss confirms that equal remedy goes beyond procedural considerations and is directly connected with choice of law. For the ILC, the sixth principle requires not only that foreign victims get equal access to the courts of the state of origin, but also that they benefit from 'the same *substantive level* of remedies' as local victims in the state of origin.[25] From this perspective, the applicable law under choice of law rules has a clear impact on equal remedy. Consider an injury suffered outside the state of origin, which triggers the rules of private international law when a lawsuit is brought in the state of origin. If the choice of law process leads to a law that is less favourable to foreign victims than the law of the state of origin (for instance, the hypothetically less favourable law of the place of injury), the objective of equal remedy is not met. Foreign victims are treated worse than victims in the state of origin as a result of the choice of law process.[26] Conversely, the objective of equal remedy is met if the choice of law process leads to the law of the state of origin because a single law applies to all victims – but it will not help them if that law does not favour compensation.

This highlights an important difference in how we think of jurisdictional and choice of law rules in light of the requirements of the ILC Principles on the

[22] See n 4 above.

[23] Uniform Law Conference of Canada, 'Uniform Transboundary Pollution Reciprocal Access Act' in Uniform Law Conference of Canada Proceedings of the Sixty-Fourth Annual Meeting (Montebello, 1982) 504, ss 2–3, reprinted in Muldoon, Scriven and Olson, *Environmental Rights in the Great Lakes Ecosystem* (1986) 369 ('Reciprocal Access Act').

[24] ibid, s 4.

[25] Commentary to the ILC Principles on the Allocation of Loss (n 6) 86, paras 5–6 (emphasis added). See also UN Watercourses Convention (n 17), Art 32 (distinguishing access to procedures and the right to claim relief).

[26] Muldoon, Scriven and Olson (n 21) 62.

Allocation of Loss. We have seen that equal access (effectively achieved through appropriate jurisdictional rules) contributes *in itself* to the availability of prompt and adequate compensation. By opening the doors of the courtrooms, they make prompt and adequate compensation possible for all victims. Equal access may not suffice if other procedural or practical obstacles stand in the way of foreign victims, but jurisdictional rules themselves can do no more than allow a court to hear their claim – the court either has or does not have jurisdiction. Achieving equal remedy through choice of law rules, on the other hand, does not necessarily ensure the availability of prompt and adequate compensation because choice of law rules can ensure equality *and at the same time* designate a law with low prospects of liability. This is due to the usual formulation of choice of law rules: a rule which disregards the contents of the potentially applicable law may designate the same law for all victims, but cannot guarantee a substantive outcome such as prompt and adequate compensation, because that depends on a substantive law which has not been applied (or even looked at) yet. Consequently, this chapter occasionally refers to 'equal remedy' and 'prompt and adequate compensation' (more accurately, the *likelihood* of prompt and adequate compensation) as two distinct but related objectives to strive for when designing choice of law rules for transboundary pollution.

For now, suffice it to say that choice of law is undeniably relevant in the ILC Principles on the Allocation of Loss – whether to ensure equal remedy or prompt and adequate compensation – even though the ILC says little on this point. We will return to this idea – and to what kind of equality it actually requires – later on.[27]

C. Implementation of Equal Remedy in Canada

There have been few Canadian initiatives to specifically implement equal remedy for foreign victims of transboundary pollution. The Boundary Waters Treaty and the International Boundary Waters Treaty Act have an equal remedy provision for water diversion.[28] The Draft Treaty on Equal Access and Remedy requires Canada to ensure that American victims of transboundary pollution are treated in a manner at least equivalent to local victims.[29] The Reciprocal Access Act provides not only that foreign victims have access to the courts of

[27] See section 4.I.D.ii.b below.

[28] International Boundary Waters Treaty Act, RSC 1985 c I-17, s 4(1); Boundary Waters Treaty (n 17), Art II, para 1.

[29] American Bar Association and Canadian Bar Association, 'Draft Treaty on a Regime of Equal Access and Remedy in Cases of Transfrontier Pollution' in American Bar Association and Canadian Bar Association, *Settlement of International Disputes Between Canada and the USA* (Chicago, Section of International Law of the American Bar Association, 1979) xiii, Art 2(a), reprinted in (2011) 35 *Canada–United States Law Journal* 9, 16–20 and Muldoon, Scriven and Olson (n 21) 365–67 ('Draft Treaty on Equal Access and Remedy').

the source province/state, but also that they have the same rights to relief as local victims.[30] Likewise, the NAAEC tasks the CEC with the consideration and appropriate development of recommendations regarding equal access and remedies.[31] These instruments were discussed in chapter three, in which it was concluded that they did not have a strong impact on cross-border environmental litigation, and that the general law of jurisdiction would apply in most cases. The same is true for choice of law.

D. Going beyond the ILC Principles on the Allocation of Loss

We have seen that the ILC Principles on the Allocation of Loss require equal remedy, and that Canada lacks a comprehensive instrument in this sense. As in the third chapter, this is not the end of the matter: choice of law rules may effectively achieve the same result even when no specific framework such as the Reciprocal Access Act is in place. The ILC refrained from prescribing a preferable approach for choice of law. Nonetheless, the ubiquity principle has emerged as a logical extension of its framework and a sound alternative to overly rigid definitions of the *lex loci delicti*.

In the next sections, I analyse the challenges of transboundary pollution in choice of law methodology (section I.D.i) and introduce the ubiquity principle, a method noted by the ILC, formally recommended by UNEP and now commonly used in Europe to deal with conflicts of laws in this area (section I.D.ii). The ubiquity principle, I argue, is the most appropriate way to deal with transboundary pollution through choice of law rules. As such, it is a useful benchmark to assess Canadian law.

i. Transboundary Pollution and the Law of the Place of the Tort

In Canada, the law applicable to torts is typically the law of the place where the tort occurred (*lex loci delicti*), understood as the law of the place where the wrongful activity occurred.[32] Many other states apply the *lex loci delicti*.[33] Localising a tort is easy when the act and its consequences occur in the same state, but again, complex torts such as those associated with transboundary pollution raise greater difficulties because the act and its consequences occur

[30] Reciprocal Access Act (n 23), s 3.

[31] North American Agreement on Environmental Cooperation (Canada, United States and Mexico) (14 September 1993, entered into force 1 January 1994) 32 ILM 1480 (NAAEC), Art 10(9).

[32] For further discussion on Canadian choice of law rules, see section 4.II.A below.

[33] For a survey, see Kadner Graziano, 'Torts' (2017) 1710–11; SC Symeonides, 'Torts and Conflict of Laws' in M Bussani and AJ Sebok (eds), *Comparative Tort Law: Global Perspectives* (Cheltenham, Edward Elgar, 2015) 47–48; SC Symeonides, *Codifying Choice of Law Around the World: An International Comparative Analysis* (Oxford, Oxford University Press, 2014) 52–58.

in different places. The issue is not to identify where the act took place, but to choose between the law of that place and the law of the place of injury. Another option is to let the court or the plaintiff decide in each case, as we will see below.

There is an inherent tension between a state's legitimate interest in regulating conduct occurring on its territory (and our own expectation that the wrong we commit will be governed by the law of the place where we acted) and the idea that tort law does not punish wrongdoers so much as it compensates victims for the damage they suffer. The first idea favours the place of acting as the default rule and the second favours the place of injury.[34] The dilemma is easily avoided at the jurisdictional stage because both the state of origin and the affected state can have an interest in hearing the dispute. It is not even necessary to speak in terms of localising environmental torts in one place or the other. Strong connections with the forum suffice. But there can only be one applicable law, hence only one place where torts occur for choice of law purposes. How to choose?

Both connecting factors have advantages and disadvantages. Applying the law of the place of injury aligns with the compensatory function of civil liability, but it burdens the judicial process when the dispute involves multiple plaintiffs in different states, whose claims are each governed by a different law. It also poses evidentiary problems if the injury is difficult to pin to a single place (long-term exposure to harmful substances, for instance). Finally, the tortfeasor may not have foreseen that an injury would occur in a given place, which makes compliance *ex ante* difficult. Applying the law of the place of acting allows tortfeasors to predict the consequences of their actions with more certainty and avoids fragmentation. But it also downplays the interest of foreign states in compensating (and possibly preventing) damage occurring on their own territory – something which the place of acting may have no interest in doing. As the High Court of Australia rightly pointed out in a famous online defamation case:

> Certainty does not necessarily mean singularity. What is important is that publishers can act with confidence, not that they be able to act according to a single legal system, even if that system might, in some sense, be described as their 'home' legal system. Activities that have effects beyond the jurisdiction in which they are done may properly be the concern of the legal systems in each place.[35]

Much can be said on the desirability and viability of either option for torts generally. Let us focus here on the particular challenges of transboundary pollution. From this perspective, no hard-and-fast definition of the *lex loci delicti* is satisfactory. Localising environmental torts at the law at the place of acting might

[34] cf Regulation (EC) 864/2007 of the European Parliament and of the Council of 11 July 2007 on the law applicable to non-contractual obligations (Rome II) [2007] OJ L199/40 ('Rome II Regulation') preamble, para 16; *Tolofson* (n 4) 1050–51.

[35] *Dow Jones & Company Inc v Gutnick* [2002] HCA 56 [24].

encourage polluters to conduct their operations in states with low environmental standards.[36] Victims thus cannot invoke the hypothetically more favourable law of the place of injury. The extent of a polluter's ability to shop its regulatory regime depends on the nature of its operations. It is illusionary if the operations involve the extraction of natural resources located only in a certain place, but it is likely if they involve human activities which can be done in alternative jurisdictions. In this context, applying the law of the place of acting imposes the weaker standards of the state of origin on the rest of the world and ignores other states' legitimate interest in activities which impact their own environment or the well-being of their population. It allows polluters to harm foreign populations while generating profit under the protection of a law which they chose by setting up their operations in a particular country.

This does not mean that the regime 'chosen' by polluters will grant them complete immunity for their actions. The law of the place of acting may be strigent: it may feature a strict liability regime, or it may not recognise statutory compliance as a defence to civil liability. And if litigation takes place in the affected state (place of injury), local environmental laws may override the law of the place of acting if the court considers them to be mandatory. In the abstract, therefore, the law of the place of acting does not always favour polluters even when it is the only connecting factor used in a choice of law rule. But it becomes problematic if other, more severe regimes exist. Polluters can then *choose* to avoid those regimes by setting up their activities in a certain place, knowing that only the law of that place will apply. The problem with the law of the place of acting lies in the choice given to the polluter, not the substantive result it leads to in any given case.

Localising environmental torts only at the place of injury, however, does not eliminate the risk that polluters shop for a favourable regulatory regime. It might in fact encourage them to conduct their operations so that the consequences occur in a neighbouring state with low environmental standards. Victims thus cannot invoke the hypothetically more favourable law of the state of origin. This hardly seems fair for foreign victims since local victims of the same polluter benefit from that higher standard.[37]

The application of the law of the place of injury raises another kind of concern in the opposite scenario, that is, when it is more favourable than the law

[36] T Kadner Graziano, *La responsabilité délictuelle en droit international privé européen* (Basel, Helbing & Lichtenhahn, 2004) 53.

[37] On the dilemma associated with both connecting factors, see Grušić, 'International Environmental Litigation' (2016) 212–13; H Muir Watt, 'Rome II et les « intérêts gouvernementaux »: pour une lecture fonctionnaliste du nouveau règlement du conflit de lois en matière délictuelle' in S Corneloup and N Joubert (eds), *Le règlement communautaire « Rome II » sur la loi applicable aux obligations non contractuelles* (Paris, LexisNexis, 2008) 132–33; H Muir Watt, 'European Integration, Legal Diversity and the Conflict of Laws' (2005) 9 *Edinburgh Law Review* 6, 18–19; H Muir Watt, 'Aspects économiques du droit international privé: réflexions sur l'impact de la globalisation économique sur les fondements des conflits de lois et de juridictions' (2004) 307 *Recueil des cours de l'Académie de droit international* 25, 269–70.

of the place of acting. At the outset, it implies that the affected state imposes on the state of origin a stronger environmental policy. This is a significant encroachment on the sovereignty of the state of origin, particularly if it affects the financial viability of its industry, although as we have seen, the affected state also has a strong interest in preventing environmental damage on its territory.

More importantly, the application of the law of the place of injury may create inequalities among victims of transboundary pollution. This is especially true for mass environmental torts which cause damage across different states. Consider a polluter operating in state *x* (place of acting) and causing pollution in states *x*, *y* and *z* (places of injury). Now consider that courts in state *x* have assumed jurisdiction and that the choice of law rule in state *x* leads to the law of the place of injury (*x*, *y* or *z*, depending on where the victim is located). In this context, the choice of law rule may create two types of inequalities. First, the choice of law rule may create inequalities between local and foreign victims. If the laws of states *y* and *z* (place of injury of foreign victims) are more favourable to compensation than the law of state *x* (place of acting and place of injury of local victims), foreign victims have an advantage over local victims. Conversely, if the laws of states *y* and *z* are less favourable to compensation than the law of state *x*, local victims have an advantage over foreign victims. Second, the choice of law rule may create inequalities among foreign victims themselves. If one of the places of injury (state *y*) has a more favourable law than the other (state *z*), applying the law of the place of injury means that victims in state *y* have an advantage over victims of the same activity in state *z*.[38]

Summing up on the pros and cons of the law of the place of acting and the law of the place of injury, the important takeaway is that a rigid definition of the *lex loci delicti* allows polluters, in one way or another, to rely on weak domestic regimes and to avoid stringent ones – either by operating in a state with low environmental standards (if the tort is located at the place of acting) or by causing damage in a state with low environmental standards (if the tort is located at the place of injury). Of course, this is only a risk, not a certainty. Either definition of the *lex loci delicti* may well designate a law

[38] While these inequalities exist among victims of the same transboundary event, there may also be inequalities between victims of transboundary pollution and victims of domestic pollution. Consider, for instance, a polluter operating in state *x* (place of acting) and causing pollution in states *x* and *y* (places of injury). Assume that the law of state *x* is more favourable to compensation than the law of state *y*. If the choice of law rule points to the hypothetically more favourable law of the place of acting, victims of transboundary pollution in state *y* receive a better treatment than victims of domestic pollution in state *y* simply because the polluter happens to operate elsewhere. This different treatment of victims of domestic and transboundary pollution is problematic because it has no obvious justification, but it is difficult to avoid. On this point, see P Hay, 'Contemporary Approaches to Non-Contractual Obligations in Private International Law (Conflict of Laws) and the European Community's "Rome II" Regulation' (2007) 7 *European Legal Forum* 135, 145; C von Bar, 'Environmental Damage in Private International Law' (1997) 268 *Recueil des cours de l'Académie de droit international* 291, 371; PH Sand, 'The Role of Domestic Procedures in Transnational Environmental Disputes' in OECD, *Transfrontier Pollution* (1977) 190.

that will in fact ensure prompt and adequate compensation. Transboundary environmental disputes do not always involve two dramatically divergent laws, one very favourable to compensation and the other not. This is particularly true for interprovincial pollution in Canada, where provinces have similar environmental laws. In such cases, the two laws may prove acceptable for victims. And if discrepancies do exist, choice of law rules may still lead to the most favourable of two laws. Foreign victims, for instance, are a good position if a choice of law rule designates the hypothetically more favourable law of the place of injury. Likewise, all victims are in a good position if the hypothetically more favourable law of the place of acting applies. But a rigid definition of the *lex loci delicti* reaches those results by coincidence rather than by design. Applying only one of the two laws in all cases *will* jeopardise equal remedy or the likelihood of prompt and adequate compensation in certain scenarios. A better design is possible. To align with the duty to ensure prompt and adequate compensation, a choice of law rule for transboundary pollution would have to remove incentives to pollute in a certain place and increase the prospects of liability as much as possible. To align with equal remedy, a choice of law rule would also have to strive for equality among victims. This is where the ubiquity principle comes into play.

ii. The Ubiquity Principle

The ubiquity principle is the practice of applying either the law at the place of acting or the place of injury, whichever is the most favourable to compensation. The tort is ubiquitous, located in every place where it manifests itself.[39] German courts have used it since the late nineteenth century, including in transboundary environmental disputes.[40] Von Hein explains that German courts developed the ubiquity principle 'because it allowed a more flexible handling of the lex loci delicti and favored the application of the lex fori'.[41] The ubiquity principle is

[39] HU Jesserun D'Oliveira, 'La pollution du Rhin et le droit international privé' in R Hueting et al (eds), *Rhine Pollution: Legal, Economic and Technical Aspects* (Zwolle, Tjeenk Willink, 1978) 98. See also A Rest, *The More Favourable Law Principle in Transfrontier Environmental Law: A Means of Strengthening the Protection of the Individual?* (Berlin, Erich Schmidt, 1980).

[40] Oberlandesgericht Karlsruhe, 4 August 1977, (1977) 23 Recht der Internationalen Wirtschaft (RIW) 718, affg Landgericht Freiburg, 10 June 1975, translated in French in [1976] 2 *Revue juridique de l'environnement* 73 (environmental damage in Germany caused by French chemical factory – French law applied because it was more favourable to the plaintiffs). For relevant cases, see A Rest, 'International Environmental Law in German Courts' (1997) 27 *Environmental Policy and Law* 409, 412–13; Rest, *The More Favourable Law Principle* (1980) 69–72; Sand, 'The Role of Domestic Procedures' (1977) 148–49; A Rest, *Convention on Compensation for Transfrontier Environmental Injuries: Draft with Explanatory Notes* (Berlin, Erich Schmidt, 1976) 61–62; SC McCaffrey, 'Private Remedies for Transfrontier Environmental Disturbances', IUCN Environmental Policy and Law Paper 8 (Morges, International Union for Conservation of Nature and Natural Resources, 1975) 40–46.

[41] J von Hein, 'Something Old and Something Borrowed, but Nothing New? Rome II and the European Choice-of-Law Evolution' (2008) 82 *Tulane Law Review* 1663, 1683.

now part of the German statute on private international law.[42] Other states have a similar rule.[43] In this kind of framework, the choice of law may belong to the plaintiff or the court.[44] The mechanics of the rule may vary. Both laws can have equal status (a positive choice is required at the outset), or one can apply by default and be displaced only by a contrary choice.[45] However the rule is structured, the idea of the ubiquity principle is to give enough leeway to choose the law that is the most favourable to compensation – either directly by applying the most favourable law, or indirectly by letting the victim choose.

The ubiquity principle is recommendable as a choice of law rule for transboundary pollution for three reasons. First, it performs a regulatory function (section I.D.ii.a). Second, it ensures equal remedy (section I.D.ii.b). Finally, it attracts consensus and is spreading around the globe – adopted in the EU, recommended by international organisations and supported by scholars (section I.D.ii.c).

a. The Regulatory Function of the Ubiquity Principle

First, the ubiquity principle is recommendable because it reduces the incentive for polluters to establish their operations in a friendly jurisdiction or to cause damage in a jurisdiction with low environmental standards.[46] This has a positive impact on victims, and possibly on the level of environmental standards themselves.

As mentioned earlier, the mobility of polluters depends on the nature of their operations. The more their operations depend on human rather than natural resources, the easier it is for them to move across jurisdictions and exploit regulatory discrepancies. The ubiquity principle eliminates that problem by applying the most favourable of two laws. Victims may not obtain prompt and adequate compensation (if, for instance, neither law is particularly favourable to it), but the likelihood of compensation may increase. Meanwhile, polluters can no longer externalise the consequences of their operations by taking advantage of a weaker law.

The ubiquity principle evidently favours victims, which raises fairness concerns. But it is not unprecedented nor illegitimate. We have seen that choice

[42] Einführungsgesetz zum bürgerlichen gesetzbuche, BGBI I 2494 (Introductory Act to the German Civil Code), s 40(1), translated in English in Basedow et al, *Encyclopedia of Private International Law*, vol 4 (2017).

[43] For a survey, see SC Symeonides, 'Private International Law: Idealism, Pragmatism, Eclecticism' (2017) 384 *Recueil des cours de l'Académie de droit international* 9, 239–44; Symeonides, *Codifying Choice of Law* (2014) 59–67, 272–75, 277–78.

[44] In certain states such as Canada, courts cannot apply choice of law rules on their own motion. Only parties can, and they might choose not to plead foreign law at all in those circumstances. Local law will then apply by default.

[45] cf Rome II Regulation (n 34), Art 8; Introductory Act to the German Civil Code (n 42), s 40(1).

[46] Y Lequette, 'Les mutations du droit international privé: vers un changement de paradigme? Cours général de droit international privé' (2017) 387 *Recueil des cours de l'Académie de droit international* 9, 523.

of law rules already play a similar role in particular areas such as consumer law, employment law, insurance law or product liability,[47] areas in which vulnerable parties can fall prey to the excesses of a globalised market. There is no reason why choice of law rules could not play a similar role in relation to environmental law,[48] particularly when the well-being of an entire population (and the planet itself) is at stake. There is nothing illegitimate about a rule which favours the interests of the victims of transboundary pollution over those of polluters[49] if it points to a law in sufficiently close proximity with the situation.

Van Loon suggests that the 'crucial role of private international law may instigate legislators to use it in order to provide citizens with a remedy for cross-border environmental harm and influence environmental conduct of economic actors across borders'.[50] Whether we ultimately enact such rules is our choice, but the regulation of transnational actors through the proxy of private law is a legitimate policy goal for private international law.[51] The ubiquity principle is simply a way to achieve that goal in relation to transboundary pollution.

This said, protecting the victims is one thing and protecting the environment is another. Yet the ubiquity principle is often described as capable of doing both. Muir Watt's account of the ubiquity principle adopted in the EU, for instance, goes beyond the protection of individual rights. She suggests that choice of law can remedy distortions of competition for public goods while avoiding the pitfalls of substantive harmonisation and preserving states' ability to pursue their own legitimate socio-economic policies.[52] A 'specifically regulatory function of the conflict rule', she writes, 'induces a profound change in the way the rule is designed; rather than attaching an appropriate connecting factor to an abstract category of issues, the rule identifies the risk of distortion and seeks the best way to correct it'.[53] This systemic perspective on choice of law rules leads Muir Watt to describe the ubiquity principle adopted in the EU as a mechanism designed not to protect victims per se, but to correct

[47] For further discussion and references to substance-oriented rules of private international law in those areas, see section 2.II.B above.

[48] O Boskovic, 'The Law Applicable to Violations of the Environment – Regulatory Strategies' in H Muir Watt and F Cafaggi (eds), *The Regulatory Function of European Private Law* (Cheltenham, Edward Elgar, 2009) 194–95.

[49] F Giansetto, 'Le droit international privé à l'épreuve des nouveaux contentieux en matière de responsabilité climatique' [2018] *Journal du droit international* 507, 528.

[50] H van Loon, 'The Global Horizon of Private International Law' (2016) 380 *Recueil des cours de l'Académie de droit international* 9, 86.

[51] Wai, 'Transnational Liftoff and Juridical Touchdown' (2002).

[52] H Muir Watt, 'Choice of Law in Integrated and Interconnected Markets: A Matter of Political Economy' (2003) 9 *Columbia Journal of European Law* 383, 393–94 and the sources cited above n 79 (ch 2).

[53] Muir Watt, 'European Integration' (2005) 20.

a particular distortion (the geographic mobility of polluters in a context of regulatory competition), to raise standards in accordance with European policy and ultimately to protect the environment.[54] As we will see below, the European legislature itself viewed the alignment of private international law with its substantive environmental policy as a fundamental justification for incorporating the ubiquity principle into the Rome II Regulation, at least as fundamental as the protection of victims per se.[55] The Permanent Bureau of the HCCH and the ILA similarly described the ubiquity principle as strengthening environmental protection.[56]

Promoting the ubiquity principle in this context assumes that the law which offers the best prospects of liability for the plaintiff is also the most protective of the environment generally. It also assumes that polluters everywhere will abide by that higher standard standard and that states will eventually adjust their own law to match it.[57] Whether the ubiquity principle can have such an effect on compliance and the level of environmental standards brings back the debate over the uncertain systemic impact of tort law on environmental protection.[58] At the very least, the ubiquity principle reduces the incentives to pollute in a place with low environmental standards, whereas discrepancies in domestic laws and a rigid definition of the *lex loci delicti* exacerbates them. This is a good beginning. It also removes incoherences in our response to global environmental challenges. Indeed, domestic measures (including civil liability) will have a role to play in the fight against transboundary pollution because international treaty-making, cooperation and harmonisation remain difficult. It would be counterproductive for a state to enact strong pollution-control measures while tolerating choice of law rules which contribute to the under-regulation of transboundary pollution. Whether the ubiquity principle ultimately raises global standards and prevents pollution is a matter of empirical research.

[54] H Muir Watt, 'Private International Law Beyond the Schism" (2011) 2 *Transnational Legal Theory* 347, 388; Muir Watt, 'Rome II' (2008) 133–34; Muir Watt, 'European Integration' (n 37) 18–19.

[55] European Commission, 'Proposal for a Regulation of the European Parliament and the Council on the law applicable to non-contractual obligations (Rome II)' COM (2003) 427 final ('Rome II Proposal and Explanatort Memorandum') 19, reprinted in (2003) 5 *Yearbook of Private International Law* 345.

[56] C Bernasconi, 'Civil Liability Resulting from Transfrontier Environmental Damage: A Case for the Hague Conference?' (1999) 12 *Hague Yearbook of International Law* 35, 80, reprinted in Hague Conference on Private International Law, *Proceedings of the Nineteenth Session: 6 to 22 June 2001*, vol 1: Miscellaneous Matters (Leiden, Koninklijke Brill, 2008) 320; ILA, 'Second Report on Transnational Enforcement of Environmental Law' (n 9) 912.

[57] For sceptical views of the Rome II Regulation in this regard, see Hay, 'Contemporary Approaches to Non-Contractual Obligations' (2007); Kadner Graziano *Responsabilité délictuelle en droit international privé* (2004) 60.

[58] For further discussion on the assumptions of civil liability regimes, see section 1.I.D.ii above.

b. Equal Remedy and the Ubiquity Principle

Second, the ubiquity principle is recommendable because it fulfils the requirement of equal remedy, even though it may not achieve perfect equality among all victims of transboundary pollution.

As explained earlier, equal remedy takes the state of origin as a point of reference to assess the treatment of local and foreign victims. Equal remedy has implications for choice of law rules because it imposes a substantive standard of protection for foreign victims (unlike equal access which is concerned with procedural and jurisdictional standards). But any choice of law rule which designates the law of the place of injury – including the ubiquity principle – may create inequalities among victims of the same activities if the law of an affected state offers better protection than the law of the state of origin or the law of another affected state. This discrepancy is hard to justify. Why should foreign victims receive better treatment for the same damage? Does it not contradict the idea of equal remedy? To answer these questions, we must determine what equal remedy actually requires or allows in terms of choice of law rules.

There are two possible ways of interpreting equal remedy in relation to choice of law rules. First, equal remedy could be interpreted as imposing the law of the place of acting in all circumstances, as some authors suggested when commenting on the Boundary Waters Treaty. All victims of transboundary pollution receive the same treatment prescribed by the law of the state of origin, even though it might deprive some victims of the hypothetically more favourable law at the place of injury and invite polluters to operate in laxer jurisdictions. On this view, the ubiquity principle contradicts equal remedy. It can lead to the law of the place of acting, but it can also lead to the law of the place of injury, which creates inequalities among victims.

Alternatively, equal remedy could be interpreted as designating any law that is *at least* as favourable to compensation as the law of the state of origin, even though it might favour some victims over others. Understood in this sense, equal remedy simply ensures that the applicable law never deprives foreign victims of the hypothetically greater benefits afforded by the law of the state of origin. It acts as a kind of public policy exception by dismissing the parts of the applicable law that go below a predefined substantive standard of protection (the law of the place of acting) and preserving the parts that go above that substantive standard.[59] On this view, the ubiquity principle becomes acceptable. Foreign victims can rely on the law of the place of acting. They can also rely on their own law if it is more favourable, no matter the differences in remedies between local and foreign victims or among foreign victims who suffer damage in different states.

[59] S Mahmoudi, 'Some Private International Law Aspects of Transboundary Environmental Disputes' (1990) 59 *Nordic Journal of International Law* 128, 134; Sand (n 38) 189.

The second interpretation is preferable. As we have seen, equal remedy exists to ensure that foreign victims, at a minimum, are not disadvantaged compared to local victims. It does not exist to ensure that all victims receive the exact same treatment. This is evident in many equal remedy provisions. The OECD Recommendation mandates a treatment 'at least' equivalent to that of local victims.[60] The OECD Secretary General mentioned the application of the law of the place of acting as only one of the solutions available to ensure equivalent treatment, and noted that states could always go beyond this minimum protection afforded to foreign victims.[61] A study of the OECD Secretariat also explained that equivalent treatment had 'particular relevance' when the law of the state of origin was more favourable than the law of the affected state.[62] The Nordic Convention similarly refers to rules that are 'no less favourable' to those of the state of origin.[63] The ILC Principles on the Allocation of Loss refer to remedies that are 'no less prompt, adequate and effective' as those of the state of origin.[64] The same goes for the IUCN Draft International Covenant on Environment and Development[65] and the ILA Toronto Rules on Transnational Enforcement of Environmental Law.[66] Equal remedy therefore admits the application of the law of the place of injury if it is more favourable to the victim than the law of the place of acting.

This interpretation of equal remedy avoids the biggest objection to non-discrimination generally, namely its insistence that local and foreign victims equally benefit from what might be a very low level of protection in the state of origin. Potential inequalities between local and foreign victims, if they exist, do not deprive local victims of any of the rights they would have in a domestic case. It is only when comparing their rights with those of other victims that we see their situation change. Foreign victims, on the other hand, would actually lose rights that they have under their home law if the hypothetically less favourable law of the place of acting applied. In this scenario, the ubiquity principle is preferable to a low baseline for all because it incentivises polluters to avoid harming people beyond the borders of the state of origin and promotes compliance with the higher standards of neighbouring states.[67] The ubiquity principle is an imperfect solution, but it is legitimate to seek higher environmental standards over a unitary solution at all costs.[68] The ubiquity principle ultimately complies

[60] OECD Recommendation (n 14), s 4(a).

[61] OECD Secretary General, 'Report on the Implementation of a Regime of Equal Right of Access and Non-Discrimination in Relation to Transfrontier Pollution' in OECD (n 14) 46–47.

[62] OECD Secretariat, 'Equal Right of Access in Matters of Transfrontier Pollution in OECD Member Countries' in OECD (n 14) 113.

[63] Nordic Convention (n 16), Art 3, para 2.

[64] ILC Principles on the Allocation of Loss (n 8) principle 6(2).

[65] IUCN Draft International Covenant on Environment and Development (n 21) 22, Art 62.

[66] ILA Toronto Rules on Transnational Enforcement of Environmental Law (n 19), rule 3(3). See also ILA Helsinki Articles on Private Law Remedies (n 19) 409; ILA Montreal Rules on Water Pollution (n 19) 544.

[67] Rome II Proposal and Explanatory Memorandum (n 55) 19.

[68] García-Castrillón, 'International Litigation Trends in Environmental Liability' (2011) 569.

with equal remedy as articulated in the ILC Principles on the Allocation of Loss. It has drawbacks for victims in certain scenarios, like any rule which leads to the law of the place of injury, but its advantages are hard to ignore.

c. Consensus Surrounding the Ubiquity Principle

Finally, the ubiquity principle is recommendable because it attracts a wide consensus among states, international organisations and scholars with respect to transboundary pollution.

At the outset, a choice of law rule tailored to a particular tort is hardly radical. There is a well-documented tendency in today's private international law to break down civil liability into discrete subfields, each governed by their own conflict rules – in other words, a move towards the specialisation of conflict rules.[69] The adoption of specific rules was in fact 'one of the most important developments in the private international law of torts' from the mid-twentieth century onwards.[70] In the EU, for instance, the Rome II Regulation contains special rules for product liability, unfair competition, environmental damage, infringement of intellectual property rights, and so on.[71] The specialisation of conflict rules often intersects with their materialisation, that is, a concern for a particular outcome in a particular area.[72]

Environmental law, however, joined this trend belatedly. In the late 1990s, the Permanent Bureau of the HCCH conducted a survey of domestic laws and noticed that only one state had adopted a specific choice of law rule for environmental damage.[73] At the time, Switzerland's 1987 *Loi fédérale sur le droit international privé* (Swiss Statute on Private International Law) allowed victims of damaging nuisances originating in real property to choose between the law of the state in which that property was located or the law of the place of injury.[74] Japan was also considering a special rule for environmental damage,[75] but ultimately did not adopt it.[76] The HCCH nonetheless pointed out that certain

[69] J Basedow, *The Law of Open Societies: Private Ordering and Public Regulation in the Conflict of Laws* (Leiden, Brill Nijhoff, 2015) para 304.

[70] Kadner Graziano (n 7) 1716.

[71] Rome II Regulation (n 34), Arts 5–12.

[72] Lequette, 'Les mutations du droit international privé' (2017) 240, 247–48.

[73] Bernasconi, 'Civil Liability Resulting from Transfrontier Environmental Damage' (1999) 74–77.

[74] Loi fédérale sur le droit international privé, RS 291 (Swiss Act on Private International Law) s 138, translated in English in (1990) 29 *International Legal Materials* 1254 and Basedow et al, vol 4 (n 7). See also former s 44 of the Introductory Act to the German Civil Code (n 42), translated in French in (1999) 88 *Revue critique de droit international privé* 870 ('intromissions emanating from real property' governed the German ubiquity principle – now governed by the Rome II Regulation).

[75] Bernasconi (n 56) 74, 76–77.

[76] Act on the General Rules of Application of Laws, ss 17–19, translated in English in Basedow et al, vol 4 (n 7) and K Anderson and Y Okuda, 'Translation of Japan's Private International Law: Act on the General Rules of Application of Laws [Hō no Tekiyō ni Kansuru Tsūsokuhō]' (2006) 8 *Asian Pacific Law and Policy Journal* 136; (2006) 8 *Yearbook of Private International Law* 427.

states had adopted variations of the ubiquity principle as the general rule for *all* torts (Italy, for instance).[77]

The HCCH's survey – and the abandonment of its own project – could be read as evidence of the difficulty of explicitly embedding environmental policy into choice of law rules. Certain states might indeed resist conflict rules guided by environmental considerations if they think that such rules would favour the interests of foreigners over those of an important local industry.[78] Lack of political interest for choice of law issues also reduces the likelihood of changes, except perhaps as part of the broader reform of an entire body of private international law.

There is cause for optimism. Environmental awareness has grown exponentially since the HCCH's work on the topic. States could decide to reform choice of law rules accordingly, particularly if they recognise the value of environmental litigation. The adoption of the Rome II Regulation in 2007 offers a useful precedent for a method which could become increasingly popular in the twenty-first century. Obviously, states with very low environmental standards can hardly be expected to enact environment-friendly choice of law rules. Doing so would indirectly impose a higher standard on their own industry when it affects victims elsewhere. There is no reason to think they will go in this direction if they have low standards to begin with – a political problem foreseen by the OECD decades ago.[79] But it stands to reason that states with high environmental standards would enact choice of law rules to ensure that their own residents can rely on those high standards when pollution originates elsewhere, or to protect foreign victims of pollution originating in their territory. The duty to ensure prompt and adequate compensation, under international environmental law, boosts the legitimacy of imposing those higher standards on foreign states through choice of law rules, because it conveys an emerging international norm rather than the unilateral policy of a single state.

The ubiquity principle also attracts consensus among organisations and experts who studied transboundary pollution. The ILC noted the practice of applying the law that is the most favourable to the victims but did not express an opinion on the matter.[80] The ILA, however, took the position that the ubiquity principle was best equipped to foster environmental protection.[81] It became the fifth of the ILA Toronto Rules on Transnational Enforcement of Environmental Law.[82] The ubiquity principle also finds support in the work of the HCCH.

[77] Bernasconi (n 56) 74–77. For a more recent survey, see the work of Symeonides (n 43).

[78] Grušić (n 3) 191.

[79] OECD Secretariat, 'Study of Some Principles for Solving Problems of Transfrontier Pollution' in OECD (n 14) 243–44.

[80] Commentary to the ILC Principles on the Allocation of Loss (n 6) 87, para 9.

[81] ILA, 'Final Report on Transnational Enforcement of Environmental Law' (n 9) 669–70; ILA, 'Second Report on Transnational Enforcement of Environmental Law' (n 9) 917. See also Société française pour le droit de l'environnement and Gesellschaft für Umweltrecht (n 21) 110, Art 30.

[82] ILA Toronto Rules on Transnational Enforcement of Environmental Law (n 19), rule 5(1).

The Permanent Bureau of the HCCH mentioned in its preliminary work that the ubiquity principle had more support in environmental law than as a general rule for all torts.[83] Experts who met in the course of the HCCH's work reached the same conclusion in the early nineties,[84] when the ubiquity principle already had doctrinal support with respect to transboundary environmental disputes.[85] Years later, the Permanent Bureau noted 'growing support' for the ubiquity principle and recommended continuing the study of its possible implementation in a global instrument, which the HCCH ultimately refused to do.[86] Despite the abandonment of the project, the HCCH's former Secretary General recently included the ubiquity principle as one of the basic building blocks of a global private international law regime for transboundary pollution.[87] René Lefeber, who first hinted at the connection between private international law and the duty to ensure prompt and adequate compensation, appeared to favour the ubiquity principle even though he did not yet consider it to be a 'procedural minimum standard' in international environmental law.[88] Today, some commentators go so far as to suggest that the ubiquity principle is 'the most widely supported criterion' in relation to choice of law for transboundary environmental damage.[89]

Two recent iterations of the ubiquity principle warrant close attention, one in the form of a binding legal instrument and the other in the form of a nonbinding recommendation: the Rome II Regulation in the EU and the 2010 UNEP Guidelines on Liability. Each can influence the development of Canadian law and other domestic legal regimes in the future.

The Rome II Regulation

In the next sections, I examine the ubiquity principle in the *Rome II Regulation* and the impact of foreign rules of safety and conduct on the applicable law, followed by concluding thoughts on the Rome II Regulation and the example it sets for other states, and in other areas of the law.

[83] Bernasconi (n 56) 87. See also ILA, 'Second Report on Transnational Enforcement of Environmental Law' (n 9) 911–12.

[84] C Zilioli, 'Choice of Law' in C von Bar (ed), *Internationales umwelthaftungsrecht*, vol 1 (Köln, Heymann, 1995) 182–88, 194; PR Beaumont, 'Private International Law of the Environment' [1995] *Juridical Review* 28, 35–36.

[85] eg GAL Droz, 'Regards sur le droit international privé comparé: cours général de droit international privé' (1991) 229 *Recueil des cours de l'Académie de droit international* 9, 285–86.

[86] Hague Conference on Private International Law, 'Should the Hague Conference Revisit the Scope and Nature of Possible Work in the Field of Civil Liability for Environmental Damage?' HCCH Prel Doc 12 (February 2010) 4–5.

[87] H van Loon, 'Principles and Building Blocks for a Global Legal Framework for Transnational Civil Litigation in Environmental Matters' (2018) 23 *Uniform Law Review* 298, 316–17.

[88] Lefeber, *Transboundary Environmental Interference* (1996) 266–67.

[89] K Fach Gómez, 'Environmental Liability' in Basedow et al, vol 1 (n 7) 659.

The Ubiquity Principle in the *Rome II Regulation*

The EU's Rome II Regulation, applicable in the EU since 2009, contains choice of law rules for extracontractual obligations (torts). Of particular interest is Article 7 of the Rome II Regulation. Article 7 incorporates the ubiquity principle in relation to environmental damage, defined as an 'adverse change in a natural resource, such as water, land or air, impairment of a function performed by that resource for the benefit of another natural resource or the public, or impairment of the variability among living organisms'.[90] In this particular context, victims can choose between the law of the country in which environmental damage occurred (the general rule in Article 4) or the law of the country in which the events giving rise to environmental damage occurred. Unlike other torts, the applicable law can never be replaced by the law of the common residence of the parties (if any) or the law of another country manifestly closely connected with the dispute. The provision reads as follows:

> 7. The law applicable to a non-contractual obligation arising out of environmental damage or damage sustained by persons or property as a result of such damage shall be the law determined pursuant to Article 4(1) [law of the country in which the damage occurs, ed], unless the person seeking compensation for damage chooses to base his or her claim on the law of the country in which the event giving rise to the damage occurred.[91]

The preamble of the Rome II Regulation makes it clear that Article 7 is explicitly driven by environmental policy:

> (25) Regarding environmental damage, Article 174 of the Treaty [new Article 191 of the *Treaty on the Functioning of the European Union*, ed], which provides that there should be a high level of protection based on the precautionary principle and the principle that preventive action should be taken, the principle of priority for corrective action at source and the principle that the polluter pays, fully justifies the use of the principle of discriminating in favour of the person sustaining the damage. The question of when the person seeking compensation can make the choice of the law applicable should be determined in accordance with the law of the Member State in which the court is seised.[92]

The rule arose from the European Commission (EC)'s concern that the exclusive application of the law of the place of injury, as generally applicable in the Rome II Regulation, 'Would give an operator an incentive to establish his facilities at the border so as to discharge toxic substances into a river and enjoy the benefit of the neighbouring country's laxer rules'.[93] Article 7 seeks to correct that problem. Because it has a universal application (it can designate the law of

[90] Rome II Regulation (n 34) preamble, para 24.
[91] ibid, Art 7.
[92] ibid preamble, para 25.
[93] Rome II Proposal and Explanatory Memorandum (n 55) 19–20.

a non-EU state),[94] the market correction operates both intra- and extra-EU and purports to discourage EU polluters from exploiting the laxer laws of other EU states and non-EU states.[95]

The scope and contents of Article 7 of the Rome II Regulation have been extensively discussed by legal scholars,[96] often positively.[97] It is not necessary to engage in another doctrinal analysis here. Suffice it to say that the scope of Article 7 is very broad. It covers environmental damage and ensuing damage to persons or property, as long as it is directly attributable to the tortfeasor[98] and does not arise from nuclear activities[99] or the exercise of public powers.[100] Claimants include victims and all other persons who seek compensation, including public authorities if their claim is civil or commercial in nature.[101] The provision applies to nuisance, negligence and other environmental causes of action.[102] It also extends to injunctions aimed at preventing future damage.[103]

[94] Rome II Regulation (n 34), Art 3.

[95] A Mills, *Party Autonomy in Private International Law* (Cambridge, Cambridge University Press, 2018) 409–10; A Mills, 'Private International Law and EU External Relations: Think Local Act Global, or Think Global Act Local?' (2016) 65 *International and Comparative Law Quarterly* 541, 565–66.

[96] eg J von Hein, 'Article 7: Environmental Damage' in G-P Calliess and M Renner (eds), *Rome Regulations: Commentary*, 3rd edn (Alphen on the Rhine, Wolters Kluwer, 2020); A Fuchs, 'Article 7: Environmental Damage' in P Huber (ed), *Rome II Regulation: Pocket Commentary* (Munich, Sellier, 2011); A Dickinson, *The Rome II Regulation: The Law Applicable to Non-Contractual Obligations* (Oxford, Oxford University Press, 2010) ch 7; M Bogdan, 'The Treatment of Environmental Damage in Regulation Rome II' in J Ahern and W Binchy (eds), *The Rome II Regulation on the Law Applicable to Non-Contractual Obligations: A New International Litigation Regime* (Leiden, Martinus Nijhoff, 2009); M Bogdan, 'Some Reflections Regarding Environmental Damage and the Rome II Regulation' in G Venturini and S Bariatti (eds), *Liber Fausto Pocar*, vol 2: New Instruments of Private International Law (Milan, Giuffrè, 2009); W Posch, 'Some Observations on the Law Applicable to Transfrontier Environmental Damage' in M Hinteregger (ed), *Environmental Liability and Ecological Damage in European Law* (Cambridge, Cambridge University Press, 2008); T Kadner Graziano, 'The Law Applicable to Cross-Border Damage to the Environment: A Commentary on Article 7 of the Rome II Regulation' (2007) 9 *Yearbook of Private International Law* 71.

[97] Von Hein, 'Article 7' (2020) 650–51 and the sources cited by the author.

[98] Rome II Regulation (n 34) preamble (para 17), Art 4(1).

[99] ibid, Art 1(2)(f).

[100] ibid, Art 1(1).

[101] On the notion of 'civil and commercial matters' in this context, see Fach Gómez (n 89) 661–62; Grušić (n 3) 199–204; G Betlem and C Bernasconi, 'European Private International Law, the Environment and Obstacles for Public Authorities' (2006) 122 *Law Quarterly Review* 124.

[102] P Torremans et al, *Cheshire, North & Fawcett: Private International Law*, 15th edn (Oxford, Oxford University Press, 2017) 829; Dickinson, *The Rome II Regulation* (2010) para 7.14. But see J Hill and M Ní Shúilleabháin, *Clarkson & Hill's Conflict of Laws*, 5th edn (Oxford, Oxford Univesity Press, 2016) para 5.57; J Hill and A Chong, *International Commercial Disputes: Commercial Conflict of Laws in English Courts*, 4th edn (Oxford, Hart, 2010) para 15.1.65; A Rushworth and A Scott, 'Rome II: Choice of Law for Non-Contractual Obligations' [2008] *Lloyd's Maritime and Commercial Law Quarterly* 274, 283.

[103] Rome II Regulation (n 34), Arts 2(2), 3.

The notion of 'event giving rise to damage' is liberally interpreted. In the landmark *Milieudefensie* case, the Hague District Court held that Netherlands-based Royal Dutch Shell (RDS) had an obligation to reduce its CO_2 emissions by a net 45 per cent in 2030 compared to 2019 levels.[104] Plaintiffs (various environmental organisations and individuals) elected Dutch law as the place of acting pursuant to Article 7 of the Rome II Regulation. RDS pleaded that its corporate policy for the Shell group of companies, alleged by plaintiffs to be incompatible with global climate targets, did not constitute an 'event giving rise to damage' under Article 7 of the Rome II Regulation.[105] That event, RDS argued, was the actual CO_2 emissions which occurred around the world. The Court rejected RDS's argument. The Court recalled that climate change due to CO_2 emissions was 'environmental damage' under the Rome II Regulation.[106] The Court then found that RDS's corporate policy in the Netherlands was an independent cause of climate change-related damage suffered by Dutch residents.[107] The Court also held that Dutch law could alternatively apply as the law of the place of injury under Articles 4 and 7 of the Rome II Regulation, since the class action sought to protect the interests of Dutch residents.[108]

Beyond the intricacies of its application, the most striking feature of the Rome II Regulation is the explicit reference to three environmental principles in its preamble: precaution, corrective action and polluter-pays. These open-ended principles have become familiar to environmental and public international lawyers. But they have had little place so far in private international law which, while not devoid of overarching principles nor disinterested with substantive objectives such as the protection of weaker parties, tends to shy away from voicing direct policy objectives through conflict rules. The preamble of the Rome II Regulation deviates from this instinctive position and articulates a clear regulatory objective aligned with substantive law,[109] also described as an 'indirect better law approach' combining unilateral choice with the more favourable law in order to achieve a certain result.[110] The EC describes its regulatory objective as the need 'to establish a legislative policy that contributes to raising the general level of environmental protection, especially as the author of the environmental damage, unlike other torts or delicts, generally derives an economic benefit from his harmful activity'.[111] This regulatory stance does not come from

[104] Rechtbank Den Haag, 26 May 2021, *Milieudefensie et al v Royal Dutch Shell plc*, ECLI:NL:RBDHA:2021:5339 (*Milieudefensie*) (English court translation available online).
[105] ibid paras 4.3.2, 4.3.6.
[106] ibid para 4.3.2.
[107] ibid paras 4.3.4–4.3.7.
[108] ibid para 4.3.8.
[109] Mills, *Party Autonomy in Private International Law* (2018) 409.
[110] R Michaels, 'Private International Law and the Question of Universal Values' in F Ferrari and DP Fernández Arroyo (eds), *Private International Law: Contemporary Challenges and Continuing Relevance* (Cheltenham, Edward Elgar, 2019) 163–64.
[111] Rome II Proposal and Explanatory Memorandum (n 55) 19.

any single approach deemed desirable in domestic law, but from EU treaties and directives – a form of supranational law.[112]

Contrary to other substance-oriented conflict rules (consumer and employment contracts, for instance), Article 7 of the Rome II Regulation does not favour the victims only for the sake of favouring the victims. It ultimately purports to have a systemic impact beyond the protection of individual rights – a bold proposition discussed earlier in this chapter. Indeed, the EC's Rome II Proposal and Explanatory Memorandum makes clear that the provision has two equally important objectives: 'the point is not only to respect the victim's legitimate interests but also to establish a legislative policy that contributes to raising the general level of environmental protection'.[113] In other words, the Rome II Regulation favours the victims partly on the assumption that their interest in compensation aligns with the EU's substantive interest in protecting the environment.[114] Victims effectively become private attorneys general,[115] the agents of European public policy.

The fairness of a built-in pro-victim/environment bias within choice of law rules can be questioned, and Article 7 of the Rome II Regulation undeniably creates uncertainty for defendants. Defending claims under the law of an objectively foreseeable foreign jurisdiction is one thing; having to comply with the environmental laws of all states that could potentially be the *loci delicti* is quite another. This is a key issue in climate change litigation: an operator in the United States might anticipate that its activities will cause damage in Canada or Mexico, but not necessarily anywhere else. The Rome II Regulation, however, does not contain a foreseeability exception to counterbalance uncertainty – an absence criticised by some.[116] Defendants who cause mass environmental damage may have to defend themselves under the law of an unforeseen state, and possibly several laws if damage simultaneously occurs

[112] Consolidated Version of the of the Treaty on European Union [2008] OJ C115/13, Art 191; Directive 2004/35/EC of the European Parliament and of the Council of 21 April 2004 on environmental liability with regard to the prevention and remedying of environmental damage [2004] OJ L143/56 ('Environmental Liability Directive').

[113] Rome II Proposal and Explanatory Memorandum (n 55) 19.

[114] Mills (n 95) 410. But see T Nissen, 'Critique de l'article 7 du règlement Rome II: étude du dommage environnemental en droit international privé' (master thesis, Université catholique de Louvain, 2015) 39; F Grisel, 'Analyse critique de l'article 7 du Règlement du 11 juillet 2007 sur la loi applicable aux obligations non-contractuelles (« Rome II »)' (2011) 88 *Revue de droit international et de droit comparé* 148, 161–63 (both noting that plaintiffs' choice under Art 7 of the Rome II Regulation may not necessarily coincide with EU environmental policy).

[115] O Boskovic, 'Le contexte transnational en matière de responsabilité climatique' in M Hautereau-Boutonnet and S Porchy-Simon (eds), *Le changement climatique, quel rôle pour le droit privé?* (Paris, Dalloz, 2019) 201; Lequette (n 46) 523; Muir Watt, 'Beyond the Schism' (n 54) 424, fn 377; Muir Watt, 'Rome II' (n 37) 134.

[116] This was criticised: SC Symeonides, 'The American Revolution and the European Evolution in Choice of Law: Reciprocal Lessons' (2008) 82 *Tulane Law Review* 1741, 1768; SC Symeonides, 'Rome II and Tort Conflicts: A Missed Opportunity' (2008) 56 *American Journal of Comparative Law* 173, 211.

in different states or if victims in a single state make a different choice of law in their respective proceedings. Hence the Rome II Regulation is said to have significant implications for climate change litigation against corporations based in Europe and causing damage elsewhere.[117]

Rome II Regulation's lack of predictability in environmental matters, however, is not an accident. It is one of the objectives precisely because it is the only way to stop polluters from taking advantage of a weaker law.[118] Introducing a foreseeability exception would frustrate the objective because it can take decades to understand the full scope of environmental problems. Polluters could easily plead ignorance and remain governed by the favourable law of the place where they chose to operate. While it is common knowledge that pollution can have disastrous impacts across borders, those impacts may be extremely diffuse and the science behind them may still be in flux, such that considerable debate will arise over what the polluter could have known. In climate change litigation, for instance, a foreseeability exception could easily override the law of the place of injury in a particular case, even if most scientists agree on the existence of human-induced climate change generally. The ubiquity principle admittedly deprives polluters of a defence against the application of the law of the place of injury when that law sets a higher standard than the law of the state in which they operate. It also means that polluters may be found in breach of a law which they had not considered. Taken as a whole, however, the Rome II Regulation does not lead to total unpredictability for polluters because it limits the array of potentially applicable laws in other ways. Damage must be direct.[119] Public policy and the overriding mandatory provisions of the forum may also intervene in the choice of law process.[120]

Foreign Rules of Safety and Conduct

Article 7 of the Rome II Regulation is supplemented by another provision which impacts transboundary environmental litigation. Article 17 of the Rome II Regulation provides that 'In assessing the conduct of the person claimed to be liable, account shall be taken, as a matter of fact and in so far as is appropriate, of the rules of safety and conduct which were in force at the place and time

[117] Von Hein (n 96) 652; M Byers, K Franks and Andrew Gage, 'The Internationalization of Climate Damages Litigation' (2017) 7 *Washington Journal of Environmental Law and Policy* 295–96, fn 139, citing S Goldberg and R Lord, 'England' in R Lord et al (eds), *Climate Change Liability: Transnational Law and Practice* (Cambridge, Cambridge University Press, 2011) 484. On climate change litigation and the Rome II Regulation, see *Milieudefensie* (n 104) paras 4.3.1–4.3.7, 4.4.44–4.4.48; Boskovic, 'Responsabilité climatique' (2019) 200–203; Giansetto, 'Responsabilité climatique' [2018] 525–29.

[118] E Guinchard and S Lamont-Black, 'Environmental Law, the Black Sheep in Rome II's Drive for Legal Certainty? Article 7 of Regulation (EC) No 864/2007 on the Law Applicable to Non-Contractual Obligations' (2009) 11 *Environmental Law Review* 161, 170.

[119] Rome II Regulation (n 34) preamble (para 17), Art 4(1).

[120] ibid, Arts 16, 26.

of the event giving rise to the liability'.[121] Rules of safety and conduct include public law provisions contained in environmental statutes and designed for local incidents.[122]

Foreign rules of conduct and safety affect the operation of the ubiquity principle. If a victim chooses the law of the country in which the event giving rise to liability occurred (place of acting), the rules of safety and conduct which were in force at the place of acting are necessarily part of the applicable law.[123] But if a victim chooses the law of the country in which the environmental damage occurred, courts may then take into consideration the rules of safety and conduct in force at the place of acting at the time of the events.[124] This intrusion of foreign rules of conduct and safety into the applicable law comes with an important caveat: courts must take foreign rules of safety and conduct into account as a matter of fact, but do not have to apply them as a matter of law.

This distinction becomes particularly important if a foreign polluter relies on an administrative authorisation (permit, licence, certificate, etc) issued in the place of acting in order to escape liability under the law of the place of injury.[125] In this scenario, the polluter is allowed to operate in one state but causes damage in another. Authors generally treat administrative authorisations as rules of safety and conduct under Article 17 of the Rome II Regulation because they result from the application of public environmental regulation.[126] The question becomes whether courts should defer to the regulatory policy of foreign states (expressed through authorisations to operate) if they lead to damage in the forum, and the law of the forum would normally apply.

This debate precedes the Rome II Regulation.[127] Inspired by pre-Rome II jurisprudence from Austria and Germany, the literature suggests that foreign licences must meet three conditions in order to be taken into consideration under Article 17 of the Rome II Regulation: (1) the operation of the facility complies

[121] Rome II Regulation (n 34), Art 17.

[122] Fach Gómez (n 89) 665; Bogdan, 'Treatment of Environmental Damage in Rome II' (2009) 227; Bogdan, 'Reflections Regarding Environmental Damage' (2009) 103.

[123] eg *Milieudefensie* (n 104) para 4.4.44.

[124] For various possible scenarios, see Von Hein (n 96) 666–69.

[125] Article 17 of the Rome II Regulation, however, is neutral and can therefore operate in other scenarios, for instance when the law of the place of acting is more stringent than the law of the place of injury: C Kessedjian, 'Questions de droit international privé de la responsabilité sociétale des entreprises: rapport général' in C Kessedjian and H Cantú Rivera (eds), *Private International Law Aspects of Corporate Social Responsibility* (Cham, Springer, 2020) 47; Symeonides, 'Rome II and Tort Conflicts' (2008) 213–14.

[126] García-Castrillón (n 12) 574. See also Von Hein (n 96) 664–65; Fach Gómez (n 89) 666; Fuchs (n 96) 217; Dickinson (n 96) para 7.29. But see G van Calster, *European Private International Law* (Oxford, Hart, 2013) 174; E Rehbinder, 'Extra-Territoriality of Pollution Control Laws from a European Perspective' in G Handl, J Zekoll and P Zumbansen (eds), *Beyond Territoriality: Transnational Legal Authority in an Age of Globalization* (Leiden, Martinus Nijhoff, 2012) 151.

[127] ILA, 'Second Report on Transnational Enforcement of Environmental Law' (n 9) 920–26; Bernasconi (n 56) 92–95.

with public international law; (2) the conditions of issuance of the foreign licence match the ones found in local law; and (3) plaintiffs had a chance to take part in the foreign proceedings leading to the attribution of the licence.[128] The first condition refers to due diligence and other primary norms of international environmental law; the second condition refers to substantive reciprocity; and the third intersects with equal access.

The test is fact-driven, but it is doubtful that a foreign authorisation can exonerate polluters altogether when they are otherwise liable under the law of the place of injury (assuming that the plaintiff chose that law to govern the claim).[129] Courts have the discretion to take foreign authorisations into account as a matter of fact, but only when they consider it appropriate to do so. The EC's Rome II Proposal and Explanatory Memorandum explains that foreign rules of safety and conduct could factor when 'assessing the seriousness of the fault or the author's good or bad faith for the purposes of the measure of damages'.[130] These are questions of degree, which suggest that the EC did not contemplate total exoneration, at least not systematically. Total exoneration would also be inconsistent with the Environmental Liability Directive, which allows EU states to relieve legally authorised operators from bearing the costs of remedial actions (also called the permit defence) but does not require them to do so.[131] Ultimately, it would be odd if Article 7 of the Rome II Regulation aligned with EU environmental policy (particularly the polluter-pays principle) while Article 17 was interpreted as providing a complete safe harbour for polluters.[132] Ultimately, however, the interaction of both provisions with respect to foreign authorisations remains unclear in practice due to the scarcity of case law.[133]

[128] Von Hein (n 96) 671–72; I Kunda, 'Policies Underlying Conflict of Law Choices in Environmental Law' in V Sancin (ed), *International Environmental Law: Contemporary Concerns and Challenges* (Ljubljana, Založba, 2012) 525; García-Castrillón (n 12) 575.

[129] After the ECJ issued its judgment on jurisdiction in *Bier*, Dutch courts held that a French authorisation to discharge pollutants did not relieve the defendant from liability in the Netherlands: Hoge Raad der Nederlanden, 23 September 1988, *Mines de potasse d'Alsace SA v Onroerend Goed Maatschappij Bier BV et al*, (1988) Rechtspraak van de Week (RvdW) No 150, translated in English in (1990) 21 *Netherlands Yearbook of International Law* 434. See also *Milieudefensie* (n 104) paras 4.4.44–4.4.448 (on the indemnifying effect of the European Emissions Trading Scheme and other permits and obligations in relation to Royal Dutch Shell's global CO_2 emissions).

[130] Rome II Proposal and Explanatory Memorandum (n 55) 25.

[131] Environmental Liability Directive (n 112), Art 8(4)(a).

[132] O Boskovic, 'Droit international privé et environnement' in *Juris-classeur environnement et développement durable*, fasc 2030 (1 September 2014) para 51.

[133] cf Case 115/08 *Land Oberösterreich v ČEZ as* [2009] ECR I-10265 [135], [139]–[40]. In *ČEZ*, the ECJ held that the EU principle of non-discrimination based on nationality prevented Austrian courts from discriminating, under Austrian substantive law, between local and foreign authorisations in the availability of defences to a nuisance claim against the operator of a Czech nuclear power plant. This oft-cited case does not, however, involve the Rome II Regulation or a conflict of laws, as Austrian courts were applying Austrian law at that point of the proceedings.

Conclusion on the Rome II Regulation

Article 7 of the Rome II Regulation innovates on several fronts. It acknowledges the problems associated with a rigid definition of the *lex loci delicti* in cases of transboundary pollution – in the European context, the problems associated with the exclusive designation of the law of the place of injury. It demonstrates certain states' willingness to openly imbue choice of law rules with substantive objectives such as the compensation of victims and the protection of the environment. It also reflects their belief that the ubiquity principle aligns with those objectives. This is a welcome development which should inspire states outside the EU.

The ubiquity principle also continues to be discussed in the EU. In September 2020, the Committee on Legal Affairs of the European Parliament (EP) issued a draft report and recommendations to the EC on the topic of corporate due diligence and corporate accountability for business-related human rights violations.[134] The draft report proposed, along with a new Directive, amendments to the Brussels I Recast Regulation and the Rome II Regulation. New Article 6a of the Rome II Regulation on business-related civil claims for human rights violations would have allowed victims to choose between four laws: the law of the place of injury and the law of the place of acting (as in Article 7), but also the law of the place where the parent company is domiciled or the law of the place where it operates (if the parent company is not domiciled in a member state).[135] In March 2021, the EP adopted a resolution which called upon the EC to craft a directive on the topic, but made no mention of an amendment to the Rome II Regulation.[136] Whether a standalone choice of law rule will eventually reappear on the legislative radar remains to be seen. Alternatively, however, debates might focus on a *remodelled* Article 7 which would go beyond environmental damage and encompass all business-related human rights violations.[137]

The 2010 UNEP Guidelines on Liability

The UNEP Guidelines on Liability are the most recent attempt from an international organisation at implementing the ubiquity principle in choice of law

[134] European Parliament, 'Draft Report with recommendations to the Commission on corporate due diligence and corporate accountability' 2020/2129(INL).

[135] ibid 30–31.

[136] European Parliament, 'Resolution of 10 March 2021 with recommendations to the Commission on corporate due diligence and corporate accountability' 2020/2129(INL).

[137] E Álvarez-Armas, 'Potential Human-Rights-Related Amendments to the Rome II Regulation (II): The Proposed Art. 6a; Art. 7 is Dead, Long Live Article 7?' (Conflict of Laws, 27 January 2021), available at conflictoflaws.net. Article 7 had already been criticised for singling out environmental damage and ignoring other types of damage caused (often simultaneously) by transnational corporations: LFH Enneking, 'The Common Denominator of the Trafigura Case, Foreign Direct Liability Cases and the *Rome II Regulation*: An Essay on the Consequences of Private International Law for the Feasibility of Regulating Multinational Corporations Through Tort Law' (2008) 16 *European Review of Private Law* 283, 310–11.

rules for environmental damage.[138] In 2008, shortly after the ILC finalised the Principles on the Allocation of Loss and the UNGA commended them to the attention of governments, UNEP convened a consultative meeting of government officials and experts to discuss the development of liability guidelines. UNEP sought to assist states in developing domestic laws on liability and compensation for environmental damage, at the request of developing states who felt that they lacked the appropriate framework.[139] Two years of work followed and UNEP finally adopted the UNEP Guidelines on Liability at its 2010 meeting in Bali, alongside the UNEP Guidelines on Access to Justice.[140] In its resolution, UNEP recalled the thirteenth principle of the Rio Declaration on liability and compensation and reiterated that liability regimes were an important part of domestic environmental protection arsenals.[141]

The UNEP Guidelines on Liability share many of the features of the ILC Principles on the Allocation of Loss and come from a major UN agency. Importantly, the thirteenth guideline explicitly endorses the ubiquity principle:

> Subject to domestic laws on jurisdiction and in the absence of special rules established by contract or international agreement, any claim for compensation that raises a choice-of-law issue should be decided in accordance with the law of the place in which the damage occurred, unless the claimant chooses to base the claim on the law of the country in which the event giving rise to the damage occurred.[142]

Commentary on this provision is sparse (both from UNEP itself and legal scholars), but this thirteenth guideline essentially replicates the essence of Article 7 of the Rome II Regulation and the ubiquity principle. Of course, the UNEP Guidelines on Liability should be taken for what they are, that is, soft law. UNEP made sure to mention that they were voluntary and did not set a precedent for the future development of international law.[143] They clearly did not have a major impact. The UNEP Guidelines on Access to Justice, adopted at the same time, overshadowed the UNEP Guidelines on Liability to the point

[138] Guidelines for the development of domestic legislation on liability, response action and compensation for damage caused by activities dangerous to the environment, UNEPGC Dec SS.XI/5 B in UNEP Governing Council, 'Report of the Governing Council/Global Ministerial Environment Forum on the work of its eleventh special session' UN Doc A/65/25 (2010) ('UNEP Guidelines on Liability') 16.

[139] United Nations Environment Programme, 'Report of the consultative meeting of government officials and experts to review and further develop draft guidelines for the development of national legislation on liability, redress and compensation for damage caused by activities dangerous to the environment' UN Doc UNEP/GC/25/INF/15/Add.3 (2009).

[140] UNEP Guidelines on Liability (n 138).

[141] ibid 16 (resolution of the Governing Council, preamble), citing Rio Declaration on Environment and Development (13 June 1992) UN Doc A/CONF.151/26/Rev.1(Vol 1) ('Rio Declaration') principle 13.

[142] UNEP Guidelines on Liability (n 138) guideline 13.

[143] ibid 16 (resolution of the Governing Council, para 1). This was apparently done to avoid interfering with ongoing negotiations on a liability regime for biosafety: E Mrema, 'UNEP GCSS-11/ GMEF: Building Confidence in the Multilateral System' (2010) 40 *Environmental Policy and Law* 136, 138.

where the words 'Bali Guidelines' often refer only to the former.[144] Nonetheless, the UNEP Guidelines on Liability should not be neglected. Even non-binding guidelines are noteworthy in an area where documents such as the OECD Recommendation and the Nordic Convention achieve surprisingly global recognition and influence multiple international conventions and domestic initiatives. And unlike the ILC Principles on the Allocation of Loss, the UNEP Guidelines on Liability delve straight into the choice of law problem. They provide an important piece of the puzzle for states seeking to strengthen environmental rights through domestic law.

Together with the Rome II Regulation, the UNEP Guidelines on Liability reflect a new way of approaching transboundary pollution through choice of law. Canada, however, has not yet followed the EU's example nor UNEP's recommendations. The next section exposes the current situation and prospects in Canadian private international law.

II. THE LAW APPLICABLE TO TRANSBOUNDARY POLLUTION IN CANADIAN PRIVATE INTERNATIONAL LAW

In this section, I argue that Canadian private international law does not completely meet the choice of law requirements associated with the duty to ensure prompt and adequate compensation. Courts in common law provinces apply the *lex loci delicti* (the law of the place where the tort occurs) when the case does not fall under the Reciprocal Access Act, but they rigidly define the place where complex torts occur for choice of law purposes. This exercise will likely result in the application of the law of the place of injury, to the exclusion of the law of the place of acting. In Quebec, the CCQ offers both options, yet courts tend to favour the law of the place of acting when the case involves multiple victims located in different states. The law of the place of injury is considered an exception which depends on foreseeability.

The drawbacks associated with each connecting factor, both generally and in relation to transboundary pollution, were described above. It was also argued that any rigid definition of the *lex loci delicti* fails to comply with the requirements of the ILC Principles on the Allocation of Loss because it does not ensure equal remedy, allows polluters to take advantage of weaker legal regimes and reduces the likelihood of compensation in certain scenarios. The law of the place of injury is problematic if foreign victims get a lesser treatment than local victims when they sue in Canada. The law of the place of acting is problematic if all victims, while being equal, have lower prospects of compensation as a result of the polluter's choice to operate in a weak jurisdiction.

[144] eg U Etemire, 'Insights on the UNEP Bali Guidelines and the Development of Environmental Democratic Rights' (2016) 28 *Journal of Environmental Law* 393.

In the next sections, I analyse the operation of choice of law rules in Canada, explain why their result is unsatisfactory in light of the above considerations, and provide the justification for an environmental reform of Canadian choice of law. I analyse the *lex loci delicti* and its application in transboundary environmental disputes (section II.A). I also analyse various mechanisms designed to override the applicable law when necessary, including on the basis of public policy (section II.B). I finally address the extraterritorial scope of Canadian environmental statutes, insofar as they contain statutory causes of action which plaintiffs can invoke in private litigation (section II.C). Indeed, even if Canadian law applies as a result of choice of law rules, several statutory causes of action are limited to local plaintiffs or subject to constitutional constraints on their extraterritorial application. The last section argues that Canadian environmental statutes do not adequately protect litigants in cases of transboundary pollution.

A. Designating the Law Applicable to Transboundary Pollution

This section examines the law applicable to transboundary pollution in light of the ubiquity principle used in the EU and recommended by UNEP. Environmental torts typically invoked by plaintiffs in private litigation (and already introduced in chapter three) include civil liability and neighbourhood disturbance in Quebec, as well as negligence, nuisance, trespass, strict liability (*Rylands v Fletcher*) and breach of riparian rights in the rest of the country.

Contrary to jurisdiction, choice of law is approached here without distinguishing foreign victims of pollution originating in Canada and local victims of pollution originating abroad. The third chapter treats the two scenarios separately for jurisdictional purposes because the relevant connecting factors are different: foreign plaintiffs will rely on the presence of the polluter in Canada whereas local plaintiffs will rely on the occurrence of a tort there. Choice of law, by contrast, comes down to the place of the tort in both cases. It may result in inequalities between local and foreign victims, but the relevant connecting factor remains the same: the place of the tort. The two scenarios are therefore discussed together, with appropriate distinctions when necessary.

In the next sections, I examine the *lex loci delicti* as applied in common law provinces (section II.A.i). I also examine the choice of law rules contained in the Reciprocal Access Act and their relationship with the common law in the four provinces that adopted it (section II.A.ii). I finaly delve into Quebec's particular iteration of the *lex loci delicti* (section II.A.iii).

At the outset, it is important to remember that Canadian courts cannot raise foreign law on their own motion if parties choose not to plead foreign law. Local law will then apply by default, regardless of choice of law rules.[145] Should the

[145] CCQ (n 4), Art 2809, para 2; *Threlfall v Carleton University* 2019 SCC 50 [26]; *Tolofson* (n 4) 1053.

ubiquity principle find its way into Canadian law, a plaintiff-initiated choice of law would sit better with the existing framework than a court-mandated one. Alternatively, a court could conceivably decide for itself the most favourable law *after* a party raises the choice of law issue.

i. Choice of Law in Canadian Common Law

Courts in common law provinces apply the *lex loci delicti* – the law of the place where the tort occurred – in transboundary environmental disputes. The crux of the matter consists in determining whether the tort occurs at the place of acting or the place of injury. This tension is at the heart of private international law since the Supreme Court of Canada issued its judgment in *Tolofson*.[146]

I explain below the choice of law rule articulated in *Tolofson* (section II.A.i.a), its approach towards pure transboundary damage (section II.A.i.b), its application to transboundary pollution (section II.A.i.c) and its implications for equal remedy and prompt and adequate compensation (section II.A.i.d).

a. *Tolofson* and the Law of the Place of the Tort

Prior to 1994, Canadian courts applied the English common law rule formulated in *Phillips v Eyre*.[147] A remedy was available in Canadian courts for an injury caused by an act committed abroad only if the act: (1) would have been civilly actionable in the forum if it had been committed there; and (2) was unjustifiable under the law of the place where it had actually been committed.[148] The rule spawned many controversies and uncertainties over the years, particularly with respect to car accidents.[149] The emphasis on the law of the forum under the first branch of the rule recalled a bygone era in which civil law served a punitive function akin to criminal law, which applied strictly territorially.[150] The rule was also thought to encourage reprehensible forum shopping.[151]

Courts seised with transboundary environmental disputes in the 1970s and 1980s would have likely applied the *Phillips v Eyre* rule in such a context.[152] This is what Justice Ritchie of the Supreme Court of Canada did in *Interprovincial Co-operatives*. Recall that the case involved a Manitoba environmental statute,

[146] *Tolofson* (n 4).

[147] *Phillips v Eyre* (1870) LR 6 QB 1, 28–29.

[148] *Samson v Holden* [1963] SCR 373, 378–79; *McLean v Pettigrew* (1944) [1945] SCR 62, 76–77.

[149] For a historical account of the law in England and in Canada, see *Tolofson* (n 4) 1039–46.

[150] UK Law Comission and Scottish Law Commission, 'Private International Law: Choice of Law in Tort and Delict' (UK Com No 193, Scot Com No 129, 1990) 7.

[151] *Tolofson* (n 4) 1052.

[152] See by analogy *Boslund v Abbotsford Lumber, Mining and Development Co* [1925] 1 DLR 978, 980–81 (BC SC), affd (1925) [1927] 1 DLR 279 (BC CA) (fire spreading from British Columbia into the state of Washington – action by American plaintiffs maintainable in British Columbia because the defendant's acts were wrongful in both jurisdictions).

the Fishermen's Assistance and Polluters' Liability Act, which created liability for damage caused to Manitoba fisheries by contaminants discharged in provincial waters or carried from elsewhere into those waters. The Act also provided that an authorisation granted by the authorities of the place where the discharge had occurred could not relieve the defendant from liability in Manitoba.[153] Adhering to the justifiability standard in the second part of the rule, Justice Ritchie found that the polluting activities were justified under the law of the place of acting because the defendants were licensed in Ontario and Saskatchewan. Hence Manitoba could not, by imposing liability on the defendants under the Act, deprive them of rights validly acquired in their home province.[154]

The dissenting judges in *Interprovincial Co-operatives*, led by Chief Justice Laskin, relied on *Moran* (a jurisdictional case)[155] to find that the tort had occurred in Manitoba. This meant that Manitoba had not legislated extraterritorially when it enacted the Fishermen's Assistance and Polluters' Liability Act.[156] The reasons of the dissenting judges foretold a different approach to choice of law in tort.[157] In the decades that followed, some authors relied on *Moran* to suggest that the *lex loci delicti* or the law of the most substantially affected state would apply in a transboundary environmental dispute, without insisting on civil actionability under the law of the forum when the forum was not the place of acting.[158] Choice of law rules, however, remained unchanged.

The Supreme Court of Canada broke free of the *Phillips v Eyre* rule in *Tolofson* (1994).[159] English courts had already changed the rule to one of double civil actionability[160] and shortly before *Tolofson* was decided, double actionability was abolished altogether by statute in the United Kingdom.[161] The Supreme Court of Canada, led by Justice La Forest, completely rejected the double-barrelled approach as it stood in Canada. The Court noted that the rule inappropriately asked the courts to pass judgment on activities occurring

[153] The Fishermen's Assistance and Polluters' Liability Act, SM 1970 c 32, s 4(2).

[154] *Interprovincial Co-operatives Ltd v R* (1975), [1976] 1 SCR 477, 521–23 (Ritchie J, concurring).

[155] *Moran v Pyle National (Canada) Ltd* (1973) [1975] SCR 393.

[156] *Interprovincial Co-operatives* SCC (n 154) 500–01 (Laskin CJC, dissenting) and the comments of SGA Pitel et al, *Private International Law in Common Law Canada: Cases, Text and Materials*, 4th edn (Toronto, Emond, 2016) 681.

[157] J Blom, 'The Conflict of Laws and the Constitution – Interprovincial Co-Operatives Ltd. v. The Queen' (1977) 11 *UBC Law Review* 144, 156.

[158] JA Gallob, 'Birth of the North American Transboundary Environmental Plaintiff: Transboundary Pollution and the 1979 Draft Treaty for Equal Access and Remedy' (1991) 15 *Harvard Environmental Law Review* 85, 103–07; CA Cooper, 'The Management of International Environmental Disputes in the Context of Canada-United States Relations: A Survey and Evaluation of Techniques and Mechanisms' (1986) 24 *Canadian Yearbook of International Law* 247, 276; A Rest, *International Protection of the Environment and Liability: The Responsibility of States and Individuals in Cases of Transfrontier Pollution* (Berlin, Erich Schmidt, 1978) 141.

[159] *Tolofson* (n 4).

[160] *Boys v Chaplin* [1971] AC 356, 388 (HL).

[161] Private International Law (Miscellaneous Provisions) Act 1995, ss 10–13; *Lucasfilm Ltd v Ainsworth* [2011] UKSC 39 [78]–[80].

in foreign countries. Its focus on the *lex fori* undermined the territoriality principle in the name of now-obsolete considerations such as the dominance of the British colonial empire, the superiority of its laws and the impracticability of proving the domestic law of distant states.[162] The Court also rejected the uncertainty associated with the American doctrine of the proper law of the tort.[163]

The Court replaced the double-barrelled approach with the *lex loci delicti* on the basis that it met normal expectations and that it was certain, easy to apply, predictable and in line with a growing international consensus.[164] Importantly, the Court associated the *lex loci delicti* with 'the law of the place where the activity occurred' (for instance, where a car accident occurs).[165] As the Court would explain in a subsequent case, 'the rationale for the rule is that in the case of most torts, the occurrence of the wrong constituting the tort is its most substantial or characteristic element, and the injury or consequences are typically felt in the same place'.[166] This is why it made sense for the Court to locate torts at the place of acting.

b. The Treatment of Pure Transboundary Damage in *Tolofson*

In *Tolofson*, the Supreme Court of Canada recognised two broad sets of circumstances calling for adjustments to the *lex loci delicti*.[167] The first concerns a small subset of international cases – but not interprovincial ones – in which the *lex loci delicti* works an injustice justifying the application of local law instead.[168] The second is more relevant for our purposes because it has to do with pure transboundary damage. In an oft-quoted statement, Justice La Forest explained that complex torts are not easily localised in a single place for the purposes of identifying the *lex loci delicti*:

> From the general principle that a state has exclusive jurisdiction within its own territories and that other states must under principles of comity respect the exercise of its jurisdiction within its own territory, *it seems axiomatic to me that, at least as a general rule, the law to be applied in torts is the law of the place where the activity occurred, i.e., the* lex loci delicti. *There are situations, of course, notably where an act occurs in one place but the consequences are directly felt elsewhere, when the issue of where the tort takes place itself raises thorny issues. In such a case, it may well be that the consequences would be held to constitute the wrong. Difficulties may also*

[162] *Tolofson* (n 4) 1052–53.
[163] ibid 1055–57.
[164] ibid 1049–51.
[165] ibid 1050.
[166] *Éditions Écosociété Inc v Banro Corp* 2012 SCC 18 [50]. See also *Club Resorts Ltd v Van Breda* 2012 SCC 17 [37]; *Castillo v Castillo* 2005 SCC 83 [27] (Bastarache J, concurring).
[167] Justice La Forest also opened the door to a public policy exception overrriding the *lex loci delicti* in international cases: *Tolofson* (n 4) 1054–55.
[168] *Tolofson* (n 4) 1054.

> *arise where the wrong directly arises out of some transnational or interprovincial activity. There territorial considerations may become muted; they may conflict and other considerations may play a determining role.*[169]

The Court strongly suggests here that when an act and its consequences occur in different states, the *lex loci delicti* is the law of the place of injury. This is a significant departure from the Court's general understanding of the *lex loci delicti* as the law of the place of acting. Justice La Forest's statement, however, raises more questions than answers. It implies that 'torts arising directly from transnational/interprovincial activity' are somehow different from transboundary torts, but does not explain what the difference might be. Transboundary pollution, to name one example, can certainly be both. Nor does it explain the circumstances in which the damage will indeed constitute the wrong for choice of law purposes. Justice La Forest himself mentioned libel as a tort potentially occurring at the place of publication.[170] Subsequent jurisprudence confirmed that in this context, the *lex loci delicti* is indeed the law of the place of publication, that is, where the defamatory statement is communicated and its reputational effects are felt.[171] But the law is not always as clear for other torts.[172] As the Ontario Superior Court of Justice noted, '*Tolofson* clearly recognizes the complexities of trans-border torts and refrains from making a definitive statement that the place of the tort is always where the harm was suffered'.[173]

The localisation of torts for choice of law purposes came back to the Supreme Court of Canada in *Éditions Écosociété* and *Breeden* (2012), two cross-border defamation cases.[174] The debate on the appropriate choice of law rule for defamation stemmed from the fact that the *lex loci delicti* would lead to the application of different laws in different courts if a defamatory statement was published in multiple places, thus favouring libel tourism – a situation further exacerbated if the statement was posted online and made available worldwide.[175] In a lengthy obiter, Justice LeBel, writing for the Court in *Éditions Écosociété*, questioned whether the *lex loci delicti* (defined in this context as the law of the place of publication) or the law of the place of the most substantial harm to

[169] ibid 1050 (emphasis added).

[170] ibid 1041–42.

[171] *Haaretz.com v Goldhar* 2018 SCC 28 [84]–[88]; *Breeden v Black* 2012 SCC 19 [32]–[33]; *Éditions Écosociété* (n 166) [62].

[172] eg *Barrick Gold Corporation v Goldcorp Inc* 2011 ONSC 3725 [645]–[655] (where the Ontario Superior Court of Justice referred both to a 'defining activity' test and a 'consequences felt' test to localise the torts of inducing breach of contract, interference with contractual relations and conspiracy).

[173] *Silver v Imax Corporation* (2009) 86 CPC (6th) 273, 324 (Ont Sup Ct), leave to appeal to Ont Div Ct refused 2011 ONSC 1035.

[174] *Breeden* (n 171); *Éditions Écosociété* (n 166).

[175] eg J Walker, *Castel & Walker: Canadian Conflict of Laws*, vol 2, 6th edn (Markham, LexisNexis, 2005) (loose-leaf updated 2021) § 35.8.

the reputation should apply to cross-border defamation claims.[176] Justice LeBel refused to give a definite answer.

The Court's restraint makes sense because the two cases did not hinge on choice of law. They involved the jurisdiction of Ontario courts and the doctrine of *forum non conveniens*. The law applicable to the dispute was merely one of the factors to be considered in deciding whether to decline jurisdiction in favour of another state, and Ontario law applied under either choice of law rule. Yet the Court seemed particularly interested in the issue. Unfortunately, its lengthy detour into *Tolofson*'s territory only caused more confusion, providing 'a good example of why common law courts should limit their reasons to the issues that are necessary to decide the case before them'.[177] In *Tolofson*, the Court had left the door open to an injury-based definition of the *lex loci delicti* for certain torts. Arguably, the caveat was not so much an exception to the *lex loci delicti* as a different way of localising certain torts in order to identify the *lex loci delicti* – in other words, a different interpretation of the same choice of law rule.[178] The Court, however, went further in *Éditions Écosociété*: it interpreted *Tolofson*'s caveat as opening the door to brand-new choice of law rules for certain torts, but did not settle the issue.[179]

Uncertainty persisted after *Éditions Écosociété*. In 2015, the Court declined to hear a case involving the localisation of the tort of conversion for choice of law purposes, in spite of the appellant's invitation to reassess choice of law rules for torts.[180] The Court signalled then its reluctance to revisit the issue. This reluctance became clearer when the Court issued its opinion in *Haaretz.com* (2018), a case involving jurisdiction over online defamation and incidentally the applicable law, as part of the *forum non conveniens* analysis. Parties had squarely debated the relevance of the *lex loci delicti* in their written submissions.[181] The Court had a good opportunity to revisit Justice La Forest's caveat in *Tolofson* and to determine whether to deviate from the *lex loci delicti* or its dominant interpretation in certain cases, as suggested by Justice LeBel in *Éditions Écosociété*.

Seven of the nine judges reaffirmed the *lex loci delicti* in defamation disputes (again, defined in this context as the law of the place of publication). Justice Côté, also writing for Justices Brown and Rowe, was not convinced of the need

[176] *Éditions Écosociété* (n 166) [49]–[62]. See also *Breeden* (n 171) [32]–[33].

[177] B Kain, EC Marques and B Shaw, 'Developments in Private International Law: The 2011–2012 Term – The Unfinished Project of the *Van Breda* Trilogy' (2012) 59 *Supreme Court Law Review (2d)* 277, 299.

[178] Walker, *Canadian Conflict of Laws*, vol 2 (2005) § 35.8 (noting that Justice La Forest seemed 'prepared to consider the place of injury, that is, where the harm ensued, as the place of tort').

[179] *Éditions Écosociété* (n 166) [50]–[51].

[180] *Coady v Quadrangle Holdings Ltd* 2015 NSCA 13 [57]–[60], [70]–[78], leave to appeal to SCC refused [2015] 2 SCR vi.

[181] *Haaretz.com* (n 171) (Factum of the Appellant, paras 78–88; Factum of the Respondant, paras 112–40).

for a new rule on the facts of the case. She did not wish to discourage the Court to hold otherwise in a later case, but only on the basis of proper evidence and submissions.[182] Justice Karakatsanis agreed with 'much of [her] reasoning', which presumably includes the appropriate choice of law rule since her reasons do not refer to this issue.[183] Chief Justice McLachlin and Justices Moldaver and Gascon, dissenting on other points, expressly maintained the *lex loci delicti*.[184] Only Justices Abella and Wagner (as he then was), concurring in the result, would have replaced it with the law of the place of substantial harm to the reputation in the context of defamation.[185]

Haaretz.com thus reinforced the status of the *lex loci delicti* as the choice of law rule for torts, absent future changes in the defamation context. Unfortunately, none of the five sets of reasons clarified *Tolofson*'s caveat on pure transboundary damage. This is disappointing because online defamation is certainly one of the thorny situations that would have preoccupied Justice La Forest in *Tolofson*. Justice Abella briefly made the parallel,[186] but her proposal for a new choice of law rule pre-empted further discussion on the localisation of torts under *Tolofson*'s framework. More fundamentally, her reasons suggest, as did Justice LeBel's in *Éditions Écosociété*, that *Tolofson* opened the door to different choice of law rules for certain torts, as opposed to an injury-based definition of the *lex loci delicti* in cases where consequences constitute the wrong.[187] The rest of the bench made no comment on this point. Accordingly, it remains unclear whether *Tolofson*'s caveat supports alternative choice of law rules or simply alternative methods of localisation (and in the latter case, for which torts).[188]

c. *Tolofson* and Transboundary Pollution

Going back to transboundary pollution, we must conclude that the choice of law rule remains the *lex loci delicti* for now, for lack of a clear, alternative choice of law rule. The question becomes where environmental torts occur for choice of law purposes. Transboundary pollution is a perfect illustration of the kind

[182] ibid [84]–[94] (Côté J).
[183] ibid [99] (Karakatsanis J, concurring).
[184] ibid [196]–[204] (McLachlin CJ, Moldaver and Gascon JJ, dissenting).
[185] ibid [104]–[19] (Abella J, concurring), 144–46 (Wagner J, concurring). Justice Abella would have employed the substantial harm to reputation test jurisdictional purposes as well: ibid [120]–[130] (Abella J, concurring). Justice Wagner, by contrast, would have adopted the test for choice of law purposes only: ibid [147]–[149] (Wagner J).
[186] *Haaretz.com* (n 171) [111]–[112] (Abella J, concurring).
[187] ibid.
[188] B Shaw and S Robinson, '*Goldhar v. Haaretz.com*: A Product of the Supreme Court's Unfinished Project to Reform Canadian Private International Law' (2019) 49 *Advocates' Quarterly* 143, 166. On the questions raised by *Tolofson* in this regard, see SGA Pitel and NS Rafferty, *Conflict of Laws*, 2nd edn (Toronto, Irwin Law, 2016) 268–70; SGA Pitel and JR Harper, 'Choice of Law for Tort in Canada: Reasons for Change' (2013) 9 *Journal of Private International Law* 289, 295–96.

of thorny situations contemplated by Justice La Forest in *Tolofson* because the act occurs in one place and its consequences occur elsewhere. In these circumstances, the *lex loci delicti* could be the law of the place of acting (aligning with *Tolofson*'s definition of the place where a tort generally occurs), but it could also be the law of the place of injury.

The localisation of torts does not follow strict or arbitrary rules. The analysis should focus on where each tort crystallises, that is, where a cause of action exists.[189] Jurisdictional rules have a certain relevance in this inquiry. The Supreme Court of Canada explained in *Haaretz.com* that 'In circumstances where the *situs* of the tort leads to the assumption of jurisdiction in the chosen forum, *lex loci delicti* will inevitably also point to the chosen forum on the question of applicable law'.[190] Should a court assume jurisdiction on the basis that the plaintiff suffered damage in the province (hence that a tort occurred there in the sense of *Moran* and *Club Resorts*), the *lex loci delicti* would likely be the law of the forum. Courts also sometimes rely on jurisdictional precedents to localise torts for choice of law purposes,[191] a possible side-effect of the much larger body of case law pertaining to jurisdiction. This said, the processes of assuming jurisdiction on the basis of a tort occurring in the forum (*Club Resorts*) and of identifying the *lex loci delicti* (*Tolofson*) remain conceptually distinct.[192] A single applicable law implies that there can only be one place where a tort occurs. Jurisdictional rules call for no such restriction: two states may well have a sufficient interest to hear the dispute if some element of the tort occurred there, without even concluding that the entire tort occurred there. Thus, 'what is meant by the place of a tort can be different in the jurisdiction context than in the choice of law context'.[193] A standalone analysis is required, even though it may borrow from jurisdictional precedents.

Courts seised with allegations of negligence, nuisance, trespass, strict liability (*Rylands v Fletcher*) or breach of riparian rights related to transboundary pollution would apply the law of the place where the injury was suffered. Again, we should distinguish negligence and property torts.

The Law Applicable to Negligence

Negligence depends on an injury which constitutes the tort.[194] In this context, the *lex loci delicti* is the law of the place where the injury occurred. This is consistent

[189] In the jurisdictional context, see the sources cited above nn 321–23 (ch 3).

[190] *Haaretz.com* (n 171) [90].

[191] eg *Thorne v Hudson Estate* 2017 ONCA 208 [7]–[11], leave to appeal to SCC refused [2017] 3 SCR x.

[192] *Moran* (155) 397; SGA Pitel and V Black, 'Assumed Jurisdiction in Canada: Identifying and Interpreting Presumptive Connecting Factors' (2018) 14 *Journal of Private International Law* 193, 196–97.

[193] SGA Pitel and V Black, 'Assumed Jurisdiction in Canada: Identifying and Interpreting Presumptive Connecting Factors' (2018) 14 *Journal of Private International Law* 193, 197. See also Pitel and Rafferty, *Conflict of Laws* (2016) 269; Walker, vol 2 (n 175) § 35.8.

[194] In the jurisdictional context, see the sources cited above n 353 (ch 3).

with the view of the dissenting judges in *Interprovincial Co-operatives*, who relied on *Moran* to find that the cause of action had arisen in Manitoba, where the effects of the pollution had been felt.[195]

Post-*Tolofson* case law supports this proposition. In product liability cases, courts follow the logic of *Moran* and locate negligence at the place of injury for choice of law purposes. In *Lilydale Cooperative* (2013), the plaintiff, an Alberta company, had bought a fryer from the defendant, an Ontario company. The fryer had later caused a fire in the plaintiff's plant in Alberta. The plaintiff sued in negligence. The Ontario Superior Court of Justice applied the law of Alberta because the damage had occurred there.[196] In *Ostroski* (1995), the plaintiff had been injured at her residence in Pennsylvania when the chair manufactured by the Ontario defendants had tipped over. Again, the General Division of the Ontario Court of Justice applied the law of Pennsylvania because the damage had occurred there.[197] In *Shane* (2003), the Ontario Superior Court of Justice hinted – in the context of a *forum non conveniens* analysis – at the possibility that Ontario law could govern the issue of the negligent design and manufacture of a tractor built in England and destroyed by fire in Ontario.[198] So did the Alberta Court of Queen's Bench in *Fort Hills Energy*.[199] The Supreme Court of the Northwest Territories left the door open to a similar reasoning in *Stewart* (1996).[200] None of these cases discusses whether *Moran*'s foreseeability requirement also applies in the choice of law context, such that the law of the place of injury would only apply if the manufacturer could reasonably foresee that the product would be used or consumed there. In *Ostroski*, however, the Court quoted *Moran* and held that Pennsylvania, and not Ontario, was a place 'substantially [a]ffected by the defendant's activities or its consequences and the law of which is likely to have been in the contemplation of the parties'.[201]

The jurisprudence of the Ontario Court of Appeal confirms the importance of the place of injury in identifying the law applicable to negligence. In *Leonard* (1997), the plaintiffs had been involved in a car accident during a high-speed police chase which had begun in Ontario and then crossed over into Quebec.[202] They sued the police officers and the person they were chasing for negligence. The Ontario Court of Appeal had to locate the tort of negligence in either Quebec or Ontario in order to identify the *lex loci delicti*. The Court held that the tort had occurred in Quebec because the injury had occurred there.[203]

[195] *Interprovincial Co-operatives* SCC (n 154) 501 (Laskin CJC, dissenting).

[196] *Lilydale Cooperative Limited v Meyn Canada Inc* 2013 ONSC 5313 [9]–[23], affd 2015 ONCA 281.

[197] *Ostroski v Global Upholstery Co* 1995 CarswellOnt 874 [5]–[15] (Westlaw) (Ont Gen Div).

[198] *Shane v JCB Belgium NV* 2003 CanLII 49357 [48], [50–51] (Ont Sup Ct).

[199] *Fort Hills Energy LP v Jotun A/S* 2019 ABQB 237 [147]–[157].

[200] *Stewart v Stewart Estate* [1996] 8 WWR 624, 631 (NWT SC). See also *Ross v Ford Motor Co* (1997) [1998] NWTR 175, 180–81 (NWT SC).

[201] *Ostroski* (n 197) [13].

[202] *Leonard v Houle* (1997) 36 OR (3d) 357, 363 (Ont CA), leave to appeal to SCC refused [1998] 1 SCR xi.

[203] ibid 364.

For the Court, no wrong existed without an injury. Plaintiffs sued because they had suffered an injury in Quebec, not because the police had breached whatever duty they might have had in Ontario.[204] The analogy with transboundary pollution is admittedly imperfect because *Leonard* involved a car chase across Ontario and Quebec which had resulted in an accident in Quebec – in other words, both the act (or part thereof) and the damage had occurred in Quebec. Nonetheless, *Leonard* was cited and applied in *Lilydale Cooperative*, a product liability case in which the allegedly negligent act had occurred entirely elsewhere.[205]

Das (2018) illustrates a similar principle.[206] Victims of the tragic collapse of the Rana Plaza building in Bangladesh sued Loblaws – a Canadian retailer that purchased clothes from a manufacturer operating in the Rana Plaza – and a company retained by Loblaws to perform audits of factories in Bangladesh. Among the many disputed issues was the law applicable to claims in negligence and vicarious liability against Loblaws. The plaintiffs argued that Loblaws' alleged wrongful conduct (acquiring knowledge of the working conditions in Bangladesh and signing contracts regarding its operations in Bangladesh, for instance) had occurred in Ontario, where it operated. Hence, Ontario law governed the claims even though the resulting injury had occurred in Bangladesh. The trial judge rejected the argument. Citing *Moran*, Justice Perell held that Loblaws' wrongdoing had 'occurred in Bangladesh, the country substantially affected by its acts or omissions and the country whose citizens suffered the consequences of the wrongdoing'.[207] Hence the *lex loci delicti* was Bangladeshi law.[208] The Ontario Court of Appeal affirmed Justice Perell's judgment and recalled that the injury in Bangladesh had 'crystallized the alleged wrong' there.[209] Both courts relied on *Leonard* in their reasons.[210]

Summing up, the above cases strongly suggest that the law applicable to a negligence claim – the *lex loci delicti* under *Tolofson* – is the law of the place of injury. Courts might revert to the law of the place of acting under *Tolofson* if too many victims rely on too many different laws in the same litigation, making the judicial process impracticable, but cases show no sign of such 'exception within the exception' outside Quebec.[211]

[204] ibid 364–65.

[205] *Lilydale Cooperative* (n 196) [23].

[206] *Das v George Weston Ltd* 2018 ONCA 1053, leave to appeal to SCC refused 38529 (8 August 2019).

[207] *Das v George Weston Limited* 2017 ONSC 4129 [248], affd 2018 ONCA 1053, leave to appeal to SCC refused 38529 (8 August 2019).

[208] ibid [265].

[209] *Das* ONCA (n 206) [90]–[91].

[210] ibid [90]; *Das* ONSC (n 207) [241].

[211] The Quebec Court of Appeal has developed such a rule in its interpretation of Art 3126, para 1 CCQ. For further discussion on this point, see section 4.II.A.iii below.

The Law Applicable to Property Torts

Although authorities are scant, the *lex loci delicti* of property torts is likely the law of the place where the injury occurred.[212] This is because trespass, nuisance, strict liability (*Rylands v Fletcher*) and breach of riparian rights all involve interference with property. And even if 'the wrongful act takes place in a different jurisdiction [than where the property is situated], the location of the property is probably still the weightiest factor in determining the *lex loci delicti*'.[213]

d. Implications for Equal Remedy and Prompt and Adequate Compensation

The outcome of the choice of law analysis is clear enough, but the rules themselves are unsatisfactory in the context of transboundary pollution because courts have to separate the components of various torts and choose one among them – most likely environmental damage itself – in order to identify the *lex loci delicti*. There is a difference between applying one law at a time (which choice of law ought to do) and claiming that only one connecting factor is appropriate in all cases. Fundamentally, locating torts at the place of injury is not illogical: it aligns with the idea that civil liability focuses on the damage rather than the wrong, and that the affected state has a strong interest in protecting its population and its environment from pollution originating in other states. It can very well lead to prompt and adequate compensation in some cases.

The problem is that this definition of the *lex loci delicti* does not always ensure equal remedy, nor does it always give victims the benefit of the more favourable law (a debatable, but legitimate objective in environmental matters as it is in other areas involving a weaker party). Foreign victims suing Canadian polluters in Canadian courts are in a good position if the law of the place of injury is more favourable to compensation than the law of the place of acting. This scenario ensures equal remedy – understood as a minimum standard – because the remedies available to foreign victims are at least equally prompt, adequate and effective as (and in fact better than) the ones available to local victims. This scenario also increases the prospects of compensation. The same goes when local victims sue foreign polluters in Canadian courts, in circumstances where local law is more favourable than the law of the place of acting. But the opposite scenario (where the law of the place of acting is more favourable than the law of the place of injury) puts foreign victims at a disadvantage compared to local victims when they sue Canadian polluters in Canadian courts. The same discrepancies occur when local victims sue foreign polluters in Canadian courts in circumstances where the law of the place of acting is more favourable than local law. This undermines equal remedy and does not favour compensation.

[212] In the jurisdictional context, see the sources cited above n 354 (ch 3).

[213] Pitel et al, *Private International Law* (2016) 680. See also R Mortensen, 'Homing Devices in Choice of Tort Law: Australian, British, and Canadian Approaches' (2006) 55 *International and Comparative Law Quarterly* 839, 854.

More fundamentally, it incentivises polluters to direct the consequences of their operations in a jurisdiction with weaker standards.

Interpreting the *lex loci delicti* as referring to the law of the place of acting instead of the law of the place of injury would solve the issue of equal remedy. It would also avoid the practical problems associated with the application of multiple laws to multiple victims in the same proceedings. But it would create an incentive for polluters to establish their operations in laxer jurisdictions, which is at odds with the duty to ensure the availability of prompt and adequate compensation. It would also make *Tolofson*'s caveat on pure transboundary damage disappear and indirectly overrule jurisprudence which, as we have seen, suggests that certain torts do occur at the place of injury for choice of law purposes. Valuable considerations support the law of the place of acting as a general choice of law rule for torts.[214] *Tolofson* made it clear (as a general rule, subject to exceptions) and, as we will see, the Quebec Court of Appeal showed a similar inclination. But the interests of victims and the protection of the environment should prevail in the specific context of transboundary pollution. They favour neither the law of the place of injury nor the law of the place of acting alone.

The *lex loci delicti* as applied by courts in common law provinces thus fails to meet the UNEP Guidelines on Liability and the broader consensus surrounding the ubiquity principle. Even worse, the law on this point is plagued with uncertainty. The above critique assumes that courts would indeed rely on *Moran* and *Tolofson* to locate environmental torts at the place of injury. It is likely, but few authoritative statements exist on this point. More than 20 years after *Tolofson*, and even after *Haaretz.com*, the Supreme Court of Canada has yet to define what it meant with its caveat on transboundary torts. It is not certain that the law of the place of injury will apply, and the workings of a foreseeability requirement (a possible by-product of the analogy with *Moran* in product liability cases) also remain unclear. A Quebec scholar who endeavoured to compare the rules of private international law throughout Canada could only reach one conclusion when it came to the law applicable to transboundary torts at common law: '*Au final, la solution n'est pas claire*' ('ultimately, the solution is not clear').[215]

Statutory reform is the most straightforward option to correct the course. It has been considered in the past: the Manitoba Law Reform Commission recommended a legislative iteration of the *lex loci delicti*,[216] and two authors called for the ULCC to adopt uniform choice of law rules for torts.[217] Choice of law

[214] For further discussion on this point, see section 4.I.D.i above.

[215] C Emanuelli, *Étude comparative sur le droit international privé au Canada* (Montreal, Wilson & Lafleur, 2019) para 509.

[216] Manitoba Law Reform Commission, 'Private International Law' (Com No 119, 2009) 8–9.

[217] Pitel and Harper, 'Choice of Law for Tort in Canada' (2013) 308.

rarely makes its way into the political agenda, but with sufficient pressure from scholars and law reform bodies, it might. And as global environmental issues increasingly take centre stage, special choice of law rules for environmental damage could be part of the discussion.

In the absence of statutory reform, an authoritative follow-up to *Tolofson* remains a possibility. A case involving a complex tort (other than defamation) could make its way to the Supreme Court of Canada. Faced with a choice between the law of the place of acting and the law of the place of injury, and assuming a party raises the choice of law issue, the Court could decide to adopt the most favourable of the two laws as the *lex loci delicti*.

A reform initiated by the judiciary is entirely conceivable. Choice of law in common law provinces is primarily judge-made.[218] The Supreme Court of Canada has not shied away from major reforms of private international law in the last 30 years, including choice of law rules. In *Tolofson*, the Court repudiated decades of choice of law jurisprudence in order to accommodate the modern needs of society.[219] In *Haaretz.com*, four judges left the door open to the overhaul of *Tolofson* in defamation cases,[220] and two judges actually made the leap.[221] Introducing the ubiquity principle is a less drastic change to the current framework because it continues to rely on the place of the tort. It simply changes the way we approach its localisation in a small subset of cases. The Supreme Court of Canada would need to adapt, expand or distinguish *Tolofson* (depending on its interpretation of Justice La Forest's caveat on pure transboundary damage) but not overrule it altogether. Its bedrock principles would remain intact.

Jennifer Orange's proposal in the context of human rights litigation offers a useful basis for discussion in this context. In a paper published in 2001, Orange explains that the *lex loci delicti* falls short of ensuring justice for victims of serious human rights violations committed abroad when their home law does not provide for adequate civil remedies.[222] She focuses on torture – an example she readily describes as 'extreme'[223] – but her point extends to other areas as well. Courts, she argues, ought to interpret *Tolofson* as affording enough flexibility to disregard foreign law when its application would undermine peremptory norms of public international law such as the prohibition of torture.[224]

[218] *Haaretz.com* (n 171) [144] (Wagner J, concurring).

[219] *Tolofson* (n 4) 1047.

[220] *Haaretz.com* (n 171) [91]–[93] (Côté J), [99] (Karakatsanis J, concurring).

[221] ibid [104]–[119] (Abella J, concurring), [144]–[146] (Wagner J, concurring).

[222] JA Orange, 'Torture, Tort Choice of Law, and *Tolofson*' in C Scott (ed), *Torture as Tort: Comparative Perspectives on the Development of Transnational Human Rights Litigation* (Oxford, Hart, 2001).

[223] ibid 323.

[224] The Supreme Court of Canada later held that 'Canada is not obligated by the *jus cogens* prohibition on torture to open its courts so that its citizens may seek civil redress for torture committed abroad': *Kazemi Estate v Islamic Republic of Iran* 2014 SCC 62 [157]. Orange's broader argument that courts should depart from the *lex loci delicti* when it violates a peremptory norm of public international law nonetheless remains valid.

According to Orange, this flexibility might operate as 'a direct public policy exception to the sole possible *lex loci delicti* or as a principle of choice between two or more plausible *lex loci delictis*'.[225] The first option is the most obvious way of disregarding the applicable law when peremptory norms of public international law are at stake, particularly as Justice La Forest seemed prepared to consider 'injustice' and the 'breach of some overriding norm' as reasons to deviate from the general choice of law rule introduced in *Tolofson*.[226] The second option is more wide-ranging and also more useful for our purposes. Orange points out that certain human rights cases may feature two plausible *lex loci delictis*, when an act in one place cause damage in another. In such circumstances, 'it would be faithful to *Tolofson*'s own general reasoning and its specific data to draw on overriding norms for aid in making principled choices between more than one plausible *lex loci delicti* for a given torture tort claim'.[227] Ultimately, she says, international human rights law should tip the balance in favour of the law that is the most conducive to compensation.[228] Orange's second option builds on *Tolofson*'s flexibility to introduce the ubiquity principle in substance if not in name. Although Orange focuses on torture as a tort, this second option is particularly relevant for transboundary pollution since there are two places where the tort potentially occurs (the place of acting and the place of injury).

Orange's analysis offers two important lessons in the context of transboundary pollution. First, public international law should factor in the identification of the *lex loci delicti*. When a tort conceivably occurs in more than place, the *lex loci delici* should favour compensation in order to give effect to a substantive policy articulated in international environmental law – equal remedy and the duty to ensure prompt and adequate compensation. Second, statutory reform is ideal,[229] but the common law affords courts enough flexibility to adopt the ubiquity principle without having to wait for political momentum that may never come.

Reform would bring Canadian private international law in line with a growing international consensus. The Supreme Court of Canada mentioned on numerous occasions the growing importance of environmental protection.[230]

[225] Orange, 'Torture' (2001) 322.

[226] *Tolofson* (n 4) 1047, 1054. On peremptory international law as overriding norms in the *Tolofson* framework, see C Nwapi, 'Tort Choice of Law and International Fundamental Norms: A Case Study of Canada and the United States' (2013) 1 *Afe Babalola University Journal of Sustainable Development Law and Policy* 54, 60–61; C Nwapi, 'Litigating Extraterritorial Corporate Crimes in Canadian Courts' (doctoral thesis, University of British Columbia, 2012) 455–56.

[227] Orange (n 222) 321–22 (emphasis omitted).

[228] ibid 322.

[229] ibid 294, 323.

[230] *British Columbia v Canadian Forest Products Ltd* 2004 SCC 38 [7]; *Imperial Oil Ltd v Quebec (Minister of the Environment)* 2003 SCC 58 [19]; *114957 Canada Ltée (Spraytech, Société d'arrosage) v Hudson (Town)* 2001 SCC 40 [1]; *R v Hydro-Québec* [1997] 3 SCR 213, 293–97; *Ontario v Canadian Pacific Ltd* [1995] 2 SCR 1031, 1075–76.

Instruments such as the Rome II Regulation or the UNEP Guidelines on Liability respond to those preoccupations by translating them into a workable choice of law framework. Courts would be wise to consider them as part of the incremental evolution of private international law.

Leaving aside the common law, it is necessary to examine the statutory choice of law rules found in the Reciprocal Access Act and the Civil Code of Quebec.

ii. Choice of Law in the Reciprocal Access Act

The common law rule set out in *Tolofson* applies in all Canadian provinces except Quebec, but the Reciprocal Access Act also contains statutory choice of law rules. In Ontario, Manitoba, Nova Scotia and Prince Edward Island, the Reciprocal Access Act requires courts in the state of origin to always apply their own law.[231] The ULCC designed this provision to provide legal certainty: polluters on both sides of the border would expect the application of their home law, and victims would know precisely which law would apply should they choose to sue polluters where they operate.[232] In this sense, the Reciprocal Access Act reflects pre-*Tolofson* tendencies to apply local law in tort disputes under the double actionability/justifiability rule.

The interaction between the Reciprocal Access Act and the common law is unclear. The ULCC intended to supplement existing rights, not replace them.[233] Years later, however, *Tolofson* brought about radical changes in the choice of law process. It rejected the *lex fori* orientation of the prior rule and made the *lex loci delicti* prevail. The choice of law provision contained in the Reciprocal Access Act contracts sharply with the common law post-*Tolofson*. The Act imposes local law, which effectively coincides with the law of the place of acting in the context of the Act, which secures jurisdiction in the state of origin. *Tolofson*, by contrast, acknowledges that the law of the place of injury might govern the dispute when the act and the injury occur in different states. This is an irreconcilable conflict.

It seems clear that the Reciprocal Access Act overrides *Tolofson*, subject to constitutional constraints. No province amended its statute after the judgment. Clear legislation trumps the common law,[234] and the Reciprocal Access Act is unambiguous. It admits no judicial discretion and leaves no room for alternative connecting factors.

[231] Reciprocal Access Act (n 23), s 4.

[232] Uniform Law Conference of Canada, 'Uniform Transboundary Pollution Reciprocal Access Act: Prefatory Note' in Uniform Law Conference of Canada Proceedings of the Sixty-Fourth Annual Meeting (Montebello, 1982) 503.

[233] Reciprocal Access Act (n 23), s 6.

[234] *Canada (Attorney General) v Thouin* 2017 SCC 46 [19]; *Lizotte v Aviva Insurance Company of Canada* 2016 SCC 52 [56].

Yet there may be an argument that the rigidity of the Reciprocal Access Act makes it unconstitutional with respect to *interprovincial* pollution. *Tolofson* made clear that 'an attempt by one province to impose liability for negligence in respect of activities that have taken place wholly in another province by residents of the latter or, for that matter, residents of a third province, would give rise to serious constitutional concerns'.[235] In other words, applying the law of the forum when the tort occurred wholly in another province amounts to an improper extraterritorial application of provincial law (which the Canadian constitution prohibits[236]). The necessary implication is that a province cannot validly impose its own law by statute in such circumstances.

The constitutional requirements for choice of law remain nebulous, precisely because the Supreme Court of Canada stopped short of defining them in *Tolofson*.[237] Arguably, the judgment did not (and ought not) constitutionalise the *lex loci delicti* between Canadian provinces.[238] This has been a prevailing view among scholars.[239] It is also reflected in the Court's willingness to consider other connecting factors for defamation,[240] and its assertion that the Constitution does not require uniformity in conflict rules.[241]

In the end, the Reciprocal Access Act is likely to be constitutionally valid. Courts must apply a law that has some connection to the dispute, not necessarily the *lex loci delicti*.[242] When courts apply their own law pursuant to the *Reciprocal Access Act*, an important part of the dispute – the polluting activity – has a connection with the forum. The law of the forum is not applied simply because it is the law of the forum. This is sufficient for constitutional purposes. It follows that Ontario, Manitoba, Nova Scotia and Prince Edward Island can validly impose their own law by statute when pollution originates in their territory. Meanwhile, courts in the affected state remain free to apply whatever law they deem appropriate, again subject to constitutional constraints.[243]

[235] *Tolofson* (n 4) 1066 (emphasis added).

[236] Constitution Act 1867, 30 & 31 Vict c 3, s 92; *Club Resorts* (n 166) [21]; *British Columbia v Imperial Tobacco Canada Ltd* 2005 SCC 49 [26]–[27]; *Unifund Assurance Co v Insurance Corp of British Columbia* 2003 CSC 40 [50]–[51].

[237] J Blom, 'Constitutionalizing Canadian Private International Law – 25 Years Since *Morguard*' (2017) 13 *Journal of Private International Law* 259, 288; Pitel and Harper (n 188) 306–08.

[238] *Castillo* (n 166) [351] (Bastarache J, concurring); *British Columbia v Imperial Tobacco Canada Ltd* 2004 BCCA 269 [171] (Rowles J, concurring), affd 2005 SCC 49.

[239] C Walsh, 'Territoriality and Choice of Law in the Supreme Court of Canada: Applications in Products Liability Claims' (1997) 76 *Canadian Bar Review* 91, 113, reprinted in J Ziegel (ed), *New Developments in International Commercial and Consumer Law* (Oxford, Hart, 1998); JG Castel, 'Back to the Future! Is the "New" Rigid Choice of Law Rule for Interprovincial Torts Constitutionally Mandated?' (1995) 33 *Osgoode Hall Law Journal* 35, 63–66. But see J Herbert, 'The Conflict of Laws and Judicial Perspectives on Federalism: A Principled Defence of *Tolofson v. Jensen*' (1998) 56 *University of Toronto Faculty of Law Review* 3, 45.

[240] *Haaretz.com* (n 171); *Éditions Écosociété* (n 166).

[241] *Club Resorts* (n 166) [21].

[242] Castel (n 239) 66.

[243] MI Jeffery, 'Transboundary Pollution and Cross-Border Remedies' (1992) 18 *Canada–United States Law Journal* 173, 177; Uniform Law Conference of Canada (n 232) 503.

Constitutional problems aside, however, the choice of law provision in the Reciprocal Access Act effectively amounts to imposing the law of the place of acting, and with it, the concerns associated with a rigid localisation of environmental torts for choice of law purposes.

iii. Choice of Law in the Civil Code of Quebec

A different choice of law framework applies in Quebec. As this section demonstrates, it does not share all the defects of the common law, but it treats victims of transboundary pollution less favourably than the Rome II Regulation or the UNEP Guidelines on Liability nonetheless.

Quebec's CCQ follows the logic of *Tolofson* and departs from an earlier ruling of the Supreme Court of Canada which had introduced the pre-*Tolofson* common law double actionability/justifiability rule into Quebec civil law,[244] much to civilists' dismay.[245] Article 3126, para 1 CCQ brings back the *lex loci delicti* in the province. It states that the law of the place of acting governs the issue of civil liability, except when a foreseeable injury appeared in another state, in which case the law of the place of injury may apply:

> **3126.** The obligation to make reparation for injury caused to another is governed by the law of the State where the act or omission which occasioned the injury occurred. However, if the injury appeared in another State, the law of the latter State is applicable if the author should have foreseen that the injury would manifest itself there.
>
> In any case where the author and the victim have their domiciles or residences in the same State, the law of that State applies.[246]

Like Article 3148 CCQ (jurisdiction), Article 3126 CCQ (choice of law) encompasses neighbourhood disturbance and civil liability claims. As explained in chapter three, neighbourhood disturbance can lead to injunctive relief and damages, and is often invoked alongside civil liability.[247] In *Uashaunnuat*, the Supreme Court of Canada characterised the Innus' claims in civil liability and neighbourhood disturbance as a personal action for jurisdictional purposes (and ultimately characterised the entire claim as a non-classical mixed action because it also sought the recognition of *sui generis* Aboriginal rights).[248] The Court made no comment on choice of law rules but its characterisation of the Innus' claims makes it unlikely that Article 3097 CCQ (which determines

[244] *O'Connor v Wray* [1930] SCR 231, 248–49.

[245] P-A Crépeau, 'De la responsabilité civile extracontractuelle en droit international privé québécois' (1961) 39 *Canadian Bar Review* 3.

[246] CCQ (n 4), Art 3126.

[247] See the text accompanying n 189 (ch 3) above.

[248] *Newfoundland and Labrador (Attorney General) v Uashaunnuat (Innu of Uashat and of Mani-Utenam)* 2020 SCC 4 [58].

the law applicable to 'real rights and their publication')[249] would apply over Article 3126 CCQ (which determines the law applicable to 'the obligation to make reparation for injury caused to another').[250] Different rules apply, however, for claims related to defective products[251] or raw materials originating in Quebec.[252]

With Article 3126, para 1 CCQ, the Quebec legislature framed the place of acting as the default connecting factor for civil liability and left the door open to the law of the place of injury, subject to a foreseeability requirement.[253] The Quebec Court of Appeal, however, strongly defers to the default rule. In *Wightman* and *Giesbrecht*, it held that the law of the place of injury applies only exceptionally under Article 3126, para 1 CCQ,[254] and not when it leads to a chaotic result because of the number of victims spread across multiple states.[255] In doing so, the Court gave particular weight to how the Supreme Court of Canada had defined the *lex loci delicti* in *Tolofson*,[256] as well as the underlying principle of order in Canadian private international law.[257]

The Quebec Court of Appeal understandably strove for a pragmatic, orderly and judicially convenient solution in complex cases involving many victims – a large group of wronged creditors in *Wightman* and the victims of a plane crash in *Giesbrecht*. The Court made a good case for the law of the place of acting in such context, but it read too much into Article 3126, para 1 CCQ. First, the injury exception is not really an exception to a general principle, but a different connecting factor triggered by a different fact pattern (an act and an injury occurring in different states).[258] The so-called exception arguably loses its exceptionality if that fact pattern occurs frequently. Second, the CCQ makes no distinction between foreseeable damage to victims in a single state and foreseeable damage to victims in multiple states.[259] How can the court force the

[249] CCQ (n 4), Art 3097, para 1 ('Real rights and their publication are governed by the law of the place where the property concerned is situated').

[250] For an argument in this sense, see G Goldstein and E Groffier, *Droit international privé*, vol 2: Règles spécifiques (Cowansville, Yvon Blais, 2003) para 477.

[251] CCQ (n 4), Art 3128.

[252] ibid, Art 3129.

[253] HP Glenn, 'Droit international privé' in Barreau du Québec and Chambre des notaires (eds), *La réforme du Code civil*, vol 3 (Quebec, Presses de l'Université Laval, 1993) 737.

[254] *Wightman c Widdrington (Succession de)* 2013 QCCA 1187 [183]–[184], leave to appeal to SCC refused [2014] 1 SCR xiii. This was technically obiter, as the Quebec Court of Appeal applied the rules of private international law in force at the time of the event, prior to the adoption of the CCQ in 1994: ibid [99].

[255] *Giesbrecht c Succession de Nadeau* 2017 QCCA 386 [28], leave to appeal to SCC refused [2017] 3 SCR vii; *Wightman* (n 254) [192].

[256] *Giesbrecht* (n 255) [21]–[22].

[257] *Wightman* (254) [192], relying on *Tolofson* (n 4) 1058.

[258] In *Giesbrecht*, the Quebec Court of Appeal made a brief parallel between *Tolofson*'s caveat (transboundary torts and inherently transnational/interprovincial activity) and Art 3126 CCQ's injury exception: *Giesbrecht* (n 255) [21], fn 17.

[259] G Goldstein, 'Le caractère « exceptionnel » frappe encore! Une nouvelle victime par ricochet: la clause d'exception de l'art 3082 CCQ' (2018) 96 *Canadian Bar Review* 402, 406–08.

application of the law of the place of acting in certain disputes but not others, given the clear wording of Article 3126, para 1 CCQ?[260]

Dubious interpretation aside, *Wightman* and *Giesbrecht* suggest that the law of the place of acting will apply by default when a polluter causes injuries in multiple states and all victims sue in Quebec. The injury exception, however, remains crucial in transboundary environmental disputes involving a single victim or multiple victims in a single state. Article 3126, para 1 CCQ does not specify who can invoke this exception, but its logic is to benefit plaintiffs by giving them the option to invoke the hypothetically more favourable law of the place of injury. In *Wightman*, the Quebec Court of Appeal blamed the defendants for trying to strategically avoid liability by invoking the law of the place of injury (Ontario). It explained that

> The rule of the place of the injurious act to determine the applicable law was designed and accepted by certain legislators (particularly in Europe) in order to protect victims and facilitate their access to a court likely to provide them with adequate compensation.[261]

The Court held that the injury exception in article 3126 CCQ reflects the same concern.[262]

Article 3126, para 1 CCQ, however, does not explicitly allow plaintiffs to choose between the most favourable of two laws, unlike the ubiquity principle incorporated in the Rome II Regulation. A literal reading indicates that Article 3126, para 1 CCQ *requires* the application of the law of the place of injury when the tortfeasor could have foreseen that an injury would occur there.[263] In other words, complex torts are always governed by the law of the place of a foreseeable injury rather than the law of the place of acting. At the same time, the Quebec Court of Appeal implied in *Wightman* that defendants could not rely on the injury exception to avoid the law of the place of acting because the exception existed to protect victims (not to mention that it would be odd for a defendant to plead that it had foreseen the damage associated with its own conduct in order to make a case for the injury exception). Plaintiffs, on their part, will presumably rely on the injury exception only if it leads to a more favourable law than the law of the place of acting. Article 3126, para 1 therefore effectively provides them with an option – the law of the place of acting applies, unless they choose to plead the law of the place of injury and establish that the defendant could have foreseen the injury.

The court could always raise the hypothetically less favourable law of the place of injury (and the foreseeability of that injury) on its own motion if

[260] For an alternative approach to address the problem of indirect victims in *Giesbrecht*, see ibid 408–10.

[261] *Wightman* (254) [193] (unofficial English translation available online on CanLII).

[262] ibid.

[263] eg *Surin c Puma Canada Inc* 2017 QCCS 3821 [24].

it thought that the law of the place of acting cannot apply, but that would contradict the rationale of Article 3126, para 1 CCQ. If a defendant cannot rely on the injury exception, then the court should not raise it on its own motion when it benefits the defendant. This is particularly true if the law of the place of injury is foreign law. A party would then have to plead its contents for the court to apply it,[264] which brings us back to square one – a defendant pleading the hypothetically less favourable law of the place of injury to avoid or limit liability.

The person who chooses to raise the injury exception bears the onus of establishing foreseeability.[265] Courts assess foreseeability on an objective standard ('should have foreseen'),[266] but may also consider the defendant's actual knowledge.[267] Unsurprisingly, pollution dispersed across large geographical areas raises the greatest difficulties. A Canadian business operating at the border can easily determine whether its activities will impact people in the United States, except perhaps when science is inconclusive. But the analysis becomes increasingly difficult as transboundary pollution becomes more diffuse. Climate change litigation involving local greenhouse gas emitters and foreign victims, for instance, would not necessarily lead to the law of the place of injury. A defendant might convince the court that it could not anticipate the damage caused, either because available information did not reveal any damage in the jurisdiction or because no scientific evidence indicated that its operations harmed the environment.

Overall, Article 3126, para 1 CCQ comes closer to the rationale of the ubiquity principle and the requirements of the duty to ensure prompt and adequate compensation than its common law counterpart because it openly admits the application of the law of the place of injury as an alternative for plaintiffs. This fulfils the equal remedy requirement in the ILC Principles on the Allocation of Loss[268] and ultimately removes some of the incentives for polluters to take advantage of a weaker legal regime. The default stance in favour of the place of acting entails that foreign plaintiffs who sue Canadian

[264] CCQ (n 4), Art 2809 and the sources cited above n 145.

[265] *Royal Bank of Canada c Capital Factors Inc* 2013 QCCS 2214 [70]. Scholars have different views on this point: cf C Emanuelli, *Droit international privé québécois*, 3rd ed (Montreal, Wilson & Lafleur, 2011) para 567, fn 2138 (the person who invokes foreseeability must prove it); Walker, vol 2 (n 175) § 35.6 (victim/plaintiff must prove foreseeability – alternatively, presumption that the damage was foreseeable unless the defendant proves otherwise); Goldstein and Groffier, *Droit international privé*, vol 2 (2003) para 466 (victim/plaintiff must prove foreseeability); JA Talpis and JG Castel, 'Le Code civil du Québec: interprétation des règles du droit international privé' in Barreau du Québec and Chambre des notaires (n 253) 890 (defendant must prove unforeseeability in order to avoid the law of the place of injury).

[266] *British Airways, plc c Option Consommateurs* 2010 QCCA 1134 [9]; Emanuelli, *Droit international privé québécois* (2011) para 567. See also *Royal Bank of Canada* (n 265) [81].

[267] *Recherches internationales Québec c Cambior Inc* 1998 CanLII 9780 [60] (Qc Sup Ct); Emanuelli (n 265) para 567. But see Talpis and Castel, 'Interprétation des règles du droit international privé' (n 265) 890 (foreseeability must only be assessed objectively).

[268] ILC Principles on the Allocation of Loss (n 8) principle 6(2).

polluters benefit from equally prompt, adequate and effective remedies as Canadian plaintiffs suing Canadian polluters, even if their own law is less advantageous. The possibility of applying the law of the place of injury entails that foreign plaintiffs do not lose the benefits of their own law if it is more favourable, even though different plaintiffs might receive different treatment under their own laws.

At the same time, Article 3126, para 1 CCQ is more restrictive than the ubiquity principle incorporated in the Rome II Regulation or the UNEP Guidelines on Liability. Foreign victims who wish to invoke the hypothetically more favourable law of the place of injury against local polluters – and local victims who wish to invoke their own law against foreign polluters – must establish foreseeability. Article 3126 CCQ also refers to an injury *caused* to another person and *appearing* in another state – concepts that are difficult to reconcile with transient forms of transboundary pollution. Article 3126 CCQ contrasts with the plaintiff-friendly approach to product liability claims under Article 3128 CCQ, where the legislature chose not to adopt a defence of commercialisation or foreseeability which would have allowed manufacturers to escape the law of the place of acquisition of the product if they did not expect the product to be used there.[269] Polluters, by contrast, can evade the law of the place of injury when foreseeability is too difficult to establish in court.

Courts could conceivably interpret foreseeability as a mere prima facie requirement. In other words, plaintiffs would simply have to demonstrate that the defendant's activities reasonably could have *some* consequences across the border. This requirement would easily be met if, for instance, a watercourse flowed from state x to state y. The very presence of a watercourse would then suffice to establish foreseeability and trigger the law of the place of injury,[270] and the exact cause of the damage suffered in state y (ie, causation) would be left for trial. But again, even a prima facie foreseeability requirement is problematic when the pollution is more diffuse than in this example. Victims of climate change, for instance, will struggle to meet their burden against foreign greenhouse gas emitters.

Summing up, it will remain difficult for many litigants to rely on the law of the place of injury instead of the law of the place of acting under Article 3126, para 1 CCQ, especially now that the Quebec Court of Appeal has tightened the exception in *Wightman* and *Giesbrecht*. A judicial reform seems unlikely. Quebec private international law is almost entirely codified. Courts can hardly build a true ubiquity principle from Article 3126, para 1 CCQ, particularly given the Quebec Court of Appeal's judgments in *Wightman* and *Giesbrecht*. The only realistic option would be for the Quebec legislature to formally

[269] CCQ (n 4), Art 3128. See also Swiss Act on Private International Law (n 74), ss 135(1)(b) (consent exception); Convention on the Law Applicable to Products Liability (2 October 1973, entered into force 1 October 1977) 1056 UNTS 187, Art 7 (foreseeability exception).

[270] Goldstein and Groffier (n 250) para 477.

implement the ubiquity principle and bring the CCQ in line with the UNEP Guidelines on Liability. This proposition has support in the literature. At least four prominent Canadian scholars recommended an elective solution to favour the victim in environmental matters. When the CCQ came into force, Talpis and Castel argued that the legislature should have introduced a special regime allowing victims to elect the law of the residence/establishment of the polluter or the law of the place of injury. An elective solution, they said, would help develop a stronger body of environmental law.[271] Similarly, Goldstein and Groffier favoured the ubiquity principle due to the special attributes of transboundary pollution.[272]

The import of the ubiquity principle would be especially intuitive as Book Ten of the CCQ already borrows from the Swiss Act on Private International Law.[273] The Swiss Act also contains a special rule for nuisances emanating from real property, which could just as easily be incorporated into the CCQ with the necessary adaptations.[274] Borrowing from EU instruments is not unprecedented either as the CCQ follows in some respects the 1980 Rome Convention on the Law Applicable to Contractual Obligations.[275] Finally, the CCQ is already familiar with the idea of letting the victim choose the applicable law: Article 3128 CCQ lets the victim choose between the law of the manufacturer's establishment/residence and the law of the place of acquisition of the product to govern the liability of the manufacturer of movable property.[276] Article 3128 CCQ is not a perfect example of the ubiquity principle as traditionally understood in the context on transboundary pollution, because it does not use the place(s) of a cross-border tort as connecting factors (even though the fault might occur at the manufacturer's establishment/residence and the injury might occur at the place of acquisition). The idea, however, remains the same: to let the victim choose the most favourable of two laws to govern a particular

[271] Talpis and Castel (n 265) 891–92 (advocating for the application of the law of the place of residence/establishment of the polluter or the law of the place of damage, at the victim's choice).

[272] Goldstein and Groffier (n 250) para 477. See also JA Talpis and G Goldstein, 'Analyse critique de l'Avant-projet de loi du Québec en droit international privé' (1989) 91 *Revue du Notariat* 456, 510, 518 (criticising the legislature's failure to adopt the most favourable law principle for all torts in the draft bill that preceded the CCQ, and suggesting special rules for certain torts, along the lines of the choice of law rule for product liability).

[273] Ministère de la Justice du Québec, *Commentaires du ministre de la Justice: le Code civil du Québec, un mouvement de société*, vol 3 (Quebec, Publications du Québec, 1993) 1040; J Talpis and G Goldstein, 'The Influence of Swiss Law on Quebec's 1994 Codification of Private International Law' (2009) 11 *Yearbook of Private International Law* 339, 370.

[274] Swiss Act on Private International Law (n 74), s 138.

[275] Ministère de la Justice du Québec, *Commentaires du ministre de la Justice* (1993) 1034–35; Convention on the Law Applicable to Contractual Obligations (19 June 1980, entered into force 1 April 1991) 1605 UNTS 59.

[276] CCQ (n 4), Art 3128. See eg *Zurich Insurance Company Ltd c Volvo Group North America* 2020 QCCS 483 [98]–[114].

kind of dispute, when the legislature deems it necessary to correct imbalances and favour compensation.[277]

Quebec missed a chance to innovate when it failed to adopt a specific choice of law rule for environmental damage. Twenty-five years later, the ubiquity principle has proliferated. International organisations and legal scholars have accepted its application in transboundary environmental disputes. Quebec, like the common law, should follow.

B. Displacing the Applicable Law

In certain circumstances, the law normally designated by choice of law rules (*Tolofson* or the CCQ) can be displaced in favour of another: foreign law can be displaced by local law (section II.B.i) and any law can be displaced by a mandatory provision of foreign law (section II.B.ii). This is unlikely to be a major issue in most transboundary environmental disputes. Very few cases admit the displacement of the designated law. Some of the exceptions below also overlap with rules on the enforcement of foreign judgments discussed in chapter three, or the built-in caveats in *Tolofson* discussed earlier in this chapter. The Reciprocal Access Act, however, does not formally incorporate any of the exceptions below.

i. Displacement of Foreign Law

When choice of law rules lead to foreign law, courts may invoke the public law exception (section II.B.i.a) or the public policy exception (section II.B.i.b) to apply their own law instead.[278] In addition, the CCQ contains a mechanism to replace the applicable law with another law that is more closely connected with the dispute (section II.B.i.c).

a. Public Law Exception to the Applicable Law

The public law exception to the enforcement of foreign judgments (examined in chapter three) can also be framed as a choice of law rule, in the sense that courts must apply local law when the claim involves foreign penal laws, tax laws or

[277] Z Jianing and G Goldstein, 'Analyse comparative de la loi chinoise de 2011 portant sur les conflits de lois à la lueur du droit international privé québécois' (2014) 48 *Revue juridique Thémis de l'Université de Montréal* 329, 376. cf K Thomassin and M Boodman, 'Choice of Law and Manufacturer's Liability in Quebec' in TL Archibald and RS Echlin (eds), *Annual Review of Civil Litigation 2012* (Toronto, Carswell, 2012) 228.

[278] For further discussion on mandatory local laws, which, unlike the public law/public policy exception, override the entire choice of law analysis in favour of local law, see section 4.II.C.i below.

other public laws.[279] In other words, courts will refuse to directly apply foreign public law, just as they refuse to indirectly apply it through the enforcement of a foreign judgment based on foreign public law. The implications of the public law exception were addressed in chapter three, in relation to the enforcement of foreign judgments.[280] The same conclusions apply here: the *Ivey* case supports the proposition that courts will not refuse to apply foreign environmental law simply because it is public in nature.[281] Only the assertion of a true sovereign power will trigger the exception. Likewise, nothing in the CCQ precludes the application of all foreign public laws. Article 3080 CCQ provides that when the law of a foreign state applies, it applies to the exclusion of its own rules of private international law.[282] This wording arguably excludes other implicit carve-outs, such as foreign public law as a whole.[283]

b. Public Policy Exception to the Applicable Law

The public policy exception can also displace foreign law, perhaps more efficiently than the public law exception. The public policy exception was also addressed in chapter three in relation of the enforcement of foreign judgments.[284] Similar considerations apply at the choice of law stage,[285] except that in this context, both the victim and the polluter can rely on the exception.

First, polluters could rely on the public policy exception to avoid overly *stringent* foreign environmental laws which would normally apply under choice of law rules. The current scope of the public policy exception makes this argument difficult, but not impossible. In *Ivey*, Ontario courts declined to apply to public policy exception in the enforcement context,[286] but the dispute involved a close neighbour (the state of Michigan) with a familiar legal system. As explained in chapter three, it made sense for Canadian courts to stress the importance of comity and cooperation with the United States, but they would not necessarily adopt the same stance towards all legal systems.

[279] A Dickinson, 'Acts of State and the Frontiers of Private (International) Law' (2018) 14 *Journal of Private International Law* 1, 10; A Briggs, 'The Revenue Rule in the Conflict of Laws: Time for a Makeover' [2001] 2 *Singapore Journal of Legal Studies* 280, 295–96.

[280] For further discussion on the public law exception to the enforcement of foreign judgments, see section 3.II.C.ii.a above.

[281] *United States of America v Ivey* (1996) 30 OR (3d) 370 (Ont CA), leave to appeal to SCC refused [1997] 2 SCR x.

[282] CCQ (n 4), Art 3080. cf Swiss Act on Private International Law (n 74), s 13 (expressly providing that foreign law is not excluded simply because its provisions have a public law character).

[283] G Laganière, 'Dialogue des systèmes en droit international privé: l'application et la reconnaissance du droit public étranger au Québec' in J Torres-Ceyte, G-A Berthold and C-A Péladeau (eds), *Le dialogue en droit civil* (Montreal, Thémis, 2018) 41–44.

[284] For further discussion on the public policy exception to the enforcement of foreign judgments, see section 3.II.C.ii.b above.

[285] At common law, see *Das* ONCA (n 206) [96]; *Block Bros Realty Ltd v Mollard* (1981) 122 DLR (3d) 323, 329 (BC CA). In Quebec, see CCQ (n 4), Arts 3081; *RS v PR* 2019 SCC 49 [53]–[54].

[286] *United States of America v Ivey* (1995) 26 OR (3d) 533, 554 (Ont Gen Div), affd (1996) 30 OR (3d) 370 (Ont CA), leave to appeal to SCC refused, [1997] 2 SCR x.

Second, victims could rely on the public policy exception to avoid overly *lenient* foreign laws which contradict basic environmental principles.[287] This is a plausible argument in light of multiple pronouncements in favour of environmental protection by the Supreme Court of Canada.[288] Public policy in this scenario might even include fundamental precepts of international environmental law.[289] But again, such cases will be exceptional and quite fact-specific because transboundary environmental disputes rarely implicate basic morality to a point where the public policy exception comes into play in one way or the other.

c. Quebec's Residual Escape Clause

Finally, the CCQ contains a residual escape clause to counteract the abnormal application of choice of law rules. Article 3082 CCQ provides that another law can apply if the dispute is only remotely connected with the designated law and more closely connected to another.[290] The provision ensures proximity but applies only in 'rare, exceptional and truly extraordinary' cases.[291] This provision is unlikely to play a determinative role in transboundary environmental disputes. Indeed, Article 3126 CCQ can lead to the law of the place of acting or the law of the place of injury, and both places are sufficiently closely connected to the dispute to prevent the application of Article 3082 CCQ.

ii. Mandatory Foreign Laws

Courts may also displace the applicable law by applying mandatory *foreign* laws. This technique recalls the consideration of foreign rules of conduct and safety under Article 17 of the Rome II Regulation.[292] Canadian courts, for instance, may refuse to enforce contracts that require the parties to breach foreign law

[287] Goldstein and Groffier (n 250) para 477.

[288] *British Columbia v Canadian Forest Products Ltd* 2004 SCC 38 [7]; *Imperial Oil Ltd v Quebec (Minister of the Environment)* 2003 SCC 58 [19]; *114957 Canada Ltée (Spraytech, Société d'arrosage) v Hudson (Town)* 2001 SCC 40 [1]; *R v Hydro-Québec* [1997] 3 SCR 213, 293–97; *Ontario v Canadian Pacific Ltd* [1995] 2 SCR 1031, 1075–76. In Quebec, however, the notion of international public policy ('public order as understood in international relations') is more restrictive than domestic public policy: CCQ (n 4), Arts 3081, 3155(5°); *RS* (n 285) [53].

[289] Boskovic, 'Droit international privé et environnement' (2014) para 50. On public international law and its impact on the public policy exception, see also M Lehmann, 'Regulation, Global Governance and Private International Law: Squaring the Triangle' (2020) 16 *Journal of Private International Law* 1, 28–29; C Fresnedo de Aguirre, 'Public Policy in Private International Law: Guardian or Barrier?' in V Ruiz Abou-Nigm and M Blanca Noodt Taquela (eds), *Diversity and Integration in Private International Law* (Edinburgh, Edinburgh University Press, 2019) 354–56; J Blom, 'Public Policy in Private International Law and Its Evolution in Time' (2003) 50 *Netherlands International Law Review* 373, 395–97.

[290] CCQ (n 4), Art 3082.

[291] *Giesbrecht* (n 255) [35] (translation).

[292] Rome II Regulation (n 34), Art 17.

in order to perform their obligations.[293] They may also refuse to issue an order requiring a person residing in a foreign jurisdiction to break the law of that jurisdiction.[294]

In Quebec, Article 3079 CCQ is more explicit and wide-ranging, but equally exceptional. It admits the application (not just the consideration) of mandatory foreign laws when legitimate and manifestly preponderant interests require it.[295] The dispute must be closely connected with the foreign state and the court must have considered the purpose of the foreign law and the consequences of its application.[296] The test is extremely stringent. Despite several attempts, no litigant has met its requirements since it came into force in 1994.

Deferring to mandatory foreign laws fosters international comity by recognising the interest of foreign states in promoting their own legislative policies. But this deference stops when the interests of the forum begin, or even when the two have equal weight. Early cases required Quebec courts to balance foreign bank secrecy precluding the administration of evidence against the principles of full disclosure and an open justice system. The latter prevailed on the basis that they were matters of public concern in Quebec.[297] Assessing the legitimate and preponderant character of mandatory foreign laws and balancing them against the forum's own interests thus necessarily go beyond the parties' own rights. It also involves important public – some would say political[298] – considerations.

The door to foreign mandatory laws may not be as tightly shut to environmental protection as it is to foreign bank secrecy. The expression of a strong legislative preference for environmental protection in a foreign state could supplant an overly lenient local law precisely because the environment is a matter of public concern.[299] A court might consider that the interests at stake are sufficiently legitimate and manifestly preponderant under Article 3079 CCQ if they concern the well-being of a large population and the state's duty to ensure prompt and adequate compensation. Defendants would undoubtedly raise countervailing considerations related to the forum's economic and industrial policy, but the argument is at least conceivable in law.

Defendants too can rely on Article 3079 CCQ in transboundary environmental disputes. In proceedings brought in Canada and hypothetically governed by

[293] *Gillespie Management Corp v Terrace Properties* (1989) 62 DLR (4th) 221, 222 (BC CA) (Southin JA, concurring).

[294] *Frischke v Royal Bank of Canada* (1977) 17 OR (2d) 388, 399 (Ont CA). cf *Google Inc v Equustek Solutions Inc* 2017 SCC 34 [44]; *R v Spencer* (1983) 145 DLR (3d) 344, 352–53 (Ont CA), affd [1985] 2 SCR 278.

[295] CCQ (n 4), Art 3079.

[296] ibid.

[297] *Globe-X Management Ltd (Proposition de)* 2006 QCCA 290 [43]–[48], leave to appeal to SCC refused, [2006] 2 SCR xiii; *Banque Paribas (Suisse) SA c Wightman*, 1997 CanLII 10291, 2–7 (Qc CA).

[298] G Goldstein, 'La condition incertaine des lois de police étrangères et du secret bancaire en droit international privé québécois' (1997) 76 *Canadian Bar Review* 449, 460.

[299] See by analogy J Talpis and SL Kath, 'The Exceptional as Commonplace in Quebec *Forum Non Conveniens* Law: *Cambior*, A Case in Point' (2000) 34 *Revue juridique Thémis* 731, 861–62.

the law of the place of injury, foreign defendants may attempt to plead that they are formally authorised to operate under their own law. This issue was hinted at earlier in this book, both in relation to the public policy exception to the enforcement of foreign judgments,[300] and the Rome II Regulation.[301] In Canada, the question remains: can the law of the place of acting (where a licence was issued) override the law of the place of injury and exonerate the defendant on the basis that it is mandatory?

In a domestic scenario where a defendant has an administrative authorisation or complies with the law, the answer is no. Compliance with statutory requirements does not preclude civil liability, and vice versa.[302] Defendants can invoke administrative authorisations in some circumstances, but those authorisations hardly confer absolute immunity. Quebec's Environment Quality Act, for instance, precludes injunctions against polluters when they comply with all the provisions of a certificate of authorisation.[303] Yet plaintiffs can always seek to invalidate the certificates themselves.[304] They can also still rely on general causes of action such as civil liability and neighbourhood disturbance.[305] Likewise, the defence of statutory authority gives tortfeasors a chance to escape liability for nuisance when a statute clearly authorises the activity and the nuisance which arises from the activity is practically impossible to avoid,[306] but the defence remains narrow, and better suited to public bodies owing their existence to a statute than private defendants.[307] Those few examples show

[300] For further discussion on the public policy exception to the enforcement of foreign judgments, see section 3.II.C.ii.b above.

[301] For further discussion on foreign rules of safety and conduct in the Rome II Regulation, see section 4.I.D.ii.c above.

[302] On the relationship between civil liability and statutory requirements in civil and common law, see *Kosoian v Société de transport de Montréal* 2019 SCC 59 [48]; *Infineon Technologies AG v Option consommateurs* 2013 SCC 59 [96]–[98]; *St Lawrence Cement Inc v Barrette* 2008 SCC 64 [32]–[36]; *Ryan v Victoria (City)* [1999] 1 SCR 201 [29]; *The Queen v Saskatchewan Wheat Pool* [1983] 1 SCR 205, 225–27; *Morin v Blais* (1975) [1977] 1 SCR 570, 579–80.

[303] Environment Quality Act, CQLR c Q-2 ('Quebec Environment Quality Act'), s 19.7.

[304] *Centre québécois du droit de l'environnement c Oléoduc Énergie Est Ltée* 2014 QCCS 4147 [49]–[56]; *Calvé c Gestion Serge Lafrenière Inc* [1999] RJQ 1313, 1318–20 (Qc CA).

[305] *Regroupement des citoyens contre la pollution c Alex Couture Inc* 2006 QCCS 950 [69]–[73], affd 2007 QCCA 565; *Entreprises BCP Ltée c Bourassa* (1984) 14 CELR 144, 147 (Qc CA).

[306] *Ryan* (n 302) [54]–[56]; *Tock v St John's Metropolitan Area Board* [1989] 2 SCR 1181, 1224–25. Similar principles apply in Quebec: *Ouimette c Canada (Procureur géneral)* [2002] RJQ 1228, 1250–51 (Qc CA), leave to appeal to SCC refused [2003] 1 SCR xv.

[307] L Collins and H McLeod-Kilmurray, *The Canadian Law of Toxic Torts* (Toronto, Canada Law Book, 2014) 162–63. Most provinces, however, have also enacted 'right-to-farm' legislation which explicitly relieves agricultural owners and operators from civil liability for normal agricultural practices: see eg Farming and Food Production Protection Act 1998, SO 1998 c 1, s 2; Act respecting the preservation of agricultural land and agricultural activities, CQLR c P-41.1, ss 79.17–79.19.2; Farm Practices Protection (Right to Farm) Act, RSBC 1996 c 131, s 2. For a critique, see L Alford and S Berger Richardson, 'Right-to-Farm Legislation in Canada: Exceptional Protection for Standard Farm Practices' (2019) 50 *Ottawa Law Review* 131.

that so-called licences to pollute do not always have a determinative impact on civil liability in domestic law.[308]

The Supreme Court of Canada's judgment in *Interprovincial Co-operatives* suggests that the same is true with respect to transboundary pollution.[309] Manitoba's legislation provided that an authorisation granted by the authorities of the place where the discharge had occurred (in that case, two neighbouring provinces) could not relieve the defendant from liability in Manitoba.[310] Although the majority of the Court invalidated the statute, six judges (three in the majority and three dissenting) found that the defendants' licence to operate in Ontario and Saskatchewan did not shield them from common law liability in Manitoba.

Justice Pigeon held that a province could not 'validly license on its territory operations having an injurious effect outside its borders so as to afford a defence against whatever remedies are available at common law in favour of persons suffering injury thereby in another province'.[311] The reasoning was predicated on his opinion that only the federal legislature had jurisdiction over interprovincial matters, such that only it could have validly exonerated the defendants from the consequences of their conduct in Manitoba. But Chief Justice Laskin, dissenting with Justices Judson and Spence, reached the same conclusion through a different route, and commented on the common law along the way. First, Chief Justice Laskin held that a licence issued to the appellants either under provincial *or* federal legislation '[did] not have an extra-territorial reach to entitle each of them with impunity to send their pollutants into the waters of another province'.[312] He concluded with an *obiter* suggesting that the Fishermen's Assistance and Polluters' Liability Act may not have been necessary, as 'there is bound to be doubt whether a foreign jurisdiction can license the pollution of waters in a neighbouring state so as to provide a defence to an action brought in the latter for injury to property therein'.[313]

Administrative authorisations therefore do not exonerate polluters from the consequences of their conduct felt outside the province. Victims of transboundary pollution can still claim any remedy available under the applicable law. Simply, that same law will also determine whether and how to recognise administrative authorisations in local courts.[314]

[308] The same is true in several other legal systems: D Howarth, 'Environmental Law and Private Law' in E Lees and JE Viñuales (eds), *The Oxford Handbook of Comparative Environmental Law* (Oxford, Oxford University Press, 2019) 1116; M Hinteregger, 'Environmental Liability' in Lees and Viñuales (ibid) 1041.

[309] *Interprovincial Co-operatives* SCC (n 154).

[310] Fishermen's Assistance and Polluters' Liability Act (n 153), s 4(2).

[311] *Interprovincial Co-operatives* SCC (n 154) 511 (Pigeon J).

[312] ibid 499 (Laskin CJC, dissenting).

[313] ibid 506 (Laskin CJC, dissenting).

[314] Goldstein and Groffier (n 250) para 477.

C. Extraterritorial Application of Statutory Causes of Action

It is assumed in this book that the applicable law, designated by choice of law rules, would provide a remedy for environmental damage. At a minimum, this remedy would come from general civil liability regimes found in most legal regimes. But environmental statutes can also contain causes of action (also known as citizen suit provisions) that supplement or overlap with general civil liability regimes. These provisions have several uses. They can turn a violation of regulatory standards into an actionable wrong without having to prove fault, add or remove defences and limitations to liability, provide particular remedies such as injunctive relief, etc. They give more teeth to environmental law,[315] especially since the mere breach of a statutory duty does not always entail liability.

Statutory causes of action, however, do not always indicate clearly whether and how they apply to transboundary pollution. As the Secretariat of the CEC notes, 'the usual emphasis on territorial application of laws may cause environmental laws to be written and/or interpreted with a focus on the internal, rather than foreign, effects of the activities regulated by the laws'.[316] Foreign victims of pollution originating in Canada may not have access to statutory causes of action under the same conditions as local victims even if Canadian law governs their claim, which threatens equal remedy. Likewise, local victims of pollution originating elsewhere may not be able to invoke statutory causes of action against foreign polluters even if Canadian law applies to their claim.

These issues relate to extraterritoriality, but the terminology remains controversial. The authors of an extensive study of extraterritoriality in Canada distinguish true extraterritorial jurisdiction from extraterritorial effects and extended territorial jurisdiction.[317] The first concept refers to the exercise of state power entirely beyond borders, in foreign states or in the global commons. The second concept refers to domestic measures having a ripple effect beyond borders. The third concept refers to the application of domestic laws to a situation that has local *and* extraterritorial aspects. Whether this last scenario should also be labelled 'extraterritorial' is open for debate because it may still involve strong connections with the forum,[318] but it is unquestionably the

[315] See generally J Boyd, 'A Statutory Solution to Ontario's Environmental Class Action Problem: Section 99(2) of the *Environmental Protection Act*' (2019) 14 *Canadian Class Action Review* 421, 425–30.

[316] Secretariat of the Commission for Environmental Cooperation (n 370) 244.

[317] S Coughlan et al, *Law Beyond Borders: Extraterritorial Jurisdiction in an Age of Globalization* (Toronto, Irwin Law, 2014) ch 4.

[318] As Seck explains, 'continued reference to extraterritoriality in relation to home state jurisdiction may serve only to disguise the existence of real territorial links that provide a solid if preliminary justification for the reasonable exercise of home state jurisdiction'. SL Seck, 'Home State Responsibility and Local Communities: The Case of Global Mining' (2008) 11 *Yale Human Rights and Development Law Journal* 177, 186–87. See also SL Seck, 'Moving Beyond the E-Word in the

most relevant for our purposes because transboundary pollution concerns, at a minimum, one state of origin and one affected state.

Extraterritoriality looms large in international environmental law. It is a recurring theme in the ongoing discussion of business and human rights, as developed states face increasing pressure to regulate the activities of their corporations abroad. Extraterritoriality is also at the heart of trade disputes over unilateral state actions to protect the environment.[319] And of course, extraterritorial concerns are raised whenever it is suggested that states have a responsibility to protect the environment of foreign populations or the global commons.

In Canada, extraterritoriality stands at the crossroads of private international law, public international law, constitutional law and statutory interpretation. *Private international law* determines whether local law applies to private disputes with a foreign element (or whether local statutes are considered mandatory such that they apply regardless of choice of law rules). *Public international law* sets out the ground rules governing whether and to what extent states can assert their legislative or enforcement jurisdiction.[320] *Constitutional law* distributes these powers to the units of the federation. Indeed, only the federal legislature has the power to enact extraterritorial legislation,[321] and only if expressly stated or necessarily implied. Finally, canons of *statutory interpretation* help determine whether a statute is clear enough to apply extraterritorially (the presumption against extraterritoriality).[322]

This section unravels some of the conceptual challenges associated with the extraterritorial application of environmental law in private litigation, bearing in mind the states' duty to ensure equal remedy and prompt and adequate compensation to all victims of transboundary pollution. The focus of this section therefore remains on private international law and incidentally on the principles of constitutional law and statutory interpretation that are relevant to this inquiry.[323] It begins with a primer on the complex relationship between extraterritoriality and choice of law (section II.C.i) and then turns to statutory causes of action in Canada (section II.C.ii).

Anthropocene' in DS Margolies et al (eds), *The Extraterritoriality of Law: History, Theory, Politics* (Abingdon, Routledge, 2019).

[319] See generally B Cooreman, *Global Environmental Protection Through Trade: A Systematic Approach to Extraterritoriality* (Cheltenham, Edward Elgar, 2017).

[320] *R v Hape* 2007 SCC 26 [57]–[66]; *Case of the SS Lotus (France v Turkey)* (1927) PCIJ Rep Series A No 10, 18–21.

[321] Statute of Westminster 1931, 22 & 23 Geo V c 4, s 3; *Hape* (n 320) [66].

[322] *Society of Composers, Authors and Music Publishers of Canada v Canadian Association of Internet Providers*, 2004 SCC 45 [54]–[55].

[323] On the public international law of jurisdiction and the prosecution of extraterritorial environmental offences by Canadian authorities, see Nwapi, *Litigating Extraterritorial Corporate Crimes* (2012) ch 4; AM Manirabona, *Entreprises multinationales et criminalité environnementale transfrontalière: applicabilité du droit pénal canadien* (Cowansville, Yvon Blais, 2010).

i. Extraterritoriality and Choice of Law

Reconciling choice of law theory with the extraterritorial application of regulatory laws (including environmental statutes) is a difficult task.[324] As Riles notes:

> When regulators or market participants make a claim about the application of one or another body of law to a given party or transaction, they are already making an implicit claim about what the scope of their domestic law should be. Whether they recognize it or not, they are making a [conflict of laws] argument.[325]

But this argument is often buried in a statutory interpretation exercise that fails to consider other states' interest in applying their own regime.[326] The terminology used by the courts exacerbates the confusion. In Canada, the notion of a 'real and substantial connection' has split into two different branches – one expressing constitutionally imposed territorial limits on provincial powers (the constitutional branch) and the other expressing an organising principle for all conflict rules (the private international law branch).[327] The use of a single expression for two very different concepts testifies to the close but potentially confusing[328] relationship between extraterritoriality and choice of law.

Leave public authorities out of the equation and difficulties remain. Suppose that an individual relies on a local statutory cause of action and the claim has a foreign element. It is tempting to conclude that the statutory cause of action will apply only if choice of law rules lead to local law. But the problem is thornier than it seems. Should the court determine whether the statute expressly or implicitly applies to this fact pattern and ignore the presence of an equivalent regime elsewhere? Should it first identify the applicable law under choice of law rules?

The law on this point is straightforward in Quebec. Article 3076 CCQ provides that 'rules of law in force in [the province] which are applicable by reason of their particular object' override conflict rules altogether. The analysis focuses on whether 'vital interests' are at stake,[329] such that a local rule applies directly to an international fact pattern. The common law is less principled towards this issue. *Paniccia* is a good example.[330] The case involved a

[324] See generally M Hook, 'The Conflict of Laws as a Shared Language for the Cross-Border Application of Statutes' in M Douglas et al (eds), *Commercial Issues in Private International Law: A Common Law Perspective* (Oxford, Hart, 2019); R Michaels, 'Towards a Private International Law for Regulatory Conflicts?' (2016) 59 *Japanese Yearbook of International Law* 175.

[325] A Riles, 'Managing Regulatory Arbitrage: A Conflict of Laws Approach' (2014) 47 *Cornell International Law Journal* 63, 89.

[326] ibid 90–91.

[327] *Club Resorts* (n 166) [22]–[43].

[328] E Edinger, '*Club Resorts Ltd. v. Van Breda*: Extraterritoriality Revisited' (2014) 55 *Canadian Business Law Journal* 263, 279–80.

[329] *B(G) c C(C)* [2001] RJQ 1435, 1440 (Qc CA). See also *United European Bank and Trust Nassau Ltd c Duchesneau* 2006 QCCA 652 [56]–[58].

[330] *Paniccia v MDC Partners Inc* 2017 ONSC 7298.

secondary market misrepresentation class action brought in Ontario under the Ontario Securities Act[331] against a company trading its shares on Canadian and American markets. The defendants argued that Ontario courts could not hear the claims of Canadian purchasers of shares traded in the United States, because choice of law rules required the exclusive application of American law to those claims. The Ontario Superior Court concluded that Ontario courts were bound to apply Ontario law because the Ontario Securities Act applied extraterritorially in these circumstances.[332] Justice Perell held that

> it would be an example of juridical irony for a court then or now to conclude on the one hand that [the Act] can apply extra-territorially but to conclude on the other hand that the choice of law rule mandates that [the Act] does not apply with respect to the defendant's shares that traded outside of Ontario.[333]

Justice Perell ultimately ruled that Ontario law applied and that Ontario was an appropriate forum.

Paniccia ties the choice of law analysis with the extraterritorial scope of the Ontario Securities Act itself: local law applied because the 'long arm' of the Ontario Securities Act extended to shares traded on both local and foreign stock markets (as opposed to shares traded entirely on foreign markets).[334] Translated into choice of law terms, this reasoning seems to imply that regulatory legislation is overriding and mandatory, or that it constitutes a unilateral choice of law rule which systematically designates local law and makes it applicable extraterritorially. Article 3076 CCQ provides a principled framework to deal with this problem in conflict of laws terms, but the common law is not so clear. As *Paniccia* shows, lines are easily blurred between what we describe as the 'extraterritorial application' of regulatory statutes in private litigation and the choice of law analysis.

The next section examines statutory causes of action in Canadian environmental legislation, whether they apply *before* the entire choice of law process (as overriding mandatory rules of the forum) or *after* choice of law rules designate the law of a Canadian province which includes a statutory cause of action.

ii. Statutory Causes of Action in Canada

Certain statutory causes of action may be available to victims of transboundary pollution in Canada. To account for constitutional constraints, a distinction must be made between federal (section II.C.ii.a) and provincial law (section II.C.ii.b). Final remarks on prompt and adequate compensation will follow (section II.C.ii.c).

[331] Securities Act, RSO 1990 c S.5, ss 138.1–138.14.
[332] *Paniccia* (n 330) [81]–[97].
[333] ibid [92].
[334] ibid [79], [89]. cf *Yip v HSBC Holdings plc* 2017 ONSC 5332 [240], affd 2018 ONCA 626, leave to appeal to SCC refused, 38331 (28 March 2019).

a. Federal Law

Federal environmental law contains two noteworthy causes of action. First, the Canadian Environmental Protection Act (CEPA) – the centrepiece of federal environmental policy – allows any person suffering loss or damage resulting from a violation of the Act to seek compensation or injunctive relief from the courts.[335] Victims can also recover loss or damage to property at the sentencing stage of a penal prosecution.[336] Second, the Fisheries Act enables licensed commercial fishermen to recover losses of income suffered as a result of the unauthorised deposit of a deleterious substance in water frequented by fish.[337]

To determine whether CEPA and the Fisheries Act apply in transboundary environmental disputes, two scenarios must be distinguished: foreign victims suing in Canada for pollution originating in Canada and local victims suing in Canada for pollution originating abroad.

Foreign Plaintiffs in Canada

The statutory cause of action in the Fisheries Act is clearly inapplicable in the first scenario – foreign victims suing in Canada for pollution originating in Canada. Foreign victims are not licensed commercial fishermen in Canada and the prohibition of deleterious substances applies only to Canadian fisheries waters.[338] CEPA, however, imposes no particular requirement on the identity of plaintiffs: all persons may initiate proceedings in Canada. Nor is CEPA's definition of environment limited to Canada.[339] Foreign plaintiffs may therefore sue Canadian polluters under CEPA. The presumption against extraterritoriality does not come into play because applying CEPA to local polluters can hardly be considered extraterritorial – this is simply a matter of equal remedy for foreign victims of transboundary pollution.

Canadian Plaintiffs in Canada

The opposite scenario – local victims suing in Canada for pollution originating abroad – is more difficult because it involves the application of domestic legislation to polluters that are presumably already regulated elsewhere. This was the essence of Teck Cominco's contention in *Pakootas*: the smelter was regulated by Canadian authorities and operated with permits issued under Canadian law,

[335] Canadian Environmental Protection Act 1999, SC 1999 c 33 (CEPA), ss 39–40. See generally M Valiante, '"Welcomed Participants" or "Environmental Vigilantes"? The CEPA Environmental Protection Action and the Role of Citizen Suits in Federal Environmental Law' (2002) 25 *Dalhousie Law Journal* 81.

[336] ibid, s 292.

[337] Fisheries Act, RSC 1985 c F-14, s 42(3).

[338] ibid, s 34(1); Secretariat of the Commission for Environmental Cooperation (n 370) 244–45.

[339] CEPA (n 335), s 3(1); *R v Hydro-Québec* [1997] 3 SCR 213, 262 (Lamer CJC and Iacobucci J, dissenting).

with no possibility of even obtaining similar permits from American authorities as a foreigner.[340]

Arguably, the statutory causes of action in CEPA or the Fisheries Act can apply to foreign polluters in relation to damage suffered in Canada. The *Edwards* case supports this view.[341] The dispute involved the private prosecution of a violation of the Fisheries Act (a regulatory offence).[342] In Canada, anyone[343] who believes that a person has committed a federal indictable offence within the territorial jurisdiction of a court may present the information to a judge, who may issue a summons or a warrant to compel that person to answer charges.[344] The private prosecution of environmental offences rarely succeeds, not least because public prosecutors have virtually unfettered discretion to take over the proceedings or withdraw the charges at any time after information is sworn,[345] and have done so in the past.[346] Stays of proceedings have tempered the expectations of environmental lawyers over the years,[347] but private prosecutions remain a useful tool to draw attention to environmental issues.[348]

In *Edwards*, an environmental advocate residing in Ontario asked the courts of the province to issue a summons to DTE Energy, an electricity provider operating coal power plants in Michigan. Scott Edwards claimed that DTE Energy violated the Fisheries Act by discharging mercury into the St-Clair River separating Ontario from Michigan. A first judge refused to issue the summons. Edwards sought to compel the issuance of the summons through a mandamus application before the Ontario Superior Court of Justice. Edwards' counsel made extensive submissions on the extraterritorial application of the Fisheries Act, pleading that the court had jurisdiction on the basis of a real and substantial connection because DTE Energy's activities, albeit located in the United States, caused damage on Canadian soil. Counsel presented Edwards' claim as a mirror image of *Pakootas*, which 'tells us that our friends down south are allowing prosecutions … of people who are doing the same type

[340] *Pakootas v Teck Cominco Metals* 2004 WL 2578982, 14 (Westlaw) (ED Wash 2004), affd 452 F (3d) 1066 (2006), *certiorari* denied 552 US 1095 (2008).

[341] *Edwards v DTE Energy Co* [2008] OJ No 4433 (Lexis Advance Quicklaw) (Ont Sup Ct).

[342] Fisheries Act (n 337).

[343] Authors suggest that this may include nonresidents: Muldoon, Scriven and Olson (n 21) 151–52.

[344] Criminal Code, RSC 1985 c C-46, ss 504(a)(b), 507.1.

[345] *Canadian Broadcasting Corporation v Morrison* 2017 MBCA 36 [24]–[25]; *R v McHale* 2010 ONCA 361 [42], leave to appeal to SCC refused [2010] 3 SCR vi.

[346] eg *Labrador Métis Nation v Canada (Attorney General)* 2006 FCA 393.

[347] See generally K Ferguson, 'Challenging the Intervention and Stay of an Environmental Private Prosecution" (2004) 13 *Journal of Environmental Law and Practice* 153; BC Tingle, 'The Strange Case of the Crown Prerogative over Private Prosecutions or Who Killed Public Interest Law Enforcement?' (1994) 28 *UBC Law Review* 309.

[348] See generally J Swaigen, A Koehl and C Hatt, 'Private Prosecutions Revisited: The Continuing Importance of Private Prosecutions in Protecting the Environment' (2013) 26 *Journal of Environmental Law and Practice* 31, reprinted in A Ingleson (ed), *Environment in the Courtroom* (Calgary, University of Alberta Press, 2019); K Webb, 'Taking Matters into Their Own Hands: The Role of Citizens in Canadian Pollution Control Enforcement' (1991) 36 *McGill Law Journal* 770.

of environmental crime in the other direction'.[349] Justice Donohue granted the request for mandamus and ordered the issuance of the summons, which implied reasonable grounds that DTE Energy was breaching Canadian law by dumping toxic substances into Canadian waters. Parties ultimately reached an agreement on the reduction of mercury emissions and charges were withdrawn in 2009.[350]

The application of American law to a Canadian company in *Pakootas* received immense scholarly attention.[351] *Edwards*, by contrast, received less attention.[352] Realistically, the case offers meagre jurisprudential support for the extraterritorial application of Canadian environmental law in a private dispute. The case began with the private prosecution of a regulatory offence, not a civil claim. Neither DTE Energy nor the Attorney General made submissions on the mandamus application.[353] The reported judgment is verbatim, and Justice Donohue simply endorsed certain paragraphs of Edwards' factum as his reasons.[354] A summons says nothing about the culpability of an accused, and the case never went to trial.

Nonetheless, *Edwards* shows that Canadian courts are prepared to extend the application of federal environmental law to foreign polluters when they cause damage in Canada. It is unclear whether Justice Donohue considered that the offence had been committed in Canada or that it had been committed elsewhere and caused effects in Canada (two arguments put forward by the plaintiff in his factum[355]), but he accepted the proposition that there was a real

[349] *Edwards* (n 341) [95].

[350] M McAree and J Vince, 'When Complying with the Law in Your Own Backyard Is Not Enough: Cross-Border United States and Canada Environmental Litigation' (2013) 42 *Brief* 57, 58.

[351] eg J Ellis, 'Extraterritorial Exercise of Jurisdiction for Environmental Protection: Addressing Fairness Concerns' (2012) 25 *Leiden Journal of International Law* 397; N Craik, 'Transboundary Pollution, Unilateralism and the Limits of Extraterritorial Jurisdiction: The Second *Trail Smelter* Dispute' in RM Bratspies and RA Miller (eds), *Transboundary Harm in International Law: Lessons from the Trail Smelter Arbitration* (Cambridge, Cambridge University Press, 2006); T Kruger, 'Trail Smelter II: A Prudent Approach? From Extraterritoriality to Non-Discrimination' (2010) 43 *UBC Law Review* 109; GF Hess, 'The Trail Smelter, the Columbia River, and the Extraterritorial Application of CERCLA' (2005) 18 *Georgetown International Environmental Law Review* 1. This is but a small sample of the literature on *Pakootas*.

[352] N Hall et al, 'Great Lakes Emerging Legal Issues Regarding the International Boundary Waters Treaty and the Great Lakes Water Quality Agreement' (2010) 34 *Canada–United States Law Journal* 193, 223–24 (comments by N Hall); Kruger, 'Trail Smelter II' (2010) 141; B Benedict, 'Transnational Pollution and the Efficacy of International and Domestic Dispute Resolutions Among the NAFTA Countries' (2009) 15 *Law and Business Review of the Americas* 863, 880–81; J Gracer, D Mahony and T Dyck, 'Cross-Border Litigation Gains Traction in U.S. and Canadian Courts' (2008) 20 *Environmental Claims Journal* 181, 187–90.

[353] The pre-inquiry process to determine whether the court should issue a summons or a warrant under section 507.1 of the Criminal Code is usually held in private and in the absence of the proposed accused, with a possibility for the Attorney General to intervene: *McHale* (n 345) [48], [58]. This is not always the case for a mandamus application challenging the refusal to issue a summons or a warrant: see eg *Ambrosi v British Columbia (Attorney General)* 2012 BCSC 720.

[354] *Edwards* (n 341) [178].

[355] ibid (Applicant's Factum, paras 52, 59–65).

and substantial connection between Canada and the offence, as required by the Supreme Court of Canada in criminal matters.[356] If environmental damage suffered in Canada represents a sufficiently strong connection in that context, it may also suffice to invoke statutory causes of action against foreign polluters in civil litigation when the language of a statute allows for it. The implications, however, should not be overstated. In the United States, scholars point out that domestic environmental law seldom stretches beyond borders.[357] Likewise, *Edwards* is unlikely to herald a new era of intensive enforcement of Canadian environmental law against foreign polluters.

To conclude, CEPA applies in proceedings brought in Canada by foreign victims against local polluters. There is also a good possibility that CEPA and the Fisheries Act apply in proceedings brought in Canada by local victims against foreign polluters, as long as a sufficient connection exists with the forum.

b. Provincial Law

Eight provinces have statutory causes of action in environmental legislation, but their scope and requirements vary greatly, ranging from narrow boilerplate provisions to full-blown environmental bills of rights.[358]

In Ontario, all persons have a right to compensation for loss or damage resulting from the spill of a pollutant, which they can exercise against the owner and the person having control of the pollutant.[359] Ontario residents can also bring an action when the violation of environmental statutes threatens Ontario public resources.[360] In Quebec, injunctive relief is available to persons domiciled in the province and frequenting the place (or its immediate vicinity) in which a violation allegedly occurred.[361] In Alberta, persons who suffer loss or damage as a result of conduct that resulted in a conviction may sue the offender.[362] Injunctive relief is also available.[363] In Newfoundland and Labrador, convictions are evidence of negligence and are actionable by persons who suffer loss

[356] *R v Libman*, [1985] 2 SCR 178, 212–13.

[357] JR Nash, 'The Curious Legal Landscape of the Extra-Territoriality of US Environmental Laws' in Handl, Zekoll and Zumbansen, *Beyond Territoriality* (2012) 163–64; JR Nash, 'The Curious Legal Landscape of the Extraterritoriality of U.S. Environmental Laws' (2010) 50 *Virginia Journal of International Law* 997, 998–99.

[358] The Reciprocal Access Act (n 23) does not create any substantive right to compensation: Uniform Law Conference of Canada (n 232) 503.

[359] Environmental Protection Act, RSO 1990 c E.19 (Ontario Environmental Protection Act), s 99(2).

[360] Environmental Bill of Rights 1993, SO 1993 c 28, s 84(1); Environmental Bill of Rights – General Regulation, O Reg 73/94, s 9.

[361] Quebec Environment Quality Act (n 303), ss 19.2–19.3, para 1.

[362] Environmental Protection and Enhancement Act, RSA 2000 c E-12 (Alberta Environmental Protection and Enhancement Act), s 219.

[363] ibid, s 225. See also Water Act, RSA 2000 c W-3, s 155.

or damage as a result.[364] Nova Scotia has a similar provision, but a conviction is only prima facie evidence of negligence and the amount recoverable is limited to reasonably foreseeable loss or damage.[365] The Northwest Territories, Nunavut and Yukon guarantee their residents the right to seek compensation or injunctive relief in order to protect the environment and the public trust from contaminants.[366] British Columbia, Manitoba, New Brunswick, Saskatchewan and Prince Edward Island do not have a statutory cause of action.[367]

Again, there are two scenarios in transboundary environmental disputes: foreign victims suing in Canada for pollution originating in Canada and local victims suing in Canada for pollution originating abroad.

Foreign Plaintiffs in Canada

In the first scenario – foreign victims suing in Canada for pollution originating in Canada – plaintiffs can rely on statutory causes of action in Ontario (Environmental Protection Act only), Alberta, Newfoundland and Labrador and Nova Scotia.[368] This is perfectly acceptable because the activity which triggers the statute originates in the province. The availability of recourse, however, remains subject to the wording of the substantive obligation itself. Ontario, for instance, defines natural environment as the air, land and water *of the province*, meaning there can be no violation outside the province.[369] Foreign plaintiffs are excluded de facto whenever a statute uses such terms.[370] Alberta, Newfoundland and Labrador and Nova Scotia define the environment more generally.[371]

[364] Environmental Protection Act, SNL 2002 c E-14.2 (Newfoundland and Labrador Environmental Protection Act), s 110.

[365] Environment Act, SNS 1994–95 c 1 (Nova Scotia Environment Act), s 142.

[366] Environmental Rights Act, SNWT 2019 c 19 (Northwest Territories), s 8(1); Environmental Rights Act, RSNWT (Nu) 1988 c 83 (Supp) (Nunavut), s 6(1); Environment Act, RSY 2002 c 76 (Yukon), s 8(1).

[367] A provision similar to the Ontario Environmental Protection Act existed in Saskatchewan but was repealed when a new environmental statute came into force in 2015: The Environmental Management and Protection Act 2002, SS 2002 c E-10.21, s 15(3), repealed by The Environmental Management and Protection Act 2010, SS 2010 c E-10.22, s 100.

[368] Ontario Environmental Protection Act (n 359) ss 1(1), 99(2); Alberta Environmental Protection and Enhancement Act (n 362), s 219; Nova Scotia Environment Act (n 365), ss 3(aj), 142; Newfoundland and Labrador Environmental Protection Act (n 364), ss 2(w), 110.

[369] Ontario Environmental Protection Act (n 359), s 1(1).

[370] Jeffery (n 243) 181. But see Ontario Environmental Protection Act (n 359), s 3(2) ('No action taken under [the Act] is invalid by reason only that the action was taken for the purpose of the protection, conservation or management of the environment outside Ontario's borders'); Secretariat of the Commission for Environmental Cooperation, 'Access to Courts and Administrative Agencies in Transboundary Pollution Matters' in Commission for Environmental Cooperation, *North American Environmental Law and Policy*, vol 4 (Cowansville, Yvon Blais, 2000) 245 (noting that section 3(2) 'raises a question as to whether foreign damage can also be a basis for a statute-based damages action');

[371] Alberta Environmental Protection and Enhancement Act (n 362), s 1(t); Nova Scotia Environment Act (n 365), s 3(r); Newfoundland and Labrador Environmental Protection Act (n 364), s 2(m).

By contrast, statutory causes of action in Ontario (Environmental Bill of Rights), the Northwest Territories, Nunavut and Yukon exclude foreign plaintiffs altogether. The Quebec Superior Court also denied statutory injunctive relief under the Quebec Environment Quality Act to an American citizen who had a residence in the province but was not domiciled there in the sense of Article 75 CCQ (the domicile being a person's 'principal establishment').[372] The Secreteriat of the CEC denounced residency requirements on the basis that they reduced transboundary access to courts in North America.[373] They go against equal remedy, and removing them would help ensure prompt and adequate compensation to foreign victims of transboundary pollution.

Canadian Plaintiffs in Canada

The opposite scenario – local victims suing in Canada for pollution originating abroad – hinges on the constitutional validity of a provincial statute purporting to apply to a foreign polluter. Unlike Federal Parliament, provinces cannot legislate extraterritorially.[374] Civil causes of action are within the provinces' jurisdictional purview,[375] but like all provincial statutes, they cannot apply extraterritorially. The current test to determine whether provincial statutes have constitutionally permissible territorial reach is highly contextual. The Supreme Court of Canada insists on the presence of meaningful connections with the province and respect for the legislative sovereignty of other territories.[376] The statute's 'pith and substance' (its essential character or dominant feature) must relate to matters within provincial powers, whether tangible or intangible. Civil causes of action will comply with constitutional requirements only if there is a sufficiently strong relationship between the enacting territory, the subject matter of the legislation and the persons made subject to it.[377]

The Supreme Court of Canada examined the provincial power to regulate transboundary pollution in *Interprovincial Co-operatives* (1975).[378] The Fishermen's Assistance and Polluters' Liability Act imposed liability for damage caused to Manitoba fisheries by contaminants discharged in provincial waters or carried from elsewhere into those waters, regardless of any licences issued outside Manitoba.[379] In a 4:3 verdict, the Court invalidated the statute, albeit on two different grounds. Justice Pigeon, also writing for Justices Martland and Beetz, found that the Act did not simply protect the province's fisheries

[372] *Coalition Verte c Technoparc Montréal* 2017 QCCS 1693 [29]–[39].
[373] Secretariat of the Commission for Environmental Cooperation (n 370) 243–46. See also Muldoon, Scriven and Olson (n 21) 123–24, 351–52.
[374] See the sources cited above n 236.
[375] Constitution Act 1867 (n 236), s 92(13); *Kirkbi AG v Ritvik Holdings Inc* 2005 SCC 65 [20]; *Imperial Tobacco* SCC 2005 (n 236) [32]; *General Motors of Canada Ltd v City National Leasing* [1989] 1 SCR 641, 672–73.
[376] *Imperial Tobacco* SCC 2005 (n 236) [26]–[36]; *Unifund Assurance* (n 236) [50]–[81].
[377] ibid.
[378] *Interprovincial Co-operatives* SCC (n 154).
[379] Fishermen's Assistance and Polluters' Liability Act (n 153).

but effectively oversaw licensed activities conducted in another province. The Act was invalid because its subject matter was interprovincial and therefore fell under exclusive federal jurisdiction.[380] Justice Ritchie, by contrast, refused to endorse Justice Pigeon's reasoning because the parties had not argued the issue. Instead, he found that rules of private international law (namely the pre-*Tolofson* double actionability/justifiability rule) entitled out-of-province polluters to have their licences recognised in Manitoba. The province had therefore exceeded its jurisdiction when it nullified civil rights validly acquired in another province and entitled to recognition in Manitoba.[381] Chief Justice Laskin, also writing for Justices Judson and Spence, disagreed with both his colleagues. He defined the purpose of the Act as the compensation of damage caused to Manitoba property. The rights asserted by the defendants, he said, stemmed from a 'licence to pollute' that was devoid of extraterritorial effect. For Chief Justice Laskin, the Act could not impact extraprovincial rights which the defendants simply did not have.[382]

It is difficult to draw firm conclusions with the guidance provided in *Interprovincial Co-operatives*.[383] Black and Swan suggest that 'The several reasons for judgment deal very inadequately with the serious problem of interprovincial water pollution',[384] and one of Canada's leading constitutional scholars admitted that the *ratio decidendi* of the majority was 'not easy to encapsulate'.[385] Overall, the case suggests that provinces cannot legislate to protect their property from pollution originating in another province or state. But the different routes taken by Justices Pigeon and Ritchie on extraterritoriality, and the dissent which makes it a 3:3:1 verdict, mean that this point is not settled.[386] Even if it were, the rules governing choice of law and extraterritoriality have evolved considerably since and the precedential value of *Interprovincial Co-operatives* on this point is now doubtful.[387]

First, the Supreme Court of Canada rejected the double actionability/justifiability rule invoked by Justice Ritchie and replaced it with the *lex loci delicti*

[380] *Interprovincial Co-operatives* SCC (n 154) 505–16 (Pigeon J).

[381] ibid 516–26 (Ritchie J, concurring).

[382] ibid 481–505 (Laskin CJC, dissenting).

[383] In a later case, the Supreme Court of Canada cited *Interprovincial Co-operatives* as support for the proposition that the federal Parliament had jurisdiction over interprovincial rivers under the 'peace, order and good government' (POGG) clause of the Constitution Act 1867: *References re Greenhouse Gas Pollution Pricing Act* 2021 SCC 11 [99].

[384] V Black and J Swan, 'Concurrent Judicial Jurisdiction: A Race to the Court House or to Judgment? *Lloyd's Underwriters v. Cominco Ltd*'. (2008) 46 *Canadian Business Law Journal* 292, 292–93, fn 3.

[385] PW Hogg, *Constitutional Law of Canada*, 5th edn (Toronto, Carswell, 2007) (loose-leaf updated 2020) § 13.6.

[386] T Bradbrooke Smith, 'The Canadian Legislative Position' (1982) 5 *Canada-United States Law Journal* 66, 70; F Chevrette and H Marx, *Droit constitutionnel: notes et jurisprudence* (Montreal, Presses de l'Université de Montréal, 1982) 1178.

[387] M Olszynski, S Mascher and M Doelle, 'From Smokes to Smokestacks: Lessons from Tobacco for the Future of Climate Change Liability' (2017) 30 *Georgetown Environmental Law Review* 1, 38.

in 1995.[388] For Justice Ritchie, the polluting activities were justified under the law of the place of acting because the defendants were licensed in Ontario and Saskatchewan, and their rights were entitled to recognition in Manitoba.[389] Today, environmental torts may plausibly be located at the place of injury, as Chief Justice Laskin suggested in his dissent.[390] The law of the place of injury would be the *lex loci delicti*, and it would not matter whether the conduct was justified under the law of Ontario and Saskatchewan.

Second, the result in *Interprovincial Co-operatives* rests on a now-outdated approach to extraterritoriality. Both Justices Pigeon and Ritchie relied on the *Royal Bank of Canada* case to invalidate the Fishermen's Assistance and Polluters' Liability Act.[391] In *Royal Bank of Canada* (1913), the Judicial Committee of the Privy Council suggested that provincial statutes could not have extraterritorial effects, however incidental: a statute would be ultra vires 'inasmuch as what was sought to be enacted was neither confined to property and civil rights within the province nor directed solely to matters of merely local or private nature within it'.[392] In *Ladore* (1939), however, the same Privy Council was prepared to accept legislation which affected extraprovincial rights 'collaterally, as a necessary incident to their lawful powers of good government within the Province'.[393] Nine years after *Interprovincial Co-operatives*, the Supreme Court of Canada rejected *Royal Bank of Canada* and held that *Ladore* was correct law.[394] The Court explained that provincial statutes are valid if their 'pith and substance' is intraprovincial matters, notwithstanding that they have incidental or consequential effects on extraprovincial rights.[395] This new approach – which the Court continues to follow today[396] – differs markedly from the early cases applied by Justices Pigeon and Ritchie.

The majority reasons in *Interprovincial Co-operatives* therefore do not align with the modern 'pith and substance' approach to extraterritoriality which the Supreme Court of Canada now follows.[397] Today, the Court could well subscribe to Chief Justice Laskin's opinion on the nature of the *Fishermen Act* – a statute aimed at compensating damage suffered in Manitoba[398] – and find that its

[388] *Tolofson* (n 4).
[389] *Interprovincial Co-operatives* SCC (n 154) 521–23 (Ritchie J, concurring).
[390] ibid 500–01 (Laskin CJC, dissenting). For further discussion on the localisation of torts for choice of law purposes, see section 4.II.A.i above.
[391] ibid 511–12 (Pigeon J), 523–24 (Ritchie J, concurring).
[392] *Royal Bank of Canada v The King* [1913] AC 283, 298 (PC).
[393] *Ladore v Bennett* [1939] AC 468, 482–83 (PC).
[394] *Reference re Upper Churchill Water Rights Reversion Act* [1984] 1 SCR 297.
[395] ibid 332.
[396] *Imperial Tobacco* SCC 2005 (n 236) [28]; *Global Securities Corp v British Columbia (Securities Commission)* 2000 SCC 21 [24].
[397] R Wisner, 'Uniformity, Diversity and Provincial Extraterritoriality: *Hunt v. T&N plc*' (1995) 40 *McGill Law Journal* 759, 775–76; Blom, 'The Conflict of Laws and the Constitution' (1977) 154–56.
[398] *Interprovincial Co-operatives* SCC (n 154) 501 (Laskin CJC, dissenting).

extraterritorial impacts remain incidental, hence constitutionally permissible. This would mean that 'any corporation that builds and operates a factory discharging a contaminant into an interprovincial river takes the risk that the downstream province will legislate so as to compensate its citizens' if damage occurs.[399] This is hardly unacceptable, particularly since holders of licences are seldom, if ever, entitled to full immunity from the consequences of their operations within a province.[400]

The scope of the federal/provincial jurisdiction over transboundary pollution remains debatable and might come back under judicial scrutiny in the future. Until then, *Interprovincial Co-operatives* remains a key precedent when analysing the extraterritorial scope of provincial environmental law. It may not represent good or even intelligible law, but it still casts a long shadow.

c. Enabling Prompt and Adequate Compensation through Statutory Causes of Action

Victims of transboundary pollution should not count on statutory causes of action to supplement civil liability and increase the likelihood of compensation. Several provinces simply have no such mechanism, and the ones that do often narrow it to the extreme. Provisions triggered only by formal convictions, for instance, hardly promote a wide access to justice for the public if regulatory enforcement is lacklustre.[401] Scholars and environmental advocates have long denounced the scarcity and weaknesses of existing statutory causes of action.[402] As Wood points out, 'Their demanding prerequisites, narrow scope, and broad defences make them so unattractive that few have been commenced and none has yet produced a trial decision on the merits'.[403] The portrait is even bleaker in a transboundary context. The residency requirements imposed in several provinces prevent foreign victims from relying on statutory causes of action against local polluters.[404] Constitutional constraints may also prevent local victims from relying on statutory causes of action against foreign polluters. Those constraints, expressed in *Interprovincial Co-operatives*, may no longer exist today, but uncertainty persists.

The reform agenda is clear. Clarifying the scope of the provinces' power to regulate transboundary pollution, widening the scope of existing statutory

[399] Blom (n 157) 155.

[400] For further discussion on this point, see section II.B.ii above.

[401] On environmental law enforcement in Canada, see S Wood, 'Canada' in Lees and Viñuales, *Comparative Environmental Law* (2019) 124–25; DR Boyd, *Cleaner, Greener, Healthier: A Prescription for Stronger Canadian Environmental Laws and Policies* (Vancouver, UBC Press, 2015) 195–97.

[402] DR Boyd, 'Elements of an Effective Environmental Bill of Rights' (2015) 27 *Journal of Environmental Law and Practice* 201, 213–19; DR Boyd, *Unnatural Law: Rethinking Canadian Environmental Law and Policy* (Vancouver, UBC Press, 2003) 246–48; EL Hughes and D Iyalomhe, 'Substantive Environmental Rights in Canada' (1999) 30 *Ottawa Law Review* 229, 247–53.

[403] Wood, 'Canada' (2019) 126.

[404] Secretariat of the Commission for Environmental Cooperation (n 370) 243–46.

causes of action and adopting new ones would help ensure equal remedy and prompt and adequate compensation to all victims of transboundary pollution. In the meantime, victims can always fall back on federal legislation, free from constitutional limitations and with at least one precedent in hand (*Edwards*).

III. CONCLUSION

In this chapter, I identified the choice of law requirements associated with the duty to ensure prompt and adequate compensation and explained how they have been implemented in Canada. International environmental law has focused primarily on non-discrimination and equal remedy. And yet, equal remedy has triggered few meaningful attempts at legal reform in North America. Surely, more can be done than the Boundary Waters Treaty, the International Boundary Waters Treaty Act, the Draft Treaty on Equal Access and Remedy, the Reciprocal Access Act and the NAAEC have managed to achieve.

But again, we must ask whether general choice of law rules can respond to the concerns that prompted those isolated sparks of legal innovation, which the ILC picked up on to develop the duty to ensure prompt and adequate compensation. The regulation theory supports the assertion that choice of law rules have a regulatory impact in environmental law. They can legitimately – and openly – favour victims over polluters, increase the likelihood of compensation and (perhaps) raise environmental standards. Choice of law rules are a crucial aspect of the ILC Principles on the Allocation of Loss, even though the ILC obscured them in the name of a diversified state practice. The objectives here are twofold. First, we must ensure that foreign victims get at least the same treatment as local victims through choice of law rules. Second, we must ensure that victims can rely on a law that favours prompt and adequate compensation. The ubiquity principle has emerged as the most appropriate choice of law rule to meet those objectives. It should not come as a surprise that the EU adopted it and that UNEP now recommends its adoption in domestic civil liability regimes.

Letting the victim choose between the law of the place of acting and the law of the place of injury as the *lex loci delicti* is not a perfect solution. It may lead to fragmentation among the claims of different plaintiffs. It makes compliance harder for defendants, particularly if they cannot plead unforeseeability. But it also ensures equal remedy, favours compensation and ultimately disincentivises polluters from taking advantage of weaker legal regimes. It reflects and responds to the challenges of transboundary pollution in private international law better than any rigid definition of the *lex loci delicti* would.

The Canadian choice of law framework lags behind. Local and foreign victims have equal access to the courts, but they may be treated differently once they get there as a result of choice of law rules. Victims may also lose the benefit of the more favourable law as a result of a rigid definition of the *lex loci delicti*. This is particularly true in common law provinces. The CCQ leans closer to the ubiquity principle, but victims still face a narrowly interpreted injury exception and a foreseeability requirement. To make things worse, statutory causes of action across the country are ill-suited to transboundary environmental disputes.

The lack of clear and binding appellate case law magnifies those problems. The Reciprocal Access Act has never been judicially tested, let alone its choice of law rule (which is unsurprising given the Act's extremely narrow scope). The Quebec Court of Appeal has only dealt with Article 3126 CCQ twice, in cases that share few of the attributes of transboundary environmental disputes. The Supreme Court of Canada has never dissipated the uncertainty surrounding *Tolofson*'s adjustments to the *lex loci delicti*. Statutory reform is nowhere in sight. Victims of transboundary pollution pay the price of this uncertainty and polluters carry on.

A strong consensus has developed around the ubiquity principle. It is achievable through legislative or judicial reform – not a complete overhaul of the choice of law framework, but a surgical intervention to better deal with the peculiarities of environmental torts. This would increase the likelihood of compensation for victims of transboundary pollution who choose to sue in Canada and ultimately contribute to environmental justice.

Conclusion

I. CONCLUSIONS OF THE STUDY

THIS BOOK IDENTIFIED a duty to ensure the availability of prompt and adequate compensation for all victims of transboundary pollution. The precise status of the duty in public international law remains open for debate, but it is mentioned in numerous environmental treaties and other documents such as UNGA resolutions and soft law instruments.[1] It forms the backbone of the ILC Principles on the Allocation of Loss and should be considered an emerging principle of international environmental law.[2] A clear duty to ensure *the availability of* prompt and adequate compensation is the best that can be achieved in the current state of international law. The doctrine of state responsibility remains difficult to grasp with respect to environmental damage and equally difficult to incorporate into a treaty.[3] The doctrine of state liability is virtually non-existent.[4] Civil liability treaties are plentiful, and helpfully focus on private parties rather than states, but most do not have wide membership.[5] In this context, it is reasonable to focus, as the ILC did, on a duty to ensure prompt and adequate compensation in domestic law.

Of course, we must be careful not to read too much into the ILC Principles on the Allocation of Loss. They represent a watered-down political compromise on a historically controversial issue and states have been somewhat indifferent to their contents despite repeated calls from the UNGA. But the ILC Principles on the Allocation of Loss say more about the future of international liability law than about its current state. They may not codify existing international law, but they provide a realistic roadmap to improve the situation of victims through concepts such as equal access and equal remedy. States can discharge their obligations through a variety of means so long as prompt and adequate compensation remains available. Regulatory diversity is embraced rather than being perceived as an impediment to treaty-making. This is an important step which ought to be acknowledged.

The reader will have noticed a drastic – and perhaps challenging – shift between the first and the second part of this book. The first part addressed the vast topic of liability in international environmental law, and the second part

[1] See sections 1.II.A.i and 1.II.A.ii above.
[2] See section 1.II.A.iii above.
[3] See sections 1.I.B and 1.I.D.iii above.
[4] See section 1.I.C above.
[5] See section 1.I.D above.

then delved into the intricacies of Canadian private international law. This includes important but somewhat specific problems such as the local action rule,[6] the localisation of a tort,[7] the public law exception,[8] and the extra-territorial reach of provincial statutes.[9] It is perfectly reasonable to be well versed in international environmental law, but not in private international law, and vice versa. This shift is intended. In fact, it is the very point of this book. Translating the ILC Principles on the Allocation of Loss or the UNEP Guidelines on Liability (and everything that came before them) into a domestic regime of private international law reveals its regulatory function. It shows that we can work towards meaningful environmental justice using a very different discipline which, unlike international environmental law, addresses the public interest somewhat less directly. This book focuses on Canadian private international law, but a similar translation process can occur in any state. It can also occur with any of the substantive rules of civil liability set out in the ILC Principles on the Allocation of Loss, the UNEP Guidelines on Liability or other soft law instruments (identity of the person liable, standard of care, defences, etc).

This book identifies what the duty to ensure prompt and adequate compensation entails in terms of jurisdictional and choice of law rules in Canada. The conclusions are as follows. First, prompt and adequate compensation entails equal access to the courts for local and foreign victims. This subset of non-discrimination is discussed in chapter three. The general law of jurisdiction can achieve this result if courts have jurisdiction at the place of acting (in order for foreign victims to sue Canadian polluters) *and* at the place of injury (in order for local victims to sue foreign polluters). Jurisdiction at the place of acting does not cause much of a problem because it flows from the presence of the polluter in Canada. It does, however, imply the abolition of the local action rule, which prevents courts from hearing disputes involving foreign land.[10] Jurisdiction at the place of injury implies the recognition that the tort has occurred there, or at least that courts at the place of injury have a sufficiently strong connection with the dispute.[11] Neither is a problem in Canadian private international law. The local action rule has doubtful precedential value in tort disputes, such that the courts of a Canadian province can (and should) assert jurisdiction over a local polluter that caused damage elsewhere.[12]

Courts in all provinces can also assert jurisdiction over a foreign polluter based on damage suffered in the forum.[13] Local and foreign victims of

[6] See section 3.II.A.i.b above.
[7] See section 3.II.a.ii above.
[8] See sections 3.II.C.ii.a and 4.II.B.i.a above.
[9] See section 4.II.C.ii.b above.
[10] See section 3.II.A.i above.
[11] See section 3.II.A.ii above.
[12] See section 3.II.A.i.b above.
[13] See section 3.II.A.ii.b above.

transboundary pollution have equal access to Canadian courts insofar as jurisdiction is concerned. Residency requirements in environmental statutes and procedural mechanisms such as security for costs distinctively affect foreign plaintiffs,[14] but equal access is generally secured. Attempts to enforce a foreign judgment against a Canadian polluter, however, may trigger a debate on the public law/public policy exception.[15] Indirect jurisdiction requirements in Quebec and in New Brunswick (in an international context) may also prevent the enforcement of a judgment rendered at the place of injury,[16] but the prospects of enforcement are generally acceptable in other provinces.

Second, prompt and adequate compensation entails equal remedy for local and foreign plaintiffs and the application of a substantive law which favours compensation. This other subset of non-discrimination was discussed in chapter three. Again, the general choice of law framework can reach this result if it lets plaintiffs choose between the law of the place of acting and the law of the place of injury. This is the ubiquity principle.[17] It removes the possibility for polluters to take advantage of a weaker law and maximises victims' chances of recovery. The common law is problematic in this regard because it tends to favour a single law (place of injury).[18] Quebec civil law admits an option albeit on somewhat restrictive terms.[19] Direct implementation of the ubiquity principle into the common law framework (by statute or judicial follow-up to *Tolofson*) and the CCQ (necessarily by statute) would better fulfil the requirements of prompt and adequate compensation.

The time may be ripe for another attempt at legislative reform – a reform of a different kind than the ones contemplated in the 1970s and 1980s. Those years were fruitful in producing equal access/remedy proposals designed to be incorporated into national law, particularly with the impetus provided by the recommendations of the OECD.[20] The same was true in North America, notably with the Draft Treaty on Equal Access and Remedy and its provincial offspring, the Reciprocal Access Act.[21] The sheer number of scholarly articles published in those years signalled a strong desire to facilitate cross-border litigation in the hope that it would complement or replace state intervention in environmental matters. Enthusiasm gradually faded and private litigation revealed its limits (which, arguably, were obvious from the start but downplayed by its most enthusiastic advocates). The spirit of attempted reforms, however, remains as relevant as ever, and private litigation continues to play an important role in environmental law: to provide compensation, but also to prevent further damage and

[14] See section 3.I.B above.
[15] See section 3.II.C.ii above.
[16] See section 3.II.C.i above.
[17] See section 4.I.D.ii above.
[18] See section 4.II.A.i above.
[19] See section 4.II.A.iii above.
[20] See sections 3.I.B and 4.I.B above.
[21] See sections 3.I.C and 4.I.C above.

influence political and corporate agendas.[22] This is particularly true with the rise of climate change litigation.[23] Tort claims against the fossil fuel industry – one of the many ways to address climate change in domestic courts – offer further evidence that an approach based on civil liability is worth pursuing as a back-up to global regulatory efforts, because it has the distinct advantage of channelling liability to the persons most directly responsible for environmental damage: greenhouse gas emitters themselves.

The civil liability angle is not new: it has been studied, developed and promoted since the 1970s in relation to other environmental problems such as acid rain. In 1988, Joel Paul concluded his provocative essay on the isolation of private international law as follows:

> I write this as the air conditioner struggles vainly against the record-breaking heat-wave of the summer of 1988. Scientists tell us that this is only the beginning of a dramatic climate change contributed to by our worldwide production of chlorofluorocarbons and other compounds which deplete the ozone layer. Is it too late to reverse the effect on the ozone? Can we collectively adapt to the new climate? Is our lifestyle or our species doomed?
>
> Some people will say that these are not legitimate questions for a teacher of private international law to ask. But I say, why not?[24]

More than 30 years later, we know that the impacts of human activities on our climate go far beyond the depletion of the ozone layer, but Paul's point remains as relevant as it was back then, and the answer is equally obvious: climate change *is* a legitimate question for private international lawyers.

Climate change is perhaps the 'ultimate' instance of transboundary pollution, the one that is the most difficult to geographically pin down. This is a test for private international law, but not a death sentence. The regulation theory opens up new and promising ways of dealing with transboundary pollution – not just bilateral *Pakootas*-like disputes, but also global problems.[25] It allows us to squarely focus on jurisdictional and choice of law rules – something every state is familiar with – rather than all-encompassing and politically sensitive legal instruments designed to facilitate cross-border environmental litigation or to harmonise entire civil liability regimes. The regulation theory also shows that it is possible and legitimate to craft conflict rules with environmental objectives in mind. Whether through targeted statutory reform or judicial evolution, the promises of the regulation theory seem more realistic than the unfinished reforms of the past decades. The proposals contained in this book

[22] S Wood, 'Canada' in E Lees and JE Viñuales (eds), *The Oxford Handbook of Comparative Environmental Law* (Oxford, Oxford University Press, 2019) 118.

[23] See the text accompanying nn 92–98 (introduction) above.

[24] JR Paul, 'The Isolation of Private International Law' (1988) 7 *Wisconsin International Law Journal* 149, 178.

[25] See subsection 2.II.B above.

can certainly make their way into an ambitious treaty or model law specifically aimed at transboundary pollution, but they do not have to. This is the important takeaway.

II. CREATIVELY THINKING ABOUT LIABILITY FOR TRANSBOUNDARY POLLUTION

Two common assumptions obscure the way we think about liability for transboundary pollution, because they imply that private international law cannot regulate transboundary pollution in any meaningful way. The first assumption is that a global phenomenon (or at least one that transcends borders) requires a global legal response. Domestic regimes are but second-best options. They respond to some of the challenges of transboundary pollution, but their response is inherently chaotic and generally insufficient. They rely on a territorial understanding of the law and thus fail to grasp the *entirety* of the global problem, no matter how private international law defines their respective reach. The second assumption is that existing legal frameworks do not adequately deal with transboundary pollution because its magnitude or characteristics are unprecedented. This is particularly true for climate change. Something new is required, ideally in the form of a global regime (which then brings us back to the first assumption).

Most, if not all areas of the law, face constant pressure to stay relevant in light of new phenomena which legislatures and courts had not foreseen. New problems arise, the law adapts, and so on. But there are few areas in which we feel a need to justify our own relevance as strongly and consistently as we do in private international law.[26] Each international phenomenon brings a new wave of arguments 'pro-private international law' or 'against-private international law'. The debate focuses not on the contents of the rules themselves, but on their very legitimacy, relevance and usefulness. The Internet – described in the early days as borderless and practically immune to territorial forms of regulation – is an obvious example.[27] Decades after it went mainstream, so-called exceptionalists and unexceptionalists still debate whether Internet-based technologies have distinct and global implications that warrant an equally distinct and global form of regulation, as opposed to a web of domestic regimes held together by private

[26] As Blom puts it, 'Now and then, any conflicts teacher gets a twinge of apprehension that the entire subject may be obsolescent. A vision rises before his or her eyes of inter-jurisdictional problems all getting worked out as domestic legal regimes become more similar, remaining differences are smoothed out by internationally agreed rules, and courts become more adept at handling the few cases that still need to be brought before them. Happily, however, for those who love the subject, this vision is still far from being realized.' V Black, J Blom and J Walker, 'Current Jurisdictional and Recognitial Issues in the Conflict of Laws' (2011) 50 *Canadian Business Law Journal* 499, 522 (comments by J Blom).

[27] eg DR Johnston and D Post, 'Law and Borders – The Rise of Law in Cyberspace' (1996) 48 *Stanford Law Review* 1367.

international law.[28] Divergent characterisations of the Internet as border-free or border-bound have an impact on the kinds of legal solutions proposed to deal with its challenges. Views on the relevance or usefulness of private international law vary accordingly.[29] This is equally true for transboundary pollution, and indeed all problems described as inherently international.

The two assumptions described above, as well as the general discomfort towards private international law as a still-useful method to deal with regulatory conflicts, may explain why the discipline has not greatly factored in the legal response to global environmental problems so far – why the obstacle theory described in chapter two still prevails in the literature. Those assumptions are not inherently wrong. We may have good reasons to favour a truly global response to pollution over a variety of domestic approaches haphazardly strung together. Likewise, we may have good reasons to design new legal instruments for our day and age rather than attempt to stretch existing law in implausible ways. As Berman suggests when criticising unexceptionalist accounts of the Internet, the very idea that so-called established legal principles can apply to new international phenomena is somewhat circular because new international phenomena keep established legal principles in a constant state of flux.[30]

The problem is therefore not that the two assumptions cannot be justified with respect to liability for transboundary pollution. The problem is that they are distracting and often insufficiently nuanced. No approach based on state responsibility requires the demonstration that transboundary pollution is *inherently* international or should *always* be attributable to states, just as no approach based on domestic civil liability requires the demonstration that international law is *absolutely* ineffective and that domestic legal regimes are perfectly comfortable with the issue because *only* private parties are concerned.

This book avoids the pitfalls of an all-or-nothing approach and focuses instead on the complex and understated connections between private international law and international environmental law. Understanding the regulatory function of *private* international law with respect to transboundary pollution is impossible if we ignore the states' commitment to ensure the availability of prompt and adequate compensation, expressed through treaties, custom and soft law instruments with obvious relevance to the problem. By the same token, understanding the development of the duty to ensure prompt and adequate

[28] In the early days of mainstream Internet; cf the views of D Post, 'Against "Against Cyberanarchy"' (2002) 17 *Berkeley Technology Law Journal* 1365 and JL Goldsmith, 'Against Cyberanarchy' (1998) 65 *University of Chicago Law* Review 1199. More recently, with respect to the flow of data, cf the views of J Daskal, 'The Un-Territoriality of Data' (2015) 125 *Yale Law Journal* 326 and AK Woods, 'Against Data Exceptionalism' (2016) 68 *Stanford Law Review* 729.

[29] A Slane, 'Tales, Techs and Territories: Private International Law, Globalization, and the Legal Construction of Borderlessness on the Internet' (2008) 71 *Law and Contemporary Problems* 129.

[30] P Schiff Berman, '*Yahoo! v. LICRA*, Private International Law and the Deterritorialisation of Data' in H Muir Watt et al (eds), *Global Private International Law: Adjudication Without Frontiers* (Cheltenham, Edward Elgar, 2019) 402–04.

compensation in *public* international law is impossible if we focus only on states themselves, without acknowledging the possibility (and desirability) of holding private parties liable in domestic law, a possibility which international environmental law itself embraces.

Some will argue that domestic law can solve the liability conundrum in international environmental law. Others will disagree. But we can hardly have this conversation if we do not clearly understand how domestic environmental regimes operate in relation to one another – more specifically how private international law performs a regulatory function by coordinating various approaches to liability and environmental protection in domestic law. This regulatory function exists, and more importantly, it is informed by a duty to ensure the availability of prompt and adequate compensation for all victims of transboundary pollution. This is a sound conceptual basis for a conversation that must continue.

Bibliography

Affolder, N, 'The Market for Treaties' (2010) 11 *Chicago Journal of International Law* 160.

Alford, L and Berger Richardson, S, 'Right-to-Farm Legislation in Canada: Exceptional Protection for Standard Farm Practices' (2019) 50 *Ottawa Law Review* 131.

Álvarez-Armas, E, '(Lack of) International Jurisdiction over Third-Country Polluters: A Trojan Horse to the EU's Environmental Policy?' in J-S Bergé, S Francq and M Gardenez Santiago (eds), *Boundaries of European Private International Law* (Brussels, Bruylant, 2015) 283.

—— 'Potential Human-Rights-Related Amendments to the Rome II Regulation (II): The Proposed Art. 6a; Art. 7 is Dead, Long Live Article 7?' (Conflict of Laws, 27 January 2021), available at conflictoflaws.net.

Anderson, M, 'Transnational Corporations and Environmental Damage: Is Tort Law the Answer?' (2002) 41 *Washburn Law Journal* 399.

Arbitblit, DC, 'The Plight of American Citizens Injured by Transboundary River Pollution' (1979) 8 *Ecology Law Quarterly* 339.

Arbour, M-E, 'Liability Law and Nuisance in the Civil Law Tradition' in L Paddock, DL Markell and NS Bryner (eds), *Elgar Encyclopedia of Environmental Law*, vol 4: Compliance and Enforcement of Environmental Law (Cheltenham, Edward Elgar, 2017) 74.

Arnt Nielsen, P, 'The Hague 2019 Judgments Convention: From Failure to Success?' (2020) 16 *Journal of Private International Law* 205.

Arzandeh, A, 'The Origins of the Scottish *Forum Non Conveniens* Doctrine' (2017) 13 *Journal of Private International Law* 130.

—— *Private International Law in English Courts* (Oxford, Oxford University Press, 2014).

Baade, HW, 'Codes of Conduct for Multinational Enterprises: An Introductory Survey' in N Horn (ed), *Legal Problems of Codes of Conduct for Multinational Enterprises* (Deventer, Kluwer, 1980) 407.

Baber, WF and Bartlett, RV, *Global Democracy and Sustainable Jurisprudence: Deliberative Environmental Law* (Cambridge, MIT Press, 2009).

Banda, ML, 'Regime Congruence: Rethinking the Scope of State Responsibility for Transboundary Environmental Harm' (2019) 103 *Minnesota Law Review* 1879, 1880.

Bantekas, I, 'The Emerging UN Business and Human Rights Treaty and Its Codification of International Norms' (2021) 12 *George Mason Journal of International Commercial Law* 1.

Barboza, J, *The Environment, Risk and Liability in International Law* (Leiden, Martinus Nijhoff, 2011).

Basedow, J, *The Law of Open Societies: Private Ordering and Public Regulation in the Conflict of Laws* (Leiden, Brill Nijhoff, 2015).

Baxi, U, 'Mass Torts, Multinational Enterprise Liability and Private International Law' (1999) 276 *Recueil des cours de l'Académie de droit international* 297.

Beaumont, PR, 'Judgments Convention: Application to Governments' (2020) 67 *Netherlands International Law Review* 121.

—— 'Private International Law of the Environment' [1995] *Juridical Review* 28.

Benedict, B, 'Transnational Pollution and the Efficacy of International and Domestic Dispute Resolutions Among the NAFTA Countries' (2009) 15 *Law and Business Review of the Americas* 863.

Benidickson, J, Book Review of *The Price of Pollution: Environmental Litigation in Canada* by E Swanson and EL Hughes, (1991) 23 *Ottawa Law Review* 475.

Bergkamp, L, *Liability and Environment: Private and Public Law Aspects of Civil Liability for Environmental Harm in an International Context* (The Hague, Kluwer Law International, 2001).

Bernasconi, C, 'Civil Liability Resulting from Transfrontier Environmental Damage: A Case for the Hague Conference?' (1999) 12 *Hague Yearbook of International Law* 35, reprinted in Hague Conference on Private International Law, *Proceedings of the Nineteenth Session: 6 to 22 June 2001*, vol 1: Miscellaneous Matters (Leiden, Koninklijke Brill, 2008) 320.

Betlem, G and Bernasconi, C, 'European Private International Law, the Environment and Obstacles for Public Authorities' (2006) 122 *Law Quarterly Review* 124.

Birnie, PW and Boyle, AE, *International Law and the Environment* (Oxford, Clarendon Press, 1992).

Black, V, 'Commodifying Justice for Global Free Trade: The Proposed Hague Judgments Convention' (2000) 38 *Osgoode Hall Law Journal* 237.

Black, V and Pitel, SGA, 'Reform of Ontario's Law of Jurisdiction' (2009) 47 *Canadian Business Law Journal* 469.

Black, V and Swan, J, 'Concurrent Judicial Jurisdiction: A Race to the Court House or to Judgment? *Lloyd's Underwriters v. Cominco Ltd.*' (2008) 46 *Canadian Business Law Journal* 292.

Black, V, Blom, J and Walker, J, 'Current Jurisdictional and Recognitial Issues in the Conflict of Laws' (2011) 50 *Canadian Business Law Journal* 499.

Black, V, Pitel, SGA and Sobkin, M, Statutory Jurisdiction: An Analysis of the Court Jurisdiction and Proceedings Transfer Act (Toronto, Carswell, 2012).

Blom, J, 'Constitutionalizing Canadian Private International Law – 25 Years Since *Morguard*' (2017) 13 *Journal of Private International Law* 259.

—— 'Public Policy in Private International Law and Its Evolution in Time' (2003) 50 *Netherlands International Law Review* 373.

—— 'The Conflict of Laws and the Constitution: Interprovincial Co-Operatives Ltd v. The Queen' (1977) 11 *UBC Law Review* 144.

—— 'The *Court Jurisdiction and Proceedings Transfer Act* and the Hague Conference's Judgments and Jurisdiction Projects' (2018) 55 *Osgoode Hall Law Journal* 257.

Bodansky, D, 'Customary (And Not So Customary) International Environmental Law' (1995) 3 *Indiana Journal of Global Legal Studies* 105, reprinted in PM Pevato (ed), *International Environmental Law*, vol 1 (London, Routledge, 2018) 105.

—— 'The Role of the International Court of Justice in Addressing Climate Change: Some Preliminary Reflections' (2017) 49 *Arizona State Law Journal* 689.

Bogdan, M, 'On the So-Called Deficit of Social Values in Private International Law' in C Pampoukis (ed), *In Search for Justice: Essays in Honour of Professor Emeritus Spyridon Vrellis* (Athens, Nomiki, 2014) 31.

—— 'Private International Law as Component of the Law of the Forum: General Course on Private International Law' (2011) 348 *Recueil des cours de l'Académie de droit international* 9.

—— 'Some Reflections Regarding Environmental Damage and the Rome II Regulation' in G Venturini and S Bariatti (eds), *Liber Fausto Pocar*, vol 2: New Instruments of Private International Law (Milan, Giuffrè, 2009) 95.

—— 'The Treatment of Environmental Damage in Regulation Rome II' in J Ahern and W Binchy (eds), *The Rome II Regulation on the Law Applicable to Non-Contractual Obligations: A New International Litigation Regime* (Leiden, Martinus Nijhoff, 2009) 219.

Boskovic, O, 'Droit international privé et environnement' in *Juris-classeur environnement et développement durable*, fasc 2030 (1 September 2014).

—— 'Le contexte transnational en matière de responsabilité climatique' in M Hautereau-Boutonnet and S Porchy-Simon (eds), *Le changement climatique, quel rôle pour le droit privé?* (Paris, Dalloz, 2019) 193.

—— 'L'efficacité du droit international privé en matière environnementale' in O Boskovic (ed), *L'efficacité du droit de l'environnement: mise en œuvre et sanctions* (Paris, Dalloz, 2010) 53.

—— 'The Law Applicable to Violations of the Environment – Regulatory Strategies' in H Muir Watt and F Cafaggi (eds), *The Regulatory Function of European Private Law* (Cheltenham, Edward Elgar, 2009) 188.

Boyd, DR, *Cleaner, Greener, Healthier: A Prescription for Stronger Canadian Environmental Laws and Policies* (Vancouver, UBC Press, 2015).

—— 'Elements of an Effective Environmental Bill of Rights' (2015) 27 *Journal of Environmental Law and Practice* 201.

—— *Unnatural Law: Rethinking Canadian Environmental Law and Policy* (Vancouver, UBC Press, 2003).

Boyd, J, 'A Statutory Solution to Ontario's Environmental Class Action Problem: Section 99(2) of the *Environmental Protection Act*' (2019) 14 *Canadian Class Action Review* 421.

Boyle, A and Redgewell, C, *International Law and the Environment*, 4th edn (Oxford, Oxford University Press, 2021).

Boyle, A et al, 'International Law and the Liability for Catastrophic Environmental Damage' (2011) 105 *American Society of International Law Proceedings* 423.

Boyle, AE, 'Globalising Environmental Liability: The Interplay of National and International Law' (2005) 17 *Journal of Environmental Law* 3.

—— 'Progressive Development of International Environmental Law: Legislate or Litigate? (2019) 62 *German Yearbook of International Law* 305.

—— 'State Responsibility and International Liability for Injurious Consequences of Acts Not Prohibited by International Law: A Necessary Distinction?' (1990) 39 *International and Comparative Law Quarterly* 1.

—— 'Transboundary Air Pollution: A Tale of Two Paradigms' in S Jayakumar et al (eds), *Transboundary Pollution: Evolving Issues of Law and Policy* (Cheltenham, Edward Elgar, 2015) 233.

Boyle, AE and Bowman, M (eds), *Environmental Damage in International and Comparative Law: Problems of Definition and Valuation* (Oxford, Oxford University Press, 2002).

Bradbrooke Smith, T, 'The Canadian Legislative Position' (1982) 5 *Canada–United States Law Journal* 66.

Brearley, A, 'Reflections upon the Notion of Liability: The Instances of *Kosmos 954* and Space Debris' (2008) 34 *Journal of Space Law* 291.

Briggs, A, *The Conflict of Laws*, 4th edn (Oxford, Oxford University Press, 2019).

—— 'The Revenue Rule in the Conflict of Laws: Time for a Makeover' [2001] 2 *Singapore Journal of Legal Studies* 280.

Broms, B, 'The Nordic Convention on the Protection of the Environment' in C Flinterman, B Kwiatkowska and JG Lammers (eds), *Transboundary Air Pollution: International Legal Aspects of the Co-operation of States* (Dordrecht, Martinus Nijhoff, 1986) 141.

Brunnée, J, 'International Legal Accountability Through the Lens of the Law of State Responsibility' (2005) 36 *Netherlands Yearbook of International Law* 3.

—— 'Of Sense and Sensibility: Reflections on International Liability Regimes as Tools for Environmental Protection' (2004) 53 *International and Comparative Law Quarterly* 351.

—— 'The United States and International Environmental Law: Living with an Elephant' (2004) 15 *European Journal of International Law* 617.

Brunnée, J and Toope, SJ, 'The Sovereignty of International Law?' (2017) 67 *University of Toronto Law Journal* 496.

Burgers, L, 'Should Judges Make Climate Change Law?' (2020) 9 *Transnational Environmental Law* 55.

Byers, M, Franks, K and Gage, G, 'The Internationalization of Climate Damages Litigation' (2017) 7 *Washington Journal of Environmental Law and Policy* 264.

Calliari, E, Surminski, S and Mysiak, J, 'The Politics of (and Behind) the UNFCCC's Loss and Damage Mechanism' in R Mechler et al (eds), *Loss and Damage from Climate Change: Concepts, Methods and Policy Options* (Cham, Springer, 2019) 155.

Caputo, JA, 'Equal Right of Access in Matters of Transboundary Pollution: Its Prospects in Industrial and Developing Countries' (1984) 14 *California Western International Law Journal* 192.

Carlarne, C, 'The Essential Role of Climate Litigation and the Courts in Averting Climate Crisis' in B Mayer and A Zahar (eds), *Debating Climate Law* (Cambridge, Cambridge University Press, 2021) 111.

Carlarne, C and Colavecchio, JD, 'Balancing Equity and Effectiveness: The Paris Agreement and the Future of International Climate Change Law' (2019) 27 *NYU Environmental Law Journal* 107.

Carter, AT, 'The Boundary Waters Treaty of 1909: Does It Provide an Environmental Cause of Action?' (1975) 20 *South Dakota Law Review* 147.

Castel, JG, 'Back to the Future! Is the "New" Rigid Choice of Law Rule for Interprovincial Torts Constitutionally Mandated?' (1995) 33 *Osgoode Hall Law Journal* 35.

Chevrette, F and Marx, H, *Droit constitutionnel: notes et jurisprudence* (Montreal, Presses de l'Université de Montréal, 1982).

Choquette, C, Klaudt, D and Shay Lyne, L, 'Climate Change Litigation in Canada' in F Sindico and MM Mbengue (eds), *Comparative Climate Change Litigation: Beyond the Usual Suspects* (Cham, Springer, 2021) 153.

Churchill, RR, 'Facilitating (Transnational) Civil Liability Litigation for Environmental Damage by Means of Treaties: Progress, Problems, and Prospects' (2001) 12 *Yearbook of International Environmental Law* 3.

Collins, L and Harris, J (eds), *Dicey, Morris & Collins on the Conflict of Laws*, vol 1, 15th edn (London, Sweet & Maxwell, 2012).

Collins, L and McLeod Kilmurray, H, *The Canadian Law of Toxic Torts* (Toronto, Canada Law Book, 2014).

—— in L Paddock, DL Markell and NS Bryner (eds), *Elgar Encyclopedia of Environmental Law*, vol 4: Compliance and Enforcement of Environmental Law (Cheltenham, Edward Elgar, 2017) 85.

Collins, N, 'On the Borderline: *Pakootas*, NAFTA and the Problem of Transboundary Pollution' (2020) 47 *Ecology Law Quarterly* 251.

Colón-Ríos, J, 'Constituent Power, the Rights of Nature, and Universal Jurisdiction' (2014) 60 *McGill Law Journal* 127.

Connell, J, 'Trans-National Environmental Disputes: Are Civil Remedies More Effective for Victims of Environmental Harm?' (2007) 10 *Asia Pacific Journal of Environmental Law* 39.

Cooper, CA, 'The Management of International Environmental Disputes in the Context of Canada-United States Relations: A Survey and Evaluation of Techniques and Mechanisms' (1986) 24 *Canadian Yearbook of International Law* 247.

Coplan, KS, 'Citizen Enforcement' in LC Paddock, RL Glicksman and NS Bryner (eds), *Elgar Encyclopedia of Environmental* Law, vol 2: Decision Making in Environmental Law (Cheltenham, Edward Elgar, 2016) 416.

Coughlan, S et al, *Law Beyond Borders: Extraterritorial Jurisdiction in an Age of Globalization* (Toronto, Irwin Law, 2014).

Craik, Neil, 'Transboundary Pollution, Unilateralism and the Limits of Extraterritorial Jurisdiction: The Second *Trail Smelter* Dispute' in RM Bratspies and RA Miller (eds), *Transboundary Harm in International Law: Lessons from the Trail Smelter Arbitration* (Cambridge, Cambridge University Press, 2006) 109.

Crépeau, P-A, 'De la responsabilité civile extracontractuelle en droit international privé québécois' (1961) 39 *Canadian Bar Review* 3.

Crerar, DA, 'A Proposal for a Principled Public Policy Doctrine Post-*Tolofson*' (1998) 8 *Windsor Review of Legal and Social Issues* 23.

D'Avout, L, 'L'entreprise et les conflits internationaux de lois' (2018) 397 *Recueil des cours de l'Académie de droit international* 9.

Daskal, J, 'The Un-Territoriality of Data' (2015) 125 *Yale Law Journal* 32.

Dawson, FG and Weston, BH, '"Prompt Adequate and Effective": A Universal Standard of Compensation?' (1962) 30 *Fordham Law Review* 727.

Day Scott, R, 'The Canadian-American Boundary Waters Treaty: Why Article II?' (1958) 36 *Canadian Bar Review* 511.

De Boer, TM, 'Developments in the Law: International Environmental Law' (1991) 104 *Harvard Law Review* 1484.

—— 'Forum Preferences in Contemporary European Conflicts Law: The Myth of a "Neutral Choice"' in H-P Mansel (ed), *Festschrift für Erik Jayme*, vol 1 (Munich, Sellier, 2004) 39.

—— 'Party Autonomy and Its Limitations in the Rome II Regulation' (2007) 9 *Yearbook of Private International Law* 19.

Dickinson, A, 'Acts of State and the Frontiers of Private (International) Law' (2018) 14 *Journal of Private International Law* 1.

—— 'Cross-Border Torts in EC Courts: A Response to the Proposed "Rome II" Regulation' (2002) 13 *European Business Law Review* 369.

—— *The Rome II Regulation: The Law Applicable to Non-Contractual Obligations* (Oxford, Oxford University Press, 2010).

DiMento, JF and Doughman, PM, 'Soft Teeth in the Back of the Mouth: The NAFTA Environmental Side Agreement Implemented' (1998) 10 *Georgetown International Environmental Law Review* 651.

Dodge, WS, 'Breaking the Public Law Taboo' (2002) 43 *Harvard International Law Journal* 161.

—— 'The Public–Private Distinction in the Conflict of Laws' (2008) 18 *Duke Journal of Comparative and International Law* 371.

Dotta Salgueiro, M, 'Article 14 of the Judgments Convention The Essential Reaffirmation of the Non-Discrimination Principle in a Globalized Twenty-First Century' (2020) 67 *Netherlands International Law Review* 113.

Droz, GAL, 'Regards sur le droit international privé comparé: cours général de droit international privé' (1991) 229 *Recueil des cours de l'Académie de droit international* 9.

Dumberry, P, *The Formation and Identification of Rules of Customary International Law in International Investment Law* (Cambridge, Cambridge University Press, 2016).

Dupuy, P-M, 'La contribution du principe de non-discrimination à l'élaboration du droit international de l'environnement' (1991) 7 *Revue québécoise de droit international* 135.

—— 'Sur des tendances récentes dans le droit international de l environnement' (1974) 20 *Annuaire français de droit international* 815.

Dupuy, P-M and Viñuales, JE, *International Environmental Law*, 2nd edn (Cambridge, Cambridge University Press, 2018).

Duvic-Paoli, L-A and Viñuales, JE, 'Principle 2: Prevention' in JE Viñuales (ed), *The Rio Declaration on Environment and Development: A Commentary* (Oxford, Oxford University Press, 2015) 107.

Dwyer, G, 'Climate Litigation: A Red Herring Among Climate Mitigation Tools' in B Mayer and A Zahar (eds), *Debating Climate Law* (Cambridge, Cambridge University Press, 2021) 128.

Ebbesson, J, 'Piercing the State Veil in Pursuit of Environmental Justice' in J Ebbesson and P Okowa (eds), *Environmental Law and Justice in Context* (Cambridge, Cambridge University Press, 2009) 270.

Edinger, E, '*Club Resorts Ltd. v. Van Breda*: Extraterritoriality Revisited' (2014) 55 *Canadian Business Law Journal* 263.

'Edison Pays 300 Claims for Fallout' *Windsor Star* (7 September 1973) A3.

Ellis, J, 'Extraterritorial Exercise of Jurisdiction for Environmental Protection: Addressing Fairness Concerns' (2012) 25 *Leiden Journal of International Law* 397.

—— 'Has International Law Outgrown *Trail Smelter*?' in RM Bratspies and RA Miller (eds), *Transboundary Harm in International Law: Lessons from the Trail Smelter Arbitration* (Cambridge, Cambridge University Press, 2006) 56.

Emanuelli, C, *Droit international privé québécois*, 3rd edn (Montreal, Wilson & Lafleur, 2011).

—— *Étude comparative sur le droit international privé au Canada* (Montreal, Wilson & Lafleur, 2019).

—— 'Recognition and Enforcement of Foreign Judgments in Quebec' (2007) 9 *Yearbook of Private International Law* 343.

Emerich, Y, *Conceptualising Property Law: Integrating Common Law and Civil Law Traditions* (Cheltenham, Edward Elgar, 2018).

Enneking, LFH, 'The Common Denominator of the Trafigura Case, Foreign Direct Liability Cases and the *Rome II Regulation*: An Essay on the Consequences of Private International Law for the Feasibility of Regulating Multinational Corporations Through Tort Law' (2008) 16 *European Review of Private Law* 283.

Etemire, U, 'Insights on the UNEP Bali Guidelines and the Development of Environmental Democratic Rights' (2016) 28 *Journal of Environmental Law* 393.

Fach Gómez, K, 'Environmental Liability' in J Basedow et al (eds), *Encyclopedia of Private International Law*, vol 1 (Cheltenham, Edward Elgar, 2017) 657.

Fairley, HS, 'Private Remedies for Transboundary Injury in Canada and the United States: Constraints Upon Having to Sue Where You Can Collect' (1978) 10 *Ottawa Law Review* 253.

Fallon, M, Fauvarque-Cosson, B and Francq, S, 'Le régime du risque transfrontière de la responsabilité environnementale: en marche vers un droit spécial des conflits de lois?' in G Viney and B Dubuisson (eds), *Les responsabilités environnementales dans l'espace européen: point de vue franco-belge* (Brussels, Bruylant, 2006) 547.

Farrow, TCW, 'Globalization, International Human Rights and Civil Procedure' (2003) 41 *Alberta Law Review* 671.

Faure, MG, 'In the Aftermath of Disaster: Liability and Compensation Mechanisms as Tools to Reduce Disaster Risks' (2016) 52 *Stanford Journal of International Law* 95.

—— 'Regulatory Strategies in Environmental Liability' in H Muir Watt and F Cafaggi (eds), *The Regulatory Function of European Private Law* (Cheltenham, Edward Elgar, 2009) 129.

Fawcett, J, Ní Shúilleabháin, M and Shah, S, *Human Rights and Private International Law* (Oxford, Oxford University Press, 2016).

Feldman, EA, 'Compensating the Victims of Japan's 3-11 Fukushima Disaster' (2015) 16 *Asian-Pacific Law and Policy Journal* 127.

Ferguson, K, 'Challenging the Intervention and Stay of an Environmental Private Prosecution" (2004) 13 *Journal of Environmental Law and Practice* 153.

Ferrand-Desmars, F, 'La non-discrimination dans le traitement des dommages causés aux personnes privées par les pollutions transfrontières' (doctoral thesis, Université Paris-II Panthéon-Assas 1998).

Ferrari, F, 'Forum Shopping Despite Unification of Law' (2021) 413 *Recueil des cours de l'Académie de droit international* 13.

Fischer, JM, 'The Availability of Private Remedies for Acid Rain Damage' (1981) 9 *Ecology Law Quarterly* 429.

Fitzgerald, GF, 'The Proposed Canada–United States Transboundary Air Pollution Agreement: The Legal Background' (1982) 20 *Canadian Yearbook of International Law* 219.

Fornasier, M, 'Employment Contracts, Applicable Law' in J Basedow et al (eds), *Encyclopedia of Private International Law*, vol 1 (Cheltenham, Edward Elgar, 2017) 615.

—— 'Employment Contracts, Jurisdiction' in J Basedow et al (eds), *Encyclopedia of Private International Law*, vol 1 (Cheltenham, Edward Elgar, 2017) 624.

Foster, CE, 'Diminished Ambitions? Public International Legal Authority in the Transnational Economic Era' (2014) 17 *Journal of International Economic Law* 355.

—— 'The ILC Draft Principles on the Allocation of Loss in the Case of Transboundary Harm Arising out of Hazardous Activities: Privatizing Risk?' (2005) 14 *Review of European, Comparative and International Environmental Law* 265.

Frank, W, Bals, C and Grimm, J, 'The Case of Huaraz: First Climate Lawsuit on Loss and Damage Against an Energy Company Before German Courts' in R Mechler et al (eds), *Loss and Damage from Climate Change: Concepts, Methods and Policy Options* (Cham, Springer, 2019) 475.

French, D and Kotzé, LJ, '"Towards a Global Pact for the Environment": International Environmental Law's Factual, Technical and (Unmentionable) Normative Gaps" (2019) 28 *Review of European, Comparative and International Environmental Law* 25.

Fresnedo de Aguirre, C, 'Public Policy in Private International Law: Guardian or Barrier?' in V Ruiz Abou-Nigm and M Blanca Noodt Taquela (eds), *Diversity and Integration in Private International Law* (Edinburgh, Edinburgh University Press, 2019) 341.

Fridman, GHL, 'Where is a Tort Committed?' (1974) 24 *University of Toronto Law Journal* 247.

Fuchs, A, 'Article 7: Environmental Damage' in P Huber (ed), *Rome II Regulation: Pocket Commentary* (Munich, Sellier, 2011) 202.

Gage, A and M Byers, 'Payback Time? What the Internationalization of Climate Litigation Could Mean for Canadian Oil and Gas Companies' (West Coast Environmental Law, 1 October 2014), available at www.wcel.org/sites/default/files/publications/Payback%20Time.pdf.

Gaines, SE, 'International Principles for Transnational Environmental Liability: Can Developments in Municipal Law Help Break the Impasse?' (1989) 30 *Harvard International Law Journal* 311.

Gallob, JA, 'Birth of the North American Transboundary Environmental Plaintiff: Transboundary Pollution and the 1979 Draft Treaty for Equal Access and Remedy' (1991) 15 *Harvard Environmental Law Review* 85.

García-Castrillón, CO, 'International Litigation Trends in Environmental Liability: A European Union-United States Comparative Perspective' (2011) 7 *Journal of Private International Law* 551.

Giansetto, F, 'Le droit international privé à l'épreuve des nouveaux contentieux en matière de responsabilité climatique' [2018] *Journal du droit international* 507.

Glenn, HP, 'Droit international privé' in Barreau du Québec and Chambre des notaires (eds), *La réforme du Code civil*, vol 3 (Quebec, Presses de l'Universite Laval, 1993) 669.

—— 'Justice Louis LeBel and the Private International Law of a Diverse Federation' (2015) 70 *Supreme Court Law Review (2d)* 47.

—— 'La guerre de l'amiante' (1991) 80 *Revue critique de droit international privé* 41.

—— 'Recognition of Foreign Judgments in Quebec' (1997) 28 *Canadian Business Law Journal* 404.

Glickman, N, 'Keep Your Pollution to Yourself: Institutions for Regulating Transboundary Pollution and the United States-Mexico Approach' (1984) 25 *Virginia Journal of International Law* 693.

Goldberg, S and Lord, R, 'England' in R Lord et al (eds), *Climate Change Liability: Transnational Law and Practice* (Cambridge, Cambridge University Press, 2011) 445.

Goldie, LFE, 'International Principles of Responsibility for Pollution' (1970) 9 *Columbia Journal of Transnational Law* 283.

Goldsmith, JL, 'Against Cyberanarchy' (1998) 65 *University of Chicago Law* Review 1199.

Goldstein, G, *Droit international privé*, vol 2: Compétence internationale des autorités québécoises et effets des décisions étrangères (Cowansville, Yvon Blais, 2013).

Goldstein, G and Groffier, E, *Droit international privé*, vol 1: Théorie générale (Cowansville, Yvon Blais, 1998).

—— *Droit international privé*, vol 2: Règles spécifiques (Cowansville, Yvon Blais, 2003).

Goldstein, G, 'Le caractère « exceptionnel » frappe encore! Une nouvelle victime par ricochet: la clause d'exception de l'art 3082 CCQ' (2018) 96 *Canadian Bar Review* 402.

—— 'La condition incertaine des lois de police étrangères et du secret bancaire en droit international privé québécois' (1997) 76 *Canadian Bar Review* 449.

Gómez, MA, 'The Global Chase: Seeking the Recognition and Enforcement of the Lago Agrio Judgment Outside of Ecuador' (2013) 1 *Stanford Journal of Complex Litigation* 429.

González Campos, JD, 'Diversification, spécialisation, flexibilisation et matérialisation des règles de droit international privé' (2000) 287 *Recueil des cours de l'Académie de droit international* 9.

Gracer, J, Mahony, D and Dyck, T, 'Cross-Border Litigation Gains Traction in U.S. and Canadian Courts' (2008) 20 *Environmental Claims Journal* 181.

Grassie, SM, 'Canada and the Global Pact for the Environment: A Strategic Legal Analysis' (2019) 32 *Journal of Environmental Law and Practice* 207.

Graziano, TK, 'Products Liability' in J Basedow et al (eds), *Encyclopedia of Private International Law*, vol 2 (Cheltenham, Edward Elgar, 2017) 1413.

—— 'The Law Applicable to Cross-Border Damage to the Environment: A Commentary on Article 7 of the Rome II Regulation' (2007) 9 *Yearbook of Private International Law* 71.

—— 'Torts' in J Basedow et al (eds), *Encyclopedia of Private International Law*, vol 2 (Cheltenham, Edward Elgar, 2017) 1709.

Greco, R, 'Access to Procedures and the Principle of Non-Discrimination (Article 32)' in L Boisson de Chazournes et al (eds), *The UN Convention on the Law of the Non-Navigational Uses of International Watercourses: A Commentary* (Oxford, Oxford University Press, 2018) 325.

Grinlinton, D, 'The Continuing Relevance of Common Law Property Rights and Remedies in Addressing Environmental Challenges' (2017) 62 *McGill Law Journal* 633.

Grisel, F, 'Analyse critique de l'article 7 du Règlement du 11 juillet 2007 sur la loi applicable aux obligations non-contractuelles (« Rome II »)' (2011) 88 *Revue de droit international et de droit comparé* 148.

Grušić, U, 'International Environmental Litigation in EU Courts: A Regulatory Perspective' (2016) 35 *Yearbook of European Law* 180.

Guinchard, E and Lamont-Black, S, 'Environmental Law, the Black Sheep in Rome II's Drive for Legal Certainty? Article 7 of Regulation (EC) No 864/2007 on the Law Applicable to Non-Contractual Obligations' (2009) 11 *Environmental Law Review* 161.

Hafner, G and Buffart, I, 'The Work of the International Law Commission: From Liability to Damage Prevention' in Y Kerbrat and Sandrine Maljean-Dubois (eds), *The Transformation of International Environmental Law* (Paris, Pedone, 2011) 233.

Haibo, G, 'ILC Proposal on the Role of Origin State in Transboundary Damage' in MG Faure and S Ying (eds), *China and International Environmental Liability: Legal Remedies for Transboundary Pollution* (Cheltenham, Edward Elgar, 2008) 107.

Hall, N et al, 'Great Lakes Emerging Legal Issues Regarding the International Boundary Waters Treaty and the Great Lakes Water Quality Agreement' (2010) 34 *Canada–United States Law Journal* 193.

Hall, ND, 'Political Externalities, Federalism, and a Proposal for an Interstate Environmental Impact Assessment Policy' (2008) 32 *Harvard Environmental Law Review* 49.

—— 'Transboundary Pollution: Harmonizing International and Domestic Law' (2007) 40 *University of Michigan Journal of Law Reform* 681.

Hanson, PN, Hagen PE and Rogers, K, 'The Application of the United States Hazardous Waste Cleanup Laws in the Canada–U.S. Context' (1992) 18 *Canada–United States Law Journal* 137.

Hay, P, 'Contemporary Approaches to Non-Contractual Obligations in Private International Law (Conflict of Laws) and the European Community's "Rome II" Regulation' (2007) 7 *European Legal Forum* 135.

Heiss, H, 'Insurance Contracts' in J Basedow et al (eds), *Encyclopedia of Private International Law*, vol 2 (Cheltenham, Edward Elgar, 2017) 954.

Herbert, J, 'The Conflict of Laws and Judicial Perspectives on Federalism: A Principled Defence of *Tolofson v. Jensen*' (1998) 56 *University of Toronto Faculty of Law Review* 3.

Hess, GF, 'The Trail Smelter, the Columbia River, and the Extraterritorial Application of CERCLA' (2005) 18 *Georgetown International Environmental Law Review* 1.

Hill, J and Chong, A, *International Commercial Disputes: Commercial Conflict of Laws in English Courts*, 4th edn (Oxford, Hart, 2010).

Hill, J and Ní Shúilleabháin, M, *Clarkson & Hill's Conflict of Laws*, 5th edn (Oxford, Oxford University Press, 2016).

Hogg, PW, *Constitutional Law of Canada*, 5th edn (Toronto, Carswell, 2007) (loose-leaf updated 2020).

Hinteregger, M, 'Environmental Liability' in E Lees and JE Viñuales (eds), *The Oxford Handbook of Comparative Environmental Law* (Oxford, Oxford University Press, 2019) 1025.

Hoffman, KB, 'State Responsibility in International Law and Transboundary Pollution Injuries' (1976) 25 *International and Comparative Law Quarterly* 709.

Holly, G, 'Transnational Tort and Access to Remedy Under the UN Guiding Principles on Business and Human Rights: Kamasaee v Commonwealth' (2018) 19 *Melbourne Journal of International Law* 52.

Hook, M, 'The Conflict of Laws as a Shared Language for the Cross-Border Application of Statutes' in M Douglas et al (eds), *Commercial Issues in Private International Law: A Common Law Perspective* (Oxford, Hart, 2019) 175.

Howarth, D, 'Environmental Law and Private Law' in E Lees and JE Viñuales (eds), *The Oxford Handbook of Comparative Environmental Law* (Oxford, Oxford University Press, 2019) 1091.

Hsu, S-L, 'A Realistic Evaluation of Climate Change Litigation Through the Lens of a Hypothetical Lawsuit' (2008) 79 *University of Colorado Law Review* 701.

Hsu, S-L and Parrish, AL, 'Litigating Canada-U.S. Transboundary Harm: International Environmental Lawmaking and the Threat of Extraterritorial Reciprocity' (2007) 48 *Virgnia Journal of International Law* 1.

Hugues, EL and Iyalomhe, D, 'Substantive Environmental Rights in Canada' (1999) 30 *Ottawa Law Review* 229.

Ianni, RW, 'International and Private Actions in Transboundary Pollution' (1973) 11 *Canadian Yearbook of International Law* 258.

Imai, S, Maheandiran, B and Crystal, V, 'Access to Justice and Corporate Accountability: A Legal Case Study of Hudbay in Guatemala' (2014) 35 *Canadian Journal of Development Studies* 285.

Jayakumar, S et al (eds), *Transboundary Pollution: Evolving Issues of Law and Policy* (Cheltenham, Edward Elgar, 2015).

Jeffery, MI, 'Seeking Redress for Environmental Harm in the Context of Transboundary Pollution: Remedies, Access, and Choice of Law Considerations' in SJ Rubin and DC Alexander (eds), *NAFTA and the Environment* (The Hague, Kluwer Law International, 1996) 463.

—— 'Transboundary Pollution and Cross-Border Remedies' (1992) 18 *Canada–United States Law Journal* 173.

Jesserun D'Oliveira, HU, 'La pollution du Rhin et le droit international privé' in R Hueting et al (eds), *Rhine Pollution: Legal, Economic and Technical Aspects* (Zwolle, Tjeenk Willink, 1978) 81.

Jianing, Z and Goldstein, G, 'Analyse comparative de la loi chinoise de 2011 portant sur les conflits de lois à la lueur du droit international privé québécois' (2014) 48 *Revue juridique Thémis de l'Université de Montréal* 329.

Johnston, DR and Post, D, 'Law and Borders – The Rise of Law in Cyberspace' (1996) 48 *Stanford Law Review* 1367.

Juenger, FK, 'Mass Disasters and the Conflict of Laws' [1989] *University of Illinois Law Review* 105.

Kadner Graziano, T, *La responsabilité délictuelle en droit international privé européen* (Basel, Helbing & Lichtenhahn, 2004).

Kahl, W and Weller, M-P, *Climate Change Litigation: A Handbook* (Oxford, Hart, 2021).

Kain, B, Marques, EC and Shaw, B, 'Developments in Private International Law: The 2011–2012 Term – The Unfinished Project of the *Van Breda* Trilogy' (2012) 59 *Supreme Court Law Review (2d)* 277.

Kalavrouziotis, TA, 'U.S.–Canadian Relations Regarding Diversions from an International Basin: An Analysis of Article II of the Boundary Waters Treaty' (1989) 12 *Fordham International Law Journal* 658.

Kellman, B, 'Space: The Foulded Frontier. Adjudicating Space Debris as an International Environmental Nuisance' (2014) 39 *Journal of Space Law* 227.

Kessedjian, C, 'Questions de droit international privé de la responsabilité sociétale des entreprises: rapport général' in C Kessedjian and H Cantú Rivera (eds), *Private International Law Aspects of Corporate Social Responsibility* (Cham, Springer, 2020) 3.

Kinsch, P, 'Droits de l'homme, droits fondamentaux et droit international privé' (2014) 318 *Recueil des cours de l'Académie de droit international* 9.

King, WK, 'Transboundary Pollution: Canadian Jurisdiction (1982) 1 *Canadian–American Law Journal* 1.

Kinna, R, 'Non-Discrimination and Liability for Transboundary Acid Mine Drainage Pollution of South Africa's Rivers: Could the UN Watercourses Convention Open Pandora's Mine?' (2016) 41 *Water International* 371.

Kisiel, E, 'Law as an Instrument to Solve the Orbital Debris Problem' (2021) 51 *Environmental Law* 223.

Knox, JH, 'The CEC and Transboundary Pollution' in DL Markell and JH Knox (eds), *Greening NAFTA: The North American Commission for Environmental Cooperation* (Stanford, Stanford University Press, 2003) 80.

——, 'The Flawed *Trail Smelter* Procedure: The Wrong Tribunal, the Wrong Parties, and the Wrong Law' in RM Bratspies and RA Miller (eds), *Transboundary Harm in International Law: Lessons from the Trail Smelter Arbitration* (Cambridge, Cambridge University Press, 2006) 66.

——, 'The Neglected Lessons of the NAFTA Environmental Regime' (2010) 45 *Wake Forest Law Review* 391.

Koh, HH, 'Transnational Legal Process' (1996) 75 *Nebraska Law Review* 181.

Koivurova, T, 'The Future of the Nordic Environment Protection Convention' (1997) 66 *Nordic Journal of International Law* 505.

Kotzé, L, 'A Global Environmental Constitution for the Anthropocene?' (2019) 8 *Transnational Environmental Law* 11.

Kreuzer, K, 'Environmental Disturbance and Damage in the Context of Private International Law' (1992) 44 *Revista española de derecho internacional* 57.

Kruger, T, 'Trail Smelter II: A Prudent Approach? From Extraterritoriality to Non-Discrimination' (2010) 43 *UBC Law Review* 109.

Kunda, I, 'Policies Underlying Conflict of Law Choices in Environmental Law' in Vasilka Sancin (ed), *International Environmental Law: Contemporary Concerns and Challenges* (Ljubljana, Založba, 2012) 507.

Kysar, DA, 'The Public Life of Private Law: Tort Law as a Risk Regulation Mechanism' (2018) 9 *European Journal of Risk Regulation* 48.

Laganière, G, 'Dialogue des systèmes en droit international privé: l'application et la reconnaissance du droit public étranger au Québec' in J Torres-Ceyte, G-A Berthold and C-A Péladeau (eds), *Le dialogue en droit civil* (Montreal, Thémis, 2018) 35.

—— 'Local Polluters, Foreign Land and Climate Change: The Myth of the Local Action Rule in Canada' (2020) 16 *Journal of Private International Law* 390.

Larsen, RK, 'Foreign Direct Liability Claims in Sweden: Learning from *Arica Victims KB v Boliden Mineral AB*' (2014) 83 *Nordic Journal of International Law* 404.

Latham, M, Schwartz, VE and Appel, CE, 'The Intersection of Tort and Environmental Law: Where the Twains Should Meet and Depart' (2011) 80 *Fordham Law Review* 737.

Lee, EG and Sproule, DW, 'Liability for Damage Caused by Space Debris: The Cosmos 954 Claim' (1988) 26 *Canadian Yearbook of International Law* 273.

Lee, RJ, 'The Liability Convention and Private Space Launch Services: Domestic Regulatory Responses' (2006) 31 *Annals of Air and Space Law* 351.

Lee, S, 'Title to Foreign Real Property in Transnational Money Claims' (1995) 32 *Columbia Journal of Transnational Law* 607.

Lefeber, R, 'The Legal Significance of the Supplementary Protocol: The Result of a Paradigm Evolution' in A Shibata (ed), *International Liability Regime for Biodiversity Damage: The Nagoya–Kuala Lumpur Supplementary Protocol* (Abingdon, Routledge, 2014) 73.

—— *Transboundary Environmental Interference and the Origin of State Liability* (The Hague, Kluwer Law International, 1996).

Lehmann, M, 'Regulation, Global Governance and Private International Law: Squaring the Triangle' (2020) 16 *Journal of Private International Law* 1.

Lehmann, M and Eichel, F, 'Globaler Klimawandel und Internationales Privatrecht – Zuständigkeit und anzuwendendes Recht für transnationale Klagen wegen klimawandelbedingter Individualschäden' (2019) 83 *Rabel Journal of Comparative and International Private Law (RabelsZ)* 77.

Lequette, Y, 'Les mutations du droit international privé: vers un changement de paradigme? Cours général de droit international privé' (2017) 387 *Recueil des cours de l'Académie de droit international* 9.

Levy, T, 'NAFTA's Provision for Compensation in the Event of Expropriation: A Reassessment of the "Prompt, Adequate and Effective" Standard' (1995) 31 *Stanford Journal of International Law* 423.

Listiningrum, P, 'Transboundary Civil Litigation for Victims of Southeast Asian Haze Pollution: Access to Justice and the Non-Discrimination Principle' (2019) 8 *Transnational Environmental Law* 119.

Looper, RB, 'Jurisdiction over Immovables: The Little Case Revisited After Sixty Years' (1956) 40 *Minnesota Law Review* 191.

Mahmoudi, S, 'Some Private International Law Aspects of Transboundary Environmental Disputes' (1990) 59 *Nordic Journal of International Law* 128.

Manirabona, AM, *Entreprises multinationales et criminalité environnementale transfrontalière: applicabilité du droit pénal canadien* (Cowansville, Yvon Blais, 2010).

—— 'Toward Barrier Removal for Transnational Human Rights Litigation in Canadian Courts' in AM Manirabona and Y Vega-Cárdenas (eds), *Extractive Industrie and Human Rights in an Era of Global Justice: New Ways of Resolving and Preventing Conflicts* (Toronto, LexisNexis, 2019) 39.

Martin, J-C, 'The United Nations Compensation Commission Practice with Regards to Environmental Claims' in Y Kerbrat and S Maljean-Dubois (eds), *The Transformation of International Environmental Law* (Paris, Pedone, 2011) 25 .

Mason, M, 'Citizenship Entitlements Beyond Borders? Identifying Mechanisms of Access and Redress for Affected Publics in International Environmental Law' (2006) 12 *Global Governance* 283.

Mayer, B, *The International Law of Climate Change* (Cambridge, Cambridge University Press, 2018).

McAree, M and Vince, J, 'When Complying with the Law in Your Own Backyard Is Not Enough: Cross-Border United States and Canada Environmental Litigation' (2013) 42 *Brief* 57.

McCaffrey, SC, 'Liability for Transfrontier Environmental Harm: The Relationship Between Public and Private International Law' in C von Bar (ed), *Internationales umwelthaftungsrecht*, vol 1 (Köln, Heymann, 1995) 81.

—— 'Of Paradoxes, Precedents and Progeny: The *Trail Smelter* Arbitration 65 Years Later' in RM Bratspies and RA Miller (eds), *Transboundary Harm in International Law: Lessons from the Trail Smelter Arbitration* (Cambridge, Cambridge University Press, 2006) 34.

—— 'Private Remedies for Transfrontier Environmental Disturbances', IUCN Environmental Policy and Law Paper 8 (Morges, International Union for Conservation of Nature and Natural Resources, 1975).

—— *The Law of International Watercourses*, 3rd edn (Oxford, Oxford University Press, 2019).

—— 'The OECD Principles Concerning Transfrontier Pollution: A Commentary' (1975) 1 *Environmental Policy and Law* 2.

—— 'Trans-Boundary Pollution Injuries: Jurisdictional Considerations in Private Litigation Between Canada and the United States' (1973) 3 *California Western International Law Journal* 191.

McIntyre, O, 'The Role of Customary Rules and Principles of International Environmental Law in the Protection of Shared International Freshwater Resources' (2006) 46 *Natural Resources Journal* 157.

McNamara, P, *The Availability of Civil Remedies to Protect Persons and Property from Transfrontier Pollution* (Frankfurt, Alfred Metzner, 1981).

Merrill, TW, 'Golden Rules for Transboundary Pollution' (1997) 46 *Duke Law Journal* 931.

Michaels, R, 'Private International Law and the Question of Universal Values' in F Ferrari and DP Fernández Arroyo (eds), *Private International Law: Contemporary Challenges and Continuing Relevance* (Cheltenham, Edward Elgar, 2019) 148.

—— 'Towards a Private International Law for Regulatory Conflicts?' (2016) 59 *Japanese Yearbook of International Law* 175.

Mills, A, *Party Autonomy in Private International Law* (Cambridge, Cambridge University Press, 2018).

—— 'Private International Law and EU External Relations: Think Local Act Global, or Think Global Act Local?' (2016) 65 *International and Comparative Law Quarterly* 541.

Montjoie, M, 'The Concept of Liability in the Absence of an Internationally Wrongful Act' in J Crawford, A Pellet and S Olleson with the assistance of K Parlett (eds), *The Law of International Responsibility* (Oxford, Oxford University Press, 2010) 503.

Morriss, A, 'Supporting Structures for Resolving Environmental Disputes Among Friendly Neighbors' in J Schmandt, J Clarkson and H Roderick (eds), *Acid Rain and Friendly Neighbors: The Policy Dispute Between Canada and the United States*, revised edn (Durham, Duke University Press, 1988) 217.

Mortensen, R, 'Homing Devices in Choice of Tort Law: Australian, British, and Canadian Approaches' (2006) 55 *International and Comparative Law Quarterly* 839.

Mrema, E, 'UNEP GCSS-11/GMEF: Building Confidence in the Multilateral System' (2010) 40 *Environmental Policy and Law* 136.

Muir Watt, H (ed), 'Aspects économiques du droit international privé: réflexions sur l'impact de la globalisation économique sur les fondements des conflits de lois et de juridictions' (2004) 307 *Recueil des cours de l'Académie de droit international* 25.

—— 'Choice of Law in Integrated and Interconnected Markets: A Matter of Political Economy' (2003) 9 *Columbia Journal of European Law* 383.

—— 'European Integration, Legal Diversity and the Conflict of Laws' (2005) 9 *Edinburgh Law Review* 6.

—— 'Further Terrains for Subversive Comparisons: The Field of Global Governance and the Public/Private Divide' in PG Monateri (ed), *Methods of Comparative Law* (Cheltenham, Edward Elgar, 2012) 270.

—— *Private International Law and Public Law* (Cheltenham, Edward Elgar, 2015).

—— 'Private International Law Beyond the Schism' (2011) 2 *Transnational Legal Theory* 347.

—— 'Private International Law's Shadow Contribution to the Question of Informal Transnational Authority' (2018) 25 *Indiana Journal of Global Legal Studies* 37.

—— 'Rome II et les « intérêts gouvernementaux »: pour une lecture fonctionnaliste du nouveau règlement du conflit de lois en matière délictuelle" in S Corneloup and N Joubert (eds), *Le règlement communautaire « Rome II » sur la loi applicable aux obligations non contractuelles* (Paris, LexisNexis, 2008) 129.

—— 'Theorizing Private International Law' in A Orford and F Hoffmann (eds), *The Oxford Handbook of the Theory of International Law* (Oxford, Oxford University Press, 2016) 862.

Muir Watt, H and Fernández Arroyo, DP (eds), *Private International Law and Global Governance* (Oxford, Oxford University Press, 2014).

Muldoon, PR, Scriven, DA and Olson, JM, *Cross-Border Litigation: Environmental Rights in the Great Lakes Ecosystem* (Toronto, Carswell, 1986).

Mulvaney, JN, 'Participation by Ontario in U.S. Administrative and Judicial Proceedings' (1983) 4 *New York Law School Journal of International and Comparative Law* 553.

Munari, F and Di Pepe, LS, 'Liability for Environmental Torts in Europe: Choice of Law and the Case for Pursuing Effective Legal Uniformity' (2005) 41 *Rivista di diritto internazionale privato e processuale* 607.

Nash, JR, 'The Curious Legal Landscape of the Extra-Territoriality of US Environmental Laws' in G Handl, J Zekoll and P Zumbansen (eds), *Beyond Territoriality: Transnational Legal Authority in an Age of Globalization* (Leiden, Martinus Nijhoff, 2012) 125.

—— 'The Curious Legal Landscape of the Extraterritoriality of U.S. Environmental Laws' (2010) 50 *Virginia Journal of International Law* 997.

Nissen, T, 'Critique de l'article 7 du règlement Rome II: étude du dommage environnemental en droit international privé' (master thesis, Université catholique de Louvain 2015).

Nollkaemper, A 'Responsibility of Transnational Corporations in International Environmental Law: Three Perspectives' in G Winter (ed), *Multilevel Governance of Global Environmental Change: Perspectives from Science, Sociology and the Law* (Cambridge, Cambridge University Press, 2006) 179.

Nwapi, C, 'Litigating Extraterritorial Corporate Crimes in Canadian Courts' (doctoral thesis, University of British Columbia 2012).

—— 'Re-Evaluating the Doctrine of *Forum Non Conveniens* in Canada' (2013) 34 *Windsor Review of Legal and Social Issues* 59.

—— 'Tort Choice of Law and International Fundamental Norms: A Case Study of Canada and the United States' (2013) 1 *Afe Babalola University Journal of Sustainable Development Law and Policy* 54.

Okowa, P, *State Responsibility for Transboundary Air Pollution in International Law* (Oxford, Oxford University Press, 2000).

Olszynski, M, Mascher, S and Doelle, M, 'From Smokes to Smokestacks: Lessons from Tobacco for the Future of Climate Change Liability' (2017) 30 *Georgetown Environmental Law Review* 1.

Orange, JA, 'Torture, Tort Choice of Law, and Tolofson' in C Scott (ed), Torture as Tort: Comparative Perspectives on the Development of Transnational Human Rights Litigation (Oxford, Hart, 2001) 291.

Orlando, Emanuela, 'From Domestic to Global? Recent Trends in Environmental Liability from a Multi-Level Perspective and Comparative Law Perspective' (2015) 24 *Review of European, Comparative and International Environmental Law* 290.

—— 'Public and Private in the International Law of Environmental Liability' in F Lenzerini and AF Vrdoljak (eds), *International Law for Common Goods: Normative Perspectives on Human Rights, Culture and Nature* (Oxford, Hart, 2014) 395.

Osofsky, HM, 'Is Climate Change "International"? Litigation's Diagonal Regulatory Role' (2009) 49 *Virginia Journal of International Law* 585.

Pallemaerts, M, 'Judicial Recourse Against Foreign Air Polluters: A Case Study of Acid Rain in Europe" (1985) 9 *Harvard Environmental Law Review* 143.

Parrish, AL, 'Trail Smelter Déjà Vu: Extraterritoriality, International Environmental Law, and the Search for Solutions to Canada–U.S. Transboundary Water Pollution Disputes' (2005) 85 *Boston University Law Review* 363.

Paul, JR, 'The Isolation of Private International Law' (1988) 7 *Wisconsin International Law Journal* 149.

Peel, J, 'International Environmental Law and Climate Disasters' in R Lyster and RRM Verchick (eds), *Research Handbook on Climate Disaster Law: Barriers and Opportunities* (Cheltenham, Edward Elgar, 2018) 77.

—— 'Unpacking the Elements of a State Responsibility Claim for Transboundary Pollution' in S Jayakumar et al (eds), *Transboundary Pollution: Evolving Issues of Law and Policy* (Cheltenham, Edward Elgar, 2015) 51.

Peel, J and Osofsky, HM, *Climate Change Litigation: Regulatory Pathways to Cleaner Energy* (Cambridge, Cambridge University Press, 2017).

Péloffy, K, 'Kivalina v Exxonmobil: A Comparative Case Comment' (2013) 9 *McGill Journal of Sustainable Development and the Law* 121.

Pelzer, N, 'Facing the Challenge of Nuclear Mass Tort Proceedings' (2017) 99 *Nuclear Law Bulletin* 45.

Percival, RV, 'International Responsibility and Liability for Environmental Harm' in S Alam et al (eds) *Routledge Handbook of International Environmental Law* (London, Routledge, 2013) 681.

Perron-Welch, F and Rukundo, O, 'Biosafety, Liability and Sustainable Development' in M-C Cordonier Segger, F Perron-Welch and C Frison (eds), *Legal Aspects of Implementing the Cartagena Protocol on Biosafety* (Cambridge, Cambridge University Press, 2013) 188.

Peters, A, *Beyond Human Rights: The Legal Status of the Individual in International Law* (Cambridge, Cambridge University Press, 2016).

Phillips, C, 'Nordic Co-operation for the Protection of the Environment Against Air Pollution and the Possibility of Transboundary Private Litigation' in C Flinterman, B Kwiatkowska and JG Lammers (eds), *Transboundary Air Pollution: International Legal Aspects of the Co-operation of States* (Dordrecht, Martinus Nijhoff, 1986) 153.

Piri Damagh, M, *Prevention and Compensation of Trans-Boundary Damage in Relation to Cross-Border Oil and Gas Pipelines* (Cambridge, Intersentia, 2015).

Pitel, SGA, 'Six of One, Half a Dozen of the Other? Jurisdiction in Common Law Canada' (2018) 55 *Osgoode Hall Law Journal* 63.

Pitel, SGA et al, *Private International Law in Common Law Canada: Cases, Text and Materials*, 4th edn (Toronto, Emond, 2016).

Pitel, SGA and Black, V, 'Assumed Jurisdiction in Canada: Identifying and Interpreting Presumptive Connecting Factors' (2018) 14 *Journal of Private International Law* 193.

Pitel, SGA and Harper, JR, 'Choice of Law for Tort in Canada: Reasons for Change' (2013) 9 *Journal of Private International Law* 289.

Pitel, SGA and Rafferty, NS, *Conflict of Laws*, 2nd edn (Toronto, Irwin Law, 2016).

Plakokefalos, I, 'Liability for Transboundary Harm' in A Nollkaemper and I Plakokefalos (eds), *The Practice of Shared Responsibility in International Law* (Cambridge, Cambridge University Press, 2017) 1051.

Popovici, A, 'Le « locus delicti » en droit international privé québécois' (1982–83) 17 *Revue juridique Thémis* 463.

Posch, W, 'Some Observations on the Law Applicable to Transfrontier Environmental Damage' in M Hinteregger (ed), *Environmental Liability and Ecological Damage in European Law* (Cambridge, Cambridge University Press, 2008) 33.

Post, D, 'Against "Against Cyberanarchy"' (2002) 17 *Berkeley Technology Law Journal* 1365.

Purcell Jr, EA, 'Geography as a Litigation Weapon: Consumers, Forum-Selection Clauses, and the Rehnquist Court' (1992) 40 *UCLA Law Review* 423.

Read, JE, 'The Trail Smelter Dispute' (1963) 1 *Canadian Yearbook of International Law* 213.

Rehbinder, E, 'Extra-Territoriality of Pollution Control Laws from a European Perspective' in G Handl, J Zekoll and P Zumbansen (eds), *Beyond Territoriality: Transnational Legal Authority in an Age of Globalization* (Leiden, Martinus Nijhoff, 2012) 127.

Rest, A, *Convention on Compensation for Transfrontier Environmental Injuries: Draft with Explanatory Notes* (Berlin, Erich Schmidt, 1976).

—— 'International Environmental Law in German Courts' (1997) 27 *Environmental Policy and Law* 409.

—— *International Protection of the Environment and Liability: The Responsibility of States and Individuals in Cases of Transfrontier Pollution* (Berlin, Erich Schmidt, 1978).

—— 'Need for an International Court for the Environment? Underdeveloped Legal Protection for the Individual in Transnational Litigation' (1994) 24 *Environmental Policy and Law* 173.

—— *The More Favourable Law Principle in Transfrontier Environmental Law: A Means of Strengthening the Protection of the Individual?* (Berlin, Erich Schmidt, 1980).

Riles, A, 'Managing Regulatory Arbitrage: A Conflict of Laws Approach' (2014) 47 *Cornell International Law Journal* 63.

Robertson, D, 'Court No Closer to Fording International Flood Dispute: U.S. Trying to Change Flow of Flooding Water' *Winnipeg Free Press* (31 January 2018) 4.

Robinson-Dorn, MJ, 'The Trail Smelter: Is What's Past Prologue? EPA Blazes a New Trail for CERCLA' (2006) 14 *NYU Environmental Law Journal* 233.

Rühl, G, 'Consumer Protection in Choice of Law' (2011) 44 *Cornell International Law Journal* 569.

Rushworth, A and Scott, A, 'Rome II: Choice of Law for Non-Contractual Obligations' [2008] *Lloyd's Maritime and Commercial Law Quarterly* 274.

Sabahi, B, *Compensation and Restitution in Investor-State Arbitration* (Oxford, Oxford University Press, 2011).

Sacerdoti, G, 'Bilateral Treaties and Multilateral Instruments on Investment Protection' (1997) 269 *Recueil des cours de l'Académie de droit international* 251.

Sachs, N, 'Beyond the Liability Wall: Strengthening Tort Remedies in International Environmental Law' (2008) 55 *UCLA Law Review* 837.

Salacuse, JW, *The Law of Investment Treaties*, 3rd edn (Oxford, Oxford University Press, 2021).

Sand, PH, 'The Evolution of Transnational Environmental Law: Four Cases in Historical Perspective' (2012) 1 *Transnational Environmental Law* 183.

—— 'The Role of Domestic Procedures in Transnational Environmental Disputes' in Organisation for Economic Co-operation and Development, *Legal Aspects of Transfrontier Pollution* (Paris, OECD, 1977) 146, reprinted in PH Sand (ed), *Transnational Environmental Law: Lessons in Global Change* (The Hague, Kluwer Law International, 1999) 87.

—— 'Transboundary Air Pollution' in A Nollkaemper and I Plakokefalos (eds), *The Practice of Shared Responsibility in International Law* (Cambridge, Cambridge University Press, 2017) 962.

Sands, P and Peel, J with Fabra, A and MacKenzie, R, *Principles of International Environmental Law*, 4th edn (Cambridge, Cambridge University Press, 2018).

Sands, PJ, 'Climate Change and the Rule of Law: Adjudicating the Future in International Law' (2016) 28 *Journal of Environmental Law* 19.

—— 'Environment, Community and International Law' (1989) 30 *Harvard International Law Journal* 393.

Saumier, G, 'Le *forum non conveniens* au Québec: bilan d'une transplantation' in S Guillemard (ed), *Mélanges en l'honneur du professeur Alain Prujiner* (Cowansville, Yvon Blais, 2011) 345.

—— 'L'ouverture récente des tribunaux canadiens aux poursuites dirigées contre les sociétés mères pour les préjudices causés par leurs filiales à l'étranger' (2018) 107 *Revue critique de droit international privé* 775.

—— 'The Recognition of Foreign Judgments in Quebec – The Mirror Crack'd?' (2002) 81 *Canadian Bar Review* 677.

Schiff Berman, P, 'The Globalization of Jurisdiction' (2002) 151 *University of Pennsylvania Law Review* 311.

—— '*Yahoo! v. LICRA*, Private International Law and the Deterritorialisation of Data' in H Muir Watt et al (eds), *Global Private International Law: Adjudication Without Frontiers* (Cheltenham, Edward Elgar, 2019) 393.

Schwartz, JA, 'International Nuclear Third Party Liability Law: The Response to Chernobyl' in International Atomic Energy Agency and OECD Nuclear Energy Agency, *International Nuclear Law in the Post-Chernobyl Period* (Paris, OECD, 2006).

Scott, C and Wai, R, Transnational Governance of Corporate Conduct Through the Migration of Human Rights Norms: The Potential Contribution of Transnational "Private" Litigation' in C Joerges, I-J Sand and G Teubner (eds), *Transnational Governance and Constitutionalism: International Studies in the Theory of Private Law* (Oxford, Hart, 2004) 287.

Scovazzi, T, The Mediterranean Guidelines for the Determination of Environmental Liability and Compensation: The Negotiations for the Instrument and the Question of Damage That Can Be Compensated' (2009) 13 *Max Planck Yearbook of United Nations Law* 183.

Seck, SL, 'Environmental Harm in Developing Countries Caused by Subsidiaries of Canadian Mining Corporations: The Interface of Public and Private International Law' (1999) 37 *Canadian Yearbook of International Law* 139.

—— 'Home State Responsibility and Local Communities: The Case of Global Mining' (2008) 11 *Yale Human Rights and Development Law Journal* 177.

—— 'Moving Beyond the E-Word in the Anthropocene in DS Margolies et al (eds), *The Extraterritoriality of Law: History, Theory, Politics* (Abingdon, Routledge, 2019) 49.

Seidl-Hohenveldern, I, 'Alternative Approaches to Transfrontier Environmental Injuries' (1976) 2 *Environmental Policy and Law* 6.

Shaw, B and Robinson, S, '*Goldhar v. Haaretz.com*: A Product of the Supreme Court's Unfinished Project to Reform Canadian Private International Law' (2019) 49 *Advocates' Quarterly* 143.

Shoesmith, TM, 'Transfrontier Pollution – OECD Council Recommendation on Implementing a Regime of Equal Right of Access and Non-Discrimination in Relation to Transfrontier Pollution' (1978) 19 *Harvard International Law Journal* 407.

Singh Nijar, G, 'Civil Liability in the Supplementary Protocol' in A Shibata (ed), *International Liability Regime for Biodiversity Damage: The Nagoya–Kuala Lumpur Supplementary Protocol* (Abingdon, Routledge, 2014) 111.

Siros, SM, 'Borders, Barriers, and Other Obstacles to a Holistic Environment' (1992) 13 *Northern Illinois University Law Review* 633.

Slane, A, 'Tales, Techs and Territories: Private International Law, Globalization, and the Legal Construction of Borderlessness on the Internet' (2008) 71 *Law and Contemporary Problems* 129.

Slaughter, A-M and Burke-White, W, 'The Future of International Law Is Domestic (or, The European Way of Law)' (2006) 47 *Harvard International Law Journal* 327.

Smets, H, 'Le principe de non-discrimination en matière de protection de l'environnement' (2000) 4 *Revue européenne de droit de l'environnement* 3.

Springer, AL, *Cases of Conflict: Transboundary Disputes and the Development of International Environmental Law* (Toronto, University of Toronto Press, 2016).

Stein, RE, 'The OECD Guiding Principles on Transfrontier Pollution' (1976) 6 *Georgia Journal of International and Comparative Law* 245.

Strebel, FD, 'The Enforcement of Foreign Judgments and Foreign Public Law' (1999) 21 *Loyola of Los Angeles International and Comparative Law Journal* 55.

Suttenberg, J, 'Who Pays? The Consequences of State Versus Operator Liability Within the Context of Transboundary Environmental Nuclear Damage' (2016) 24 *NYU Environmental Law Journal* 201.

Swaigen, J, Koehl, A and Hatt, C, 'Private Prosecutions Revisited: The Continuing Importance of Private Prosecutions in Protecting the Environment' (2013) 26 *Journal of Environmental Law and Practice* 31, reprinted in A Ingleson (ed), *Environment in the Courtroom* (Calgary, University of Alberta Press, 2019) 240.

Symeonides, SC, *Codifying Choice of Law Around the World: An International Comparative Analysis* (Oxford, Oxford University Press, 2014).

—— 'Private International Law: Idealism, Pragmatism, Eclecticism' (2017) 384 *Recueil des cours de l'Académie de droit international* 9.

—— 'Result-Selectivism in Conflicts Laws' (2009) 46 *Willamette Law Review* 1.

—— 'Rome II and Tort Conflicts: A Missed Opportunity' (2008) 56 *American Journal of Comparative Law* 173.

—— 'The American Revolution and the European Evolution in Choice of Law: Reciprocal Lessons' (2008) 82 *Tulane Law Review* 1741.

—— 'Torts and Conflict of Laws' in M Bussani and AJ Sebok (eds), *Comparative Tort Law: Global Perspectives* (Cheltenham, Edward Elgar, 2015) 39.

Talpis, J, '"If I Am from Grand-Mère, Why Am I Being Sued in Texas?" Responding to Inappropriate Foreign Jurisdiction in Quebec-United States Crossborder Litigation' (Montreal, Thémis, 2001).

Talpis, J and Goldstein, G, 'Analyse critique de l'Avant-projet de loi du Québec en droit international privé' (1989) 91 *Revue du Notariat* 456.

—— 'The Influence of Swiss Law on Quebec's 1994 Codification of Private International Law' (2009) 11 *Yearbook of Private International Law* 339.

Talpis, J and Kath, SL, 'The Exceptional as Commonplace in Quebec *Forum Non Conveniens* Law: *Cambior*, A Case in Point' (2000) 34 *Revue juridique Thémis* 731.

Talpis, JA and Castel, JG, 'Le Code civil du Québec: interprétation des règles du droit international' in Barreau du Québec and Chambre des notaires (eds), *La réforme du Code civil*, vol 3 (Quebec, Presses de l'Université Laval, 1993) 801.

Thomas, E and Kebede, MT, 'One Legally Binding Provision on Civil Liability: Why It Was So Important from the African Negotiators' Perspective' in A Shibata (ed), *International Liability Regime for Biodiversity Damage: The Nagoya–Kuala Lumpur Supplementary Protocol* (Abingdon, Routledge, 2014) 125.

Thomassin, K and Boodman, M, 'Choice of Law and Manufacturer's Liability in Quebec' in TL Archibald and RS Echlin (eds), *Annual Review of Civil Litigation 2012* (Toronto, Carswell, 2012) 209.

Tingle, BC, 'The Strange Case of the Crown Prerogative over Private Prosecutions or Who Killed Public Interest Law Enforcement?' (1994) 28 *UBC Law Review* 309.

Torremans, P et al, *Cheshire, North & Fawcett: Private International Law*, 15th edn (Oxford, Oxford University Press, 2017).

United Nations, 'Press Conference on Request for International Court of Justice Advisory Opinion on Climate Change' (3 February 2012), available at www.un.org/press/en.

Valiante, M, '"Welcomed Participants" or "Environmental Vigilantes"? The CEPA Environmental Protection Action and the Role of Citizen Suits in Federal Environmental Law' (2002) 25 *Dalhousie Law Journal* 81.

Van Calster, G, 'Environmental Law and Private International Law' in E Lees and JE Viñuales (eds), *The Oxford Handbook of Comparative Environmental Law* (Oxford, Oxford University Press, 2019) 1139.

—— *European Private International Law* (Oxford, Hart, 2013).

Van de Kerkhof, M, 'The Trail Smelter Case Re-Examined: Examining the Development of National Procedural Mechanisms to Resolve a Trail Smelter Type Dispute' (2011) 27 *Utrecht Journal of International and European Law* 68.

Van Loon, H, 'Principles and Building Blocks for a Global Legal Framework for Transnational Civil Litigation in Environmental Matters' (2018) 23 *Uniform Law Review* 298.

—— 'The Global Horizon of Private International Law' (2016) 380 *Recueil des cours de l'Académie de droit international* 9.

—— 'The Present and Prospective Contribution of Global Private International Law Unification to Global Legal Ordering' in F Ferrari and DP Fernández Arroyo (eds), *Private International Law: Contemporary Challenges and Continuing Relevance* (Cheltenham, Edward Elgar, 2019) 214.

Vinogradov, SV, 'Observations on the International Law Commission's Draft Rules on the Non-Navigational Uses of International Watercourses: Management and Domestic Remedies' (1992) 3 *Colorado Journal of International Law and Policy* 235.

Voigt, C, 'International Responsibility and Liability' in L Rajamani and J Peel (eds), *The Oxford Handbook of International Environmental Law*, 2nd edn (Oxford, Oxford University Press, 2021).

Von Bar, C, 'Environmental Damage in Private International Law' (1997) 268 *Recueil des cours de l'Académie de droit international* 291.

Von Hein, J, 'Article 7: Environmental Damage' in G-P Calliess and M Renner (eds), *Rome Regulations: Commentary*, 3rd edn (Alphen on the Rhine, Wolters Kluwer, 2020) 649.

—— 'Something Old and Something Borrowed, but Nothing New? Rome II and the European Choice-of-Law Evolution' (2008) 82 *Tulane Law Review* 1663.

Walker, J, *Castel & Walker: Canadian Conflict of Laws*, 6th edn (Markham, LexisNexis, 2005) (loose-leaf updated 2020).

Wilde, M, *Civil Liability for Environmental Damage: Comparative Analysis of Law and Policy in Europe and the US*, 2nd edn (Alphen on the Rhine, Kluwer Law International, 2013).

Wolfrum, R, Langenfeld, C and Minnerop, P, *Environmental Liability in International Law: Towards a Coherent Conception* (Berlin, Erich Schmidt, 2005).

Wai, R, 'Conflicts and Comity in Transnational Governance: Private International Law as Mechanism and Metaphor for Transnational Social Regulation Through Plural Legal Regimes' in C Joerges and E-U Petersmann (eds), *Constitutionalism, Multilevel Trade Governance and International Economic Law* (Oxford, Hart, 2011) 229.

—— 'Private v Private: Transnational Private Law and Contestation in Global Economic Governance' in H Muir Watt and DP Fernández Arroyo (eds), *Private International Law and Global Governance* (Oxford, Oxford University Press, 2014) 34.

—— 'The Interlegality of Transnational Private Law' (2008) 71 *Law and Contemporary Problems* 107.

—— 'Transnational Liftoff and Juridical Touchdown: The Regulatory Function of Private International Law in a Global Age' (2002) 40 *Columbia Journal of Transnational Law* 209.

—— 'Transnational Private Law and Private Ordering in a Contested Global Society' (2005) 46 *Harvard International Law Journal* 471.

Walker, J, '*Teck Cominco* and the Wisdom of Deferring to the Court First Seised, All Things Being Equal" (2009) 47 *Canadian Business Law Journal* 192.

Walsh, C, 'General Jurisdiction over Corporate Defendants under the *CJPTA*: Consistent with International Standards?' (2018) 55 *Osgoode Hall Law Journal* 163.

—— 'Territoriality and Choice of Law in the Supreme Court of Canada: Applications in Products Liability Claims' (1997) 76 *Canadian Bar Review* 91, reprinted in J Ziegel (ed), *New Developments in International Commercial and Consumer Law* (Oxford, Hart, 1998) 237.

Wasserstein Fassberg, C, 'The Public in Private International Law' in Y Emerich (ed), *Le public en droit privé* (Montreal, Yvon Blais, 2019) 23.

Weaver, RH and Kyser, DA, 'Courting Disaster: Climate Change and the Adjudication of Catastrophe' (2017) 93 *Notre Dame Law Review* 295.

Webb, Kernaghan, 'Taking Matters into Their Own Hands: The Role of Citizens in Canadian Pollution Control Enforcement' (1991) 36 *McGill Law Journal* 770.

Welling, B and Heakes, EA, 'Torts and Foreign Immovables Jurisdiction in Conflict of Laws' (1979) 18 *University of Western Ontario Law Review* 295.

Wetstone, G and Rosencranz, A, 'Transboundary Air Pollution Between Canada and the United States' (1982) 1 *UCLA Pacific Basin Law Journal* 197.

Whincop, MJ, 'Conflicts in the Cathedral: Towards a Theory of Property Rights in Private International Law' (2000) 50 *University of Toronto Law Journal* 41.

Whytock, CA, 'Domestic Courts and Global Governance' (2009) 84 *Tulane Law Review* 67.

Whytock, CA and Burke Robertson, C, 'Forum Non Conveniens and the Enforcement of Foreign Judgments' (2011) 111 *Columbia Law Review* 1444.

Wilderspin, Michael, 'Consumer Contracts' in Jürgen Basedow et al (eds), *Encyclopedia of Private International Law*, vol 1 (Cheltenham, Edward Elgar, 2017) 464.

Willheim, E, 'Private Remedies for Transfrontier Environmental Damage: A Critique of OECD's Doctrine of Equal Right of Access' (1976) 7 *Australian Yearbook of International Law* 174.

Willis, J, 'Jurisdiction of Courts – Action to Recover Damages for Injury to Foreign Land' (1937) 15 *Canadian Bar Review* 112.

Wisner, R, 'Uniformity, Diversity and Provincial Extraterritoriality: *Hunt v. T&N plc*' (1995) 40 *McGill Law Journal* 759.

Wood, S, 'Canada' in E Lees and JE Viñuales (eds), *The Oxford Handbook of Comparative Environmental Law* (Oxford, Oxford University Press, 2019) 108.

Wood, T, 'Sticks and Carrots: *Rylands v Fletcher*, CSR, and Accountability for Environmental Harm in Common Law Jurisdictions' (2012) 91 *Canadian Bar Review* 275.

Woods, AK, 'Against Data Exceptionalism' (2016) 68 *Stanford Law Review* 729.

Xue, H, *Transboundary Damage in International Law* (Cambridge, Cambridge University Press, 2003).

Zerk, JA, *Multinationals and Corporate Social Responsibility: Limitations and Opportunities in International Law* (Cambridge, Cambridge University Press, 2006).

Zhao, H and Percival, R, 'Comparative Environmental Federalism: Subsidiarity and Central Regulation in the United States and China' (2017) 6 *Transnational Environmental Law* 531.

Ziff, B, 'Environmental Protection and the Abject Failures of the Common Law' (2020) 71 *University of New Brunswick Law Journal* 3.

Zilioli, C, 'Choice of Law' in C von Bar (ed), *Internationales umwelthaftungsrecht*, vol 1 (Köln, Heymann, 1995) 177.

Index

Lightning Source UK Ltd.
Milton Keynes UK
UKHW020051290922
409604UK00003B/197

9 781509 951154